GEORG

BRAQU

GEORGES BRAQUE

A Life

ALEX DANCHEV

Arcade Publishing
New York

FIRST U.S. EDITION

First published in the U.K. by Hamish Hamilton, a publishing division of Penguin Books, Ltd.

Library of Congress Cataloging-in-Publication Data

    Danchev, Alex.
      Georges Braque : a life / by Alex Danchev. — 1st U.S. ed.
        p. cm.
    ISBN 1-55970-743-7
    1. Braque, Georges, 1882–1963. 2. Artists—France—Biography. I. Title.

    N6853.B7D36 2004
    759.4—dc22   2004009482

Published in the United States by Arcade Publishing, Inc., New York
Distributed by Time Warner Book Group

Visit our Web site at www.arcadepub.com

10 9 8 7 6 5 4 3 2 1

EB

PRINTED IN THE UNITED STATES OF AMERICA

FOR D

I prefer the man to the artist. Cézanne was not an artist, but Manet was. If you follow me.

Braque

What we see is not what we see but who we are.

Pessoa

Portrait by Robert Doisneau (1953)

Contents

List of Illustrations

All works by Braque unless otherwise indicated.

Colour Plate Section

© Succession Picasso/DACS 2005. Photo: Solomon R. Guggen-heim Museum/David Heald).

9. *Fruit Dish and Glass*, 1912 (Private Collection. © ADAGP, Paris and DACS, London 2005).

10. *Violin*, 1914 (The Cleveland Museum of Art. © ADAGP, Paris and DACS, London 2005. Photo: The Cleveland Museum of Art, Leonard C. Hanna, Jr., Fund, 1968.196).

11. *Violin and Pitcher* , 1910 (Kunstmuseum, Basel, Switzerland. © ADAGP, Paris and DACS, London 2005. Photo: Giraudon/The Bridgeman Art Library).

12. *The Round Table*, 1929 (Phillips Collection, Washington, DC, USA. © ADAGP, Paris and DACS, London 2005. Photo: The Bridgeman Art Library).

13. *The Black Fish*, 1942 (Musée national d'art moderne, Centre Pompidou, Paris, France. © ADAGP, Paris and DACS, London 2005. Photo: Giraudon/The Bridgeman Art Library).

14. The Braque ceiling in the Louvre, 1953 (The Louvre, Paris, France. © ADAGP, Paris and DACS, London 2005. Photo: © Giraudon/The Bridgeman Art Library).

15. *The Bird and Its Nest*, 1955 (Musée national d'art moderne, Centre Pompidou, Paris, France. © ADAGP, Paris and DACS, London 2005 Photo: Giraudon/The Bridgeman Art Library).

16. *Studio VIII*, 1954–5 (Private Collection. © ADAGP, Paris and DACS, London 2005. Photo: Christie's Images Ltd).

17. A seven-colour lithograph from *Lettera Amorosa*, 1963 (© ADAGP, Paris and DACS, London 2005).

18. *The Weeding Machine*, 1961–3 (Musée national d'art moderne, Centre Pompidou, Paris, France. © ADAGP, Paris and DACS, London 2005. Photo: The Bridgeman Art Library/Peter Willi).

Black and White Plate Section

1. *Marie Laurencin and Georges Lepape at the Moulin de la Galette*, 1904 (Private Collection. © ADAGP, Paris and DACS, London 2005).

2. Marie Laurencin, *Georges Braque at the Easel*, 1904 (Private Collection. © ADAGP, Paris and DACS, London 2005).

3. Georges Lepape, *Georges Braque*, *c* .1905 (Private Collection. © ADAGP, Paris and DACS, London 2005).

4. *Large Nude*, 1908 (Musée national d'art moderne, Centre Pompidou, Paris, France. © ADAGP, Paris and DACS, London 2005).

5. *Woman*, 1908 (Whereabouts unknown. © ADAGP, Paris and DACS, London 2005).

6. *Houses at L'Estaque* (*Houses and Tree*), 1908 (Donation Geneviève et Jean Masurel. Musée d'art moderne Lille Métropole, Villeneuve d'Ascq. © ADAGP, Paris and DACS, London 2005. Photo: Philip Bernard).

7. Marie Wassilief, *The Braque Banquet*, 1917 (Courtesy Claude Bernès, Paris).

8. Greetings card: 'No Braquing any time' (© Judy Horacek www.horacek.com.au).

9. *Violin: 'Mozart/Kubelick'*, 1912 (Private Collection, Basel, Switzerland. © ADAGP, Paris and DACS, London 2005. Photo: Lauros/Giraudon/The Bridgeman Art Library).

10. *Homage to J. S. Bach*, 1911–12 (Private Collection. © ADAGP, Paris and DACS, London 2005. Photo: The Bridgeman Art Library).

11. Picasso, *The Reading of the Letter*, 1921 (Musée Picasso, Paris. © Succession Picasso/DACS 2005. Photo: RMN/J.G. Berizzi).

12. *Hesiod and the Muse*, 1932, an etching for the *Theogony* (© ADAGP, Paris and DACS, London 2005. Photo: Roger-Viollet/Rex Features).

13. A page from Braque's *Cahier* (Paris: Maeght, 1994. © ADAGP, Paris and DACS, London 2005.).

14. *Death's Head*, 1943 (The Laurens Archive. © ADAGP, Paris and DACS, London 2005).

15. *The Stove*, 1942 (Yale University Art Gallery. Gift of Paul Rosenberg and Company in Memory of Paul Rosenberg. © ADAGP, Paris and DACS, London 2005. Photo: Yale University Art Gallery.).

16. An etching for *The Order of Birds*, 1962 (© ADAGP, Paris and DACS, London 2005. Photo: Roger-Viollet/Rex Features).

17. Giacometti, *Georges Braque on His Deathbed*, 1963 (Alberto Giacometti, Georges Braque on His Deathbed, 1963. © ADAGP, Paris and DACS, London 2005).

Integrated Photographs

Frontispiece: portrait by Robert Doisneau, 1953 (© Robert Doisneau/Rapho)
1. Charles and Georges Braque at Harfleur, *c.* 1895 (The Laurens Archive).
2. Aged sixteen, playing the flute (The Laurens Archive).
3. Marie Laurencin by Man Ray, 1924 (© Man Ray Trust/ ADAGP, Paris and DACS, London 2005. Photo: ADAGP, Banque d'Images, Paris 2005).
4. Braque's Paris studio by Robert Doisneau, 1957 (© Robert Doisneau/Rapho).
5. In Sens, en route to Sorgues, near Avignon, 28 or 29 June 1914 (The Laurens Archive).
6. In his studio in the Impasse de Guelma, *c.* 1911 (© Archives Charmet/The Bridgeman Art Library).
7. A corner of Braque's Paris studio by Alexander Liberman (Research Library, Getty Research Institute, Los Angeles (2000.R.19)).
8. Braque's Fang mask (The Laurens Archive).
9. Picasso's Grebo mask (Collection Claude Picasso, Paris).
10. Snapped by Kahnweiler on the balcony of his studio in the Hôtel Roma, 1913 (Kahnweiler-Leiris Archives).
11. Picasso, *Portrait of Fernande Olivier and Georges Braque, c.* 1908–10) (Musée Picasso, Paris. © Succession Picasso/DACS 2005. Photo: RMN).
12. The corner sculpture in Braque's Hôtel Roma studio, 1914 (no longer extant; photo: The Laurens Archive).
13. The model for *Houses at L'Estaque* (1908), taken by Kahnweiler in 1910 (Kahnweiler-Leiris Archives).
14. Picasso, *Bouillon Kub*, 1912 (no longer extant; © Succession Picasso/DACS 2005. Photo: Kahnweiler-Leiris Archives).

15. With Marcelle, and Braquian table, 1946 (© David E. Scherman/Time Life Pictures/Getty Images).

16. Madame Braque by Alexander Liberman, 1953 (Research Library, Getty Research Institute, Los Angeles (2000.R.19)).

17. Portrait of Georges Braque by Pablo Picasso, 1911 (Musée Picasso, Paris. © Succession Picasso/DACS 2005. Photo: RMN).

18. Portrait of Pablo Picasso by Georges Braque, 1911 (Private Collection. © ADAGP, Paris and DACS, London 2005).

19. On the Western Front, 17 December 1914 (The Laurens Archive).

20. In Henri Laurens's studio, 1915, taken by Laurens (The Laurens Archive).

21. In his Sorgues studio, 1917 (The Laurens Archive).

22. Braque and Marcelle (and Turc) with Pierre and Henriette Reverdy, Sorgues, 1917 (The Laurens Archive).

23. Jean Paulhan in the débris of his room, Braque's *papier collé*, *Violin*, 1914, on the wall behind him (© Roger-Viollet/Rex Features).

24. Braque's *maison-atelier* near the Parc Montsouris in Paris (Direction des Archives de France / Institut français d'architecture. Archives d'architecture du XXe siècle, Paris (DAF/IFA)).

25. Georges Braque by Man Ray, 1922 (Musée national d'art moderne, Centre Pompidou, Paris, France. © Man Ray Trust/ADAGP, Paris and DACS, London 2005. Photo: CNAC/MNAN Dist. RMN).

26. With chauffeur Jean Ferrand and Simca, *c.* 1955 (courtesy Jean Ferrand).

27. In his Paris studio, *c.* 1935–6, by Brassaï (Braque in his Paris studio, Brassaï. Private Collection © Estate Brassaï/RMN. Photo: Photo RMN/Michèle Bellot).

28. Portrait of Georges Braque by Picasso, 1909 (Musée Picasso, Paris. © Succession Picasso/DACS 2005. Photo: RMN).

29. In his Varengeville dining room, 1953, by Robert Doisneau (© Robert Doisneau/Rapho).

30. Homemade palette, palette tree, lectern, and small beachscape in his Varengeville studio (The Laurens Archive).

31. The French tourists at the Gare de l'Est, Paris, before their departure for Germany in 1941 (© Roger-Viollet/Rex Features).

32. Sharing a joke with Picasso at Vallauris in the South of France in 1954, by Lee Miller (© Lee Miller Archives, England 2005. All rights reserved).

33. Etruscan antiquity in the Louvre (From a collection in the Louvre. © Photo RMN/Hervé Lewandowski).

34. The first meeting between Braque and Saint-John Perse, with Paulhan, in 1958, in front of *The Bird and its Nest*, 1955 (© ADAGP, Paris and DACS, London 2005. Photo: Courtesy of Fondation Saint-John Perse).

35. Meditating on *The Bird and Its Nest*, 1955 (© Photos12.com/ Luc Fournol).

36. In front of *The Billiard Table*, 1947–9, with oncoming birds (© ADAGP, Paris and DACS, London 2005. Photo © Roger-Viollet/ Rex Features).

37. Braque by Lee Miller, 1956 (© Lee Miller Archives, England 2004. All rights reserved).

38. With Mariette in the Paris studio, working on *Lettera Amorosa* (© Imapress/L'Illustration/Eyevine).

39. The state funeral in the Cour Carrée of the Louvre. From the cover story in *Paris-Match*, 14 September 1963 (© *Paris-Match*/ Patrice Habans).

40. The funeral at Varengeville (© *Paris-Match*/François Gragnon).

41. With *The Weeding Machine*, (1961–3), in progress (© Imapress/ L'Illustration/Eyevine).

42. The grave at Varengeville, with its lapidary legend (© Dee Danchev).

Every effort has been made to trace the copyright holders and we apologize in advance for any unintential omission. We would be pleased to insert the appropriate acknowledgement in any subsequent editions.

1. 'Everyone has his own coffee grounds': The Apprentice

He was born at Argenteuil, on the banks of the Seine, a day trip from Paris, on 13 May 1882. He was reborn at Carency, on the battlefields of the Western Front, a cannon-shot from Arras, on 13 May 1915. The first occasion was trouble-free, so far as we know, but the second was savage enough for the veteran Braque to pass it off lightly, if he mentioned it at all. He had been left for dead on the field of Neuville-Saint-Vaast, his skull shattered by a piece of shrapnel.[1] After dark, fortuitously, he was picked up by the stretcher-bearers, still unconscious but still breathing, just. For cases such as Braque's, trepanation was the recommended procedure. The drilling was done immediately, by Deladrière from Dunkirk. When it was over Braque lay in a coma for forty-eight hours. He came round on his birthday. It was 9.00 in the evening, exactly the time he was born. Recuperating, he remembered an absurdist exchange with a nurse: ' "Are you the one who's been trepanned? Take off your shoes." Would you believe it, I was wounded in the head and they wanted to look at my feet.'[2]

He nearly died in 1915. He nearly died again, of pneumonia, in 1947. Death came definitively on 31 August 1963, after a lengthy period of incubation.

Georges Braque had more life and death experience than most. Of all this living and dying, he let slip remarkably little. The authorized version – 'his testament' – comes down to us in a series of interviews he gave to the writer Dora Vallier for the upmarket *Cahiers d'Art*, in 1954; or rather in Vallier's rendition of some twelve hours of talk (punctually each evening, 6.00 till 7.00), from the notes she took on her lap.[3] Braque was always alert to the shades of names. It must have pleased him to have his thoughts gathered by a young woman with the same name as Cézanne's gardener, the noble subject of the inspiritor's last work. He vetted the text before publication, as he had stipulated, but altered nothing. He had already made himself crystal clear. In a mirror of his artistic practice, he was well rehearsed. He often worked in series, planting, grafting, pruning and training, before moving on, a process that could take many years. 'All the great artists have been great workers,' as Nietzsche knew, 'inexhaustible not only in invention but also in rejecting, sifting, transforming, ordering.'[4] So with Braque. His canvases are composts. His texts too. The account he gave to Vallier had been seeded in similar accounts given to his friend Jean Paulhan during the Occupation, and to the American curator of a large-scale retrospective at the Museum of Modern Art in New York in 1949. 'The artist is not misunderstood,' said Braque, 'he is poorly understood.'[5]

The lack of talk is something very like deference to his wishes. In life, Braque gave off a strong sense of self-containment. He lived in the castle of his skin. Even as a young man he conveyed a strict injunction: no gossip. In Braque's circle the term was expansively interpreted. Gossip covered anything that did not count. 'What counted' and what counted for nothing was a favourite discriminator. The only thing that really counted, he sometimes professed to believe, was the work. Everything but the work was gossip. Life itself was gossip. '*Conceal thy life*,' commanded Epicurus, and so Braque did.[6] Hence the injunction. Inner life was off-limits, and private life should live up to its name. 'I thought that one could do good painting without attracting attention to one's private life,' sighed Cézanne.[7] The same applied to Braque. His own was sacrosanct. It was an attitude neatly caught in retrospect by the distinguished writer-curator Jean Leymarie, who became his friend. 'There are no anecdotes,' Leymarie observed, sympathetically, of this white-out life. On further reflection: 'Of course, there are anecdotes. But they are secret.'[8]

The injunction echoes down the decades. When interviewing the artist on his early life and times for the MoMA retrospective – forty years after the fact – the well-briefed curator of the exhibition took great pains to accommodate Braque's sensitivities by tiptoeing delicately round anything remotely personal. Non-events were ratified in the book of the show: 'If he had any youthful romances, they were of little importance.'[9] In after-life, too, the story remained the same. In Argenteuil, which might have claimed him, the shabby 40 rue de l'Hôtel-Dieu where he was born and where three generations of Braques lived on top of one another has been demolished. There is an obligatory Place Georges Braque – a pitiable corner where it is not advisable to linger – but what is unknown in Argenteuil is that his parents are buried under a plain stone in the town cemetery, in a plot acquired originally by Braque's mother and now registered under the name of Eugène Gosselin (1877–1929), the artist's brother-in-law, a businessman less conspicuous in life than in death, whose mission it was to teach Braque billiards.[10] In Argenteuil, therefore, in the span of one short century, something has happened that might almost be called Kafkaesque. As the name of Braque began to grow it also began to disappear. By the time it was great it was all but invisible. When it comes to Georges Braque, public memory is patchy indeed. His birthplace is a blank spot.

What should they know of Braque who only Braque know? The authorized version of his pre-history, as Vallier puts it, is telescopic:

I've always had a feeling for painting. My father, a building contractor, liked to paint. My grandfather had also been an amateur painter. I was born in Argenteuil, at the time when the Impressionists were working there. Throughout my childhood in Le Havre, the Impressionist atmosphere prevailed . . . My artistic education? I did it all by myself with *Gil Blas* [a satirical review]. My father had a subscription. I must have been about twelve, I had been struck by Steinlen and [Toulouse-]Lautrec, I remember, but it was Lautrec I liked the best. I spent my evenings copying – by the light of an oil-lamp – the illustrations in *Gil Blas*. I even had a craze for posters. Often I used to wait until dark and go and peel off the ones I liked and for a long time I kept one of Lautrec's . . . I may still have it . . . On Sundays, my father used to hitch the horse to the cart and go and 'do landscapes'. I used to go with him and watch him work . . .

In class during drawing lessons I did nothing but barrack the teacher and mess around doing caricatures. There was nothing of any interest in my sketches, and even if there had been the teacher would not have had the wit to notice. It was scarcely any better at the [École Municipale des] Beaux-Arts in Le Havre. I must have been about fifteen when I started going to evening classes. I've always hated official painting – I still feel very strongly about that . . .

During that period I used to come to Paris in the holidays and it was then that I saw the Louvre for the first time. I remember, however, that I soon began to be more interested in the paintings in the Musée du Luxembourg. After leaving school at eighteen, I began my apprenticeship as a painter and decorator. I realized that I was not capable of winning a medal at the Beaux-Arts – which would have gained me exemption from military service – and my father decided to send me to Paris so that I could complete my apprenticeship, still because this would have made things easier with regard to military service . . . They taught me to do mock marble, mock wood, but even so I stuck it out right to the end of the apprenticeship.[11]

Braque was a Northerner born and bred. His forebears came from Haudivillers, near Compiègne, in the Oise, some 50 miles north of Paris. His great-grandfather, Pierre Braque (1799–1859), settled in Argenteuil in the 1840s. There he married Élénore Lequeux. They had four children: Frédéric, a woodcarver; Toussaint, a locksmith; Jean, a joiner and cabinetmaker; and Amédée (1830–1903), Braque's grandfather, a house painter. Amédée Braque married Louise Botel. They had three children: Achille, a joiner; Lucien, a watchmaker; and Charles (1855–1911), Braque's father, also a house painter, later a prosperous building contractor, as indicated by his proud son. Charles Braque married a local girl, Augustine Johanet (1859–1942). They had two children: Henriette (1878–1950) and her younger brother Georges.

Braque's relatives are mostly lost to history, especially on the distaff side. The young tyro painted his mother, his maternal grandmother and his cousin Louise, and preserved the evidence, despite professing his apprentice work worthless and editing it even more ruthlessly than his apprentice life. As late as the 1950s he burned a life-size *Portrait of the Artist's Mother*, possibly the last vestige of his

1. Charles and
Georges Braque at
Harfleur, *c.* 1895

Toulouse-Lautrec period.[12] It is interesting that the extant portraits concentrate on the women of the family: studies in availability, perhaps. These well-conducted women are mute. Braque gave them cameos, not speaking parts. (If that. His sister's space is void.) Nothing of their talk or temper survives in his reminiscence, evanescent as it is, save for the vague but intriguing suggestion that his mother may have been less reconciled than his father to their only son's determination not to pursue the logic of his hard-graft apprenticeship and join the family firm, but instead to brave the stew of Montmartre and find his own way to paint: to become an artist, not an artisan, if he could.[13]

His mother is otherwise an unperson. His father, by contrast, benefits in the telling and emerges a little better defined. Charles Braque inherited from his own father both his trade and his avocation: the matching traditions of house painting and Sunday painting in which his son Georges grew up. 'They worked to keep my conscience clear,' the latter remarked to Jean Paulhan.[14] One of his earliest memories was of his father telling him with pride that even Parisian artists came to paint Argenteuil, their home town, without ever mentioning what kind of painting they did. By the time young Georges could spell its name, Argenteuil and its riparian charms had been advertised, shockingly, by a new breed of open-air artists whose totem was a longhair called Claude Monet – a man in a crowd of eunuchs, in Zola's estimation. These artists practised Impressionism, a name coined in ridicule from one of Monet's paintings, his 'impression' of the rising sun. The name stuck; and so did the mud. To Charles Braque and his friends Impressionism was an offence, if not a disgrace, and they would have no truck with it. This reaction was not uncommon. At the École Municipale des Beaux-Arts in Le Havre, where Georges Braque put in a fleeting appearance a few years later, the director solemnly informed his students that Impressionism had come too late for him.[15]

Monet had been encamped at Argenteuil for much of the 1870s. One of the legends of Braque's childhood is that he caught the Impressionist-in-chief executing one of his scandalous scenes: *Sunday at Argenteuil*, as it may be, or *The Boat Rental Area*. Unfortunately the chronology fits no better than the psychology. The boy was not ready; and Monet had moved on. Confrontation or inoculation would have to wait. Georges Braque was in no sense precocious. What he did see was the construction of a mansion for a cultivated naval architect from Paris, Gustave Caillebotte, a stripling with bottomless pockets, advanced tastes in contemporary art, and remarkable foresight. It was the house rather than the contents that interested the Braques at the time; but the story had a sequel, at least for one member of the family. The naval architect left his collection to the state, which did not want it, but Gustave Caillebotte was not to be denied. His will provided not only for a permanent collection but for its exhibition, first at the Musée du Luxembourg (the national museum for living artists) and then at the last bastion of the Louvre itself. There followed a bitter rearguard action. Eventually, in 1897, a portion of the Caillebotte bequest was duly installed at the Luxembourg, in an isolation wing built for the purpose. The teenage Braque was not slow to investigate its contagious offerings. There were Monets, Renoirs, Pissarros, Manets, and, at the very bottom of the barrel, grudgingly accepted by the unenlightened functionaries of the state, two small Cézannes – Braque's first, or the first he registered. One of them was not so much an impression as a sensation of a small Mediterranean port that became a place of pilgrimage: L'Estaque.[16]

Argenteuil, meanwhile, was losing its appeal, spoiled by progress and sacked by invading armies of Parisians bent on having a good time. 'Nature is going to quit its role of the mysterious, silent nymph,' lamented *La Vie Parisienne*. 'She is going to become an inn maid, to whom travelling salesmen pay rather poor respect. They take over the country as if it were a huge "guinguette", a café-concert larger than the one on the Champs-Élysées . . . All these people come to feel the hills as if they were breasts, to tuck the forests up to the knee and ruffle the river as if the Sunday ritual was to give nature a charivari [a raucous serenade]. The mad Parisians have thrown nature into an uproar.'[17] The mad Parisians may have been good for business in some quarters, but they did not do much for house painting. For Charles Braque trade was slow. Prospects were poor. He and his extended family decided to look elsewhere. In 1890, when their youngest was eight, they left Argenteuil for Le Havre.

It was an opportune decision. *Fin-de-siècle* Le Havre was bursting at the seams, with a fast-growing population and a rush of new building. Demand for high-class painters and decorators was nearly insatiable. In order to get started, the new arrivals went into partnership: Driancourt and Braque, 33 rue Jules-Lecesne, another house demolished, this time involuntarily, by the carpet bombing of 1944. Briskly the business took off. Within three years Charles Braque was his own boss, with a loyal crew, a certain fingerprint, a growing reputation, and a burgeoning self-esteem. Soon it was said that every new property of consequence in Le Havre had the decorative stamp of Braque & Co. Forty years on, when the theatre director Armand Salacrou (a local boy made good) set about restoring the Villa Maritime, a demi-palace on the esplanade, under an aberrant coating of spinach-green paint he discovered the trademark of Charles Braque – unstinted mock wood, in yellow and brown. Salacrou, who knew his Braques, had a swift sense of *déjà vu*. It was as if the workmanship of one generation had been framed in the next. For Armand Salacrou, these 'astonishing decorations' resembled nothing so much as the canvases-to-be of Georges Braque.[18]

Charles Braque painted pictures too. For a Sunday painter, he was a serious one. If his highest aspirations were never quite fulfilled, filially they were far exceeded. How children dance to the unlived lives of their parents, observed Rilke wisely. Braque *père* took lessons from Théodule Ribot, whose stronger-voiced confederate Eugène Boudin was the one who encouraged the young Monet out of the studio and into the field, believing that 'everything painted directly and on the spot has a strength, a vigour, a vivacity of touch that can never be obtained in the studio'. Ribot and Boudin were pre-Impressionists. They ventured something, within bounds. Their idol and inspiration was Corot – Boudin considered Corot and Millet 'the two greatest individuals of our time' – for the luminescent silvery-grey that seemed to seep through his paintings, but above all for his delicacy, his maturity, and his outdoorsmanship. ('But where, monsieur, do you see that splendid tree you've put there?' Corot, taking his pipe from between his teeth and without turning round, points with the stem at an oak *behind them*.) Ribot and Boudin were both professionally versatile, a lesson well learned by the Braque succession, but what they liked to do best was paint seascapes at Honfleur and Trouville, just along the coast from Le Havre. 'It is a consolation for us to see that in spite of our advancing years we are still holding our own against the unruly and daring young people who do not want to do the same as their predecessors and who perhaps are getting a little carried away in their fracturing of colour and light.'[19]

Charles Braque himself confected rather in the manner of Corot, with a delay of about twenty years to absorb the latest developments. He did what he did well enough for his work to be represented at the conservative Salon des Artistes Français in Paris. (Did he nurse the fond hope that Georges might follow him there?) In the art world of Le Havre – a bustling enterprise – he gained substance and emi- nence, showing regularly at the Salon de la Société des Amis des Arts, and founding with other local notables the Cercle de l'Art Moderne, 'to bring the public art which is personal', whose annual exhibitions of 1906 to 1909 mustered a fine array of national talent, including Braque *père* and *fils*, introduced ritually by an elevated discourse from such as Apollinaire, on 'The Plastic Virtues'.[20]

Charles Braque's work elicited a mixed response. In the early 1900s he and his son used to exhibit regularly together at venues all over Le Havre. (Georges Braque's 'first exhibition' at the 1906 Salon des Indépendants in Paris is another example of artistic licence, or pre-historical editing.) Of one joint outing, a critic found the portrait studies by Braque junior 'interesting', and the landscapes by Braque senior 'a shade too chic'. After all, 'One must not confuse chic with style.'[21] The hauteur of the *Havre Éclair* could be withering. The inaugural exhibition of the Cercle de l'Art Moderne, on the other hand, precipitated a veritable eulogy:

But what is the very calm, very balanced, very classical Monsieur Charles Braque doing in this revolutionary company? His *gouaches, Outskirts of Le Havre*, are assuredly Impressionist, but in the best sense, in their expression, in the overwhelming charm that they convey. The new 'independents' faithful to their own system would consider him 'old hat'. Today Monsieur Braque is enjoying a success that owes nothing to snobbery. I offer hearty congratulations to this Parnassian who, falling among aesthetes of the simi- larity of difference and the difference of similarity, has preserved the charac- ter of an art inspired by nature itself, nature as seen by the vast majority, simply beautiful and beautiful once more in his rendition of it.[22]

All of which must have pleased the Parnassian exceedingly. The reaction on the lower slopes is unrecorded, as is that of the nearest and dearest member of the revolutionary company; but in later life Georges Braque is known to have kept at least two precious works in his bedroom. One was a Cézanne. The other was a small sub- Corot landscape, a bridge and boats on the Seine, in silvery-grey;

a shade too chic, no doubt, but finished and signed, in a hand very like his own, Ch. Braque.[23] Though they looked to different examples, Corot was a shared love. Braque surely knew the tree exchange. His own gamesmanship was practised indoors. 'But that light, Monsieur Braque, it's not natural.' 'And me, am I not natural?' 'But really, the light, where does it come from?' 'Ah, that's from another painting, one you haven't seen.'[24]

Le Havre was good for Charles Braque, evidently, and Charles Braque was good for Le Havre. His son's relationship with the place was rather more modest. Stupidity was not Georges Braque's forte, but as a pupil he managed a passable imitation. At the local *lycée* – when present – he was either dreamy or refractory, bored with lessons hardly begun. He reserved a special scorn for his drawing teacher, also a Sunday painter, who appears to have made the mistake of showing the boys his own work (little watercolours, much derided). The feeling was not entirely mutual, for in spite of everything Braque was placed third in conventional drawing in his first year there, sixth in hand-writing in the second, and first in hand-writing in the fourth. As for the rest, he failed to register. Neither did he take his baccalaureate. If there was no possibility of passing the exams, it would be pointless staying on to fail them. On this impeccable logic all parties, parents, teachers and the defaulter himself, amicably reached agreement. In 1899, at seventeen, Georges left without a backward glance.[25]

For two years he had been moonlighting at drawing classes at the École Municipale des Beaux-Arts down the road. The Beaux-Arts as Braque experienced it was a stuffy institution directed by another stuffy institution, Charles Lhullier, known to his legions as Father Lhullier, a figure of immense self-importance, primly censorial. The nude was clothed at the Beaux-Arts in Father Lhullier's day: models were obliged to wear a complete set of under-garments. The well-armoured director prided himself on his antique pedagogy ('the nude? yes, but after several years of plaster casts'), and he had indeed compiled a lengthy roll of honour. Among the most recent additions were two others from the town, Raoul Dufy and Othon Friesz, star pupils a little older than Braque,

2. Aged sixteen, playing the flute

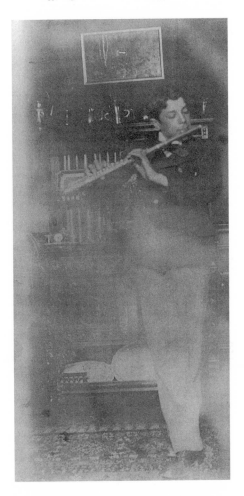

who already knew them slightly. Dufy in particular he looked up to as a real painter – 'un grand' – whose work was bought by his father.[26] Braque himself had taken flute lessons from Dufy's brother, and glimpsed a house of artistic hubbub, an inspiring notion.

Contrary to legend, Braque never studied with Lhullier himself, who died in 1898, merely with a local painter by the name of Courchet. These classes, from 8.00 till 10.00 each evening, he attended regularly, at least in body. They were not exactly do as you please, but Courchet was no doctrinaire, unlike some. The teacher was not over-burdened with academic knowledge: nor were the students. Nevertheless, week in and week out, they ploddingly followed Father Lhullier's precepts. The class would work mostly in charcoal from plaster casts of ancient sculpture: the *Hercules*, the *Satyr*, the *Gladiator*, if they were very lucky the *Medici Venus*. Every morning they had to say their prayers, as Lhullier put it, and copy one of these. In the intervals of armless torsos Braque did a little unsupervised doodling of his own. After a year or two of this he escaped the plaster casts and entered the life class, allowed at last to try his hand at drawing from the model, whatever her attire. He was not conspicuously successful. His drawing was un-distinguished, his statuary wooden and his figures lumpen. 'I couldn't portray a woman in all her natural loveliness,' as he put it afterwards. 'I haven't the skill.' Disconcerted by a live model, he had to find other stratagems and other subjects. An idea (or a rationale) began to germinate. In its final form: 'Progress in art does not consist in expanding one's limitations, but in knowing them better.' Expressed more personally, 'I don't do as I want, I do as I can.'[27] Braque's long march was to know his own limitations, and the way to work within them. At the Beaux-Arts, unrecognized and undeterred, he did what he could.

He made a better vagabond. If he missed Argenteuil, he was soon over it, and exploring the wonders of this new world: the flotsam and jetsam of the port, ships of every jib and spinnaker – inspected up close, with painterly attention, by the inquisitive land-lubber in his pocket-size sailing boat – and the sea, the sea. The young Braque dreamed like the fish. 'At Le Havre,' he remembered, 'I used to spend ages contemplating the sea. A sense of the infinite was borne in upon me and I had an obscure feel-ing of being able to get to the bottom of things . . .'[28] It was the contemplation of a lifetime, commemorated with a beautiful simplicity by the poet Jacques Prévert:

> Braque
> what was he thinking
> what was he dreaming
> in front of the sea
> that nude model[29]

The closest we may ever get to an answer has been given by the writer Francis Ponge, who observed him and worshipped him in later life. Ponge was some seventeen years younger, but he was perhaps the man with the keenest empathetic understanding of the unplumbed Braque. His writing proceeded by indirection. In the prose poem 'Seashores' he arrived, eccentrically, at an acute perception.

The sea, until she nears her limits, is a simple thing, repeating herself wave by wave. But you cannot approach the simplest things in nature without a good many formalities, the thickest things without a bit of thinning out. This – and also because he resents their oppressive immensity – is why man rushes to the edges or the intersections of the great things he wishes to define. For reason, plunged in the bosom of uniformity, gets perilously tossed about and runs into short supply: *a mind in search of concepts must, to begin with, lay in a stock of appearances.*[30]

There was more exploring, outdoors and in. Braque would go for long rides on his bike round the coast and inland, easel and paintbox slung over his shoulder, in search of the ideal motif. His early favourites were pleasant enough: the Tancarville Canal; the Seine at Harfleur, where the family rented a cottage during the summer, *à la* Monet; a quiet corner of the Côte de Grâce above Honfleur.[31] Other subjects suggested themselves by different routes. At the turn of the century his sister married a local businessman, Eugène Gosselin (he of the burial plot), and Braque made a friend of the bridegroom's brother, René, then an impoverished music student, later a distinguished cellist. In the municipal art gallery he discovered several Boudins and a Corot. (Many years later he authenticated an unsigned Boudin, remembering a wall of them from his youth.)[32] And in the municipal museum, astonished, he came upon a mummy from Antinoë, grimacing horribly at any visitor who had the nerve to approach it. Georges Braque did, gingerly. He buried the encounter for forty years.

Some of this exploring was done with classmates. Much of it was done alone, as in later life. Braque did not want for company. But he seems to have kept a certain distance, a compound of shyness (or lack of thrustfulness) and resolution, meditative instinct and athletic self-sufficiency – he swam, he rowed, he biked, he danced, he boxed, on some accounts he wrestled. His habitual detachment from schools of all sorts, from 'official painting', began young. The withdrawal bordering on self-exclusion from the *lycée* was followed by other withdrawals and other self-exclusions in other places. Yet Braque 'the solitaire' was not lonely.[33] There was something in him of Melville's *Isolato*, 'not acknowledging the common continent of men', but living on a separate continent of his own.[34] Like a true epicure – his proximate philosophy – he found happiness in freedom from disturbance. Left to his own devices, he grew. But he gained cautiously. A congenital discretion primed the slow temperament. Picasso's first mistress, the sharp-eyed Fernande Olivier, noticed this and thought him mistrustful – 'mistrustful, nimble, sly, in a word, a typical Norman' – a malicious construction, not quite right on each count, but a compelling example of the reaction an adoptive Norman Epicurean could provoke.[35]

In the evenings, before going to sleep, Braque embarked on a brief life of crime. As he confessed to Dora Vallier, he would bide his time before nipping out and peeling the posters off the wall of the sub-prefecture across the road. He collected chiefly Steinlen and Toulouse-Lautrec, especially the latter. Braque's taste in poster artists was shared by the coming Spaniard, Pablo Picasso, in his glandular fashion, who revelled in their shamelessness. (Paris outbid Barcelona in this respect, it seems, as in other sensual pleasures.)[36] Braque for his part is supposed to have had his eye on Lautrec's frequent model Jane Avril, who performed under the name 'La Mélinite', a new type of explosive, and was rumoured to exude 'a depraved virginity'. La Mélinite, however, was positively demure compared to 'La Goulue' ('The Glutton'), Louise Weber, a former flower-seller who became a panting attraction at the Moulin Rouge soon after it opened in 1889. La Goulue was a sensation. *Gil Blas* reported that 'she allows the spread of her legs to be glimpsed through the froth of pleats and reveals clearly, just above the garter, a small patch of real, bare skin'. Other accounts salivated over a more lascivious display. Lautrec's famous poster told the same tale, the action pivoting on precisely the area in question. Unless his father was a particularly vigilant censor (of which there is no sign), young Georges can hardly have missed all this as he monitored the activities of the municipal billsticker and pored over *Gil Blas* by the flickering light of the oil-lamp.[37]

By his own account he was never a great reader. That is certainly not true of the mature Braque. Of the immature one it is harder to be sure. As for Rilke's Malte Laurids Brigge at the same age, there was an element of postponement, a feeling that books were for grown-ups, and reading 'a profession one would take upon oneself, later some time, when all the professions came along, one after the other'.[38] He read in character, reading and re-reading, not widely but deeply, underground. Later he read moral philosophy in various forms, especially the briefest. Though he did not shrink from length – he read Chateaubriand's triple-decker, *Memoirs from Beyond the Grave*, three or four times – brevity was the virtue that appealed to him.[39] For Braque, the thinker should epitomize the thought. Philosophically, the décor was minimalist. He refused the sumptuous and the superficial. Gestures, moral or pictorial, had no interest for him. What seized him was the compact, often poetic, examination of moral sense and sensibility – *la sensibilité*, another key word in the Braque lexicon – especially the maxim or aphorism. For that he went to the gurus of the East and the West, Lao Tzu, Confucius, Milarepa, Parmenides, Hesiod, and the well-thumbed Heraclitus, ever-present on his bedside table.[40] Of the French, he favoured Vauvenargues over La Rochefoucauld. 'One should never judge men by what they do not know, but by what they know, and the way in which they know it' (Vauvenargues) rather than 'There are few things we should keenly desire if we really knew what we wanted' (La Rochefoucauld).[41]

In time, tutored by his friend Pierre Reverdy, Braque made the epigrammatic form his own. The museum director Jean Cassou found him in the studio one day, Vauvenargues in hand, intent on the text. He gave a short reading, carefully underlining the exactitude of expression. Cassou was struck by the elective affinities with the painter himself.

He, Braque, is one of the family of *moralistes*, adapting their laconic practice to his own working methods. A novel way of completing the jigsaw, a rearrangement of the pieces, and lo and behold a formula emerges, so carefully shorn of the superfluous, and yet so capacious, so luminous, so right, that it seems the soul of brevity. Such perfection produced by such thought. Interior, intimate, hearth thought; the thought of the solitary man making sense of the world; the thought of the craftsman in his workshop, the alchemist in his laboratory, the thinker on the cusp and in the bone.[42]

The escapist *moraliste* turned to novels, the occasional adventure, and a soupçon of de Sade, the last supplied (unsolicited) by Jean Paulhan.[43] In the 1930s he read *Travels in Tartary, Tibet and China*, a nineteenth-century odyssey to Lhasa, the home of the Dalai Lama, by Père Huc.[44] During the Phoney War he read an account of the expedition to the South Pole – to keep warm, as he drolly informed his dealer.[45] During the Occupation he read Melville (*Moby Dick*). At some point he tried Aldous Huxley, and Dickens, but was not completely satisfied: 'In *Great Expectations* Dickens persists in wanting to arrange circumstances according to probabilities instead of looking for probabilities in circumstances.'[46] 'Circumstances' were freighted with meaning for Braque. They connoted qualities, potentialities, a climate favourable for the work to ripen. 'A certain temperature must be reached to make things malleable.' Circumstances meant auspices and tolerances rolled into one. 'If Picasso and I had not met, would Cubism have been what it is? I don't believe so. That meeting was a circumstance of our life. I have even written that art is "circumstantial"; all the more so for life.'[47]

He was not above proselytizing for his enthusiasms. On the occasion of the Liberation of Paris in 1944 he gave Henri Cartier-Bresson a copy of *Zen in the Art of Archery* (even more evocative in the French: *Le Zen dans l'art chevaleresque du tir à l'arc*), a plain exposition of 'the artless art', and on the celebrated photographer's own admission permanently altered his conception of himself and his camera.[48] In the same spirit he gave *Zen in the Art of Flower*

Arrangement to his faithful studio assistant, Mariette Lachaud, who
was not so impressed. He also treated her to Dostoevsky (*White
Nights*) and Stendhal.[49] Did he see himself in these mirrors? He was
deeply interested in introspection. Stendhal for one is a wonderful
casebook of pride and vanity, 'divided between his immense desire
to please and to become famous, and the opposite mania, his delight
in being himself, in his own eyes, in his own way. He felt, deeply
embedded in his flesh, the spur of literary vanity; but he also felt a
little deeper down the strange sharp pricking of an absolute pride
determined to depend on nothing but itself.'[50] It is not too much
to believe that Braque felt something like that.

He loved poetry: the ancients (Pindar, Lucretius), the moderns
(Mallarmé, Baudelaire – he spelled it Beaudelaire), one or two in
between (Lamartine, Hölderlin); increasingly with the passage of
time, his contemporaries and collaborators (Apollinaire, Reverdy,
Ponge, Prévert, Blaise Cendrars, Max Jacob, René Char, Saint-
John Perse . . . an illustrious company). In *Gil Blas* there was
Verlaine and Rimbaud, 'the pederast assassin', hailed by the
Cézanne character in a contemporary *roman à clef* as 'the greatest
poet on earth'. Rimbaud's 'Vowels' offered the kind of lesson they
did not teach at the *lycée*:

A black, E white, I red, U green, O blue: vowels,
One day I will recount your latent births:
A – furry black corset of spectacular flies
That thrum around the savage smells;

Gulfs of shade. E – whiteness of steam and tents,
Proud glaciers' lances, white kings, quivering umbels.
I – purples, expectorated blood, the laugh of lovely lips
In anger or in the ecstasies of penitence.

U – eons, divine vibrations of viridian seas,
The peace of animal-strewn pastures and of furrows
That alchemy imprints on broad studious brows.

O – the final trump of strange and strident sounds,
Silences traversed by Worlds and Angels:
O – Omega, the violet ray of His Eyes![51]

That he could appreciate.

He could also learn a trade. He was apprenticed first to his father and then, in short order, to Rupalay and Rosney, from the school of Charles Braque, whose speciality was deceiving the eye in every way known to man.[52] Their newest apprentice received instruction in mock wood graining (he liked the undulating lines), and also in mock rosewood and oak panelling, mock parquetry, mock cornices, mock dadoes, mock corbels, mock masonry, mock marble, even mock mosaics. After that he went on to sign painting and stencilled lettering, making it leap out at the eye, just as Rupalay and Rosney prescribed.

At eighteen, in 1900, the call-up loomed. Military service was then an interminable three years, commuted to one for those able to produce a bona fide qualification from an École des Beaux-Arts or full certification as an artist-craftsman. His immediate course was easy to determine. Rupalay and Rosney might not meet the requirement for a comprehensive training. Braque was despatched to Paris to join another former member of the firm, Laberthe, who found him a little room in the rue des Trois Frères in Montmartre. He went, as he went everywhere, by bike. Eighty miles out he had a puncture. Lacking any sort of repair kit, he stuffed the offending tyre with straw from a nearby field and continued on his way. Half a century later a jocular little picture, *The Shower* (1952), unobtrusively recalled this mounted anabasis.

With Laberthe he got down to the roots. He was set to preparing colours, grinding the pigments and mixing the tones. So he embarked on that endless quest (*la recherche*) – the expression used, tellingly, by Braque himself – his initiation into matter (*la matière*), and the ingenious mixture of chemistry and cookery foundational to the craftsman's art. This was something more than vowels. It was an education in the grammar of colour. At the same time it was a roam through the periodic table of the atelier, whose alchemical tinctures included a number anathema to the purist. He discovered that all manner of things can be mixed with paint, including soil, sand, sawdust, ash, iron filings, pipe tobacco, and coffee grounds; that the oil to use as an additive is linseed or *sécatif de Courtrai*, brown or clear, exposed first to the light in order to fade; that there must be over forty shades of blue, and that he could make at least one of them appear like a puff of smoke in *The Saint-Martin Canal* (1906), a painting later owned by Alain Delon; that black, too, is a spectrum, a case study in 'the behaviour of colour', embracing such as smoked black and vine-black, tones to tantalize the nose and palate; that the grinding and mixing of colours is an art in itself, a question of temperament and 'feel' as much as pigment and proper-ties; that the artist–craftsman worth his salt is open to the elements, constantly alert to the turning of the earth; that he himself revelled in burnt sienna, partly for that reason; that powdered ceruse is too fine and needs thickening to give it more body; and that antimony is dried camel's urine – or so he told Mariette Lachaud.[53]

'Everyone has his own coffee grounds,' he would say, like a psychic. 'As for me, I read in ceruse.'[54]

Braque was well earthed. 'I work with matter and not with ideas,' he explained seriously to Dora Vallier. 'I mix and match.'

I've always been much occupied and preoccupied with matter because there is as much sensibility involved in the technique as in the rest of the picture. I prepare the colours myself, I do the grinding. I am absolutely convinced that, to get the most out of a thing, the artist must be directly involved. I remember the horrified expression of a colour merchant who, after boasting to me of the fine discrimination of his grinding, learnt that I intended to add sand. Where this feel for the grinding comes from I don't know; it's undefinable.[55]

Perhaps it was not as undefinable as all that. Still he measured his words. There are many for whom 'sensibility' would be an overstatement in this context. For Braque it had meaning, just as matter had meaning. 'The veneration of matter,' extolled Francis Ponge: 'what is more worthy of the human spirit?'[56] One of the words that meant most to Braque was an archaic one, *limon* (clay), of the kind that figured in the story of creation in the Book of Genesis. 'Man was created from the clay of the earth. I try to extract my work from the clay of the earth,' he told a friend, adding impiously, 'I have put nothing but cinders in my paintings.'[57] As Jean-Paul Sartre was quick to recognize, it was this deep-seated sympathy for the very stuff of the earth, the proclivity 'to side with things', that served to endear him to Ponge, and vice versa. Braque found in Ponge's artistic practice a certain analogue of his own: a long gestation, a concern with the simplest things, a lack of show. His 1956 homage to the living Ponge – a rarity from the painter's pen – was repayment in kind for a ream of poetic tribute. It was couched in typical form, yet somehow rather Pongean. 'Happy to declare my strong affinity with Francis Ponge, the poet who, avoiding all random speculation, has the wisdom to start from the lowest depths (nothing is lower than the earth), thereby giving himself the chance to rise. Leaving the roads and the paths, we shall follow his tracks.'[58]

The affinity between men and things was epitomized with quasi-philosophical rigour in the collaborative work of the painter and the poet called *Five Sapates* (1950), a work wholly in keeping with Braque's lifelong exploration of the way from the root to the flower. The title proposes a special kind of gift: a hidden treasure. A *sapate* is a fabulous article in a commonplace object – a diamond in an orange – the unlooked-for in the overlooked. (A reference to the Spanish equivalent of Father Christmas, when children leave their shoes – *zapatos* – out on the balcony on the eve of Epiphany, 6 January, to be filled with presents from the Three Kings.)[59] In this instance the five objects are earth, olives, jug, fish and shutter. Ponge offered a paean to each. 'The Jug' ('La Cruche'): 'No other word that sounds like jug. Thanks to that U that opens in the middle, jug sounds hollower than hollow, and so it is in its way.'[60] Braque consulted these scratchings, came to a decision – 'this book requires black and white' – and made some marks of his own.[61] The result is all they hoped: an inseparable accord, visual and visceral.

Braque passed his apprenticeship on the root. His first flower was the decoration of the Ceylon Tea House in the rue Caumartin, off the boulevard Haussmann. High up around the walls, he did a complicated frieze, 'very 1900'.[62] The frieze is long gone, but he got his certificate, and his reduction in military service, as a fully-fledged painter-decorator. House painting he could do.

As for easel painting, throughout his period of indenture he kept his hand in – laboriously – at evening classes under the benign dispensation of an old painter-instructor called Quignolot in Batignolles (near Montmartre). The time slipped by pleasantly enough. The torsos did not improve.

'Talent doesn't reveal itself in a moment,' said Chardin, his eighteenth-century predecessor, with feeling; 'judgements about one's limitations can't be reached on the basis of first efforts.'

The student is nineteen or twenty when, the palette having fallen from his hands, he finds himself without profession, without resources, and without moral character: for to be young and have unadorned nature ceaselessly before one's eyes, and yet exercise restraint, is impossible. What to do? What to make of oneself? One must either take up one of the subsidiary crafts that lead to financial misery or die of hunger. The first course is adopted, and while twenty or so come here [to Paris] every two years to expose themselves to the wild beasts, the others, unknown and perhaps less unfortunate, wear breastplates in guardrooms, or carry rifles over their shoulders in regiments, or dress themselves in theatrical attire and take to the boards. What I've just told you is the life story of Bellecour, Lekain, and Brizart, bad actors out of despair at being bad painters.[63]

And Braque? Not yet a bad painter. An unpromising one, no doubt. But an uncommonly good soldier.

2. 'Memories in anticipation':
The Confirmed Painter

The good soldier Braque reported for duty on 30 October 1902. He was drafted into the 129th Infantry Regiment and stationed, by accident or design, near Le Havre. Officially, Private (Second Class) Braque, Georges had dark hair and eyebrows, brown eyes, average forehead, strong nose, and oval face. He was 5 feet 10 inches (1.78 metres) tall.[1] Unofficially, he was in good shape. He had the build of a light heavyweight and the step of a Saturday night waltzer; a fetchingly serious mien; and for the girls who caught his eye, a spiritual smile. By profession he was a painter and decorator. On the subject of any other ambition he kept officially and unofficially mute. His muckers in barracks were Jean Dieterle, a budding dealer, and Albert Henraux, a future president of the Friends of the Louvre. They remembered his skill at rolling his own cigarettes, playing the accordion, dancing and singing songs better than anyone else. They knew he was keen on boxing. They had no idea he was intent on art.[2]

One year later he emerged, unscathed, a Corporal. Within months the student artist was promoted to Sergeant, a qualified platoon commander in the reserves. That remained his station, through successive periods of refresher training, until the general mobilization of August 1914. These military interludes were at once monotonous and distracting. Two traditional diversions lay to hand. The monotony was relieved by organizing regimental concerts. The distraction was allayed by bamboozling regimental officers, as *Le Supplément* reported in 1911:

Quite recently, the painter Georges Braque – a likable giant whose Cubist compositions are the subject of debate – had to fulfil an obligatory twenty-three-day period of service in the military. Upon his arrival at his company, the captain noticed his longish hair – not too long, of course –

and invited him to visit the barber at once. Georges Braque, however, not too keen about the idea of returning to civilian life with too military a coif, decided to keep his hair, which pleasantly complements his overall appearance, and did not go to the barber's. The captain insisted, and ordered an immediate shearing.

But the painter heroically did not hesitate to resort to lies in order to keep his hair: 'Captain, sir,' he explained, 'I lied to you. I'm not a painter, but a singer. I sing songs by Mayol [a popular *café-concert* singer whose own coif was piled improbably high]; my hair is my bread and butter. If I go back to Paris without it, I won't find any work. Please let me keep my hair . . .'

And the captain, touched, gave the painter permission to leave his hair just as it was.[3]

By the time the initial year was up, Braque knew what he wanted. He would go back to Paris and follow his star. His father was happy to provide – convinced, if he needed convincing, by the early portrait of cousin Louise.[4] He would live among fellow émigrés from Le Havre, share an unheated room in the rue Lepic with René Gosselin and his cello (and the ghost of van Gogh), and renew his acquaintance with Dufy and Friesz, the older musketeers, who had already gained admission to the studio of Léon Bonnat at the exalted École Nationale et Spéciale des Beaux-Arts.[5] More specifically he would enrol at an academy, consult the good book of the Louvre, as Cézanne advised, and become a real painter.[6] What he would paint, and how he would paint, were not the sort of questions he was yet equipped to answer. 'An aim is servitude,' he declared, after Nietzsche. He received a few ambiguous words of comfort from his mother – 'if you get disheartened, you can always stop and take over the family business' – and an unambiguous allowance from his father. He may have been cold, but he was cushioned, as the envious did not fail to notice. 'He always had a beefsteak in his stomach and some money in his pocket,' said someone sourly (and anonymously), fifty years later.[7]

Braque enrolled at the Académie Humbert, in the boulevard de Clichy, a few doors down from the Moulin Rouge, 'an academy like all the academies', he told Vallier with some disdain, 'where the teacher counted for nothing, where the students were amateurs, but which was very good for a laugh'.[8] Ferdinand Humbert who counted for nothing was an official portraitist and a member of the Institut de France, the governing body of the Beaux-Arts. He specialized in religious inspiration. His *John the Baptist* was especially popular. He was also responsible for some of the decorations in the Hôtel de Ville de Paris. Teaching was not his forte. Humbert himself was a phantom presence. He would appear for about half an hour on Saturdays, deliver a short peroration by way of 'correction générale', and disappear. On Tuesdays and Thursdays his colleagues Albert Wallet and François Thévenot held the floor. Live models of all ages wandered about completely unclothed. Classes were a mêlée, more or less creative. The students would apply themselves for forty-five minutes and then relax for fifteen. The talk was unconstrained. By tacit agreement aesthetics did not figure.

For Braque the lack of discipline was highly congenial. He found that he was permitted to work much as he pleased, with the minimum of correction, so long as he paid his fees (an annual rate of 320 francs for all-day sessions). In the same class was the eclectic subversive Francis Picabia, later an anarchist Dadaist, later still an individualist Surrealist, 'the first painter I ever knew'. Beyond that enigmatic overstatement, the encounter seems to have made little or no impression on either side – Braque off-put, perhaps, by Picabia's disdain for Cézanne as a 'fruit merchant'.[9] His neighbour at the easel was Georges Lepape, whose stylized fashion drawings would soon be the talk of the *Gazette du bon ton*. When it came to oils, Lepape was an absolute novice, bewildered by the paraphernalia of brushes and paints. He was delighted to discover his new-found friend's useful knowledge and transferable skills, and only too eager to quiz him further:

'Painting since childhood, you must have acquired a lot of experience already?'

'Yes, it's true, I have a good deal of experience.'

'And what kind of painting do you do?'

'I do a pretty good mock marble, mock wood, mock mouldings . . .' (Was he pulling my leg?)

'You have to know what you're doing, you know. There's marble of every colour and the veins, all the little veins with their different patterns; the same for wood . . . It's very hard but you learn . . . It's great!'

I didn't know what to think, because he gave every sign of being serious.

'But when will you paint here?'

'Here, never! Here I just want to draw, build, practise scales . . . Paint! That's another story . . . One must be alone, calm at home . . . or out in the country . . . but alone. Here, believe me, only scales, scales . . . scales . . .'[10]

Soon he discovered an even newer student. At the early-evening sketching sessions, which Braque usually skipped, Georges Lepape had become fascinated by a young woman of striking self-possession and accomplishment, able it seemed to capture every aspect of the model without moving her place, and apparently without effort. The awestruck Lepape recounted this to his sceptical friend and urged him to come and see for himself. Braque came and saw and was also smitten. After a few days they plucked up courage to introduce themselves. Her name was Marie Laurencin, 'Coco' to her friends, later 'Tristouse Ballerinette', the childlike but cruel mistress of 'Croniamantal', the tragic hero of *The Poet Assassinated* (1916), Apollinaire's gaudy embroidery on life and wild times, his and hers. Marie Laurencin was one year younger than Braque, though she liked to pretend it was three. She lived with her mother, Pauline, and her cat, Poussiquette. Mothers and cats were important to her. She was illegitimate, with a spicy ancestry; her cat was her mark, personal and sexual.[11] On first encounter she was captivating, an effect she took a little too much trouble to sustain.

The first time Gertrude Stein ever saw Marie Laurencin, Guillaume Apollinaire brought her to the rue de Fleurus [where Stein lived] . . . She was very interesting. They were an extraordinary pair, Marie Laurencin was terribly near-sighted and of course she never wore eye-glasses, no

3. Marie Laurencin by Man Ray, 1924

Frenchwoman and few Frenchmen did in those days. She used a lorgnette.

She looked at each picture carefully, that is, every picture on the line, bringing her eye close and moving over the whole of it with her lorgnette, an inch at a time. The pictures out of reach she ignored. Finally she remarked, as for myself I prefer portraits and that is of course quite natural, as I myself am a Clouet. And it was perfectly true, she was a Clouet. She had the thin square build of the medieval Frenchwoman in the French primitives. She spoke in a high-pitched beautifully modulated voice. She sat down beside Gertrude Stein on the couch and she recounted the story of her life, told that her mother who had always had it in her nature to dislike men had been for many years the mistress of an important personage, had borne her, Marie Laurencin.[12]

H. P. Roché, chronicler and libertine, who operated as an agent of influence in the Parisian art market, was a man with a morbid desire to seduce. Confronted with Marie Laurencin, he could hardly wait. 'All her pride was in her lower lip, her pout emotive and scornful. She had a long full plait down her back. That day, she said of some man: "He's like a bowl of flowers that never come out however much they're watered." That was how she talked. It was riveting. Then she would say of someone, as if it were the last word: "He's not at all simple." And again: "Someone without egoism is no one. But there's the style."'[13]

Braque and Lepape were overcome. 'Coco is bubbly, witty, ironic, caustic, discriminating, unpredictable and charming . . . We begged her to show us some other studies. The next day she brought in her boxes, notebooks full of drawings, watercolours, sketches, marvellous rough outlines. Imaginary scenes, too, decorated with strange animals: deer spotted with little flowers, swan-necked horses ridden by frail naked girls. Coco sought advice, criticism. She didn't rate them, she said. We did. We certainly did.'[14] She and Braque had something in common, it turned out. Marie Laurencin was another bastard Norman, with a drop of creole blood from the French West Indies. She too had made her way from Quignolot to Humbert.[15] She was forward but insecure, and for all the chatter, no featherbrain. Coco was serious about her art, if anything over-serious, and much involved in the craft; she was then learning engraving. And she was different – not quite exotic – as strange as her animal decorations.

A bond was forged. For a short but intense period in his life, the interzone between independence and acceptance, Marie Laurencin became Braque's confidante, his *accompagnatrice* in the stew of reputation and degradation that was the hillock of Montmartre. They kept company together. They drew each other, at work and at play, out on the town with Lepape (b/w pls 1 and 2). They shared jokes and secrets. They mooned about and moped around. Laurencin fancied that Braque was as prone to a certain debilitating languor as she was herself. She fed regular titbits to the gluttonous Roché. 'I've been grumpy and disagreeable for four days. Braque thinks I'm a lesbian.' 'Yesterday Braque and I were being lazy together – too lazy to do anything but fight. We didn't though. Very silly, just sitting there, each in his armchair. To amuse me he put on blue glasses. I laughed – ha ha ha ha – a man dressed as a woman – an actor with legs – legs – real legs like mine. I would have loved to run my hand over his skin – the skin of his throat.'[16]

They did not sleep together. Plainly there was an element of sexual banter and by-play in this free-spirited camaraderie – fantasy too, apparently, unless this was playing to the gallery – but it went no further. Laurencin kept the attentive Roché minutely informed of her progress in love, or confessed under his persistent interrogation; and he deposited it all, remorselessly, in the pages of his diary. In fact there was remarkably little to report. Licentious by correspondence and contrary by nature, Coco was more uninhibited in theory than in practice. Braque was not far wrong: her orientation was variable and her tastes various. (Apollinaire's collar stud featured strongly a little later.) As much as anything else, it seems, she liked to tease. They were few and far between who teased Georges Braque. Marie Laurencin was one of the first. And he enjoyed it. Indeed, the verbal was perhaps the most enjoyable aspect of a chaste liaison. Apart from that, progress was erratic and slow. This *jolie laide* was a perplexed twenty-two before she lost her virginity. The culprit or deliverer was not Braque but H. P. Roché, triumphant at last.[17]

In his twenties Braque still had a certain shyness about him. 'To see him blush when I asked permission to photograph him – and then to turn to the monster on his easel, a female with a balloon-shaped stomach – oh, it was delicious to see big, burly Braque drop his eyes and blush!'[18] Once ensconced in bohemia, however, he retained his modesty for longer than his chastity. Doubtless he was inexperienced. The young contender had many skills – he could dance a slow dance, and even a hornpipe – but fast women were not part of his repertoire. That was soon remedied. Montmartre was an unsurpassable place for the inexperienced. It was one thing to play the old hand with a callow Georges Lepape in the safety of the studio. It was quite another to tangle with '*le Malherbe de la prostitution*', otherwise known as Paulette, or a crash course in pleasure.[19]

Paulette Philippi was notorious, even in Montmartre. She was not a prostitute but a courtesan, *une femme galante*. 'Blonde, twenty-five or thereabouts, her face a little worn, a beauty beginning to fade, Greek features, soft, cynical, witty.'[20] Pungent and intelligent, Paulette was the very opposite of a dumb blonde. Her *galanterie* knew no bounds. She ran a private opium den in the rue de Douai for her friends and lovers – a who's who of café society, with a pronounced literary flavour – and their friends and lovers (all categories virtually indistinguishable as far as the hostess was concerned).[21] Paulette hated to smoke alone. There was small risk of that. The visitors who flocked to her door were well provided for. 'Sometimes one stayed for eight days, ten days,' recalled 'Baron' Mollet, Apollinaire's Sancho Panza. 'Life ceased to exist, there were no more days or nights . . . There was only one condition . . . You had to bring a basket of oysters and two litres of *mêlé-cassis* [a mixture of marc and cassis] . . . As I was working for Apollinaire, rather than make up an excuse, I got him to join in. I did him a good turn that day!'[22] Along with the smoking went the love-making. How active a participant was Braque remains suitably impenetrable, but he was certainly a regular invitee.

He occupied a special place in Paulette Philippi's affections. 'She set Braque apart,' said Roché, 'because he worked by inclination – *enough but not too much.*'[23] Making all due allowance for the inevitable occlusions and intermissions, they had a surprisingly long history. Roché saw them together at a ball in May 1906, and was still bumping into them three years later. The former occasion was the Bal des Quat'z' Arts, an event well known for its riotous behaviour.

He was dressed as a Roman, which suited him, sitting at the foot of a huge staircase, with a young blond, statuesque, in the Venus-Minerva mould, chatting. They kept being disturbed by a float from the procession that was forming. The third time it happened Braque said calmly: 'You're annoying us with your machine. If you continue I'll overturn it.'

– I bet you can't. It's too heavy! said one of the drivers who was pushing it.

– Well, we'll see . . . said Braque, getting up. He discarded his tunic, slid bare-chested under the float, on all fours, and got into position to lift it on his back. But the heavy float didn't move. Braque quickly got out, considered the matter for a moment, went back under the float, attacked at another axle, and the float rose a little.

A crowd was gathering. Bets were placed: 'Upside-down! Right way up!'

Braque had set himself a tricky task and one which he found more and more interesting. He flexed his muscles, he braced himself, he modified his tactics. Finally he raised the float on one side, a little, then a lot, and the machine tilted sharply.

No one intervened and people kept a safe distance.

– All right, Braque, shouted the driver, you've won. You've shown us you can do it. Now don't up-end the float, it'll block the procession!

Braque held the float until almost overcome, then after a momentary uncertainty lowered it gently to the ground. He crawled out, stood up, sweating profusely, satisfied, with a faint smile. I should have liked to have a photograph of him at that point.

He was given an ovation while he resumed his conversation with the Venus-Minerva.

Roché's thinly-veiled diary entry records the bittersweet aftermath of this Herculean labour. 'Opia [Paulette] is happy. One doesn't dare utter a word to Cab [Braque].' A little later Braque went off somewhere. Roché seized the opportunity to plead for an assignation with Paulette, who consented. 'She offers me the corner of her mouth. Cab came back and saw us. He must be used to it, it doesn't seem to bother him.'[24]

Braque may well have been used to it, for he and Paulette went back even further. He spent the summer of 1904 in Kergroës, near Pont-Aven, in Brittany, in the company of his friend and fellow Humbertian, the roisterous Jacques Vaillant; a student doctor, lecher and champion amateur cyclist, Ponscarme, known as Pons; another man more difficult to identify; and Paulette. He called them the Vincent Colony.[25] Pont-Aven was associated with Gauguin, not van Gogh, as Braque surely knew.[26] Apart from the cross-cultural pedigree of the place, the soubriquet was a nod to their heritage *chez* Humbert, which occupied the premises of the former Atelier Cormon, where van Gogh, Lautrec and Émile Bernard, the interpreter of Cézanne to the world, had worked twenty years earlier. The Vincent Colony took their pleasures seriously. As an earnest of things to come, Braque fretted at losing two days' work because he had run out of certain paints. He was waiting on an order of deep madder lake, crimson lake, and French ochre. ('What is colour? When you've said "red" or "green", you've said nothing. If it's a "red lake" that's one thing, if it's a "red ochre" that's another, and so on for ever more.')[27] Any frustrations were soothed by the luxuries at their disposal (as he put it), women, drink, tobacco: everything a man could desire, it seems, including opium, which he smoked with a will, work or no work.[28]

The summer of *luxe, calme et volupté* confirmed Braque in his inclination to cut loose. Over the next few months he abandoned Humbert and – as if to declare his independence – changed lodgings, renting a studio in the rue d'Orsel, opposite the Théâtre Mont-martre, where he indulged a quiet passion for period melodrama.[29] The summer fruits he destroyed, save for a portrait of a little Breton girl, modest in attitude and execution.[30] The model still reigned supreme. A little later he confided in Marie Laurencin about his feelings for Paulette. At around the same time rumour had it that he was a dope-head, spoiled for serious work. Marie Laurencin did not fall for that, and neither did Georges Braque. Thereafter, Paulette Philippi, *le sympathique Böls*, 'our opium dens, etc., etc.' all disappeared into the black hole of selective memory.[31]

He was not quite done with tuition. In May 1905 he approached the magisterial Léon Bonnat at the École des Beaux-Arts.[32] Bonnat was a pillar of the establishment, august, canonic, reactionary. He did not go to the lengths of having his palette and brushes served up each morning on a silver salver by his valet, like Jacques-Émile Blanche, but he did put on his coat and tails. His métier was bewhiskered boardroom portraiture of masterly accuracy and ex-emplary sobriety: the art of self-aggrandizement for sitter and painter alike. Bonnat could be mocked; but from a distance. Gaug-uin: 'A young Hungarian told me that he was a pupil of Bonnat's. "My congratulations," I replied. "Your master has just won the first prize in the postage stamp competition with his Salon picture." The compliment went its way; you may imagine whether Bonnat was pleased. The next day the young Hungarian was ready to fight me.'[33] Irremovable as he became, Bonnat was a considerable figure. He had an eye and a mind and a stock of strong criticism, vented regularly on selected pupils. The young Braque had the nerve to show him the portraits he had done of his own family circle. Interestingly, Bonnat saw something in them. Braque was in.

In a matter of weeks he was out again, repelled by the formality, the conformity, the academicism, the infantile sub-culture of the Beaux-Arts – and, it may be, the bite of Léon Bonnat's tongue.[34] 'His lash was good for me,' affirmed Toulouse-Lautrec. Twenty years on another pupil felt no such gratitude. Braque was with Matisse: attendance at the École should be replaced by a long free stay at the zoo. 'There, by continual observation, students would learn the secrets of embryonic life.'[35]

And so, at twenty-three, after six years of instruction, episodic yet unconfined, in art and craft and love and war, he was out on his own, free of any school or zoo: unattached, as yet, to programme or person, Paulette notwithstanding; sanguine, apparently, about paths not taken and citadels not stormed; absorbed in a project inchoate and intensely felt, monumental and individual, of timeless prospect; and wholly innocent of any scheme to realize it.[36] The nature of that project was articulated by Rilke, insofar as it was susceptible of articulation, at exactly the same juncture, and under one of the same Gods. 'Somehow I too must come to make things . . . *realities* that emerge from handwork. Somehow I too must discover the smallest basic element, the cell of *my* art, the tangible immaterial means of representation for everything . . .' Averse to articulation, the man himself was almost transcendentally vague about anything approaching a purpose. Braque the fatalist: 'It's very bad when one comes to realize that one is a painter . . . If I had an intention, it was to fulfil myself from day to day. In fulfilling myself it emerges that what I make looks like a painting. I make my path as I go, and that's that . . . It's like the alcoholic who has his little drink every morning. Me, I have my palette . . .'[37]

Palette in hand, Braque contemplated the still life on the table and the wall. 'It is well known that certain materials have a mysterious power of evocation, leaving us to discern almost human forms through their skin. So it was that the mould covering the walls of the studio I once had . . . evoked something special for me.'[38]

Sometimes he hired a model, at 7 francs an hour: previously, a serious-looking girl called Hermine, shared with his friends at the Académie Humbert; for a while, a pretty, whey-faced deaf girl with black eyes and hair, known to posterity as L.M., who dressed (when she was dressed) in purple and green.[39] Sometimes he sketched in the streets of Montmartre. He continued to destroy much of what he made.

For inspiration he went to the Louvre. 'As a young painter, I fed my curiosity and my dreams on the works of the great colourists of the past. From the Primitives to van Gogh and Boudin. There were stages . . . Raphael, Corot, Chardin, among others. It was first of all a delectation rather than a reflection.'[40] He knew what he liked. He was much taken with the phantasm of Uccello, whose awesome *Battle of San Romano* he stalked over a long period. 'He has succeeded in preserving something innocent of Gothic art and at the same time he has made a kind of puzzle of the perspective. A director of plans: look at his compositions, they are scientifically constructed . . . A director of plans and a visionary . . . And what a colourist, what a poet colourist!'[41] By contrast, he did not fall for 'the Gauguin maids in the banyan shades'. He loathed the *Mona Lisa*, 'for personal reasons', with or without moustache. The Dada gesture was not his style. Nor was he tempted to burn down the Louvre, the recurrent dream of the disaffected (even Cézanne, for all his bookish fervour).[42]

Braque was always happier among the ancients. He spent long hours in the company of the Etruscans, in particular, appraising with a decorator's eye the motifs of an amphora or an oinochoe, with their flying birds, weaving fish, engraved lines and geometrical patterns. All of this was packed away for future use. Fifty years later, after much thought, he succumbed to an honour and an institution – an invitation to decorate a ceiling of the Louvre. That venerable pile had three such commissions from the nineteenth century (by Prud'hon, Ingres and Delacroix) but none from the twentieth. Braque was moved by various considerations, but what swung it was the ceiling proposed: the Salle Henri II, the Etruscan Room. 'The undertaking would not have been viable in a room dedicated to Raphael, for example,' he told an interviewer at the time. 'Such an encounter was impossible. These Etruscan motifs, that style is very familiar to me. I was brought up among all that. And it was interesting for me to bridge the gap of thousands of years.'[43]

Raphael was not a neutral counter-example. Consciously or unconsciously, Braque adverted to another difficult passage in his pre-history. Young painters go to museums not only to excavate but also to appropriate. 'Artists loathe art museums,' as Valéry said. 'They enter them only to suffer, or as spies to make off with strategic secrets.'[44] They ransack the past masters and try on their clothes. They study by emulation. They flatter by imitation. In a word, they copy. The Louvre is a mecca for this time-honoured practice. Braque too was a copyist in his time, unofficially, until something began to go awry. Initially it seemed quite straightforward, beginning with the paintings he liked best. According to Paulhan, this meant Raphael and more Raphael. 'The first copies are excellent. The next show a distortion, which sets in, and worsens over time.' Braque's Raphaels became increasingly deformed. Soon enough – embarrassingly soon – he was stuck. In truth he appears almost as uncomfortable as a free-range copyist as he had been in the battery-farm life class. He tried alternative originals, from Corot to van Gogh, with identical results. 'Strange to relate: no matter how different the painters, in the copies always the *same* failing' – a failing never specified, but in Braque's eyes a kind of disqualification.[45]

Between the stilted and the distorted there was little to choose. As a copyist Braque was getting nowhere. It was twenty years before he had another go, just long enough for the fruit to ripen. In 1923 he produced *Woman with Mandolin*, carefully recording his inspiration on the back of the canvas: 'free study/ after Corot' – a luscious transposition, shimmery and subdued, instantly recognizable in its colouration as a Braque, subtly faithful in its radiation as a Corot, 'signed' and initialled in concord; a blend of well-remembered Corots, but above all a tribute to one of his favourite works, *Gypsy Girl with Mandolin (Christine Nilsson)* (1874), whose tattered colours could be found pinned to the back of a door in his studio. He was by no means alone in worshipping Christine Nilsson

4. Braque's Paris studio by Robert Doisneau (1957). The lower reproduction is Corot's *Gypsy Girl with Mandolin (Christine Nilsson)* (1874), one of Braque's favourite paintings. The upper reproduction, another Corot, is a detail from *The Italian Woman, Agostina* (1866). Below these are photographs of ploughs, an important theme of his late work.

and her kind. Yet it was Braque's 'secret filiation' with Papa Corot that mattered most. Apart from a felt sense of affinity with the *homme-peintre*, what Braque appreciated in Corot's meditative studio portraits was the way his models hold musical instruments but seldom play them, an abstinence imitated in *Woman with Mandolin*. Braque was bewitched by Corot's silence.[46]

In a damper studio, meanwhile, the failed copyist determined to find his own salvation. Braque passed the summer of 1905 in Le Havre and Honfleur in the company of two members of the Picasso gang – whose leader he had yet to meet – the sculptor-dreamer Manolo (Manuel Hugué) and the abecedarian theoretician Maurice Raynal, dog supplier and copywriter to the avant-garde. Raynal had fond memories of him at this time, 'determined to free himself from the heritage of the Impressionists, his easel planted on the beach, attempting to discipline the sea'.[47] His resolve quickened. 'Effectively the only way to get out of my incorrigible failing was to try to make a virtue of it.'[48] That was easier said than done. Braque's ambition still exceeded his direction. 'Renoir was triumphant,' Picasso recalled laconically, when asked about the break-out. 'We had to do something different.'[49] Braque would not be an Impressionist, not even a post-Impressionist; perhaps not a tame 'ist' of any sort. But what? For a brief and breathless interlude, a wild beast – a wild beast with velvet paws.[50]

'The moment of reflection, which was also one of choice, came with my encounter with the works of Matisse and Derain, in their Fauve period.' The Fauves or Wild Beasts leapt into public consciousness at the Salon d'Automne of 1905. In his report for *Gil Blas*, the critic Louis Vauxcelles monitored the proceedings with his usual acid wit: 'In Room VII are exhibited the works of Henri Matisse, [Albert] Marquet, [Henri] Manguin, [Charles] Camoin, [Pierre] Girieud, [André] Derain, Ramon Pichot . . . In the centre of the room, a sculpture of a child and a bust in marble by Albert Marquet, whose modelling is a delicate science. The naïvety of these busts comes as a surprise in the middle of an orgy of raw colour: Donatello amongst the wild beasts . . .'[51]

'The Impressionists' aesthetic seemed just as insufficient to us as the technique of the Louvre,' remembered Matisse, 'and we wanted to go directly to our needs for expression. The artist, encumbered with all the techniques of the past and present, asked himself: "What do I want?" This was the dominating anxiety of Fauvism. If he starts from within himself, and makes just three spots of colour, he finds the beginning of a release from such constraints.'[52] Fauvism was a mongrel movement. Indeed, it was less a movement or a school than a tendency or a coterie, a small agglomeration of adherents, of mutable faith, uneven talent and doubtful constancy. In historical perspective, it flared and died like a firework. In the hothouse Salon, its vibrant sensibility detonated like an anarchist's bomb. For every spot of blue, red or green he applied, Matisse had insults of an entirely different colour heaped upon him. Gallery-goers laughed out loud at his paintings – the noise could be heard from the street – while the critics outdid each other with their jeers. Daubs, scribbles, shapeless hotchpotch: such was the savour of critical opinion.[53] Before his elevation to poster status, Henri Matisse had a lot to endure.

Braque found himself an interested spectator at this three-ring circus, and was ripe for recruitment. Musing later on his youth:

I'm naturally drawn towards the things I like, to measure myself against the works which to me represent novelty and energy, in all humility wanting to be as good as those of the highest authority around me, that is to say the Fauves. My friends Friesz and Dufy were also going the Fauvist way. For me that 'jaunty' aspect of colour was stimulating. A reassuring physical presence. The Fauves were savages, of a sort. Impressionism had become domesticated, played out, mannered.[54]

From the lofty height of three years' seniority and a promising solo exhibition in May 1904, Friesz recalled:

Braque . . . came to see me around 1905. His father intended for him to be a decorator. Straightaway he was in touch with Matisse, and he had an intuitive grasp of the Fauve palette. Not having to clear the ground like his elders – Matisse, Derain – Braque immediately learned our trade and made the fresh contribution of his own burning faith in painting. He also contributed an exuberant character, keen to continue the fight alongside us, his seniors. I say seniors because we had already had six or seven years of trials, battles, salons, decisions, clearances and severances.[55]

The rank-conscious Friesz gave clear precedence to Matisse. So did they all. Apollinaire lauded him as Fauve of Fauves. Salmon dubbed him the Emperor and Vauxcelles the Prince. In 1907 the latter published a pecking order, with Matisse as Leader, Derain as Deputy-Leader, Dufy and Friesz as Followers, and Delaunay (aged fourteen) as Infant Fauvelet – to which was later added Marie Laurencin as Fauvette. Braque did not figure. Vauxcelles, no fool, never considered him truly one of them.[56]

Braque was not in touch with Matisse personally until several months later. They met on the eve of the other annual fixture in the artworld calendar, the Salon des Indépendants, in March 1906. Matisse was thirty-six, thirteen years older than Braque. He was both more and less than he seemed. He still had difficulty selling his work; and his life had by no means unrolled in the lotus fashion so tempting to extrapolate from his art. 'If people knew what Matisse, supposedly the painter of happiness, had gone through, the anguish and tragedy he had to overcome to manage to capture that light which has never left him, if people knew all that, they would also realize that this happiness, this light, this dispassionate wisdom which seems to be mine, are sometimes well deserved, given the severity of my trials,' he lamented in old age, the mask of serenity slipping momentarily askew.[57] But the inner turmoil was formidably concealed. His public presentation was superb. Matisse appeared impregnable.

In one of his dialogues, Plato's hero Socrates admits that 'there is one being whom I respect above all. Parmenides himself is in my eyes, as Homer says, a "reverend and awful" figure. I met him when I was quite young and he quite elderly, and I thought there was a sort of depth in him that was altogether noble.'[58] So it was with Braque and Matisse, reverend and awful, until a chasm opened between them in 1908 that was never spanned. In the formative period before that tectonic shift, the impact on Braque of his sustained encounter with Matisse was profound indeed.

Matisse had been regularly represented in the Salons since the turn of the century. His first solo exhibition in June 1904 drew an admiring 'not at all bad' from André Derain – high praise from that curled lip, whose contemporaries were usually despatched with a clever sneer.[59] Matisse's second exhibition opened just as Braque made his acquaintance, and he also appeared in the inaugural exhibition of the Cercle de l' Art Moderne at Le Havre (May–June 1906), an exhibition conceived and selected with the help of the Braque family firm. Braque knew him well, in a certain sense, before ever they shook hands. Their relationship was an unequal one – the postulant and the beatified – vital, on Braque's side, and at the same time curiously impersonal. It happened that they occasionally worked in close proximity, but never together, outdoors or in. Matisse made no effort to mentor Braque, nor to seek him out, as he did with Derain, whom he practically compelled to come and live and paint side-by-side with him (en famille, almost) for the summer of 1905, in the Mediterranean port of Collioure, near the border with Spain. 'I cannot insist too strongly that a stay here is absolutely necessary for your work – you would find yourself in the best possible conditions and you would reap pecuniary advantages from the work you could do here. I am certain that if you take my advice you will be glad of it. That is why I say to you again, come.'[60] Again, it was Matisse who recommended Derain to the python-like dealer Ambroise Vollard, a tip which led to Vollard swallowing whole the entire contents of the young Derain's studio, eighty-nine paintings and eighty drawings, for the sum of 3,300 francs, all before his twenty-fifth birthday.[61] Matisse's beneficence could be very helpful, but it was parsimoniously exercised. The Leader had a rather poor opinion of his Followers. He objected strongly to Dufy's participation in a group show; and he considered one of Friesz's later exhibitions 'shabby'.[62] It is possible that Braque too fell victim to such strictures. Whatever the explanation, he had neither summons nor introductions from the Fauve of Fauves.

Matisse's second in this incandescent experiment became a friend, for a time, though always a somewhat ambiguous one. Derain was a difficult man to know. Two years older than Braque, he lost three to military service. He re-emerged in September 1904, ravenous for the world, and almost impossibly sophisticated. His arrival in Collioure in 1905 caused a sensation. 'An apparition,' remembered the hotel potboy, 'a sort of giant' – Derain towered head and shoulders above his fellows – 'dressed all in white, with a long fine moustache, cat's eyes and a red peaked cap on his head.' He had enough luggage to fill a handcart, 'and a parasol bigger than a customs officer's umbrella'.[63] He was versed in the Cabbala, astrology, Pythagoras, Buddhism, the Tarot, numerology, Wagnerian opera, Goethe, Nietzsche, and Plotinus. He pursued a violent philosophical argument with Gertrude Stein, around her own lunch table, based on his reading of the second part of Goethe's *Faust*. (For which he received his comeuppance in *The Autobiography of Alice B. Toklas*: 'They never became friends. Gertrude Stein was never interested in his work. He had a sense of space but for her his pictures had neither life nor depth nor solidity.')[64] He liked the harpsichord, the spinet, the flute; on the phonograph he listened to music from Arabia and China. Maurice de Vlaminck, his brother-in-arms, said that he knew all the museums in Europe. He certainly knew the old Musée d'Ethnographie (now the Musée de l'Homme) at the Trocadéro, that ill-sorted, unventilated, benighted emporium of the world beyond the metropolis – the world of voodoo and juju whose masks and totems their thrilled acquisitors called *art nègre* – and he was perhaps the first to register the mind-expanding possibilities of African tribal sculpture for Parisian art.

The Fauves galvanized Braque into action. He was sufficiently encouraged to show his work at the 1906 Salon des Indépendants. Unlike the Salon d'Automne, the Indépendants involved no jury or selection committee. For the price of the 25-franc entry fee, any artist had the right to enter up to ten paintings. Braque entered seven, a mixture of landscapes from his past and still lifes from his room.[65] None excited any interest whatsoever. All were subsequently destroyed. Meanwhile, he had gone to see Friesz.

Othon Friesz, 'the head of the school of Le Havre', had his airs and graces, and his jealousies (Dufy was luckier in love, and possibly in commissions), but he was a knowledgeable painter and a conscientious instructor.[66] Advice came easily to him, as Braque knew well. After attending the opening of the Cercle de l'Art Moderne, where they were both represented, the two musketeers left Le Havre for Antwerp, where they installed themselves on the first floor of a disused casino, complete with terrace, outlook on the teeming port, and swarms of friendly mosquitoes. Side by side, they set up their easels. Over the summer of 1906, with Friesz at his elbow, Matisse on his mind, and mosquitoes buzzing in his ears, Braque practised scales in the Fauve key. After three months he could out-Friesz Friesz. For the first time he was doing work he thought worth keeping. He completed over a dozen hard-won canvases and had ideas for a dozen more (col. pl. 1).

In September he returned briefly to Paris, staying with the portraitist Alexis Axilette, a former winner of the Prix de Rome and an early enthusiast for the thundering colours of young Georges Braque – a further boost.[67] In October he was off again, on his own, migrating south for the winter, following the flock to the shores of the Mediterranean. Until then he had been no further south than the bar of the Coupole. His most immediate contact with the Midi was the work Matisse and Derain had brought back from Collioure the year before – *The Open Window*, *The Red Beach*, *The Drying of the Sails* – which Braque had studied long and hard over the last few months. 'Matisse and Derain had prepared me for the journey.'[68]

Symbolically, perhaps, he went for a different port. He chose not Collioure but L'Estaque, on the outskirts of Marseille, where the Rio Tinto zinc mines held sway. L'Estaque was Cézanne's old stamping-ground – Derain's too for a few weeks – and the site of a cheap hotel (70 francs a month). Braque stayed for five months, soaking up his surroundings like a chameleon. 'I may say that my first paintings of L'Estaque were already conceived before my departure. I took great care, nevertheless, to place them under the influence of the light, the atmosphere, and the reviving effect of the rain on the colours.' The light took his breath away. 'It's there that I felt all the elation, all the joy, welling up inside me. Just imagine, I left the drab, gloomy Paris studios where you were still working in bitumen. There, by contrast, what a revelation, what a blossoming!' For the Fauves, light was their heart's desire. Their scandalous use of colour was a means to trap it, or translate it, on to canvas. Braque tried that too, with increasing subtlety, but his own hallucination was spatial. 'There is something about the light that makes the sky of the Midi look higher, much higher than it does in the north.'[69] The yawning sky was a liberation. The corollary of that discovery was a horizon no longer fixed but free-floating. Landscape, and what counted as landscape, was then as malleable as plasticine. Sky was optional. It could be squashed to the ceiling, or squeezed out altogether. This took a while to work through, but it was not long before the effects were felt, vertiginously, within the frame.

Back in Paris, he selected six recent works for the 1907 Salon des Indépendants. Five sold immediately to the German collector Wilhelm Uhde, already a friend of Picasso and resolutely progressive, for a very respectable 505 francs. Uhde was a *dénicheur* – one of the best – a bargain-hunter, more precisely a bargain-unearther, among the upmarket unknown. The biggest bargain at the Indépendants was Braque. For Uhde it was love at first sight. His friends told him he had made a mistake; he should have bought Friesz.[70] Better yet, the sixth painting was acquired by a key figure, the masterful young dealer-in-the-making, Daniel-Henry Kahnweiler, Uhde's friend and compatriot, who was then in the process of opening his 'boutique', a tiny gallery 4 metres square sub-let from a Polish tailor in the rue Vignon, near the Madeleine, a first step on the road to pre-eminence.[71]

Braque was quietly jubilant. Satisfaction vied with relief. 'At that moment I understood that I was a painter. Until then I had not believed it.'[72] The confirmed painter left two of his visiting cards at Picasso's studio. On one he wrote 'memories in anticipation'.[73]

3. 'But that's what a nose is like!': The White Negro

He had sold. That was a necessary virtue. Actually he had sold before, just as he had exhibited before, at home. When it came to the reckoning, however, selling privately to the burghers of Le Havre counted for next to nothing. (Especially as one good burgher had only bought to demonstrate to his son the complete absurdity of modern art.) Selling publicly to the merchants of Paris, on the other hand, counted for a great deal. The market in esteem was a difficult one to crack. After a period of brisk trading, almost unnoticed, Braques were going up.

Braque ranged further than before, sometimes by train, sometimes by bike. Suitably dressed, he was not averse to the 450-mile (700-km) run from Paris to the south, very much à la mode in breeches from Samaritaine. He was still searching for the ideal

5. In Sens, en route to Sorgues, near Avignon, 28 or 29 June 1914

motif, doing 'rather geographical pictures', as Gertrude Stein aptly said, 'rounded hills and very much under the colour influence of Matisse's independent painting',[1] scenic hallucinations anchored by technicolour trees.

For the moment he was caught between public association and private depreciation. Clearly identified with the Fauves' enterprise, he joined with them again at the second Cercle de l'Art Moderne exhibition at Le Havre in June 1907, before heading south for the summer, to La Ciotat (between Marseille and Toulon), accompanied by Friesz. Outwardly all was amicable, but inwardly the Fauves were becoming fractious. The stale odour of hierarchy was unmistakable. Derain's encapsulation of Braque for Matisse at this juncture was a vintage put-down. 'It's Guillaumin [a die-hard Impressionist] a shade louder.' Ever restive, Derain himself was on the move, gathering strength to quit the pack. From nearby Cassis he fed Vlaminck news of the others: 'The Frie[s]zs, the Braques are very happy. Their idea is young and seems new to them. They'll grow out of it; there are other things than that to be done.'[2] Derain was not alone in this assessment. The jury of the 1907 Salon d'Automne peremptorily rejected all but one of Braque's submissions.

'He is finding solace after these exhibition misfortunes in the south of France,' reported Apollinaire. 'The attic of the house where he is staying contains a large number of books, and at present Georges Braque is reading the good works of the sixteenth-century polygraphs. This humanist painter has ruined his health by excessive spitting while he smokes his pipe,' he added. 'Being delicate and weakly, he should take several litres of cod-liver oil, a few glasses a day, from early November until the beginning of Spring.'[3] This little announcement was merely the *hors d'oeuvre*. Braque had entered the orbit of the heroic eccentric who was Guillaume Apollinaire, the poet who so loved art that he joined the artillery, as he said, only to be shelled and trepanned, like the painter, in the Great War, an ordeal from which he emerged an altered case, drained of devilment, the antic inspiration crushed, the pizzazz stilled. As he wrote then:

Where have Braque and Max Jacob gone
Derain with eyes grey as the dawn
Where are Billy Raynal Dalize
Whose names melancholize
Like footsteps in a cathedral
Where is Cremnitz who enlisted
Perhaps already dead
My soul is full of memories
Fountain weep for my sorrow.[4]

The elemental Apollinaire, the one behind the shadow he became, was a lyric magician, simple and sublime ('The window opens like an orange/The lovely fruit of light'), and a tonic to all who knew him.[5] Since he knew everyone, enrapturing and importuning as he went, and could pen an ode before breakfast, he was a magnificent showman of new art, the kinetic proclaimant of its makers. He proclaimed Georges Braque:

GREAT ARTIST G-RG-S BRAQUE
INVENTS METHOD
INTENSIVE CULTURE OF PAINTBRUSHES

Or, more tenderly: 'Here is Georges Braque. He leads an admirable life . . . This painter is angelic.'[6]

Braque's response was equivocal: 'I liked Apollinaire very much,' he told Vallier; 'he was a great poet and a great artist and that is what brought us together. We had a warm relationship, but I don't believe he knew much about painting. He couldn't tell a Rubens from a Rembrandt . . .'[7] Braque sided with Valéry: 'Aesthetics are not my forte; and then, how is one to talk about colour? It might reasonably be left to the blind to discuss them, just as we all discuss metaphysics; but those who have eyes know just how irrelevant words are to what they see.'[8] Practitioners would scoff at the futility of the endeavour to explicate the inexplicable, the method and the madness of the artist and his art. 'To define a thing,' said Braque, 'is to substitute the definition for the thing.'[9] Many of his fellows (painters and poets) would have agreed with him. 'If I were a believer,' he confessed once to André Malraux, 'I should think that certain paintings had been touched by Grace.' Malraux reflected wryly: 'I have never known any great painter – not one! – who hasn't told me in some way or other that the most important element in his best works, as in the masterpieces of other painters, was inexplicable – no matter whether that implied mystery or clarity.'[10]

In Braque's case, also, the belittling of the poet's art criticism has a more personal cause: it had something to do with Apollinaire's habit of reserving pride of place for Picasso, a tendency consolidated and accentuated in his later work, where Braque appears in the diminishing guise of 'corroborator' or 'verifier'.[11] Apollinaire's critical judgement was often suspect, as for example when he advanced the proposition that 'the most prominent personalities among the young new painters' of 1911–12 were Derain, Dufy, Laurencin, Matisse and Picasso, a list as surprising for its inclusion of Dufy and Laurencin (his lover) as for its notable absentee. Such things appeared in private correspondence, published after Apollinaire's death – he was swept away in the influenza epidemic of 1918 – but not before Braque's. The follow-up simply added insult to injury. 'Don't you agree,' urged Apollinaire, 'that for a new artistic conception to become established it is necessary for mediocre things to appear beside sublime ones? In this way one can measure the reach of the new beauty. It's for that reason, and on behalf of great artists such as Picasso, that I support Braque and the Cubists in my writings.'[12] Yet his public summing-up has an undeniable grandeur. Like Vasari's, his artists' biographies were brilliant exercises in mythicism. The more he had to go on, the better they became. Picasso was his ideal subject. Braque was more difficult. Yet his prognostication for Braque was as acute as it was expansive. 'They will say: Georges Braque the verifier. He has verified and will yet verify all the novelties of modern art.'[13]

Braque was well aware of the importance of fellowship in an overwhelmingly hostile world. It was not long before Louis Vaux-celles branded his work 'resolutely Kanak [Melanesian, i.e. savage], aggressively unintelligible' in the pages of *Gil Blas*.[14] It was just such criticism that made the moral support of an Apollinaire so valuable. Guillaume Apollinaire swelled a sense of destiny. He was a confidence-booster. If anyone would seize the day, he would. Seizing the day was no more than the artist's duty. Apollinaire, moreover, was a one-man artistic community: painters, poets and musicians marched together under the same banner. In this milieu Braque reached his maturity. And, as he acknowledged, the poet was a quixotic and effective sponsor. 'The poets of that time were our best disseminators: Apollinaire, Jacob, Reverdy, others besides.'[15]

In 1907 Braque had one more summer of Fauve work in him. On his return to the Midi he continued to paint 'in the coloured manner', as he put it. He was very fond of one of these paintings in particular, *The Little Bay of La Ciotat* (1907), so much so that he did something he almost never did – he bought it back. 'After its sale,' he told André Verdet, 'I felt a great sadness, a great regret. I missed it, I thought of it sometimes as of someone you love who is far away.' He was quick to deflect Verdet's suggestion of 'a shade pointillist . . .' – perhaps too quick: he had a reproduction Seurat on the wall – '. . . but very atmospheric and a study in smooth harmonies. It's a Fauve painting that doesn't roar.' In 1959 the good-tempered painting was restored to its rightful place in his dining room. Shortly afterwards he had a visitor who knew something of its past history. 'You see,' said Braque, deliberately, 'that one hasn't budged in fifty years . . . It's as fresh as it was when it was first painted.' (col. pl. 2)[16]

Back in L'Estaque, Braque broke the mould. In October 1907 he embarked on a serial treatment of the elements of that place (its houses, its trees, its roads, its viaduct) which evolved over the next few months into a style of painting that had no name, no school, no code and no precedent – painting that left his peers breathless and his critics stunned. The L'Estaque landscapes were not so much landscapes traditionally conceived as variations on the idea of landscape. Each element nested in context; but the sense of place was increasingly evanescent. 'The time came when there was no occasion for geography,' wrote Gertrude Stein.[17] The time was at hand.

Braque's rebellion had shattering implications. The sheer audacity of this work, and the cool effrontery of its maker, propelled him into partnership with Picasso. Roped together like mountaineers, in Braque's classic image, they entered into an extraordinary creative dialogue, rivalrous and unrivalled, legislating the future, vandalizing the past, completely subverting Western ways of seeing.[18] People dissolved, things disintegrated. Space itself changed shape. Time passed, Proustian fashion, within the frame. The traditions of the Renaissance were decisively overthrown. When the need arose for the newness at the heart of this project to be put into words, it was christened Cubism. If an ism can be said to be invented by a person, then Cubism was invented by Georges Braque. It was Braque who painted and exhibited the first Cubist pictures. It was Braque who established Cubist motifs. It was Braque who created Cubist space. It was Braque who demonstrated Cubist techniques. It was Braque who accented Cubist language. It was Braque who set the tone. And it was Braque who led a second revolution – the move into 3-D, making the first paper sculptures in 1911 and the first *papiers collés* (pasted papers or collages) in 1912.

Manifestly, some of these innovations might not have appeared as they did, when they did – if at all – nor with the same effect, but for Picasso, and the dynamics of their relationship. The pattern, however, is clear enough. It is not what Guillaume Apollinaire, Max Jacob, Fernande Olivier, André Salmon, Gertrude Stein and all the Picassian supremacists, past and present, have served to inculcate, or what numberless others have swallowed with their mother's milk. 'Brack, Brack, is the one who put up the hooks and held the things up and ate his dinner,' wrote Gertrude in experimental voice.[19] In the Stein house he put up the pictures. In the creative dialogue he put up the ideas. 'You can't always hold your hat in your hand,' reflected Braque characteristically: 'that's why they invented the hat stand. For me, I came to painting to hang my ideas on a nail. That allows me to change them, and to avoid fixation.'[20]

In reality, it was a relationship of equals – equals and unlikes. Their posthumous fates underscore the incompatibilities. Picasso is an industry and an archetype. His very name is a metonym for the artist-creator. Braque is a quark, dimly perceived. His elusive shade is reverenced by the cognoscenti. 'He liked his studios to face south instead of north and his skylights to be veiled with thinnish, whitish material, which filtered the light and gave it a deliquescent look. In this penumbra the artist would sit looking, as hieratical as Christ Pantocrator in a Byzantine mosaic, his Ancient Mariner's eyes fixed on his work. The monastic hush would be broken only when he got up to make a slight adjustment to this or that canvas. As a young man on my first visit to the artist's studio,' writes John Richardson, 'I felt I had arrived at the very heart of painting.'[21] Those less privileged are none the wiser. Braque had his devotees – they run from Heidegger and Beckett and Malraux to Françoise Gilot, Ellsworth Kelly and Jasper Johns – but their devotions were private.

Among scholars, corrections are being made, while the sniping continues unabated. At the official opening of the Museum of Modern Art's showstopping exhibition, 'Picasso and Braque: Pioneering Cubism', in 1989, members of the Picasso family could be heard remarking in loud voices, 'But where is Braque?'[22] The literary echo of this sort of response is not hard to find. A ditty by Telegrin Böse, a friend of the art historian Leo Steinberg:

> When a landscape produced at L'Estaque
> Reveals modernist trends in Georges Braque,
>> It takes but a minute
>> To find something in it
> For the anti-Picasso Braque claque.[23]

The deeper truth is that the revolutionary imperative was not either/or; it was both together. It was Braque–Picasso. The new order was a dual effort, with the emphasis on the effort. 'Above all we were very focussed,' reported Braque succinctly.[24] In that state of concentration they exchanged secrets. Like lovers or conspirators, their interactions were cryptic, flip, arcane, or altogether blank. This phenomenal relationship, the most phenomenal in the history of art, lasted at least six years (1908–14) on what might be called the conjugal model, and the rest of their lives (a further half-century) in remission. It has never been fully explored.

The origins of the relationship are typically obscure. There seems to be no clear recollection of their first meeting. Braque's studio in the rue d'Orsel was only about ten minutes' walk from Picasso's in the rue Ravignan (the ramshackle 'Bateau Lavoir' or laundry boat, so named for its distinctive configuration), but their beats were different, and as like as not it was only in April or May 1907 that an arrangement was made, after a little to-ing and fro-ing or polite fencing on both sides. If Braque, emboldened, decided to introduce himself to Picasso soon after he had confirmation of the sale to Uhde, that would date the visiting cards to the last week of April. In Picasso's sketchbook for the period from March to May there are the tantalizing reminders, 'Write to Braque', and, inside the back cover, 'Braque, Friday'.[25] Of this trial outing nothing is known. It may not have taken place in the studio, but rather on neutral ground, perhaps in the company of others; at any rate it seems not to have involved substantive discussion or disclosure. Both parties had reason to be a little wary. The sketchbook in question was full of outlandish studies of the female nude, exercises for what was in the process of becoming Picasso's cherished monstrosity, *Les Demoiselles d'Avignon*, while for Braque, the underdog, an initial encounter with the Spaniard of whose jinks and jugglery he must have heard so much already from Picasso's *compadre* Manolo, from Maurice Raynal, from Jacques Vaillant (who was soon to occupy another studio in the Bateau Lavoir) is not likely to have been a completely relaxing occasion.

However that may be, a connection was made. If there were other meetings at this stage, they must have been quick and few. Braque was away from Paris almost continuously, in Le Havre, La Ciotat and L'Estaque, from May to November 1907. He is thought to have passed through in time to see an exhibition of Cézanne watercolours at the Bernheim-Jeune gallery in June. From Ciotat he sent Picasso a trademark postcard – 'Greetings to you and your friends' – something more than the usual laconic 'Bonjour', or the mock-official 'Georges Braque born 13 May 1882 in Argenteuil,

Seine and Oise, sends you his kind regards'.[26] He was back again in October to investigate the Cézanne retrospective at the Salon d'Automne, returning immediately to L'Estaque in order to digest what he had seen. It was late November or early December before direct contact was re-established, with a celebrated engagement in Picasso's studio: the first summit. According to Braque, that was where the relationship effectively began.

My true meeting with him was in his studio, in the Bateau Lavoir, in front of *Les Demoiselles d'Avignon*. I was with Apollinaire. There at once I knew the artist and the man, the adventurer, in the work he set down in spite of everything, as it seemed. People have talked about provocation. For my part, I found in it an unswerving determination, an extraordinary yearning for freedom asserted with a daring, one might almost say a calm fieriness, already sure of itself . . . But Picasso was very anxious, watching for my reaction.[27]

Braque's reaction, spread at first by word of mouth, then from pen to pen, has been picked up and examined, this way and that, achieving almost the status of runecraft. It is variously recorded, translated and interpreted. A settled interpretation of sorts – or merely a truce – has been proposed quite recently by one Picasso expert, more than seventy years after the episode first came to light, but even now it is safe to say that no one knows exactly what was said, or meant, or heard. If Apollinaire was present, as Braque recalled, he remained uncharacteristically silent, then and since. The only other witness, or putative witness, was the temporary lady of the house, Fernande Olivier, who was indeed keenly interested. Fernande's own relationship with Picasso was beginning to unravel; she is one of several favourites (male and female), some passing more quickly than others, wedded in their different ways to Picasso, who were not best pleased at the irruption of Georges Braque into their lives – Fernande, Max, even Gertrude, looked askance at Braque the interloper, and at Picasso's consuming interest in his doings and sayings. 'I didn't do Cubism,' Max Jacob wrote later, '. . . because Picasso chose as his pupil not me but Braque.'[28] There are indications that the conversation was not only animated but protracted. By courtesy of Fernande, the fragment that has come down us is as follows: 'But despite your explanations,' says Braque to Picasso, 'your painting, it's as if you wanted to make us eat tow or drink kerosene.' Or, according to the dealer Kahnweiler (who was not there, but who was not far behind): 'It was as if someone was drinking kerosene to spit fire.' Or again, according to André Salmon (a consummate professional gleaner): 'It's as if you were drinking kerosene and eating flaming tow.'[29]

In Fernande's retrospective account, Braque's remark is a kind of parting shot at the end of an argument about Cubism, an argument to which we are not privy, in which the recalcitrant Norman remains (apparently) unconvinced by the visionary Malagan. His words convey his disapproval, perhaps his reproof. He then proceeds to adopt the new conception, furtively, in his own work.[30] The moral of Fernande's tale is clear. Braque is a mule, and malicious to boot. Picasso, the rascal, is a dauntless quester after artistic truth. The next episode is equally predictable. 'Fernande has buggered off with a Futurist,' Picasso told Braque. 'What am I going to do with the dog?'[31] In fact it was he who ended it, abruptly, on the pretext of her imprudent affair with a Viennese Secessionist. As was his habit, Picasso had nothing more to do with her. In her rheumatic old age, destitute, Fernande threatened to publish another volume of *Intimate Memories*. This was just the sort of thing Picasso was anxious to avoid, as Fernande well knew. Through the good offices of an old friend, she was bought off. Picasso was persuaded to part with one million francs in return for an undertaking that her memories would not appear in his lifetime. The undertaking was kept. The intercedent was Madame Braque.[32]

Precisely what Braque was reacting to is hard to determine. Picasso's studio was full of disturbing canvases, at different stages of completion. In addition to *Les Demoiselles d'Avignon*, a work perpetually reconceived and repainted, Braque may well have seen various spin-offs of that refractory process: *Three Women*, *Nude with Drapery* and *Female Nude with Raised Arms*, all towering figures, not to mention a small watercolour of a raunchy *Yellow Nude*. This was a collection of images the like of which had never been seen before in a civilized country. Its visceral impact on those who first saw it may be gauged from the mordant observation of André Derain, on witnessing the *Demoiselles* in progress, 'that painting of this sort was an impasse at the end of which lay only suicide; that one fine morning we would find Picasso hanging behind his large canvas'. (col. pl. 3)[33]

The *demoiselles* themselves are nearly 7 feet tall. They have upthrust and attitude. When they stare, they stare. They have no shame. If they are on view, then so are we. They are not to be trifled with, which is ironic, for that was exactly their original purpose. In truth the *demoiselles* are not *demoiselles* (young ladies) at all: they are whores. The painting has been gentrified, as it were, by time and title. Picasso thought of it and Braque was introduced to it as a brothel scene, *Le Bordel d'Avignon*. The prudish alternative was a fiction introduced for its first public exhibition in 1916, as a sop to polite society, at a time when even to spell out the word brothel was taboo, even if frequenting them was not. Obliged to live with the fiction, Picasso adapted it, not so subtly, to the Spanish vernacular *las chicas* (the girls). Apollinaire, Jacob and Salmon called it *Le Bordel philosophique* (*The Philosophical Brothel*), perhaps a nod to 'the philosophical boudoir' of the Marquis de Sade, a special interest of Apollinaire's. For the initiated, the amusement did not end there. Picasso himself liked to joke that he could identify some of the women. There was Max Jacob's grandmother (who came from Avignon), Fernande, and Marie Laurencin – not to mention, in later years, Madame de Gaulle, the potter's wife, and Gina Lollobrigida.[34] Which was which, he did not say. Similarly, the painting now known as *Nude with Drapery* was originally called *The Dance of the Veils* – the dance appealed to the artist's imagination – or, in Picasso parlance, *ma nue couchée* (an expression carrying the double meaning of lying down and being in bed), supposedly to indicate the ambiguity of the pose (horizontal and vertical), but surely also to comment suggestively on the status of the woman (kept and bedded).[35] That was the atmosphere of the studio. As Braque and Picasso grew closer, they took it all in almost before they had drawn breath; and what might be called the deep background of each other's work became instinctively familiar to them.

Braque was certainly not opposed to the 'primitive' or the 'tribal' as such. With Derain, Matisse and Picasso, he was in the vanguard of the appropriation of *art nègre* to atelier culture. *Art nègre* (or simply *nègres*) was common parlance, high and low, in this period. It was a form of words used blithely, and not without a certain instinctual superiority in the matter of both art and race, as a catch-all for Africa as a whole – in practice chiefly French West Africa and the Belgian Congo – and for Oceania too. When Derain was in London in 1906 he naturally visited the *musée nègre* (the British Museum, and its ethnographical collection). 'It's amazing, disturbing in its expression. But there is a double reason behind this surfeit of expression: these are forms coming from outdoors, in full light, and are meant to appear in full light. This is what we should pay attention to in terms of what we can deduce from it, in parallel. It is thus understood that the relations of volumes can express a light or the coincidence of light with this or that form.'³⁶ For the over-excited avant-garde, and not only the French, the wonderment of these objects lay in their plastic originality. The title of the seminal German work on the subject was *Negerplastik*.

The 'discovery' of *art nègre* has been claimed and counter-claimed, constructed and deconstructed, almost as often as the 'discovery' of America. The self-appointed Columbus of this enterprise was Derain's friend and neighbour, Vlaminck, whose claim was to have chanced upon three such pieces on a shelf behind the bar of a bistro in Argenteuil – of all places – one hot summer's day in a year that slips loosely from 1903 to 1905, and is most probably 1906. His eyes opened, Vlaminck liberated these and garnered more, one of which he sold to Derain for 50 francs (a Fang mask from Gabon, by the master of the close-set eyes), meanwhile channelling their influence directly into his own work, or so he said. As for the Fang mask, it is now known to be one of a series made for sale to European colonial administrators or sailors.³⁷

Braque made no claims to priority. Specimens of *art nègre* had been exhibited in the museum at Le Havre as early as 1904, if not

6. In his studio in the Impasse de Guelma, *c.* 1911

earlier. In 1905 he bought his first tribal mask – Tsogo (Gabon), expression unreadable – from a sailor or a friend of his father's.[38] In 1910 he acquired a better one, authentic Fang, impressively bearded and whitened with kaolin (p. 57); and in 1911 'a superb Senufo object, of uncertain function', from the Ivory Coast.[39] The two masks are visible on the wall in a contemporary photograph of his studio in the Impasse de Guelma, together with his stock company of musical instruments and other paraphernalia: an African harp (to the left of the masks; one of two in his possession), a violin, a bandurria (to the right), a guitar (on the shelf by his shoulder, half-obscured by the bellows of a concertina), some music, or music paper (propped behind the guitar), a rack of pipes (suspended on the wall below the violin), the inevitable jug, a vase of flowers that have seen better days, and an instrument that looks suspiciously like a thermometer (near the pipes). The artist himself is seen playing his habitual accordion. In 1912, on a celebrated shopping expedition – 'la chasse aux nègres' – he and Picasso cleaned out the traders of Marseille. Picasso reported gleefully to Kahnweiler on his purchases,

7. A corner of Braque's Paris studio by Alexander Liberman. On the left, six flower prints; below them a reproduction of a Renoir nude, part of the inspiration for some muscular nudes of his own painted in the 1920s. On the far right, a colour reproduction of van Gogh's *Sunflowers* (1889) and a photograph of a detail from the St John fresco (1353) by Matteo da Viterbo on a wall in the Palace of the Popes in Avignon, a sacred place for Braque. The white Fang mask hangs above a small collection of *art nègre*, two Braque fish sculptures, bowls and pitchers, a guitar, and an African harp.

among them 'a fine mask and a woman with big tits and a young boy'. Braque too got a good haul.[40] He returned the next year, with Derain and without Picasso, to winkle out a few more.[41] He now had at least three Bambara statuettes from Mali (Western Sudan), an effigy from the Lower Congo, and two small sculptures that have eluded identification, repatriated to Paris and clustered in a corner of his studio-eyrie on the top floor of the threadbare Hôtel Roma in the rue Caulaincourt. Kahnweiler recorded his impressions of an ascent:

8. Braque's Fang mask (32 cm high)

9. Picasso's Grebo mask (37 cm high)

10. Snapped by Kahnweiler on the balcony of his studio in the
Hôtel Roma, 1913

Endless steps – women in their slips going to fetch their hot water – at
the very top the studio. A glass cage – a lighthouse. A luminous brightness,
a balcony all round which overlooks Paris. A great many works: painted,
pasted, reliefs in wood, in paper or in cardboard. Lots of little objects on
the walls and on the tables. Braque sings as he works, like a housepainter.
With the aid of binoculars (he spent his childhood in Le Havre), he points
out to visitors the town of Argenteuil, cradle of his family, lying on the
slopes of the hills in the distance. Oh, the gentle countryside of the
Ile-de-France.[42]

Finding an acolyte from Czechoslovakia installed hopefully on one of the lower floors, Braque advised the proprietor to put up a sign saying 'Cubists on every floor.'[43]

When it came to *nègres*, then, Braque was something of a *dénicheur* himself. He certainly helped to raise the quality of his friends' collections. For Picasso there was a competitive element in this too. Glee doubled, no doubt, if his bearded mask was better than Braque's – and redoubled if he could do more adventurous things with it. Picasso could not bear to lose. More importantly, he could not bear to withdraw. He had to compete. One of his biggest complaints about Braque was that 'he did not like to fight', a charge to which Braque was quite content to plead guilty.[44] Inescapably for Picasso it was all rough and tumble. Braque had the power of abstention; and as time went by, the gift of seclusion.

Paradoxically, they fought all their lives about the fight. That was somewhere near the crux of the exchange in Picasso's studio among the Egyptians, as they were known to the artist's nonplussed associates. At that stage Braque could scarcely contemplate the *chicas* and their kind with any sort of equanimity. No one could – not even their maker. Nevertheless, he was not totally unprepared. *Art nègre* had been broached before, in one way or another. (Did Picasso share with Braque his '*cartes nègres*', the little treasure-trove of postcards of carefully posed African women, statuesque and sharp-breasted, that has recently come to light among his effects?)[45] Braque had already seen Matisse's daring *Blue Nude* (1907) up close, and been vastly impressed. The horror in the studio has been overdone. Braque's figure of speech about fire-eating was a jibe about shock tactics – wilfulness – and an alert about backlash. Braque once said to John Richardson that Picasso had set out to shock, but had not been prepared for the consequences.[46] As he probably knew, Picasso had been bruised by the response among his friends and acquaintances – a procession of ill-concealed bafflement and dismay – and Braque himself had just been burned, more publicly, by the rejectionist jury at the Salon d'Automne.

Typically, Braque seems to have taken issue most directly with an aspect of the making, challenging Picasso about the nose of one of the *demoiselles*: not the notorious *quart-de-brie* or wedge-shaped 'sideways nose' of the women looking directly out of the picture, a disjunction that repelled everyone else, but the 'high-bridged proboscis' of the two more transgressive figures on the right. To this Picasso apparently replied, 'But that's what a nose is like!'[47]

The two men must have said a lot more to each other than that about the making and unmaking of these paintings, but we are condemned to fragments and reports, as Braque in his prophesying old age foresaw. 'Things were said with Picasso during those years that no one will ever say again, things that no one could ever say any more, that no one could ever understand . . . things that would be incomprehensible and which gave us such joy . . . and that will end with us.'[48] Historically, however, there is an imbalance in the evidence. The noise from Picasso tends to drown out Braque. Picasso's characteristic mode of intervention was single-burst point-scoring. He was a riddler. 'Braque and James Joyce,' he said to Gertrude Stein, 'they are the incomprehensibles whom anybody can understand.' His best sallies were models of economy. 'Braque always has the cream.'[49] Sometimes, with trusted interlocutors, he was more garrulous. He talked because he liked talking; but in his own fashion he also talked for the record. He loved paradox. The paradox of Picasso is that tape recorders, even notebooks, were banned in his presence, and yet there was a collusive expectation of a lien on posterity. One of his biographers told him that he was like a native who didn't want to be photographed. He agreed immediately. 'Exactly!'[50] Nothing could be further from the truth. He wanted to be photographed, recorded, noted, fêted – presented and preserved – on his terms. No one strikes a better attitude, on and off camera, than 'Don Misterioso'. In the early days, before there were Brassaïs and Cartier-Bressons around, Picasso took the photographs himself. Here too he was ahead of the game. He turned his best tricks with crafty *mise-en-scène* – Braque as barman – but his favourite genre was self-portraiture.

Braque's noiselessness – his Sphinxian quality – facilitated Picasso's monopolization of all the parts. How did Braque's fire-eating remark gain such currency at the time, given that it did not appear in print until nine years later, in 1916, and then only

11. Picasso, *Portrait of Fernande Olivier and Georges Braque* (c. 1908–10). A confusing title. The woman in this photograph is not Fernande. It is sometimes said that the man on the right is Braque, wearing one of his favourite hats, but everything about the figure suggests otherwise (including the awkwardly perched hat). The barman, however, does look like Braque; and the unidentified man looks remarkably like Derain.

in German? The most likely explanation is that it was repeated by Picasso. (The least likely explanation is that it was repeated by Braque.) Picasso hated people laughing at his work, or being lost for words; he had too much of that over the previous few months. If he was disappointed in Braque's reaction, he gave no sign of it. Contrary to the impression conveyed by Fernande, and powerfully reinforced by Kahnweiler, there was no strain or hiatus in the relationship.[51] Rather the reverse: the dialogue broadened and deepened. On reflection, the remark was strangely apropos. Picasso may well have relished it. He may also have spun it. In that case the notion that Braque was hesitant, that he was 'unconvinced' or 'undecided' or somehow opposed, originates with Picasso.

In fact Braque was on to something else: the L'Estaque landscape variations were begun before ever he set foot in Picasso's studio. But the pivotal importance of those works took a long time to sink in. Key canvases disappeared from view in private collections for much of the twentieth century, which did not help Braque's case in the arguments over precedence.[52] Over the next few months his answer to the work he had seen was anything but hesitant, as Picasso soon discovered. In the matter of the nose – according to Picasso

– Braque conceded the argument. 'Later, Braque said to me: "It had to be that way." '[53]

According to Picasso, history is a one-way street. Picasso contrived to represent Braque, to speak for him in his absence, literal and metaphorical: a slippery process, begging the question of what is lost and gained in translation. The response to *art nègre* is a case in point. Twenty years on (when he was finishing *Guernica*), Picasso regaled André Malraux with his epiphany of 1907, and what followed from it:

When I went to the Trocadéro, it was disgusting. The Flea Market. The smell. I was all alone. I wanted to get away. I didn't leave. I stayed. I stayed. I understood that it was very important: something was happening to me, don't you think?

The masks weren't like any other pieces of sculpture. Not at all. They were magic things. But why not the Egyptian pieces or the Chaldean [Babylonian]? We hadn't realized it. Those were primitives, not magic things. The *nègres* were *intercesseurs* [intercessors], I've known the word in French ever since. Against everything; against unknown, threatening spirits. I was still looking at fetishes. I understood: I too am against everything. I too believe that everything is unknown, is an enemy! Everything! Not the details – women, children, animals, tobacco, playing . . . but the whole! With the *nègres*, I understood what sculpture was to them. Why sculpt like that and not some other way. They weren't Cubists after all! Since Cubism didn't exist. Clearly some characters had invented the models, and others had imitated them, tradition, no? But all the fetishes were used for the same thing. They were weapons. To help people avoid coming under the influence of spirits any more, to become independent. Tools. If we give spirits a form, we become independent. Spirits, the subconscious (people still weren't talking about that very much), emotion – it's the same thing. I understood why I was a painter. All alone in that awful museum, with masks, redskin dolls, dusty manikins. *Les Demoiselles d'Avignon* must have come to me that very day but not at all because of the forms: because it was my first exorcism-painting, yes! . . .

That's also what separated me from Braque. He loved the *nègres*, but as I told you: because they were good sculptures. He was never in the least bit afraid of them. Exorcisms didn't interest him. Because he wasn't affected by what I called 'Everything', or life, I don't know, the Earth? what surrounds us, what isn't us; he didn't find that hostile. And imagine! not even foreign! He was always at home . . . Even now . . . He doesn't understand these things at all: he's not superstitious!

Then, there was another thing. Braque paints in reflective mode. For me, for my preparation, I need things, people. He's lucky: he never knew what curiosity was. People stupidly mistake it for indiscretion. It's a disease. A passion, because it has advantages too. He doesn't know life; he never felt like doing everything with everything . . .[54]

Doubts have been expressed about the authenticity of this bravura account, a scepticism only strengthened by what is now known of Malraux's penchant for self-invention and for a kind of Cubistic collage of his own – his wife said that he ran up a book as a dressmaker runs up a frock.[55] Nevertheless it has become as totemic in its way as the objects it evokes. For Picasso they are *intercesseurs*, real presences, apotropaic creations charged with significance; lightning conductors for bad medicine; insurance against the evil eye. For Braque they are sculptures, when all is said and done. The inference is unavoidable. Certain things Picasso was privy to (says Picasso) were beyond Braque's ken. Braque was not only noiseless but bloodless too. Veracity was not Picasso's strong suit. He was a consummate self-publicist. 'You can't be a sorcerer all day long,' he remarked knowingly to Malraux.[56]

Braque's offering on the subject is a study in self-restraint. After underlining the impact of Cézanne, he told Vallier: 'The *masques nègres* also opened a new horizon for me. They allowed me to make contact with instinctive things, direct appearances which went against false tradition [conventional perspective, for example], which I hated.'[57]

Braque was more restrained in mind than in body. He was reticent, always, and yet eloquent in his fashion. He was recessive, but also image-conscious. In the pre-war period he cut a dash by design. The public Braque was part strongman, part dare-devil, part minstrel. André Salmon recorded: 'The gang set out, passengers to Batignolles-Clichy-Odéon, Georges Braque enlivening the journey with the sounds of his accordion, then a little-regarded instrument.'[58] He was powerfully physical, and in the early days of their friendship Picasso made comic drawings of an imaginary school for physical culture that they would found; there was talk of getting Picasso tattooed with a Cubist still life on his barrel chest when they visited Le Havre together in 1912.[59] Sparring and dancing kept him light on his feet. He enjoyed his reputation as a boxer. One evening the word went round that Braque was boxing at the Cirque d'Hiver, near the Place de la République. A crowd of painters deserted their posts at the Café du Dôme and rushed over to see him, but it was a false alarm. Whether or not he had ever been in the ring with a professional boxer he admired (an Englishman), as rumour had it, he easily outclassed the amateurs Derain and Roché. The latter recorded their humiliation:

I found myself . . . facing Braque, squared up, fifteen pounds heavier than me, and I was afraid. I felt his science and his strength. My slender arms were longer and quicker than his. I had only the recourse of the weak: continuous attack. With all my power I threw about fifteen punches which I thought were well-prepared, to the jaw, to the heart, to the back . . . except all of these punches landed on Braque's gloves, or on his forearms which he used like a pigeon's wings. Not one went home. His hands fluttered around his face like butterflies and his elbows went down all along his sides and hugged his sternum. I couldn't take any more. Was he now going to punish me . . . ?

'I've just missed my chance,' said Braque. 'I'll try again later.'

Fortunately Derain intervened: 'You look tired, Roché, and Braque doesn't. And I'm tired of doing nothing. Let me carry on with him?'

And I had the pleasure of seeing an assault between two heavyweights, Braque and Derain. The latter threw massive punches, with all his great strength, and he weighed fully ten pounds more than Braque. But he soon had to appreciate that not one of his punches landed, that Braque intercepted them all, that Braque hit him when he wished, where he wished, without trying, and that he was playing with him, waiting for more serious opposition than the two of us. And Derain was, in his turn, worn out.[60]

The boxing champions of the day had at least one thing in common: the colour of their skin. Boxers were *nègres*, too, and they caused a similar sensation. *Les Soirées de Paris* waxed lyrical over a match between Joe Jeannette, who resembled 'a Cubist dog from East Africa', and Sam Langford, 'a skull in which a candle occasionally flickered'. *L'Écho des sports* trumpeted the latest passion: 'to pass for a negro'.[61] The one who caught the eye of the Picasso gang was Sam MacVea, 'the Black Napoleon of the ring', an African American in Paris; not merely because he frequented the Ermitage, their headquarters, but because he looked like Braque. The painter himself would have dearly loved to pass for a professional boxer. In later life Picasso took great delight in boasting, 'We were constantly mistaken for boxers. Even taxi drivers would give us . . . a free ride'.[62]

Could Braque achieve *négritude*? His friends thought so. Georges Lepape had noticed the resemblance a few years before (b/w pl. 3). 'Braque is athletic: swimming, boxing – which he practises regularly with his friend André Derain – and . . . tap dancing! In Le Havre, from childhood, English sailors taught him the art of the jig. He accompanies himself whistling softly between his teeth. Tip . . . tap . . . tip . . . tap . . . TAC!'[63] Under the pseudonym of 'La Palette', André Salmon was even more explicit in a profile for *Paris-Journal*:

Isn't he a black king (a giant king) come to whiten himself at the École des Beaux-Arts? Insufficient laundering! Georges Braque went to other steam baths to cleanse himself of tradition. If he didn't invent Cubism, he is the one who has popularized it, after Picasso, but before Metzinger. I don't believe any other painter loves painting with a love as violent as this good colossus, who hides a bushman head of hair under a Tyrolean-style hat.

In bed in his garret at siesta time, Georges Braque mentally piles up the cubes that will very soon designate *Man with Violin* or *Torso of the Virgin*. This painter willingly practises wrestling, skating, the trapeze, and, every morning before painting, he keeps his hand in with a punchbag. In his own way a dandy, he buys Roubaix suits returned from America, by the dozen, maintaining that the long passage at the bottom of the hold nicely alters the fit and gives the cloth an unrivalled suppleness.

Braque approved. 'I read the cameo about me in *Paris-Journal*,' he wrote to Kahnweiler. 'It's not lacking in vividness. All that's missing is the accordion.'[64]

4. 'Mon vieux Wilbourg': The Encounter with Picasso

At this time Braque was hooked on the tall tales of Colonel William F. Cody, alias Buffalo Bill, and his buckskin-clad sidekick, affectionately known as 'pard' (partner). He collected each thrilling instalment and passed them on, with proper ceremony, to the wide-eyed young son of his best friend, the sculptor Henri Laurens.[1] Picasso, too, was a fan, Buffalo Bill joining Sherlock Holmes and Nick Carter in the tin bath that served as a receptacle for his penny dreadfuls. He sometimes signed himself *ton pard* in his letters to Braque, and he executed an official portrait of Buffalo Bill, Cubist-style.[2] Braque's cryptic *papier collé*, *The Draughtboard: 'Tivoli-Cinema'* (1913), many-layered and full of object-apparitions, features as one of its pasted papers a programme of coming attractions. Among the headlines are the words COW-BOY and PARDO, the ending of the latter masked by a strip of the familiar mock wood – a teaser for Pablo.

The ideal reader of this work, and the preview audience of one, was Picasso; and vice versa. Braque and Picasso did not make work solely for each other's delectation, but that was an important consideration. For Picasso, Braque's good opinion was powerful reinforcement. He was impatient to get it and often relayed it straight to Kahnweiler, the recipient of their canvases and confidences. 'I'm waiting for you already and I hope that soon I'll have the pleasure of seeing you. Kahnweiler told me that you've seen my Céret paintings. You must tell me what you think above all of the biggest with a violin whose intentions you must have understood.' The violin painting, inscribed JOLIE Eva (PRETTY Eva), was a hymn to Picasso's new love, Eva Gouel (Marcelle Humbert), successor to Fernande; in great secrecy they had eloped together to Sorgues, the Cubist hideout near Avignon.[3] 'Very pretty,' Braque replied straight-faced. 'The violin especially seemed to me a canvas of prime importance – very, very pretty. She's all of a piece. I'm hoping to come across lots like that on my way to Sorgues.' Picasso immediately informed Kahnweiler: he had heard from Braque; 'he speaks most favourably of the paintings I sent you from Céret'.[4]

For Braque, the relationship was a further step towards self-definition. Valéry wrote sympathetically of the young Baudelaire: 'his problem must have posed itself in these terms: "How to be a great poet, but neither a Lamartine, nor a Hugo nor a Musset?"'[5] Braque's problem must have posed itself in analogous terms: How to be a great painter, but neither a Picasso, nor a Matisse nor a Derain? Braque had a mind of his own, as Françoise Gilot re-marked. Yet he was also eager to engage. André Salmon, the perky participant-observer turned serial memoirist of Picasso's circle, wrote later that the young Braque was 'perpetually in quest of a comrade with whom to work out seductive solutions to the insol-uble'.[6] Famously, Picasso was a finder. ('In my opinion to search means nothing in painting. To find, is the thing.') Braque was a searcher. He saw that for his purposes the one to engage was Picasso. He realized almost immediately what David Sylvester noted sixty years later. 'In any event, Picasso *is* the issue, Picasso is the one to beat, Picasso is the fastest gun in the West.'[7]

Picasso's pet-name for Braque was 'Vilbour' or 'Wilbourg' – 'mon vieux Wilbourg' ('Wilbourg, old boy') – after Wilbur Wright, one half of the flying record-breakers of the day, Picassified, owing to the difficulty they had in pronouncing the original.[8] The real Wilbur became something of a folk hero in France from the time of his public exhibition flights near Le Mans in 1908 until his early death (from typhoid fever) in 1912. Replicas of his familiar green cap, known as a Vilbour, were sold all over Paris. The man himself had an image curiously like Georges Braque's: steadfast, self-reliant, practical. He was a doer, not a talker. 'The only birds who speak are parrots; they can't fly very high.' The French aviator Léon Delagrange, who saw Wright in action, believed he was 'the most beautiful example of strong character that I have ever seen. In spite of the sarcastic remarks and jokes, in spite of the traps laid for him on every side, in spite of the offers and challenges people made to him, over a period of years this man never faltered; sure of himself and his genius, he kept his secret.'[9] Picasso's use of his name for Braque reached a crescendo in 1911–12, when Braque's pioneering paper sculptures apparently reminded him of the equally amazing and equally flimsy contraptions flown by the Wright brothers in their efforts to go further, faster, higher than anyone had been before without feathers, utilizing as it seemed only a few spars and struts held together with a dab of glue. Such mock bird constructions achieved the first powered, controlled flight: an assault on their medium of which the space-obsessed Braque must have been proud. He and Picasso – who appears to have escaped the tit-for-tat soubriquet Orville – took a keen interest in these developments and often went to watch the aviators at Issy-les-Moulineaux, an aerodrome on the outskirts of Paris. 'If one plane wasn't enough to get the thing off the ground,' said Picasso, 'they added another and tied the whole thing together with bits of string and wood, very much as we were doing.'[10]

The pet-name, and Braque's adoption of it, spoke of a genuine affection, a fraternal bond; a keen regard – more than for any other living artist save Matisse, with whom Picasso did have a bond of sorts, a function of respect over time, but never the taproot of connectedness, the lived experience, he had with Braque; an acknowledgement of mettle, and above all a shared sense of mission (inchoate as that might be), experimentation, transgression, insubordination.[11] Shared fun – naughtiness – was a vital component of their understanding, and a yardstick for life. Hélène Parmelin, who had a good ear for the utterances of the older Picasso, records him lamenting that 'these days people don't want painting: they want art ... One has to know how to be vulgar. When I was with Braque, we would say: there's the Louvre, and there's Dufayel [a department store, complete with imitation Henri II sideboards]. And we would judge everything according to that. It was our way of judging the painting that we were looking at. We would say: that, no, that's still the Louvre ... but there, there's a tiny little bit of Dufayel!'[12]

The paper sculptures themselves have disappeared. The *catalogue raisonné* of Braque's work (a compilation as inadequate as it is incomplete, forty years after his death) merely observes, 'it is thought that all Braque's paper sculptures were destroyed', a voice that conveys the passivity of the enterprise only too well.[13] It seems that Braque did not take any special care to conserve them. Picasso kept his in boxes. When he gave his cardboard guitar to the Museum of Modern Art in New York in 1973, it was in a box from the Old England clothing shop in Paris, labelled 'deux pantalons rouges' (two pairs of red trousers), sent to the artist in 1913. It had survived sixty years of upheavals and migrations, two world wars, two wives, innumerable mistresses, and passing fashions.

Braque liked sculpting, in every medium, but for him it was essentially a diversion from his real work. 'A painter becomes a sculptor out of curiosity to see what really happens behind his painting,' said Henri Laurens shrewdly.[14] Braque was first and last a painter. His bursts of sculptural activity were more or less enforced breaks, for inspiration or relaxation. As for the works in paper, he made them and he moved on. They were more in the nature of puzzles to solve than objects to display (cling as they might to the wall), bearing the same relation to his artistic purpose as a chess problem to the game itself. The early reports of Christian Zervos, founding father of *Cahiers d'Art*, were reliably based on conversations with Braque himself. Zervos dated to 1911 'the first paper sculptures Braque dreamt up and soon abandoned, because he saw them only as an experience that would enrich and organize his painting'. Later on Braque said much the same to John Richardson. The sculptures helped him solve pictorial problems. They fed into the new system of representation that was Cubism. If they paved the way for the *papier collé* – the big breakthrough, as Braque saw it – 'so much the better: there was no deliberate intention behind it'.[15]

Braque sometimes availed himself of an assistant, an employee of Kahnweiler's, to help him with the mounting of his paper sculptures, and with the pasting of his *papiers collés* after he had pinned everything into place. Pasting was a surprisingly tricky operation. 'Don't think it's easy to paste papers without having them buckle,'

Picasso advised Pierre Daix, 'especially when you're using different kinds of paper. It's Braque who knew how to do that, because in his family they knew how to do that sort of thing.'[16] Picasso also had an assistant, it turns out, whose name was Georges Braque. Even so Picasso had trouble with his pasting. In consequence a number of his *papiers collés* are also *papiers épinglés*: they are pasted *and* pinned. As for the decorator Braque, throughout his life he sought the help of collaborators for processes with which he was not completely familiar, such as engraving or glass-making, and for special commissions such as the Louvre ceiling. The collaborators had to have a particular bent and a sympathetic disposition. They might be fellow artists (Jean Bazaine and stained glass) or more often master craftsmen: the engraver Jean Signovert; the lithographer Henri Deschamps; the printer Aldo Crommelynck. All of these men emerged with a powerful admiration for Georges Braque.[17] He may have glimpsed the flower, but he never forgot the root. Such a connoisseur of *faux bois* was bound to appreciate an assistant called Boischaud (hot wood). Boischaud, moreover, not only knew how to paste mock wood. He also knew how to sign mock signatures. In the artist's absence, at Kahnweiler's behest, he occasionally signed a Braque or a Picasso on the back of the canvas: *faux boischaud*.[18]

An isolated photograph of Wilbourg's 'little paper scaffoldings' shows a corner relief in his Hôtel Roma studio – the eyrie where Kahnweiler had noticed all manner of reliefs, in wood, paper, and cardboard – completed on or after 18 February 1914, the date of *Le Matin*, the newspaper at the base of the construction; made of paper and cardboard, some of it shaded and painted; cut and shaped and curled; glued and pinned together; and held as if in suspension in a corner of the room.[19] What it is a sculpture of, or what it represents, is not immediately obvious. In its general configuration it is rather like a still life – rather like the more durable sculptures made by Henri Laurens soon afterwards – and the upright form in newspaper, presumably a bottle, conceivably an overweight wind instrument, bears the cropped legend ART. Other announcements are equally brief. The headline that sticks out from *Le Matin* is

12. The corner sculpture in Braque's Hôtel Roma studio, 1914

TU DOIS (you must, you should, you owe): a neatly tailored admonition, as it appears, but inscrutable then and impenetrable now.

Whether this was typical of the constructions made two or more years earlier, we cannot be sure. According to Douglas Cooper, whose *château des cubistes* in the South of France boasted a fine collection of Braques (including his first *papier collé*), and who had the opportunity to talk to the artist at length about them, Braque's earliest sculptures were constructions or cut-out models of a single object (a guitar, a violin), in a single medium (paper or cardboard), which was then painted; and indeed Braque himself sometimes referred to them as *papiers peints*, painted papers.[20] Apart from Kahnweiler, Picasso, Laurens and a few other intimates, hardly anyone can have seen them at the time – they were never sold or exhibited – but one who did was the future corner constructivist, Vladimir Tatlin, who made the rounds of the Paris studios in April

1914 and took the idea back to Moscow with him. Picasso for his part was much seized by them. Cooper thought that he simply followed Braque's example. This sounds suspiciously like corroboration or verification in reverse, but it seems to accord with his initial practice – before he launched into the brightly painted bronze and the perforated absinthe spoon – except that his sculptures, often guitars, were more akin to bas-reliefs (placed against a flat wall) rather than corner ones, with a form of back-board acting almost like a mount or a face, from which protruded other elements or features.

Such constructions more closely matched the architecture of Braque's paintings than the pattern of his sculptures. They harked back to the mould-breaking work of 1907–8: the landscape variations, punctiliously derived from the model in L'Estaque and scrupulously deformed in the studio in Paris. The fierce originality of those customized, progressively cubified, canvases lay in the way in which they were built up. Consciously following in the footsteps of Cézanne, Braque opened his campaign by abandoning Renaissance perspective. Meeting the demands of traditional perspective, the perspective of the famous railway lines that 'vanish' to a point far away, had always been a burden to him:

the whole Renaissance tradition is antipathetic to me. The hard-and-fast rules of perspective which it succeeded in imposing on art were a ghastly mistake which it has taken four centuries to redress: Cézanne and, after him, Picasso and myself can take a lot of the credit for this. Scientific perspective is nothing but eye-fooling illusionism; it is simply a trick – a bad trick – which makes it impossible for an artist to convey a full experience of space, since it forces the objects in a picture to disappear away from the beholder instead of bringing them within his reach, as painting should.

'Mechanized as it is, that perspective never yields full possession of things,' he told Vallier. 'It proceeds from one point of view and doesn't depart from it. And yet, the point of view is a very small thing. It's as if someone were to spend all his life drawing profiles

13. The model for
Houses at L'Estaque
(1908), taken by
Kahnweiler in 1910
(compare col. pl. 4)

pretending that man has only one eye.' When you begin to think like that, he added, 'everything changes, you have no idea how much!' Perspective, as John Berger has said, is not a science but a hope.[21]

The notion of 'possessing' things, of bringing them within reach, was now central to Braque's thinking. The lure of the Midi and the revelation of the meridional light had waned. 'I would have had to push on to Senegal,' was his laconic reflection. 'One can't rely on more than ten months of enthusiasm.'[22] The paroxysm of Fauvism was over. The many-changing colours left the world as it was. Vermilion doesn't do everything, as Friesz was heard to remark. In retrospect Braque was inclined to minimize it as a phase he went through, underplaying both his ardour and his output. Braque fostered the impression that he painted rather few Fauve canvases – 'hardly more than twenty' – yet Douglas Cooper remembered him in 1935 fetching at least thirty out of a dark corner of his studio, in order to sign and date them ('some by guesswork') for his one and only Fauve exhibition, at the Galerie Pierre [Loeb], in 1938; and in the post-war period no fewer than sixty-five were authenticated for the phantom *catalogue raisonné*.[23] Whether or not he was ever a true Fauve, the Fauvist experience had more significance for him than he ever cared to admit.

Part of the explanation for the unspoken discrepancy may lie in Braque's dealings with Henri Matisse. For all his largeness of spirit, Matisse brooked no insubordination in the ranks. There is a ring of truth to the quip that he could not see a movement without wanting to become leader of it. As new allegiances formed over the winter of 1907–8, his ascendancy was in jeopardy, and he knew it. 'Poor, patient Matisse,' wrote the visiting American Gelett Burgess, 'breaking his way through this jungle of art, sees his followers go whooping off in vagrom [vagrant] paths to right and left. He hears his own speculative words distorted, misinterpreted, inciting innumerable vagaries . . . What wonder Matisse shakes his head and does not smile!'[24] Matisse was an uncomfortable leader. Braque was an uncomfortable follower. A parting was inevitable. Braque never fully acknowledged his early dependence on Matisse's example. Cooper had some more indiscretions: 'Braque . . . seems to have felt that he could no longer work alongside of such a dogmatic personality as Matisse,' he recorded in 1958, four years after Matisse's death. 'As Braque remarked to me recently, "I came to realize that Matisse's much-vaunted sense of colour was little more than the clever application of a scientific formula." '[25] Braque could never have said such a thing in public, even perhaps in private (or what passed for private with Douglas Cooper), while Matisse was alive. As soon as the coast was clear, Cooper wrote it all down for a lecture at the Louvre.

As for his métier, Braque's appreciation deepened. He was looking into rather than at. He began to absorb himself in the fundamental problem that is the materialization of space on canvas. How to convey the 'full experience'? Lost in space, painting was a paper tiger. The traditional chiaroscuro satisfied him no better than the traditional perspective. 'I was told: shading-in will do. No, in the first instance what counts is the thinking one does. I tried to think it out.'[26]

What Braque was after was not entirely clear at first, to him or to others. 'He looks at Nature in order to possess it emotionally,' recorded Gelett Burgess, after an interview with the artist (his first) in April 1908. In the course of the interview Braque talked a lot about giving volume to things; to keep Burgess on his toes, he also mentioned 'the search for violence'. He spoke of his quest for non-illusionistic three-dimensionality: relief without trompe-l'œil, as he later explained. It was to Burgess that he confessed his inability to portray a woman in all her natural loveliness – 'I must, therefore, create a new sort of beauty, the beauty that appears to me in terms of volume, of line, of mass, of weight, and through that beauty interpret my subjective impression. Nature is a mere pretext for a decorative composition, plus sentiment. It suggests emotion, and I translate that emotion into art. I want to expose the Absolute, and not merely the factitious woman.'[27] (Deprecation of the facitious was a recurrent theme. When Braque saw a retrospective of Fauve painting in 1951 he said that he could no longer rekindle his earlier enthusiasm. Even the best work of Matisse and Derain struck him as 'disappointingly factitious'.)[28] The point at issue became one of Braque's cardinal precepts. The new sort of beauty had to be graspable. 'It is not enough to let people see what one paints. You even have to let them touch it.'[29]

Braque gave Burgess an ink drawing of a work completed just in time for the 1908 Salon des Indépendants, a three-in-one *Woman* (b/w pl. 5), missing presumed destroyed, which he exhibited together with some landscapes. In the drawing, the woman-forms are rough-hewn, sculptural, though the volumes are hatched with some intensity; the faces are stylized, but barely mask-like (and the noses hardly developed at all); the hands and feet are square-cut Picasso-primitivist; the postures are reminiscent of Cézanne's bathers.[30] No visual record exists of the painting, which was apparently very similar. Among the 'slick well-licked candy-box nudes' at the Indépendants, as Burgess's companion Inez Haynes Irwin noted, it caused quite a stir. One critic christened it *Hunger, Thirst, Sensuality*. 'A woman – if one may call her such – is eating her right leg, drinking her blood, and with her left hand . . . No, I could never tell you where her left hand is wandering, no doubt in memory of Titian.'[31] The great majority were hostile, if not vitriolic. 'Is not the painter Braque making fools of us?' The intuitive Apollinaire, who was keeping a close eye on the painter's progress, did not think so.

The big composition of Monsieur Georges Braque seems to me to be the most original effort of this Salon. Certainly the distance travelled by the artist between the tenderness of *The Dale* [one of the landscapes] and the new composition is considerable. And yet these pictures have been painted at an interval of only six months. There is no point in dwelling on the summary expression of this composition, but we must recognize that Monsieur Braque has steadfastly realized his will to construct. The science of construction confronts the painter with many problems that are not yet resolved. Monsieur Braque has courageously taken on several of them. It is merely one eventful stage in the proud ascent of an artist who, no doubt, we will soon find less anxious.[32]

Surprisingly, *Woman* was not alone. Braque had been working all winter on another figure, described by Inez Haynes Irwin as '[a] fearful picture of a woman with exposed leg muscles; a stomach like a balloon that's begun to leak and sag; one breast shaped like a water pitcher, the nipple down in the corner; the other growing up near the shoulder somewhere; square shoulders.'[33] This was the *Large Nude*, his modernist odalisque, his body-building *Blue Nude*, his counterpart *nue couchée*: a civilized response to savage customs (b/w pl. 4). Experimentally, the *Large Nude* models more than the eye should see (her left buttock comes round to join her right thigh), but this boldness cannot resolve her existential dilemma – to stand, seen from the side, or to lie, seen from above? Doughty as she is, she remains strangely undetermined, at once clod-hopping and 'ungrounded', in John Richardson's word, a gigantic study for a finished work that never came. The painter must have regarded it as a comparative failure; there were no more figures for another two years, and then they emerged much changed. 'In my youth I had made lots of portraits, almost all destroyed. Fundamentally, it never really moved me and when I did figures during the period of our Cubist researches it was like still lifes.' Still life was safer. 'A portrait is a job in which there is always something wrong with the mouth,' said Braque. 'Show a bourgeois the most advanced art you like, and he is delighted; but just you touch his mug and there's Hell to pay.'[34]

As for the figure, so for the landscape. In escaping from the straitjacket of traditional perspective, Braque sought also to escape the illusionism that went with it: the illusion of reality seen at a distance as if through a window. This had implications for how he set about his work. 'I bid farewell to the vanishing point. And, to avoid a projection towards infinity, I interpose closely spaced overlapping planes, so that it is understood that one thing is in front of another instead of distributed in space . . . Rather than starting with the foreground, I would concentrate on the centre of the picture. Soon I even reversed the perspective, the pyramid of forms, so that it would come towards me, and end up at the spectator.'[35] Instead of receding tidily into space in the prescribed manner, the forms in Braque's paintings advanced disconcertingly towards the viewer. Landscapes became landslips, as though bearing witness to some underground volcanic activity or process of erosion. Topography yielded to insecurity. The old order was subverted. Far from receding, houses and trees asserted themselves, in their quiet way, reclaiming inalienable rights to light, space and a certain dignity. Studying this work, Matisse observed acutely that Braque's houses (or rather the signs used to represent them) were employed formally, 'to let them stand out in the ensemble of the landscape', and at the same time morally, 'to develop the idea of humanity which they stood for'.[36] In late 1907 there was still a vestige of sky. During the summer of 1908, when he returned once more to the well-trodden model (this time with Dufy in tow), the sky disappeared altogether, in favour of an 'all-over' background with pictorial protrusions (b/w pl. 6). Traditional landscape space met the same fate as traditional perspective. The sky was not seen again for another twenty years.

Keen to make the strongest possible showing at the 1908 Salon d'Automne, Braque submitted six of his L'Estaque landscapes. On the jury were Guérin, Marquet, Matisse and Rouault, among whom Matisse was the dominant personality. Collectively that groupuscule rejected Braque's whole submission. In such cases, according to the rules of the Salon, each member of the jury was entitled to 'retrieve' one rejected work; Guérin and Marquet alone elected to do so, thus keeping two in play. This was too much for Braque, who withdrew them all (which was not according to the rules of the Salon), and laid the blame firmly at Matisse's door. Louis Vauxcelles later recounted how Matisse told him at the time, '"Braque has just sent in a painting made of little cubes." . . . In order to make himself better understood (for I was dumbfounded . . .), he took a piece of paper and in three seconds he drew two ascending and converging lines between which the little cubes were set, depicting an Estaque of Georges Braque, who, incidentally, withdrew it from the Grand Palais on the eve of the opening.'[37] The painting in question was almost certainly *Houses at L'Estaque* (1908), as yet unexhibited but neither unseen nor unheard (col. pl. 4). Long after the dust had settled, Matisse remembered it as 'really the first picture constituting the origin of Cubism . . . We considered it as something quite new, about which there were many discussions'. Later still he let slip a further significant detail. He had seen it, not in Braque's studio, but in Picasso's. 'I saw the picture in the studio of Picasso, who discussed it with his friends.'[38] Picasso had borrowed it to study and to learn. Great artists are sharp critics. Matisse and Picasso knew well enough that there was a new gun in town – slower, perhaps, but dangerous.

The quickest reaction to the showdown at the Salon d'Automne came from the nimble Kahnweiler, who tore up his schedule and offered Braque an instant one-man show. The offer was cordially accepted, and on 9 November 1908 the historic Exposition Georges Braque opened at the claustrophobic Galerie Kahnweiler: twenty-seven recent paintings, mostly still lifes and landscapes, including the refugees from the Salon, plus *Woman*, retitled *Nude Woman*. This was the world's first exhibition of 'Cubist' art. It confirmed Braque to himself, and to perspicacious others, as the pathfinder of the avant-garde. Of no small consequence, it did something similar for Kahnweiler, a fisherman like St Peter, as he said, fishing for men rather than works.[39] And it gave Apollinaire a platform from which to wax lyrical about the angelic artist and his amazing artistry, in a specially commissioned preface to the catalogue.

Here is Georges Braque. He leads an admirable life. He strives with passion for beauty and he attains it, apparently without effort. His compositions have the harmony and fullness one was expecting. His decorations testify to a taste and a cultivation underwritten by instinct. Reaching within himself for the elements of the synthetic motifs he paints, he has become a creator. He no longer owes anything to his surroundings. His spirit has deliberately challenged the twilight of reality and here elaborates in plasticity, within himself and beyond himself, a universal renaissance. He expresses a beauty full of tenderness and the mother-of-pearl of his paintings lends iridescence to our understanding. An all-too-rare lyricism of colour fills him with enthusiastic harmonies, and St Cecilia herself plays on his musical instruments . . .[40]

Serious commentary soon followed. Vauxcelles bit his tongue. 'Monsieur Georges Braque is a very daring young man . . . He despises form, reduces everything, places and figures and houses, to geometrical schemas, to cubes. Let us not make any fun of him, since he comes in good faith. And let us wait.' Immediately below this review, on the same page of *Gil Blas*, was a report on another daring exhibition, headlined 'La Conquête de l'air' ('The Conquest of the Air'), with an intriguing sub-heading: 'Wilbur Wright gagne le prix de la hauteur' ('Wilbur Wright wins the prize for height') – the height he attained in an exhibition flight at Le Mans – the origin of the identification. On the works themselves, the most discerning contribution was made by Charles Morice, formerly a mentor to Gauguin. The terms of Morice's reflections were an uncanny echo of the terms used by Braque himself:

Visibly, he proceeds from an *a priori* geometry to which he subjects all his field of vision, and he aims at rendering the whole of nature by the

combinations of a small number of absolute forms. Cries of horror have
been uttered in front of his figures of women: 'Hideous! Monstrous!'
This is a hasty judgement. Where we think we are justified in looking
for a feminine figure, because we have read in the catalogue *Nude Woman*,
the artist has seen simply the geometrical harmonies which convey to
him everything in nature; to him, that feminine figure was only a pretext
for enclosing them within certain lines, for bringing them into relation
according to certain tonalities . . . Nobody is less concerned with psychology than he is, and I think a stone moves him as much as a face. He
has created an alphabet of which each letter has a universal acceptance.
Before declaring his book of spells hideous, tell me whether you have
managed to decipher it, whether you have understood its decorative
intentions. These strange signs, which I am unable either to praise or to
condemn, remind me of an admirable and useful saying of Carrière's:
'Think of what it would be like as a statue.'[41]

He showed again at the 1909 Indépendants − two paintings
(the new limit) − a still life, since destroyed, and a half-landscape
half-seascape now known as *Harbour*.[42] *Harbour* and its ilk crowned
Braque's systematic investigation of Cézanne and the secret something in his painting, the most scrupulous inquiry into the art of
one master by another in the modern era.[43] The shock of recognition that he experienced on encountering Cézanne in strength at
the legendary retrospective of 1907 must have been profound.
Fifty-six oil paintings, a year after his death: 'One needs a long,
long time for all of this,' Rilke wrote to his wife, Braque-like, from
his own plunge into it. 'When I remember the puzzlement and
insecurity of one's first confrontation with his work . . . And then
for a long time nothing, and now suddenly one has the right
eyes . . .'[44] For Braque himself, deep immersion in Cézanne was a
revelation of affinity and a process of anamnesis, a 'memory' of
what he did not know he knew. 'The discovery of his work
overturned everything,' he told Verdet. 'I had to rethink everything. I wasn't alone in suffering from shock. There was a battle to
be fought against much of what we knew, what we had tended to
respect, admire, or love. In Cézanne's works we should see not

only a new pictorial construction but also – too often forgotten – *a new moral suggestion of space.* I myself didn't understand that until later.'[45] The almost molecular structures, the elisions and occlusions, the scepticism towards representation, as T.J. Clark puts it, perception getting in the way of definition – that is the lode Braque mined from Cézanne.[46]

'In moments of doubt,' Matisse told one interviewer, 'when I was still searching for myself, frightened sometimes by my discoveries, I thought: "If Cézanne is right, I am right." . . . Cézanne, you see, is a sort of god of painting.' For Picasso he was another kind of *intercesseur,* 'like a mother who protects her children'.[47] But it was Braque who saw himself as son and heir.

The right eyes were not yet widely available. Braque's latest work left Vauxcelles fulminating about *bizarreries cubiques,* more unintelligible than ever. 'Here we have someone, Pascal would have said, who abuses the geometrical turn of mind.' Morice was still wondering whether Braque was anything more than bastard Cézanne. Meanwhile, one development did not escape his notice. 'The uncompromising, the absolutely devoted ones, who formerly accepted the tryanny of Matisse, have rejected it. Today, in effect, if not by his own admission and theirs, the head of the bold ones is Monsieur Georges Braque.'[48] This was gratifying; but the brickbats were obtuse and the bouquets meagre. Enough was enough. Following Picasso's example, Georges Braque bade farewell to the Salons until after the First World War. He did so with the connivance of Kahnweiler, and an understanding between them that they would do business together from then on.[49]

Braque's relationship with Kahnweiler was a boon for both men. Surface bonhomie notwithstanding, it was not always friction-free. Kahnweiler was a businessman, not a philanthropist, and Picasso, for all his wiles and demands, was better business. Faster production at higher prices made irrefutable arithmetic. The dealer may have blenched at *Les Demoiselles d'Avignon* but he knew a goldmine when he saw one. In keeping perhaps with these priorities, in his conversation and in his writing Kahnweiler had a tendency to misprize Braque, especially in his conversations with Picasso.

Picasso confirms what I had thought: no one has truly understood his painting. 'My paintings,' he says, 'were painted to make men's imaginations work, but they didn't work.' He says that Rembrandt would be very surprised if he knew what we feel in front of his paintings. 'Besides, all these museum paintings are stupid. A Titian: a naked woman on a bed and a man playing a trumpet' – he is thinking of the painting in the Prado, I believe, in which an organist is shown next to a nude – 'and yet it's magnificent.'

He says that Braque never did anything like that. 'With him, it's the painting that dominates. He arranges the surfaces.'

Picasso means – and I am of the same mind – that Braque never had the incredible urge to invent new signs that drove him. 'To make men's imaginations work.'[50]

On his side Braque monitored the dealer's operations in his interest very carefully. He was not averse to disputing Kahnweiler's choice of exhibitions abroad, or making sharp remonstrance over business practice. 'Your stupefaction seems to me exaggerated,' he wrote, after a disagreement over the pricing of a work for a show in Amsterdam. 'I don't mind telling you that mine was equally so, when you told me that the price of 100 francs made you sick. Now you ask me not to do any business elsewhere, and then in one fell swoop you take away the means for me to compensate a little for the very modest prices you give me. Your demands are truly confusing. I hope then that in future you will show a little more goodwill since I accede with such good grace to all your demands, and our dealings will be very clear-cut and everything will go well . . .'.[51]

Everything went well enough for Braque to sign an exclusive contract, for one year in the first instance, in November 1912. The contract provided for Braque to sell and Kahnweiler to buy his entire production at fixed prices on a scale according to canvas size (see Appendix A), ranging from 75 francs for smaller works of 41 × 33 cm (known in the trade as a number 6) to 400 francs for larger works of 130 × 97 cm (a number 50). Drawings were normally priced at 40 francs. *Papiers collés* clearly merited a separate clause:

'drawings with paper wood, marble or any other accessories', 50 to 75 francs according to size. As for the profit in it, Kahnweiler's mark-up was simply calculated: it was 100 per cent. By agreement with his artists, he simply doubled the cost price. A discount of 20 per cent was offered to other dealers (if they were lucky) and to a few favoured clients. None of this was written down.[52]

In monetary terms such a contract gave Braque a measure of security undreamt of by most of his peers. But others did better – much better. Derain signed a similar document a few days later. His prices ranged from 125 to 500 francs. Picasso followed, with a more elaborately drawn agreement rewritten by the artist himself (excluding commissions for portraits and decorations, for example, and maintaining the right to keep a certain element of his production for himself). His prices ranged from 250 to 1,500 francs, albeit fixed for three years rather than one. There is no indication that he discussed these figures with Braque. One-upmanship took many forms; and Picasso craved preference. The following year Kahnweiler signed up Gris, Vlaminck, and Léger. Then he stopped.[53] This was an exclusive stable.

Equally confidential, though of considerable interest to the others, was Matisse's position. It was almost as bad as they suspected. Matisse had signed a contract with Bernheim-Jeune three years earlier, in 1909, a commercial breakthrough for the successors of Cézanne. His prices then ranged from 450 to 1,875 francs, dwarfing Braque's, and comfortably exceeding even Picasso's. Furthermore, Matisse retained a 25 per cent interest in the profits from all sales, and pioneered the right to accept commissions outside the contract. He was therefore free to paint *The Dance* (1910) for the Russian merchant Shchukin, and free also to negotiate a price of 14,000 francs for his trouble.[54] Financially, too, Matisse was not a man to be taken lightly.

Coming under Kahnweiler's umbrella yielded ancillary benefits even before the advent of the written agreement. Kahnweiler paid the rent, literally and figuratively, more or less on demand. In times of need he could also be induced to convert payment into a stipend (some 200 francs a month in 1911). And he provided a kind of refuge-cum-surgery for battered paintings. Despatching some canvases from their other outstation at Céret, in the French Pyrenees, Braque warned him that one of them needed minor surgery: 'The large still life needs to have a strip of canvas added at the bottom. I'm sending it to you as is, since I don't have the proper materials at hand. Pig fair great rejoicing for Céret.'[55] This was *Pedestal Table* (1911), the descriptive title supplied by the dealer rather the artist, who usually referred to his work simply as still life or landscape, as the case might be, with a number to indicate its size and value (see Appendix A). Sometimes there was a telegraphic description ('mandolin-player'); more rarely, a little local colour. 'I am in the process of doing . . . an Italian emigrant standing on the bridge of a boat with the harbour in the background, and I hope that neither war nor famine will tear the palette from my hands.' It is doubtless symptomatic that there is no work of that description in Kahnweiler's inventory. There is a *Portuguese*, with which he is sometimes confused, but there is no Italian.[56] *Pedestal Table* had no such mongrel pedigree. Braque merely designated it an NM 50, that is to say a *nature morte* of 116 × 81 cm, for which Kahnweiler would pay some 400 francs. Arrayed on the table, tipped up for our inspection, is a fantastical array of staves and scrolls. The longer one looks, the more things emerge; but the facets of these things are redistributed across the surface of the picture, as if beamed down, higgledy-piggledy, from above. But below the table-top something unforeseen occurred. Georges Braque, geometrician, ran out of space. To gain a few more centimetres at the bottom of the picture, he unfolded the lower edge of the canvas from its stretcher, and continued to paint. Hence the need for an additional strip of canvas. Kahnweiler appears to have followed his instructions, mounting it on a slightly taller stretcher, and in effect lining the exposed bottom edge of the original.

'A picture remaining in its frame was a thing that had always existed,' wrote Gertrude Stein in her own inimitable fashion, 'and now pictures commenced to want to leave their frames and this also created the necessity for Cubism.' Life, still and other, had been reframed. As Braque summarized for Jean Paulhan: 'Whilst I tackled the foregrounds first, I needed frames with depth to assist the movement [backwards]. Then I started with the backgrounds: little by little I got nearer; I got hold of those vanishing frames, which project the canvas [forwards].'⁵⁷ Traditional frames lead in, as if entering a tunnel. They act like a viewfinder, guiding the viewer into the painting, and at the same time isolating and distancing the view. 'Reverse section' frames thrust out, as if perching on a cliff edge.⁵⁸ They serve to combat the isolation and the distance. The painting surfaces from the depths. It is projected, extruded almost, into the living world of the viewer. It is no longer a picture-window but a picture-object. It thereby fulfils its highest calling. Framed or unframed, the picture-object (*tableau-objet*) was for Braque and Picasso an ideal of what their art should be – not a confidence-trick on the eye, like Impressionism or wallpaper, where we make as if to see the sun, the haywain, or the wall; instead, *painting*. The picture-object is not an apple-illusion but a paint-mark. Be it ever so reminiscent of an apple, the very madeleine of an apple, it remains a construction: a thing of beauty, perhaps, but not a fruit substitute. One of Braque's earliest maxims was that 'the aim is not to reconstitute an anecdotal fact but to constitute a pictorial fact'. A Braque or a Picasso was not to be seen as a representation-of, but as a thing in itself. The idea has been plagiarized by artists ever since. Also the maxim. Frank Stella, in the argot of the 1960s: 'My painting is based on the fact that only what can be there *is* there. It really is an object . . . What you see is what you get.'⁵⁹

In this sense Braque's and Picasso's canvases were more interventions than decorations. 'Painting is not made to decorate apartments,' Picasso declared heatedly in 1945. 'It is an instrument of offensive and defensive war against the enemy.'⁶⁰ The enemy was various. Cubist works seem to speak a new language, and a private one at that, but Braque and Picasso had no interest in being unintelligible. They wanted to communicate, and they needed to sell. Competitive games-playing was a vital ingredient of brotherly love and brotherly living. With their paints and their accessories – their toys – they played learning games and language games. Their one-upmanship, on each other and the rest of the world, is unsurpassed. Cubism was fun, or it was nothing. The brothers were never po-faced, which is more than can be said for their critics. Nor were they merely jokers. A *Man with a Guitar* (col. pl. 7) was not a prank. Braque and Picasso were each in their different ways deadly serious. What they were serious about was an approach to reality as they saw it, a point on which they both insisted. 'Under different appearances,' Matisse once said, 'Cubism is a sort of descriptive realism.' In Braque's notebook the maxim about letting people touch what one paints is affixed to the telling masthead of 'Reality'. The difficulty lay, once again, in the materialization. 'It's not a reality you can take in your hand,' said Picasso, as if in response. 'It's more like a perfume . . . The scent is everywhere but you don't quite know where it comes from.'[61]

Nevertheless there is something familiar about the man with a guitar. He is an icon. His presence is almost axiomatic. It anticipates Raymond Chandler's formula for the hardboiled genre. 'When in doubt have a man come through the door with a gun in his hand.'[62] Substituting guitar for gun, there is a Chandleresque aspect to the tale of the Braque–Picasso. The usual suspects – guitars, violins, bottles, glasses, playing cards, grapes, pipes, and other such low life – rounded up from the bars and the cafés; the débris of their rooms; the peeling paper, the chipped paint, the chair caning, the bits of old rope . . . Cubism was a harboiled genre, and Braque and Picasso were hardboiled too, within limits.[63] Pictorially, they drank like fish – everything from *vieux marc* to bottles of Bass – they did *café concerts*, they did gambling, they did kitchen knives and banderillas. They were particular about their weapons. They did not do guns. Picasso for one could surely have made something of them, however much his attention was riveted on the plastic possibilities of female attributes and orifices. Guns were not part of the culture, perhaps, though the artists themselves had a snappier line to deliver. 'It is not necessary to paint a man with a gun,' said Picasso. 'An apple can be just as revolutionary.'[64]

These may have been natural subjects, but the process of selection was also a matter of preference – self-expression – something Braque and Picasso were extremely reluctant to acknowledge, let alone explain. Braque was as pleased as St Cecilia with his *Still Life with Musical Instruments*, painted possibly during the summer of 1908, possibly even earlier in the year, and exhibited at the Galerie Kahnweiler (col. pl. 6). He regarded it as his first truly Cubist work and kept it with him all his life. It gave him one of his pivotal subjects and the project one of its signal themes.[65] Even more than the houses, the instruments press forward, clamouring to be played. 'It's as if the artist were behind rather than in front of the canvas, pushing everything outwards,' Braque remarked of certain of Cézanne's works.[66] He made the technique his own.

Braque's explanation of why he painted so many musical instruments is an interesting one: 'firstly because I was surrounded by them, and then because their forms, their volumes, came under the heading of still life, as I saw it. I was already moving towards tactile space, manual space as I prefer to call it, and the distinctive feature of the musical instrument as an object is that it comes alive to the touch'. Coming alive to the touch is a deft bit of business, derived perhaps from a fragment of Heraclitus, who makes a suggestive comparison between bending a bow and a lyre.[67] The 'playing' of the archer and the musician, and the notion of a resistant instrument, might well have captured Braque's metamorphic imagination. Gris said that guitars were for Braque what Madonnas had been for the Italian primitives. Even in his own terms, it barely hints at the visual 'rhyming' of musical forms, where for instance the symbol for playing *forte* (*f*) rhymes with the sound hole of the stringed instrument, or the staves of sheet music rhyme with the grain of the mock wood, an effect achieved by dragging a decorator's steel comb through the wet paint – a technique that so delighted Picasso when Braque showed it to him that he went one better and combed a mock moustache – not to mention the plastic possibilities of the curvaceous instruments themselves.[68]

> I am the lute. If you wish to describe
> my body, with its beautiful arching stripes:
> speak of me as you would of a ripe
> full-bodied fig.[69]

14. Picasso, *Bouillon Kub* (1912).
The beginning of a duel with
Braque

Braque described no bodies. In general he was as mute as he was musical. It is precisely this blank non-explanation that has found favour with his successors. Georges Braque was the master of modernist deadpan.

Play was competitive. Picasso began to experiment with stencilled letters and brand names early in 1912 in the lost painting *Bouillon Kub*, a reference to the famous stock-cube made by the German company Maggi, and a pun on the image and the essence of more than one art. A few weeks later Braque produced *Violin: 'Mozart/Kubelick'* (b/w pl. 9). The billing recalled a recital by the Czech violinist Jan Kubelík (his name misspelled by the artist) at an Ingres retrospective in Paris the previous year – an event Braque could have attended – when Kubelík played Ingres' favourite pieces of Mozart, on Ingres' own violin. MOZART KUBELICK also replied to BOUILLON KUB. Picasso's little Kub was outfaced by Braque's big Kubelick.

Braque went further. Mozart may or may not have meant much to Picasso, who was inclined to bluff about his ignorance rather than his knowledge. Ingres meant a great deal, as Braque had cause to know. There was a seasoning of Ingres in the Cubist soup.

'Those who think Cubism is a con are completely mistaken,' Apollinaire had written a few months earlier. 'They simply demonstrate that if the lesson of Ingres has not been lost on these artists, the public and many writers on art have not understood it at all.'[70] But that was a plea for the so-called Salon Cubists, spearheaded by the intellectually over-determined Gleizes and Metzinger, the Danton and Robespierre of the Cubist revolution, whose derivative canvases and restrictive theories were anathema to Braque.[71] Their book of words, *Du Cubisme* (1912), enlisted Leonardo da Vinci and Michelangelo, and barely condescended to Braque and Picasso. Here was material for Braque's antipathy to principles and definitions. 'Look at the daubs it engendered.'[72] Picasso, keen enough to ask Kahnweiler when it would appear, was similarly disappointed. Gleizes and Metzinger remained permanently beyond the pale. 'Those who go before turn their backs on the followers. That's all the followers deserve.'[73] Was 'la leçon d'Ingres' a lesson in deformation, or deviation – a shared joke, or a bone of contention? Ingres in his time had delivered himself of some memorable sallies – 'there is no black in nature' – a mode much imitated by Picasso ('there are no feet in nature'). He and Braque liked to say the same thing about the Braque *nature morte* phase, as Wyndham Lewis called it. 'There is no Cubism . . .'[74] Perhaps Ingres was another of the things that passed between them that no one will ever fully understand. In the wake of the war, it was not long before Braque was making disparaging remarks about Picasso's 'Ingres period'.[75] He could easily have kidded him on the subject much earlier (and in better humour). Braque himself had a certain stake in the use and abuse of Ingres, according to a curious episode he related to John Richardson:

Oddly enough, I have a liking for Ingres, but there is no logic in my preferences. You must admit that his portraits have an amazing conviction and force; there's even something impressive about the man's frigidity. Incidentally, my admiration for Ingres was responsible for my break with the Fauves, or rather with their leader Matisse. Matisse wouldn't tolerate a neophyte like myself upholding the merits of an artist who hadn't received the official stamp of his approval and, after a stormy luncheon, we didn't speak for about ten years. The irony is that in the end Matisse grew to admire Ingres, as his work shows clearly.[76]

On this occasion Ingres had more than a lesson to offer. 'Le violon d'Ingres' makes a play on words that must have pleased Braque immensely. In French, it is an expression for a secondary activity or hobby, an expression itself derived from Ingres' passion for the violin – the violin that Kubelík actually played at the recital. Well before it became attached to Man Ray's scandalous photograph in 1924, the expression was employed in equally scandalous fashion in print. One review of the 1919 Salon d'Automne described Picasso as an artist 'who will always suck at the violin of Ingres'.[77]

Never one to duck a challenge, Picasso responded with *Still Life on a Piano* (1912), a painting he had been tinkering with for some months. He had started it the summer before, in Céret; the freehand lettering CER[ET] GRAN[DES] FÊTES is just visible on the far left of the canvas (recalling the festival of St Ferréol, a popular brigand saint, whose image may have appealed to the artist). Picasso seems to have reworked some portions at a later stage, crowning his efforts with the four bold stencilled letters CORT in the top left-hand corner. What to make of CORT? It may continue the Céret train of thought by alluding to the processions (*cortèges*) which were an important part of the festival. More pertinently, it may announce the name of Alfred Cortot, pianist and conductor, presiding over the teeming life on the piano. In June 1911, shortly before Picasso started work on this painting, Cortot had featured at the première of Déodat de Séverac's *Cerdaña* suite, a celebration of traditional ways of life in the Cerdaña region of Catalonia, for the Société Nationale de Musique in Paris. The composer Séverac had settled in Céret. Once spoken of in the same breath as Debussy and Ravel, he was familiar with the maquis of Montmartre, and even the inside of the Bateau Lavoir. Séverac and Picasso were mates. At around the same time as Picasso was putting the finishing touches to *Still Life on a Piano* he drew a neat little Cubist *Pianist with Music by Déodat de Séverac*.

As for Braque, if he had not met Séverac before, they soon got acquainted around the tables of the Grand Café, Céret, in the course of the five months that the artist spent in the town during the latter part of 1911. Braque claimed that he could play Beethoven's symphonies on his accordion. He could read music. He had studied the flute. He mustered a rowdy piano. It is difficult to believe that he did not have a go on the other instruments that passed through his paintings. He supplied Picasso with sheet music for *papiers collés*. He was well versed in both popular and classical composers. For Braque there was no hierarchy of genres. 'There is art of the people and art for the people, the latter an invention of the intellectuals. I don't think Beethoven or Bach dreamt of establishing a hierarchy when they drew inspiration from popular tunes.'[78] His favourites were eighteenth-century French (Couperin, Rameau) or honorary French – Bach, his great love. Among contemporaries, he liked Debussy, and paid painterly tribute to him. He became friendly with Auric and Milhaud; he had an ambivalent relationship with Poulenc, at least on Poulenc's side; and he was perhaps as close as any man to the troublous, lovable Erik Satie ('Ce bon Satie!'). He would certainly have been familiar with Cortot.

Culturally, therefore, Picasso undertook to beat Braque at his own game. Cort(ot) yoked personal association, local custom, regional particularism and national tradition, in one polyphonic painting. To cap it all, or rub it in, he inserted a linguistic riddle-me-ree. *Cort* is the root of the Spanish word for short, or cut off; if its masculine form, *corto*, is spoken aloud, it sounds like the pianist's surname. Could his French friend solve this? Maybe he could. The French *court* is not so far removed from the Spanish *cort* (or the Catalan *curt*). And Braque had picked up more of the language of the street in Céret than is commonly realized. He knew, for instance, the names of the instruments in the typical Catalan cobla or little orchestra, in particular the tenora, and the names of the tunes they played. 'I will remember all my life the instrument which is called a tenora,' wrote Max Jacob; 'it is long like a clarinet and can compete, says a musician, with forty trombones. Its sound is dry, like the bagpipes.'[79] In fact the tenora is longer than the average clarinet, with a wider bell; in the scrum of Cubist compositions its plainest distinguishing feature is the mouthpiece, whose widening flange projects emphatically from the body of the instrument. On close inspection, Braque's clarinets often turn out to be tenoras (or their older sisters).[80] It is but another example of the comprehension test set by Braque and Picasso that it took some eighty years to re-establish that distinction. The Museum of Modern Art's baldly mistaken *Clarinet* (1913) has now been retitled *Still Life with Tenora*. The Tate's heavily camouflaged *Clarinet and Bottle of Rum on a Mantelpiece* (1911) is looking increasingly insecure.

Musically and linguistically, Braque knew more than he let on. Between the brothers, reading music took on a whole new meaning. Playing on words was Picasso's *violon d'Ingres*. But the notes were Braque's.

5. '*I* am Madame Braque': Partnership and Marriage

In his later years Picasso was fond of joking about how much Braque owed to him. This was a well-polished routine. He had given Braque three things, he would say, the *papiers collés*, a dog, and Marcelle, the best woman in Paris. The *papiers collés* were over, the dog was dead, there remained only Marcelle, and look what has become of her.[1] The joke, like many of Picasso's jokes, was a serious one, because Picasso himself half-believed it, and because it soon found its way back to Braque. And Picasso did indeed introduce Braque to Marcelle, who became his wife.

Braque was not the only one. Picasso liked to fix up his friends. On the whole he preferred that they did not get married. Why get married, after all, only to get divorced later? But he did want them to live happily, if not ever after. He also preferred to have slept with the women before passing them on. It was not his invariable practice, but it added considerably to his satisfaction with a job well done. He had slept with Alice Géry before proposing her to Derain (notwithstanding that she was already married to the actuary Maurice Princet, the so-called mathematician of Cubism). On the other hand he had not slept with Marie Laurencin before proposing her to Apollinaire. Whether he had slept with Marcelle Lapré before proposing her to Braque is an open question, but given the trajectory of the relationship between the two men we might well have heard more about it if he had.[2]

In fact Marcelle was not Picasso's first choice for his friend in need. One of Max Jacob's cousins owned a Montmartre cabaret called, appropriately, 'Le Néant' ('Nothingness'). The proprietor had an attractive daughter. A visit was called for. A mobilization order went out. Formal dress was decreed. The cabaret and the girl were besieged by the Picasso gang in all its glory – top hats, coats, canes. The splendour of their attire made a good impression. The looseness of their behaviour did not. As the night wore on, Braque's prospects steadily deteriorated. In the early hours of the morning the party was asked to leave. By this time their rented finery was only a blur. Everything in the cloakroom looked the same. The gang helped themselves to whatever came to hand and rolled home. Henceforth, the establishment, the proprietor and his daughter were off-limits. The cabaret had lived up to its name.[3]

After this fiasco, Picasso had to think again. He came up with Marcelle, then known as Madame Vorvanne. Madame Vorvanne was no stranger to the demi-monde of Montmartre. Like Fernande Olivier, she had modelled for Kees Van Dongen, who lived at the Bateau Lavoir in 1906–7, and who left an unregarded portrait of her. The portrait is flattering but formulaic: it is Van Dongen in hot lips and black lashes mode, bearing a remarkable likeness to all the others he produced. Marcelle had also modelled for the irresistible Modigliani, whose Roman head she recalled tenderly to her dying day – 'How handsome he was, Modigliani . . .' – much to her husband's irritation. She is supposed to have sewn Modigliani's shroud.[4] She already knew Fernande, who had trodden the same path, and other members of *la bande à Picasso*, notably Max Jacob, whom she addressed in honorific terms as 'the magus'.[5] Chaperoned by Fernande, she went through another rite of passage, taking tea with Gertrude Stein, and emerging more or less unscathed (and forgotten). She also knew Marthe Duverger, who lodged at the same boarding house, and who married Braque's soulmate Henri Laurens. Clearly it was time for her to know Braque.

She was three years older than he. Marcelle Vorvanne was born Octavie Eugénie Lapré on 23 July 1879 in Paris. The adoption or imposition of different names was common practice for women at that time, usually at the behest of their menfolk, and regardless of marital status. Marcelle's menfolk are more shadowy than most. Monsieur Vorvanne has disappeared without trace. Her father's identity is not recorded on her birth certificate. Her mother was Eugénie Lapré, a thirty-year-old upholsterer, who lived in the rue St Dominique in the 7th arrondissement, not far from the Invalides. Her forebears, it is said, came from Burgundy. If Eugénie Lapré

15. With Marcelle, and Braquian table, 1946

was a single parent, she seems to have coped remarkably well. Marcelle's biggest vice was chain-smoking. She was known to the relatives of Braque's studio assistant as *Tabac Blond* (Light Tobacco). To all outward appearances tobacco was the only light thing about her. Bodily, she and Braque were a study in contrasts. Duncan Grant, one of the beautiful people of Bloomsbury, thought them 'a strange couple' for precisely this reason. 'But perhaps their mutual passion for the sea explains it.' Curiously enough, Max Jacob's nickname for Marcelle was 'the little sea-monster', on account of her protuberant blue eyes. Regrettably, she could not swim. Every year Braque tried to teach her, and every year he almost succeeded by the end of the summer.[6] In reality she hugged the ground. She was short and plump when they met and as time went on she got shorter and plumper – 'rounder than round', said Mariette Lachaud, the studio assistant, who loved them both.[7] She was usually to be found under

16. Madame Braque
by Alexander
Liberman, 1953

a capacious hat. Clothes were a problem, solved or concealed for a while by Mariette's grandmother, a former dressmaker to Sarah Bernhardt. But in the end, no amount of dressmaking could conceal the truth. The beauty of this couple was Braque.

Marcelle has left a faint spoor, but there is every indication that she was happy in her skin. She seems also to have been happy to submerge herself in Braque. For richer or poorer, she remained very much herself – a real woman of the people – no airs and graces.[8] Nina Kandinsky wanted to call her memoirs *I and Kandinsky* until it was pointed out to her that *Kandinsky and I* might be more apropos. Marcelle Braque would never have perpetrated such a solecism, nor thought to write her memoirs. Her discretion matched his. In the annals of Braque she is characteristically off-camera: she did not like to have her picture taken. One of Gertrude Stein's clever friends, Miss Mars, propounded the view that there were three types of women: the *femme décorative*, the *femme d'intérieur*, and the *femme intrigante*.[9] Miss Mars and company were quite sure that Fernande was a *femme décorative*. In spite of her adventurous youth, or perhaps because of that very experience, Marcelle was a *femme d'intérieur*. If she did not have the cultivation or incisiveness of Paulette Philippi – omitted from Miss Mars's typology – she did not have Paulette's habits either. She was not without resources of her own. The photographer Alexander Liberman was a sensitive observer of Marcelle and her ménage. He found 'a small, serious woman, with extraordinarily tender, perceptive blue eyes. Under her smart, simple hat the eyes and the nervous curve of her mouth expressed intelligence and wit. She is adored by their friends and amuses them with countless anecdotes. Music plays an important part in her life – her favourites . . . are Bach, Vivaldi, Mozart, and Buxtehude; she owns Erik Satie's piano.'[10] She fed the photographer chilled Muscadet and warmed biscuits, a combination he appreciated. Marcelle specialized in feeding people what they liked: for H. P. Roché, iced cider; for Herbert Read, raspberry jam and brown bread; for Brassaï, a simple grill doused in calvados; for Martin Heidegger, only the best white wine. She herself gorged on books – she and Braque read aloud to each other – and like Braque, she administered some to Mariette, beginning with Zola (*The Dream*), and moving on to Lamartine (*Jocelyn*) and Bernardin de Saint-Pierre (*Paul and Virginia*). She was voluble with intimates like the art-loving priest Père Couturier, or the master printer Fernand Mourlot, or the brilliant young painter Nicolas de Staël. 'Watch out,' she warned de Staël with a characteristically shrewd appraisal, 'you staved off poverty all right, but do you have the strength to stave off riches?'[11] Out in the world she held her peace; but she was not easily overborne. She had a strong faith: stronger, or more conventional, than Braque's. In Varengeville their house was near the church; the priest, Lecoque, knew them both well. Braque, he thought, 'was well on the way towards saintliness', though 'we never discussed religion. He had a religious sense, but practised accidentally; there are so many ways to pray! He had his pew in church, but I saw Madame Braque there much more often.'[12]

Braque was not properly speaking an unbeliever, he was more of an agnostic with spiritual tendencies. He knew several art-loving religious men.[13] They would talk about life; and the life of the religious order was not dissimilar to his own. He seldom went to church, or rather to church services – he did not attend his nephew's first communion – but that did not stop him making a number of objects for church use: a tabernacle with a boned bream-like fish for the well-stocked church at Assy in the Haute-Savoie, at the instigation of Père Couturier, who sometimes came to stay with the Braques in the 1950s; a stained-glass window with a trademark Braque bird for the chapel in the grounds of the foundation established by his last dealer, the vaulting Aimé Maeght, at Saint-Paul-de-Vence, in the paradisal hills above the French Riviera ('it's probably because I know it too well,' said Braque, 'but it bothers me that when I go to the House of God it's Matisse that lets me in'); a triptych of stained-glass windows and a replica of the fish tabernacle for the chapel of St Dominique at Varengeville; and a stained-glass window of the Tree of Jesse and a tabernacle of the Last Supper for Lecoque's church of St Valery, a commission offered and accepted at Marcelle's instigation.[14]

Contemplating his work, Couturier too sensed that Braque had evolved further than many. 'I feel in it a marvellous (admirable) *humanity* that moves me: a certain kind of gaze (that a man fixes on things) testifying to a tenderness of heart, and an elevation of spirit.'[15] For his part Braque professed suitably elevated views about *l'art sacré*. 'The moment that religious art is reduced "to the level of the common man", it's no longer an act of faith, it's an act of propaganda.'[16] In practice, however, it is difficult to tell his religious art from his non-religious art. St Dominique in stained glass bears a striking resemblance to a billiard table on canvas, performing similar tricks in space (though it looks as if the table might snap shut and the saint take wing). Both have humanity. Both were cherished by the artist. Patrick Heron, a longtime acolyte, had a profound feeling for this very Braquian ethic of enhancement:

The kind of life which he bestows on his coffee-pot or coffee-grinder, his table, his chair and window, is just the sort of life we feel these things are really living! The personality with which Braque invests his jug is something that the jug possesses in its own right. In other words, Braque divines the essential spirit – one might almost call it 'the soul' – of each object that he paints.[17]

Never well adjusted to doctrine or system, Beaux-Arts or Bon Dieu, Braque looked East for enlightenment. From a comparatively young age he had a deep love of the *Tao Te Ching*.[18] He relished its serenity and quietude, and was instantly at home with its fragmentary form. Ruminating on the words, and the space between the words, he found a kind of affirmation. 'One who knows does not speak; one who speaks does not know.' What matters is self-knowledge. 'He who knows others is clever; he who knows himself has discernment. He who overcomes others has force; he who overcomes himself is strong.' The greatest journey is the interior one. 'Without stirring abroad,' says Lao Tzu, 'one can know the whole world.'

> Without looking out of the window
> One can see the way of heaven.
> The further one goes
> The less one knows.
> Therefore the sage knows without having to stir,
> Identifies without having to see,
> Accomplishes without having to act.[19]

In the later stages of his life Braque found himself almost instinctively in harmony with the teachings of Zen Buddhism – so much so that in 1960 a special edition of *Le Tir à l'arc* (*Archery*) was published, a manuscript 'illuminated' by Georges Braque, interleaving extracts from Eugen Herrigel's original distillation of Zen and the art of archery with selections from Braque's thoughts and aphorisms, chosen by the principal ambassador of Zen to the West, D. T. Suzuki, in conjunction with Herrigel himself.[20] What did Braque find in Zen? According to Braque, reassurance. When asked about influence, he demurred. 'Do these ideas of mine derive from Zen Buddhism? I don't think so. True, I have read a lot about Zen

Buddhism, but I'm convinced that this philosophy hasn't influenced my way of thinking or my work. On the other hand, I have been deeply interested to find how closely certain tenets of Zen Buddhism correspond to views that I have held for a long time. For me this is reassuring, no more than that.'[21] Influence is perhaps as hard to concede as it is to specify. Even reassurance has its importance, however, and it recurs. Kahnweiler made exactly the same claim with regard to Cubism and *art nègre*: that Braque and Picasso were not so much influenced as 'reassured', artistically, by the strange looks and perceptual leaps of *les nègres*.[22] With the passage of time *les chinois*, *les tibétains* and *les maîtres du Zen* were added to the rich stockpile that was Braque's prajna: 'the highest power of intuition which sounds the depths of our soul-life'.[23]

Suzuki tells us that the origin of Zen is to be sought in the Supreme Perfect Enlightenment attained by the Buddha as he sat under the Bodhi-tree near the city of Gaya. 'The content of this Enlightenment was explained by the Buddha as the Dharma [crudely, truth] which was to be directly perceived, beyond limits of time, to be personally experienced, altogether persuasive, and to be understood each for himself by the wise. This meant that the Dharma was to be intuited and not to be analytically reached by concepts.'[24] In other words Buddhists hold that the intellectual process – mere reason – cannot comprehend what is most funda- mental. That requires a power of intuition possessed by spirit, a power of grasping something instantly and directly, in its totality and in its individuality. The name given to this power is prajna. Prajna cannot be taught and learned in the way that we are accus- tomed to teaching and learning. It is awakened by solitary medi- tation and quickened by self-realization. When the student is ready, the master is there; but the last word in Zen instruction is silent.

The young poet Antoine Tudal was not the only one to see something of the Zen master in Georges Braque – and to feel that he himself had been taught a lesson in living. For Jean Paulhan, Braque's extraordinary quality came from 'a metaphysical sense of the world, a sort of genius, comparable to Heraclitus or Lao Tzu, that he himself apprehends only sketchily and imperceptibly, and that is anyway almost inapprehensible, inexpressible'. Francis Ponge called him a Master of Life.[25] Regarding his stained-glass window of St Dominique, Braque observed, 'People said to me: "But he doesn't look like a saint!" I replied: "Saintliness is what one makes of it." What counted for me about the figure of Dominique was the bearing of a man who was marching towards something . . . And who, other than God, knew what?' It is not that but *towards* that, he used to repeat, koan-like, to the painter Jean Bazaine. 'Creation,' Bazaine added, 'is what happens in the space opening *towards that*: *that* being happily out of reach.'[26]

Braque habitually refused the '*maître*'. 'I cannot be a master, in the normal sense of the word. For me painting is a perpetual adventure. Each time I begin a canvas, I never know how it will end. In those conditions, what could I teach?' In the perpetual adventure of becoming, the utterance of the Zen masters had a powerful appeal for him. He relished the combination of the mystic and the matter-of-fact, the propensity for 'contradiction' or negation, often paradoxical, and the absolute refusal to explain. Graphic irrationalities abound in Zen. They find an echo in Braque. 'Empty-handed I go and yet the spade is in my hands; I walk on foot, and yet on the back of an ox I am riding: When I pass over the bridge, lo, the water floweth not, but the bridge doth flow.' (Fudaishi) 'The frontiers are the limits of resistance. The lake asks its shores to contain it.' (Braque) 'If you have a staff, I will give you one. If you have not, I will take it away from you.' (Basho) 'I love the rule that corrects the emotion. I love the emotion that corrects the rule.' (Braque)[27]

'Echo answers echo. Everything reverberates.'[28]

There were artist-echoes too. It is related, as Suzuki says, that Ŏkubo Shibun, famous for painting bamboo, was requested to execute a wall-picture of a bamboo forest. He consented, and after much labour produced a magnificent bamboo forest painted entirely in red. When it was delivered, his patron marvelled at the artist's extraordinary skill and called on him to thank him. 'Master, I have come to thank you for the picture; but, excuse me, you have painted the bamboo red.' 'Well,' cried the master, 'in what colour would you desire it?' 'In black, of course,' replied the patron. 'And who ever saw black-leaved bamboo?' answered the artist. It is also related that Jean Paulhan once showed Braque a fake Braque – 'fake but very well forged, including the signature. What a face he made.'

Paulhan: 'Well, they certainly are *your* colours: this brown isn't wrong, nor this violet.'

Braque: 'They really are my colours.'

P: 'It's your composition: they really are your brush-strokes; it's your atmosphere.'

B: 'No doubt about it.'

P: 'You could have painted it.'

B: 'Do you think I'm not capable of doing fake Braques?'

P: 'What have you got against it?'

B: 'It's that it would be rather the opposite of a Braque.'

P: 'How do you mean?'

B: 'I'll tell you: it's beautiful.'[29]

According to Suzuki, Zen in painting is an attempt to catch the spirit as it moves. 'Everything becomes, nothing is stationary in nature.' Conventional representation and slavish imitation are beside the point.

Let us instead create living objects out of our own imagination. As long as we all belong to the same universe, our creations may show some correspondence to what we call objects of nature. But this is not an essential element of our work. The work has its own merit apart from resemblance. In each brush-stroke is there not something distinctly individual? The spirit of each artist is moving there. His birds are his own creation.[30]

In 1911 the spirit of the artist was moved to paint a demure Cubist *Girl with a Cross* (col. pl. 5), a picture of luminescence, and a multiple departure from his normal practice. It is a portrait that proclaims itself. This is not a still life, it says, though the head carries the implications of a jug, and the shoulder a pot. It has an explicitly religious dimension. The aberrant attribute itself – the cross – is rendered naturalistically rather than *cubisté*. It might almost cast a shadow, like the famous nail, on which he hung his ideas.[31] The girl has a wreath of daisies (*marguerites*) in her hair; allegorically she is the chosen type of female innocence and meekness. St Marguerite was a virgin martyr who got the better of a dragon. Braque flatly rejected allegorical interpretation of his paintings. He would doubtless have said that there were a lot of daisies for the time of year, or that he was interested in the texture of the flower. An alternative legend is that Olybrius, governor of Antioch, captivated by Marguerite's beauty, sought her hand in marriage. Rejected, he threw her into a dungeon, where the devil appeared before her in the form of a dragon. She held up the cross and the dragon fled. It is sometimes said that the dragon swallowed her, and that she made her escape by using the cross to puncture its stomach – a variant that neatly anticipates Braque's fascination with the transformational possibilities inherent in any given object. The mixture of piety and corporeality seems just right for his very own girl with a cross. Marcelle concentrated on protecting and insulating Braque. 'With Picasso you can never afford to give an inch,' she remarked to John Richardson.[32]

Picasso painted his women incessantly. He also took care to paint his dealers. Braque did neither. After his apprentice work, he fought shy of portraiture. 'Make a portrait! And of a woman in an evening dress for example. No, I'm not domineering enough.' The live model, loose in the studio, was unsettling, corrupting – and material for some ribald artistic in-joking with Picasso. The parable of Puvis de Chavannes, on a postcard: 'The model was sacred to Puvis and when he couldn't resist he went alone into an alcove ad hoc. I beat nature . . . said the master happily.'[33] Even in the absence of the model, there were other pitfalls. Picasso's portraits of women often tend to be exercises in self-regard. 'They're all Picassos,' said Dora Maar. 'Not one is Dora Maar.' These portraits insist on their paternity. Picasso's Dora Maar is precisely that: Picasso's. The sitter is immortalized but possessed; and immortality is a dubious pleasure, as the angry Dora Maar made very clear. 'Do you think I care? Does Madame Cézanne care? Does Saskia Rembrandt care?'[34]

Braque himself was not practised in the art of self-regard. He was too conscious of his limitations. 'For me Cubism, or rather my Cubism, is a means that I created in my own way, the aim of which was above all to bring painting within my gifts.'[35] As far as portraits were concerned, the generic problem had been solved. A Cubist torso was perfectly conceivable. Was this the moment? Marcelle beckoned. Braque's ideal model was an ex-model. She and he had decided to make a new beginning. It was wholly in keeping that the decision was not taken quickly. Braque cultivated the wisdom of slowness, in Milan Kundera's epic phrase. In life as in art, he could not be rushed or forced. 'It takes me weeks to make up my mind which groups of bottles will go well with a particular tablecloth,' said the Italian master of the *natura morta*, Morandi. 'Then it takes me weeks of thinking about the bottles themselves, and yet often I still go wrong with the spaces. Perhaps I work too fast?' For Braque there could be only one answer to that question. He measured not in weeks but in years.

He met Marcelle in 1908. Still in 1909 he was to be seen squiring Paulette about town, even at events such as a lecture by Apollinaire at the Indépendants. By 1910 things were apparently moving in Marcelle's favour. But there was another obstacle: Braque's parents, above all his father, unmet and perhaps unreconciled. Charles Braque had recently retired from his decorating business in order to concentrate on his own canvases. That pleasure was cruelly denied him. Early in 1910 he was taken ill with an undisclosed condition. After a year of 'painful illness' he died in January 1911, in a psychiatric hospital in Sceaux, south of Paris. He was fifty-five. The death notices recognized an *artiste-peintre* – a small crumb of posthumous comfort.[36] He was buried in Argenteuil, his son at the graveside.

Braque did not tell Picasso about his father. Yet the death of the fathers was in some fashion shared between the sons. Two years later, in 1913, Picasso's father died. Picasso immediately informed Braque, who responded with a declaration unique in his chronically abbreviated correspondence:

My dear friend. I was very painfully surprised to get your letter on Wednesday and I much regret not having been by your side to tell you how I share your grief. I'm thinking a lot about you and if you find a moment write to me I'll be happy. My thoughts are with you. With affection.[37]

Perhaps Braque found a greater freedom after his father's death, but it was a grim release. He was first detained by an irksome bout of military service. Liberty regained, he spent much of the rest of 1911 in Céret, where he and Marcelle tried joint housekeeping for the first time. The experiment was a success. On his return to Paris, in January 1912, they moved in together, occupying two studio apartments in a building overrun with artists in the Impasse de Guelma, off the Place Pigalle. Gino Severini, the suave Italian Futurist on the floor below, ardent for contacts, was thrilled to discover that the fellow practising the accordion directly overhead was none other than Georges Braque, who took an interest in his work and introduced him to his friend Picasso.[38]

From that day forward, apart from the intermission on the Western Front, Braque and Marcelle were inseparable. (They were always Braque and Marcelle, even to each other.) They were *complice* – the word most often used by those who knew them – meaning that there was a closeness between them, a dash of comfortableness, a rock-solidness rarely encountered round the corner from the Moulin Rouge.[39] They were not married, officially, until 1926, but she had taken his name from the outset.[40] The painting was timed to celebrate that bright beginning. And if this is indeed 'Madame Braque', in portraiture she has a distinguished ancestry. The girl with a cross has the characteristic lean of another painter's lady – as iconic as an apple – Hortense Fiquet, Madame Cézanne.

They were *complice*, also, with another couple. The Braques and the Laurenses together forged an intimate bond. This was perhaps the nearest Braque ever came to a gang of his own. In the early days in Montmartre they could wave to each other from their respective back windows. On Sunday mornings Braque would call on Laurens, with his invariable greeting, 'What's new?', and the two men would talk about the work – Braque once drawing an explanatory diagram on Laurens's studio wall – or about the pleasures of life: boxing, cycling, cars. They shared a certain approach to the task in hand, an approach grounded in respect for *matière* and *métier* (Laurens confessed to an almost superstitious belief in the *matière*), and a conviction that the quality of the work depended fundamentally on the humanity of the worker.[41] They also shared a sense of humour. On one occasion when Laurens was making a sculpture of a boxer, they hired a live one and invited him to strike a pose. The boxer raised his guard. 'Box!' commanded Laurens. 'Against who?' asked the boxer, bewildered. 'Against no one. Box on your own,' Laurens replied. He turned to Braque. 'Look, this man is sculpting his adversary in space.' Some time later the boxer returned to see the finished work. He was overcome. 'So that's me,' he marvelled. 'No,' said Laurens, 'It's the other fellow.'[42]

'Madame Braque', however, was a contested position. When Jean Paulhan's celebratory *Braque le patron* was first trailed in article form, in 1942, the author received a word of congratulation from Picasso: 'I'm happy that justice has been done to the woman who loved me best.'[43] This was by way of being a recapitulation of one of Picasso's best-known sallies, that of Braque as his wife, or ex-wife.[44] The theme had a number of variations. Apart from the obvious conclusion to be drawn about Braque's lack of *cojones*, it served naturally to domesticate and relegate. Braque was cast in the role of follower, if not camp-follower, and (in jealous moments) imitator.[45] It has been taken to imply that, by contrast with Picasso, Braque had a more 'female' sensibility or style. Whatever that might mean, it was evidently not a compliment. Nor was it purely a symptom of Picasso's strutting machismo. Saul Steinberg remarked that the best dealers have a distinctly fictional quality. Part of Daniel-Henry Kahnweiler's fictional quality was his *alter ego* as an intellectual, a Brahmin of European culture. As a dealer he had a well-established *Ostpolitik* even before the First World War. He was also a merchant of ideas – it was Kahnweiler who translated

Braque's early 'Thoughts and Reflections on Painting' into German.[46] His first treatise on the Cubist revolution, published in 1916,
established the intimacy between Braque and Picasso as the heart
of the project, and at the same time placed considerable emphasis on
their differences of temperament. His expression of these differences
seemed only to give credence to Picasso's jibe. 'Admittedly,' he
wrote, 'Braque's art is more feminine than Picasso's brilliantly
powerful work.' In their cross-cultural partnership, the Frenchman
played the 'gentle moon' to the Spaniard's 'radiant sun'. These
effusions were deleted from later versions, but the demarcation
according to temperamental and national characteristics remained.
The 'lucid' Frenchman produced 'tranquil' Braques, while the
'fanatically searching' Spaniard produced 'nervous and turbulent'
Picassos.[47] And Kahnweiler was not the only one to practise this sort
of pseudo-psychoanalysis. Uhde considered that Braque brought to
'the spiritual union' a great sensitivity, Picasso a great artistic gift. If
there was a gendered sub-text here, it was overlaid with a rather
lumpen class consciousness. Braque's temperament was 'clear,
measured, bourgeois'; Picasso's, 'sombre, excessive, revolutionary'.[48] Not even 'pard' was immune from incipient feminization.
According to Paulhan, Buffalo Bill's pard was 'l'ignoble Calamity',
Calamity Jane.[49]

On the conjugal model, then, it seems there is ample scope to
identify Braque as the woman of the pair. Picasso's suggestive
prompting bore fruit. And yet, as John Richardson has underlined,
it is never wise to take Picasso too literally. Many of his most
celebrated sallies had in common a convenient reversibility. He
spoke for effect, especially in interviews. He could never remember
whether he had said 'I don't look, I find' or 'I don't find, I look' –
'not that it makes much difference'.[50] In similar fashion, the case of
'Madame Picasso' involved a classic role reversal. On one occasion
when Braque was hospitalized, Picasso was refused permission to
see him. 'The nurse wouldn't let me into his room,' he fumed.
'She said Madame Braque was with him. She didn't realize that *I*
am Madame Braque.'[51]

For Marcelle, in the early days, being with Braque meant being with Picasso too, and long hours sitting at the bottom of the stairs to the studio, not daring to interrupt their discussions.[52] What were they discussing? Theory and mock theory. They were fascinated by certain ideas or expressions. Limbering up for the *papier collé*, 'the inimitable' in art was one. 'If you are painting a newspaper held in someone's hands, should you take pains to reproduce the words PETIT JOURNAL, or reduce the business to sticking the newspaper itself on to the canvas?'[53] 'The elimination of the subject' was another.[54] 'Squaring the circle' was a third. Braque found it all but impossible to complete the corners of a traditional rectangular canvas to his satisfaction. They were left out, or left over, far removed from the *foyer d'intensité*, as he called it, the very heartbeat of the work; that patch of radiance, like the 'little patch of yellow wall' in Vermeer, the trigger for Proustian rhapsody – in Braque humanized, as if the picture-object itself had had a CAT scan and the vital organs had been illuminated accordingly. By comparison the corners were inert.[55] (Though Braque's corners tended to be more finished than Picasso's, one of the telltale differences between them even at their most interchangeable.)[56]

Therein lay the challenge. Braque began experimenting with an oval, and found that the work gained a three-dimensional effect. Cubist canvases had come to be dominated by the pyramid shape that acted as a kind of armature on which the composition was built up. Paradoxically, the oval format helped him to recover a sense of the vertical and the horizontal, thus squaring the circle, or at any rate the oval. 'We made experiments,' Picasso told Roland Penrose. 'The squaring of the circle was a phrase that excited our ambitions. To make pictures was less important than to discover things all the time.'[57]

Braque and Picasso were both prone to refer to 'the laboratory' of their experiments; but both cautioned against thinking in terms of exact calculations or straightforward appropriations, mathematical or metaphysical, particularly the speculative geometry of 'the fourth dimension', or the transcendental philosophy of 'the inner eye', which so excited some of their contemporaries. Braque made his own mathematics. 'A lemon next to an orange ceases to be a lemon and an orange in order to become fruit. Mathematicians follow this rule. So do we.'[58] If he latched on to the idea of tactility and the expression 'tactile space' from somewhere else, it is most likely to have been the Cartesian concept of vision modelled after the sense of touch. Descartes said that the blind 'see with their hands', an idea widely available in the intellectual culture.[59] It is just possible that Braque picked it up from Henri Poincaré – a polymath much in vogue at the time – perhaps by listening to the café-table exposition of Maurice Princet, a fellow-traveller in both worlds, and watching him lay out some of the problems on paper.[60]

Braque was susceptible to the formal properties of script; he liked the look of Princet's maths and Satie's scores (and his father's wood grain) as a calligrapher might like the look of a medieval manuscript. Satie himself never ceased to wonder that marks on paper could stand for musical sounds in time, an observation that might have been made by his friend the painter.[61] For all he was branded a 'gentleman rhomboidian' by Vauxcelles, the fact remained that Braque could read the scores (and the grain) but not the maths.[62] He and Picasso always scoffed at the fourth dimension and the mediumistic baggage it carried with it. If there was something in the way in which any of these doctrines were couched that was worth stealing, or borrowing for a while, they were not about to own up to it. 'Mathematics, trigonometry, chemistry, psycho-analysis, music and whatnot have been related to Cubism to give it an easier interpretation. All this has been pure literature, not to say nonsense, which brought bad results, blinding people with theories,' declared Picasso. 'But of what use is it to say what we do when everybody can see it if he wants to?'[63] Braque admired Gris, significantly, not for his rigour, but for his ability to transcend his theoretical approach. 'Of course even he was often led astray by science.' He liked to tell the story of visiting Gris's studio and being shown a canvas that he did not much care for. To cover his embarrassment he said, 'Down there, in that corner, there's some-thing that looks odd to me.' Gris fished out his preparatory sketches. 'Of course,' he cried, re-examining them, 'I made a mistake.' 'Be careful,' cautioned Braque. 'If you make a mistake you could easily paint three bowls in an apple.'[64]

Braque and Picasso did not confine themselves to theory. They also engaged in practical criticism. 'Just imagine,' Picasso recalled, 'almost every evening, either I went to Braque's studio or Braque came to mine. Each of us *had* to see what the other had done during the day. We criticized each other's work. A canvas wasn't finished unless both of us felt it was.' Standards were high. 'With Braque, when we were looking at pictures, I would show my canvases and say, "Is that woman right? Can she walk down the street? Is that a woman or a painting?" I would say: "Does that one smell under the arms? What I want is for it to smell under the arms." So we would look and say: "Yes, that one smells a bit." Or again we would say: "No, that one doesn't smell much!"'[65] Einstein once said that physics does not tell us how soup tastes. These paintings do.

Animal instinct took different forms. 'I remember one evening I arrived at Braque's studio,' continued Picasso. 'He was working on a large oval still life with a package of tobacco, a pipe, and all the usual paraphernalia of Cubism.'

I looked at it, drew back and said, 'My poor friend, this is dreadful. I see a squirrel in your canvas. Braque said, 'That's not possible.' I said, 'Yes, I know, it's a paranoiac vision, but it so happens that I *see* a squirrel. That canvas is made to be a painting, not an optical illusion. Since people need to see something in it, you want them to see a package of tobacco, a pipe, and the other things you're putting in. But for God's sake get rid of that squirrel.' Braque stepped back a few feet and looked carefully and sure enough, he too saw the squirrel, because that kind of paranoiac vision is extremely communicable. Day after day Braque fought the squirrel. He changed the structure, the light, the composition, but the squirrel always came back, because once it was in our minds it was almost impossible to get it out. However different the forms became, the squirrel somehow always managed to return. Finally, after eight or ten days, Braque was able to turn the trick and the canvas became again a package of tobacco, a pipe, a deck of cards, and above all a Cubist painting.

Picasso told Françoise Gilot the squirrel story to demonstrate just how close they had been. 'At that time our work was a kind of laboratory research from which every pretension or individual vanity was excluded. You have to understand that state of mind.'[66] There was a moment – a utopian moment – when both high-contracting parties were prepared to contemplate something very like a merger. The moment was lost; but the impulse was real, and the feeling to a surprising degree mutual. Each of them recounted that moment:

Braque:

[We] were engaged in what we felt was a search for the anonymous personality. We were inclined to efface our own personalities in order to find originality. Thus it often happened that amateurs mistook Picasso's paintings for mine and mine for Picasso's. This was a matter of indifference to us because we were primarily interested in our work and in the new problem it presented.

Talking to Vallier he went even further.

You see, when Picasso and I were very close, there was a time when we had trouble recognizing our own canvases . . . I judged that the personality of the painter ought not to intervene and that therefore the paintings should be anonymous. It was I who decided canvases should not be signed and for a while Picasso did likewise. The moment someone could do the same thing as me, I thought that there was no difference at all between the paintings and that there was no need for them to be signed. Afterwards I understood that all that wasn't true and I started signing my canvases again. Picasso for his part had done the same. I understood that without "tics", without a trace of individual personality, self-revelation is not possible.[67]

Picasso:

People didn't understand very well at the time why very often we didn't sign our canvases. Most of those that are signed we signed years later. It was because we felt the temptation, the hope, of an anonymous art, not in its expression but in its point of departure. We were trying to set up a new order and it had to express itself through different individuals. Nobody needed to know that it was so-and-so who had done this or that painting. But individualism was already too strong and that resulted in a failure, because after a few years all Cubists who were any good at all were no longer Cubists. Those who remained Cubists were those who weren't really true painters. Braque was saying the other day, 'Cubism is a word invented by the critics, but we were never Cubists.' That isn't exactly so. We *were*, at one time, Cubists, but as we drew away from that period we found that, more than just Cubists, we were individuals dedicated to ourselves. As soon as we saw that the collective adventure was a lost cause, each one of us had to find an individual adventure.[68]

The canvases were signed on the back rather than the front. This was determined on aesthetic grounds as well as artistic principles. At the time the two men thought that the signature did not 'hold up'. This was a key phrase in Braque's lexicon, and a vital consideration, almost a moral obligation, in his code.[69] He told Gris, who believed him, that 'the signature was an alien element in the composition, that it did not blend in with the whole'.[70] The signature upset the picture. In a word, it did not go. There are other cases, especially perhaps in the radical simplifications of abstract art (which Braque tended to see as a contradiction in terms), where one might well reach a similar conclusion. Barnett Newman's scribbled 'Barnett Newman' is a blemish on a Barnett Newman – in his case a deliberate ploy, a calculated intrusion of the alien element, precisely in order to assert 'the self' of the artist in the process of creation. Other artists, Newman thought, 'stamp on a symbol as if it were outside the picture. I try to do it when I sign my paintings.'[71]

Anonymity was to some extent assured. Between 1910 and 1914, as a rule, Braque and Picasso did not exhibit. Their work could be seen only by aficionados and only in Kahnweiler's back room. If the dealer in effect underwrote their production, he also made sure to monopolize their presentation. Braque made no more appearances as a 'front' for Picasso – taking the heat in the Salons – the calculation proposed by a feline Max Jacob to account for their alliance. In this schema, at once absolutist and reductionist, Picasso was God (*le Grand Annonciateur*) and Braque his disciple (*le Grand Adepte*).[72] Proselytism, however, was not the good soldier's strong suit. Braque stayed at home. Isolated examples of his work appeared, fleetingly, in Amsterdam, Munich, Prague, or Moscow, but in New York he was unknown and in Paris he was invisible. Kahnweiler bought what he made. Discriminating collectors bought what Kahnweiler showed them. But Kahnweiler was deliberately trying to build up his stock, *à la* Vollard, in the confident expectation that it would appreciate; and as far as Braque was concerned discrimination was at a premium. The major foreign collectors of Cubism in the pre-1914 period were the Czech Vincenc Kramář and the Russian Sergei Shchukin, both of whom had a blind spot about Braque. (Shchukin bought fifty-one Picassos and only one Braque.)[73] In Paris, Picasso's most munificent patrons were Leo and Gertrude Stein, but

Gertrude Stein always says that Cubism is a purely Spanish conception and only Spaniards can be Cubists and that the only real Cubism is that of Picasso and Juan Gris. Picasso created it and Juan Gris permeated it with his clarity and his exaltation. To understand this one has only to read the life and death of Juan Gris by Gertrude Stein, written upon the death of one of her two dearest friends, Picasso and Juan Gris, both Spaniards.[74]

The unassuming Roger Dutilleul was almost alone in collecting both Picasso and Braque with equal assiduity from the outset, starting with *Houses at L'Estaque* from the 1908 exhibition, and often buying as soon as the paint was dry. By the time war broke out he had amassed some twenty-five works by each artist, wedged into his small apartment, which came to resemble nothing so much as a Cubist composition in 3-D, as the walls gradually thickened with layer upon layer of superimposed canvases. For the rest, as bold as he might be, Braque existed in cultural limbo. In Anatole

17. Portrait of Georges
Braque by Pablo Picasso
(1911)

France's 'modern' novel *The Revolt of the Angels*, serialized in *Gil
Blas* in 1913, the acme of advanced taste is an expressed preference
for Matisse and Metzinger over Delacroix and Raphael.[75] At the
famous Armory Show in New York the same year, visitors could
easily have come away with the impression that Cubism was a
movement dominated by Duchamp and Picabia – who was there,
alone of the avant-garde, industriously promoting Picabia.[76]

Picasso and Braque were thrown on their own resources.
Anonymity *à deux* was anonymity shared. The sharing was joyful.
They tried on each other's clothes. In the blue mechanics' overalls
favoured by Braque – but without the hazel bowler and yellow
clodhoppers he also affected – they went cap in hand to Kahnweiler
at the end of the month to seek a wage for their labour. 'Patron!
We've come for our pay!'[77] They took photographs of each other
in Braque's army uniform, Sergeant Braque with a faraway look in
his eye, Sergeant Picasso swaddled but steadfast, a ritual copied fifty
years later by Jasper Johns and Robert Rauschenberg, the Braque
and Picasso *de nos jours*, in their Manhattan warehouse studios.
They tried each other's national dishes, or mock dishes. 'Picasso

18. Portrait of Pablo Picasso
by Georges Braque (1911)

and I do a lot of cooking,' Braque informed Kahnweiler from Sorgues. 'The other evening we had *ajo blanco* [literally, white garlic], a Spanish dish as its name suggests. We very much regretted that you were not here to share with us this modest but delicious dessert-soup. (In case you might be tempted, here is the recipe.) One or two bowls of water per person, several cloves of garlic, almonds, and, on serving, throw some grapes in the water (above all do not cook). Try it, it makes you laugh a lot. I plan to get my revenge.' The *ajo blanco*, he added helpfully, makes a powerful insecticide.[78]

They also tried each other's styles. Unlike Johns and Rauschenberg, Braque did not put the finishing touches to any Picassos, or vice versa, so they both maintained. Rather, they exchanged fingerprints, playfully perhaps, but with a mighty purpose. Braque even put on a Spanish accent.[79] If Picasso was a vertical invader, as John Berger has suggested, then Braque was a horizontal raider. The vertical invader appears in the writings of Ortega y Gasset on the modern European masses. 'The European who is beginning to predominate . . . must then be, in relation to the complex civilization into which he has been born, a primitive man, a barbarian appearing on the stage through the trap-door, a "vertical invader".'[80] Picasso appeared on the European stage through the trap-door of Spain. He became honorary president of the School of Paris, he lived and died on French soil, yet he remained existentially an outsider, a foreigner. He was in France, for seventy years, but not of it. With a select few, he was not above joking about national styles in painting, at French expense. 'The French, at heart, they're peasants.'[81] Much as he abhorred German militarism and national socialism, fundamentally, *la patrie* failed to connect; he was not about to risk his life, and his country was elsewhere. Picasso was always fearful of xenophobia – fear given colour during two world wars – but his condition was irremediable. He was not French. He was, as he signed himself once to Braque, his blood up from the bullfight, 'ton Picasso artiste-peintre espagnol'.[82] He was apt to be possessive about his turf. Braque's adoption of the tenora was a kind of covert operation in Spanish territory, recognizable only by the initiated, an in-joke. But from Céret in the summer of 1911 he raided the citadel of Spanishness, bull fighting, and produced a work that was as plain a declaration as his letter of condolence: *Still Life with Banderillas*, complete with the painted letters [TO]RERO (bullfighter) and two crossed banderillas in dynastic alliance.[83]

The reciprocal masterpieces that issued out of their cohabitation in Céret testify to a wondrous equipoise in an idiom so novel and a duo so variant. 'As we saw clearly later,' said Braque delphically to Vallier, 'Picasso is Spanish, and I'm French; we know all the differences that that entails, but during those years the differences didn't count.'[84] Picasso's Braquian *Landscape at Céret* matched Braque's Picassian *Rooftops at Céret*. Picasso's Braquian *Accordionist* matched Braque's Picassian *Man with a Guitar* (col. pls 7 and 8). These ravishing paintings – sensuous, mysterious vibrations of a newly visible world, blueprints for what Baudelaire called the secret architecture of the work – crept up on the imagination of the West and took root. Forty years later *Man with a Guitar* and two or three other canvases of this period were praised to the skies by the exacting Clement Greenberg. The same man and the same impedimenta are at the heart of Albert Murray's ruminations on 'the visual equivalent to blues composition': the creative process as a form of play, the ornamental and ritual emphasis, the disposition to make any raw material into aesthetic statement, the essence of the work (and the identity of the artist) consisting not in choice of subject matter or title but in interpretation, or reinterpretation.[85] In André Breton's quintessential Surrealist romance *Nadja*, first published in 1928, when the unearthly Nadja ('I am only an atom respiring at the corner of your lips') visits the narrator or Breton-figure at home, she recognizes 'in a painting by Braque the nail and the string, outside the central figure, which have always intrigued me'.[86] The painting is *Man with a Guitar*; the nail and the string mementos of a bygone age, when a picture told a story – an anecdote – say, *Martyrdom of St Sebastian*. The Cubist works offer nothing so tidy. There is no inference to draw (*Reclining Nude*) or narrative to complete (*Woman Reading a Letter*). There is no conventional resolution, no end. Indeed there is no beginning either. In Braque as in Beckett, we are treated to slices of speechlessness. 'To restore silence is the role of objects,' asserted Beckett. 'I like only two things, silence and music,' asserted Braque.[87] We look to these speechless objects, not for an explanation, but for insights. It is not a matter of quartering the canvas systematically, as if deciphering hieroglyphics; it is more like caving. 'We start from the surface,' in John Berger's brilliant exposition, 'we follow a sequence of forms which leads into the picture, and then suddenly we arrive back at the surface again and deposit our newly acquired knowledge upon it, before making another foray.'[88]

Making a foray is a resonant metaphor. Jean Paulhan made one of his own. Arriving home in the early hours, he realized that he would have to negotiate a room of spectacular clutter in order to reach the bed. He was anxious not to wake his wife. He decided to switch on the light for a split second, fix the obstacles in his mind's eye, and then proceed as best he could in the dark. 'I managed some curious falls (sketches for falls): when my hand, after having followed the outline of some piece of furniture, abruptly lost contact, going astray in the shadows (and I felt suddenly isolated from the world of things). Another clock chimed two, as my hip recognized a table corner: even the time was out.' Part-way across, it comes to him that what he is doing, out of time in this defamiliarized chamber, is a kind of slow-motion space-walk through a Braque – he is clambering about inside the picture.

It will be said that I couldn't see. On the contrary. I had seen all my obstacles perfectly, I had never seen them so well, I saw them almost too well, by that blinding light – as if they had never yet been there; as if they had just been created; as if they had created themselves! . . . One might even say that I saw them from all sides at the same time. For now at last I recognized the back and the sides as well, or as ill, as the front, and I was no less familiar with the bottom of the table than the top. I wasn't content with their aspect: I wanted to grasp their inspect. (Can one say *inspect*?) I had been immersed in it. I had digested it. (Like a woman who chooses a diamond in a jeweller's window, and then, to possess it for a moment, closes her eyes.) I had believed in it.[89]

'Rather than ask of a Cubist picture: Is it true? Or: Is it sincere? One should ask: Does it continue?' says John Berger.[90] *Man with a Guitar* and its ilk are bottomless. That is the art of the *longue durée*. Braque's painting takes time in this sense too: the time it takes to make a foray, to show how the things become things, to grasp a handful of inwardness. It is the grin, long after the cat has vanished.

There was one more high summer of conjugal Cubism. In 1912, after much importuning – a perennial theme in the relationship: Picasso pursued Braque as relentlessly as he did any woman, and over a far longer period – Braque took a neighbouring house in Sorgues and they resumed their discussions. The laboratory was as busy as ever, but domestically the correlation of forces had changed. The position of Madame Braque had been filled, permanently, by Marcelle. Whatever Duncan Grant may have thought, the strangest thing about them as a couple was that, amidst so much artistic unbuttoning, they were completely faithful to each other for over fifty years. Braque was not short of offers to spend the afternoon with one young woman or another – 'failing you', as he would say to Marcelle. It was a standing joke between them.[91] Within the household, Mariette Lachaud joined her mother Amélie (the cook) in Braque's employ in 1930 at the age of sixteen and served him

faithfully till the end, as chaste as she was devoted. She graduated
from studio assistant to ministering angel and photographic docu-
mentarist – never to mistress. Her relationship with Braque (and
with Marcelle) was very different from that of Lydia Delectorskaya
and Matisse. Faced with an ultimatum from his wife, 'Choose
between that girl and me,' Matisse is supposed to have informed
her after due reflection that he had decided to keep Lydia, because
she was a big help in preparing his income tax returns.[92] Braque
never sought such assistance. Picasso meanwhile had abandoned
Fernande and installed Eva in her place. This was all one to Braque
but not to Marcelle, who was fond of Fernande and found Provençal
exile with Eva something of a trial. 1912 was a hot summer. When
the mistral got up, they would go for walks in single file, Marcelle
delighted in recalling, Braque leading the way, strong against the
wind, accompanied by the second of Picasso's gifts, Turc, a
crosspatch bulldog, increasingly deaf, that once sank its teeth into
Henri Laurens's wooden leg; then Marcelle and Eva; with a miserable Picasso bringing up the rear, herded by his beloved dog Frika,
a mixed-up Breton spaniel and German shepherd, not long for this
world.

In 1913 a spate of deaths and illnesses in Picasso's camp meant
that their summer was cancelled. In 1914, a few days after an
Austrian archduke was shot by a Serbian student in Sarajevo, they
reconvened in Provence, Braque in Sorgues, Picasso in Avignon,
and Derain in nearby Montfavet. 'Picasso is frequenting the cream
of Avignon society,' Braque told Kahnweiler – a note that would
recur.[93] Braque for his part spent most of the time renovating his
property, rather grandly called the Villa Bel-Air, 'a Japanese farm
with good old-fashioned whitewashed walls like in France'. On
25 July it was finally done and he could look forward to some peace
and quiet in the studio. Three days later Austria declared war on
Serbia. Russia mobilized along the German and Austrian frontiers.
On 1 August Germany declared war on Russia. In the chancellories
of Europe an invasion of Belgium was expected hourly.

In the studios of Provence news travelled slowly. 'I am working,'
Braque reported to Kahnweiler that morning, 'quite content to be

finally settled in my own place.'[94] While he worked, a general mobilization had been announced. Braque and Derain leapt to do their patriotic duty. The next day they boarded a train at Avignon. Marcelle was stunned; she could hardly speak. Picasso went with them to the station. Years later he delivered himself of his notorious parting shot: 'On 2 August 1914 I took Braque and Derain to the station at Avignon. I never saw them again.'[95]

6. 'If I should Die out there': The Great War

As Braque and Derain journeyed north, on 3 August, they heard that Germany had declared war on France and invaded Belgium. The Schlieffen Plan had been put into action: the German army would wheel through Northern France, as impervious to restraint as an ironclad revolving door, and step out at Paris. A febrile nationalism masked French consternation. Victory is certain, they would say in the trenches, 'as long as the civilians hold out'.[1] The two painters travelled on to rejoin their regiments, Braque in Le Havre, Derain in Lisieux. For the latter it was the beginning of a long trail of marginal utility. Derain was not cut out for military service. His war was a desolate affair, by turns boring and annoying, as interminable as it was undistinguished.

Braque's war was different.

He was lucky at first. He was not immediately thrust into action but retained in Le Havre and then despatched to the relative calm of Lyon for specialist training on the coffee mill – soldiers' slang for the machine-gun. On 14 November his luck ran out. He was promoted Sub-Lieutenant and sent forward. The German advance had been checked, perilously, within sight of the Eiffel Tower. In a flurry of improvisation Joffre had succeeded in jamming the door on the Marne. For this there was a price to be paid. France was haemorrhaging. In the first five months of the war one in three French combatants was killed or wounded. Casualties in August alone were close to 300,000. Sub-Lieutenant Braque was sorely needed. He found himself on the Somme, in the Maricourt sector, not far from Mametz Wood. 'I'm now in the firing line,' he wrote to Picasso on 29 November. 'I had my baptism about a week ago . . . There's been a lot of fighting here and we've taken up guard among dead Boches and also unfortunately some [French] marines. Now the area is fairly calm. You can't imagine what a battlefield is

19. On the Western Front, 17 December 1914

like with the uprooted trees and the earth dug up by the shells.' He closed with the familiar repetitions of the field postcard:

I shake your hand.
Health is excellent
and morale too.

In January 1915 he was still in the thick of things. 'I've been at the front two months,' he informed Apollinaire, with a touch of pride. 'We've had some pretty serious engagements with the Germans.' With the volunteer artilleryman he was a little more uninhibited:

Health is good and morale excellent.
I shake your hand like a brother in the trenches.
Vive la France.[2]

Two months was a long time and 'pretty serious engagements' an understatement. The order to attack had come on 17 December. Braque led his platoon over the top. In the teeth of the guns he gave a good account of himself, but the attack, like so many attacks, failed. The regimental history speaks of heavy losses. That very day he sent a souvenir photograph back to Marcelle, a portrait from the front. He looks sleepless but unbowed. He has seen things he never thought to see. He is still focussed. 'A vigorous officer, commanding his platoon well, dedicated. Shows willing.'[3] His military dossier is a paean of praise to his drive and his fortitude. Braque had the right temperament for trench warfare. War is as much waiting as fighting, or what passes for fighting. Trench warfare was ritualized waiting, in unspeakable conditions, interspersed with bouts of loosely choreographed blood-letting, dignified by the ballet-masters as a strategy of attrition. 'Memory of 1914. Joffre's only concern was to redo the battle paintings of Vernet.'[4] The general had his château, but for soldiers and sub-lieutenants the Somme was a charnel house. Battles were not battles traditionally conceived, but siege offensives of indeterminate compass, competitions in exhaustion. Sooner or later the ghoulish performance was repeated, often over the same ground. The intermissions stopped the guns but not the putrefaction. Prolonged inactivity ground men down as surely as predicted offensives. 'The action is a series of desperate acts that allow us to maintain hope,' Braque recorded later in his epigrammatic notebook. 'Few men's courage is proof against protracted meditation unrelieved by action', as Melville says.[5] His morale remained excellent, in spite of all. The whine of bullets became stamped on the grey matter of his brain, as on the wax of a gramophone record. From the sound of a shell he developed the ability to gauge its trajectory and estimate its point of impact. This deadly contest of expectation brought tactility to the battle space. 'The artilleryman *touches* the target. (The trajectory is the extension of the arm.) Units of tactile measurement: the foot, the cubit, the thumb . . .'[6] Being shelled is the stock-in-trade of the infantry soldier.

Braque knew his trade: a bloodier métier. If he was courageous, his courage was an expression of professional conscience.[7] The much-vaunted *élan vital* of the French army was every bit as mystical as the fourth dimension. In every avant-garde, constancy counted for more than charisma. Lieutenant Braque led dependably. His men followed soberly. Through the blasted waste of the Western Front he showed them how to be brave enough. 'I'm not looking for exaltation. Fervour will do for me.'[8]

Braque's regiment sat tight in the same sector for another three months. In early May 1915 they were moved into Artois, north of Arras, in preparation for a large-scale French offensive against the heavily defended villages screening Vimy Ridge. After losing all element of surprise, the offensive was conducted under a merciless enemy bombardment. On 11 May the regiment was committed in the vicious fighting for Neuville-Saint-Vaast. It was here, on this quaking field, that Braque abruptly lost the battle of expectation. In the hail of shells, one toppled him. No-man's-land gained another involuntary citizen. A lifetime later, shortly before his death, he summoned Apollinaire to testify, as if on his behalf, from 'the shadow of my love', the poems that the ardent *artiflot* composed for Louise de Coligny-Châtillon (Lou) at precisely that moment. Braque selected, edited, and illustrated the book he made. The title he chose was *If I Should Die Out There*.

> If I should die out there at the front,
> You would weep for a day, beloved Lou
> And then my memory would burn out like a
> Shell bursting on the front lines,
> A shell pretty as mimosas in bloom.[9]

After several hours marooned in no-man's-land the stretcher-bearers brought him in, pulverized and oblivious. If they had not stumbled upon him, he would have died out there, joining the other 17,000 mashed on that bloody midden. By an inch, he survived. In the fullness of time he returned to active duty, but not to the front line.

He was awarded the Croix de Guerre, first with bronze star, then with palm, and appointed Chevalier of the Legion of Honour.

The citations agree: 'An officer full of drive, seriously wounded, leading his platoon with the greatest bravery in the assault on the German trenches.'[10] In an empathic rumination on the real presence of Braque's *natures mortes*, Giacometti would imagine him,

disarmed in front of the things he's interrogating, trying to save these fleeting flowers, trying to capture on canvas for a little longer, as long as possible, a bit of all these things and himself and others. Trying to salvage something from the immense gaping darkness that surrounds them, that eats into them on all sides, but no! It's not the flowers, it's us and the paintings that are the fragile ones. The flowers themselves continue impassively to grow and their darkness is not ours.[11]

Braque kept his darkness to himself. In the immediate aftermath of the action at Neuville-Saint-Vaast one assumption prevailed, even in his own unit. *Left for dead* means what it says. With brisk efficiency the regiment set his affairs in order. His batman retrieved his papers and forwarded them to his next of kin. For a fleeting instant Braque joined the missing of the Somme. Magnificently, Marcelle refused to believe it. Next came a report that he had been wounded . . . seriously . . . but no indication that on 13 May he had come back to life, unable to see his hand in front of his face. 'At that moment, he was on the point of cursing his fate: a thick fog obscured everything in his vision. He hardly dared believe the doctor when the latter explained to him that it was only a temporary condition.'[12] Temporary blindness was a poor state for a painter.

Marcelle had to wait until the very end of the month before her faith was vindicated. At last she received word that he was recovering after holes had been drilled in his skull in order to relieve the pressure: trepanation was a brutal procedure.[13] He was out of danger and about to be moved to Paris, in the first instance to the Hôtel Meurice, commandeered for the convalescent. Word quickly spread. Gris sent bulletins to Kahnweiler, sheltering in neutral Switzerland. 'We knew that he had been wounded, but for a whole fortnight we did not know just what had happened. While he was on the danger list he kept it all quiet. He's a wonderful person. I have been terribly worried on his account, for you know how fond I am of him.' Marcelle screwed up courage for her first sight of him since he had left for the Front. 'I was afraid of finding him so badly wounded,' she remembered, 'that I wouldn't be able to hide my despair.' So afraid was she that she asked Picasso to come with her. When they got to the room she sent Picasso in first. He was out in a trice. 'Come quickly,' he called. 'It's OK.'[14]

Picasso saw Braque again in June 1915, it transpires, at an emotional reunion. His eve-of-war *boutade* has been subject to some fanciful over-interpretation. The two men did not quarrel on the station platform, about pacifism, socialism, or anything else; they parted the best of friends. 'And there was nothing between us there/ That might not still be happily ever after.'[15] Picasso may even have painted him a characteristic farewell, *Head of a Soldier in a Képi*. In a certain sense there was nothing to discuss. War was a circumstance of life, as Braque would have said. They both knew full well that there was no question of Picasso trying to join up and no question of Braque trying not to. They were destined for long periods of separation. They were about to move into different orbits, socially as well as professionally. There were frictions and resentments: deep resentments. But the differences between them were not easily reducible to the ancient schisms of combatant and non-combatant, belligerent and non-belligerent, nor to any simple-minded opposition of right and left. There were other sallies, from both sides, repeated by those who were happy enough to see the end of Picasso's 'Braque period', the most concentrated and fruitful of his whole career.[16] Whatever they may have said in public, Picasso and Braque remained closely involved in each other's works and days (and prices).[17] When Braque's fate was still unknown, in May 1915, Picasso was driven to beseech Roché, then employed as secretary to the commander of the Invalides, to see if he could discover any information. 'Braque is wounded that's all I know . . . Perhaps with the help of your general you could telegraph to find out some news and how he is. I would be very grateful to you . . . You know my friendship for Braque.'[18] That was in private. At Gertrude Stein's, meanwhile, he played the cynic.

20. In Henri Laurens's studio, 1915, taken by Laurens

'Will it not be awful when Braque and Derain and all the rest of them put their wooden legs up on a chair and tell about their fighting.'[19]

Braque for his part was in no condition to tell about anything. He spent the rest of the year in and out of hospital, recovering himself and reclaiming his world. He was tough, as Gris remarked; constitutionally he seems to have taken the shelling and the trepanning in his stride.[20] Psychologically it was more difficult. Re-entry was a lesson in acceptance. Not surprisingly, he had done no painting on active service. He had more urgent concerns, as he once said to Richardson. He had been in the mincing machine for the best part of six months. What is more, unlike most of the artist irregulars, he was an officer; he had an example to set and a platoon to look after. Gunner Derain and Sapper Léger saw a lot of war – not for want of trying to find cushier billets: draughtsman, writer, cyclist or chef, suggested Léger, perhaps even camouflage – but they did not have Lieutenant Braque's responsibilities.[21] He had done his duty. Now he was anxious to resume his work. Marking time – more waiting – was excruciating. The work was suffering, and so was he. 'It wasn't so much the wound that I suffered,' he told André Verdet later, 'but the impossibility of painting for those long months. It was more the mental than the physical wounding. In 1945, when I was ill again, the inactivity drove me crazy. What use would I be, deprived of painting?' To Vallier he said, eloquently, 'I wanted to continue, to get my ideas clear by working.'[22]

In January 1916 he reported to the depot of a new regiment at Bernay, in Normandy, still evidently unfit for duty. Instead of being discharged, as he hoped, he was given a further six months' convalescent leave. He returned to his old stamping-ground in Sorgues and rather gingerly re-entered the studio he had abandoned eighteen months earlier. 'It remains only to pick up the brushes again which won't be long now,' he said, without conviction.[23] By the middle of May he had made a tentative start on some still lifes. Braque was never a war artist.

At the same time he was in negotiation with a new dealer. In the market for modern art there was a vacuum to be filled. Kahnweiler, a German national, was a casualty of war. He had been forced to leave the country, his stock had been sequestered, and he was the cynosure of some ugly talk about Cubism, spelled Kubism, as *l'art boche* (Kraut art) – at best a deviant tendency, at worst a conspiracy to undermine French civilization, in league with Wagner, Nietzsche and the depraved Bouillon Kub, first looted and then banned for the duration of the war. After Braque left Avignon in August 1914, Marcelle had been questioned by the police. 'What is your husband's profession?' 'He is a painter,' she replied. 'No, madame,' she was told severely. 'He is a Cubist!'[24]

Into the breach stepped Léonce Rosenberg. Rosenberg's flagship enterprise was the Galerie de l'Effort Moderne. If the Galerie Kahnweiler was an exclusive boutique, a club for the connoisseur, the GEM was a department store, with aggressive promotions and a calculating house style (large canvases discouraged). Léonce Rosenberg was an opportunist with a mission. He wanted to corner the market in Cubism. He also wanted to brand it. Rosenberg's Cubism, like Campbell's soup, was a more or less homogeneous product – or, as he liked to say, movement – defined principally as the Cubism produced by Rosenberg's Cubists. His methods were unedifying. He was not above making insinuations about *marchands boches* (dealers) and the taint of sausage and sauerkraut, or fomenting trouble between artists. 'At this moment,' he wrote to Braque in 1919, 'P[icasso] has two *bêtes noires* . . . you and I myself. You because you dare to compete for the championship prize, me, because I ceaselessly and implacably demonstrate with works to hand that he alone does not represent the sum total of twentieth-century painting.'[25] The terms of his contracts were stringent, but he bought freely: too freely. Buying power exerted a strong attraction. Gris was nearly destitute in 1914; Laurens lived as frugally as a monk; even Derain offered to sell at any price. Rosenberg specialized in menaces and messianism, with a ready line in faux-Braque philosophizing ('I love the sentiment that humanizes the rule').[26] In this fashion he bagged a large number of Cubists, Braque included.

Braque signed a contract with Rosenberg in November 1916. Both were keen to do a deal, Rosenberg perhaps the keener. Braque laid low was still Braque, and Braque was a catch. Gris was already indentured. His advice was unequivocal: the only truly indispensable names for anyone who wanted to capture the movement were Picasso and Braque.[27] Given the pertinacity of the dealer, the terms of the contract suggest that Braque was regaining his strength. He preserved for himself more discretion than was customary with the Galerie de l'Effort Moderne. Strictly speaking it was a 'preferential agreement' rather than a commercial treaty, allowing Rosenberg first choice of the works proposed by Braque – not a right to his entire production – while committing the dealer to a minimum purchase of 1,000 francs per month. (Rosenberg's normal practice was to specify a maximum rather than a minimum figure.) The prices were at least respectable. Canvases for which Kahnweiler had paid 75 to 400 francs four years earlier now ranged from 150 to 1,100 francs (see Appendix A). Both the rates and the range compared favourably with any other artist under contract with the GEM. Léger, clearly a coming force, negotiated rates of 200 to 800 francs the following year, but mortgaged himself to Rosenberg in the process. The unworldly Laurens submitted willingly to a draconian regime at sweat-shop prices (200 to 500 francs for sculptures). Gris did likewise (40 to 350 francs).[28] The worldly Picasso, on the other hand, played the field. He sold to Rosenberg, among others, but cannily declined to sign a contract. Picasso could do this. He had muscle and guile and *réclame*. He had not been shelled or trepanned or detained. For Picasso there had been no interval.

Despite his braggadocio, Léonce Rosenberg had his uses. The GEM provided a shop window for his artists. He gave them individual exhibitions. He commissioned studies of their work. *Georges Braque* appeared in 1920, a picture book headed by some preternaturally well-informed 'Notes on the art of Braque' by Roger Bissière. The information came from conversations with the subject. Bissière (or Braque) laid emphasis on the artist's dedication and abnegation – 'gaining in depth what he was losing in brilliance' – that is, on the moral purpose of his way.

Braque is perhaps the first among the moderns to have glimpsed the poetry that comes from the *beau métier*, from a body of work made with love and patience, without the interference of a preconceived sensibility. He has understood that humane work, long caressed, ultimately bears the imprint of the care which surrounded his [painter-decorator] beginnings, and yields a moving humanity I cannot describe. Instead of letting himself go with the seductive effects of a brush stroke, with the endless tricks of the palette, instead of abandoning himself to his indefinable gifts, he is wary of them and wants to abide by the strictest disciplines . . . Braque has never forgotten his origins. Above all he has wanted only to be a workman, convinced that the rest would come by degrees.[29]

This set the tone and the parameters of much subsequent comment. It was somehow typical of a work under the imprint of the GEM that it was such a thumpingly hard sell. Rosenberg subscribed to the blatant school of product placement. Yet there is no denying he took a risk. However immovable the merchandise – not a single piece was sold at Laurens's exhibition in 1920 – he was for a while the sustainer, the insurer, at a time when insuring Cubists was by no means a secure occupation. Already in 1918, with the inanities of *l'art boche* ringing in the ears, Ozenfant and Jeanneret (better known as Le Corbusier) published their 'Purist' manifesto, *After Cubism*, vapourings about 'the modern spirit' and 'the conception' ('the simultaneous effort of reason and sensibility realizes *the conception*'), spiced with a haughty disdain for the over-rated ornamentalism they hoped to supersede: 'simple paintings by good painter-decorators smitten with form and colour'.[30] There was no mistaking the identity of the painter-decorator. In 1920 came the Dadaist manifesto, from Picabia. Dada didn't care. According to Picabia the Cubists were little better than pornographers and profiteers. They had 'cubed negro sculptures, cubed violins, cubed illustrated newspapers, cubed shit, cubed the profiles of young girls, and were now cubing money'.[31] The knives were out. In 1925 a poll was conducted for the artists to be included in any future national museum of modern art. The top ten, in order of precedence, turned out to be Matisse, Maillol, Derain, de Segonzac, Picasso, Utrillo, Rouault, Bonnard, Braque and Vlaminck. Cubism was represented here only by Picasso and Braque. The next ten contained one Cubist (or Tubist), Léger. Leading exponents such as Gleizes, Gris, Laurens, Lipchitz and Metzinger did not figure in the first thirty. The results were indicative. At the official exhibition of 'Fifty Years of French Painting', held the same year, all Cubists except for Picasso and Braque were kept out of the selection.[32] If Cubism was no longer a dirty word, it was not yet a bankable one.

Over the period 1916–20, as Braque navigated a new kind of no-man's-land, Rosenberg bought the bulk of his output: fifty-seven paintings, nineteen *papiers collés*, and several works on paper. None of these emerged until late 1917. Early 1916 was a false start.[33] Braque spent the last six months of that year immured in the depot at Bernay commanding a training company, still unsure of his status, still unable to paint. On New Year's Eve he went to a banquet in Paris in honour of Apollinaire ('hors-d'œuvre cubistes, orphistes, futuristes, etc.'). The two old comrades attended in identical uniform, down to the bandaged head in honour of King Shell, the fraternity of the trepanned.[34] The proceedings were suitably boisterous. Apollinaire wrote afterwards to Maurice Raynal, in the ossuary of Verdun, that his dinner was 'exactly what it should have been, a magnesium flash, explosive, dangerous, brief, carried to the brink of paroxysm. The air was thick with menacing stumps.'[35]

The unmissable event in his social calendar came a fortnight later, on 14 January 1917, when 'the admirers of the painter Braque' organized a banquet for him too (b/w pl. 7). The venue was Marie Wassilieff's studio-canteen on the avenue du Maine in Montparnasse. The Russian Wassilieff was a diminutive ball of fire, an intimate of Max Jacob's and a lover of Leon Trotsky's. She had enrolled briefly at the Académie Matisse before starting her own Académie Russe, subsequently transformed into the Académie Wassilieff, where a professor by the name of Léger relieved the students of 5 francs every time he corrected their work. The war ruined the Académie, but Wassilieff reopened each evening as a kind of soup kitchen-cum-drop-in-centre for the international flotsam and jetsam of the unmobilized, a raffish bunch whose star turns were Modigliani, Picasso and Zadkine, attended by the favoured, the besotted, and the rejected but hopeful. There was entertainment at Marie Wassilieff's every night of the week, but the Braque banquet was an extra-special occasion. With appropriate ceremony an organizing committee was formed, consisting of Apollinaire, Gris, Jacob, Matisse, Metzinger, Picasso, the poets Paul Dermée and Pierre Reverdy, Matisse's former pupil and Braque's future friend Walter Halvorsen, and Wassilieff herself, the moving spirit. Invitations were sent out to thirty-five guests, among them Friesz and Dufy, at 6 francs per head, wine and champagne inclusive. In an effort to avert any bad behaviour, Modigliani was specifically asked not to attend. There were crowns of gold for the homecoming heroes, Braque and Marcelle. The table was laid with a black cloth, blue plates and red napkins; the walls covered in *art nègre* hangings; the light shrouded in red. Wassilieff cooked the food – turkey – great big birds served in the magnificent Russian bowl she also used for her ablutions. Matisse served 'with the sang-froid of a Socrates'.[36] Everything went smoothly until half-way through the meal, when the door was flung open and a crowd of drunken revellers spilled in. At their head, singing an Italian song, was Modigliani. The organizers froze. Seated at the table was Béatrice Hastings, Modigliani's former lover, with her new beau, Alfredo Pina, a hot-headed sculptor. Pina produced a revolver and took aim at his rival. The intrepid Wassilieff launched herself at Modigliani and bundled him downstairs. The door to the studio was locked from the inside. Picasso pocketed the key.

The banquet resumed. Further mayhem was happily avoided. Wassilieff proposed a toast to the victorious Braque, and entertained the guests with her Cossack 'dance of the little fish'. Braque had had little enough of lionization. That night he drank his fill. The artists present paid tribute. Max Jacob did a brilliant impersonation of Braque's mother, whom he had never met. Braque himself joined Wassilieff in a belly-dance which brought the house down. The merry-making continued until six in the morning, at which hour the guest of honour could still be seen prancing around with Derain, brandishing the bones of the turkeys they had eaten. He looked happy again.[37]

To return once more to the depot after this was a considerable let-down. 'I'm still doing nothing and it pains me to lose so much time. I've always thought of the winter as the dead season, well that consoles me a bit.' The sum total of that season's work was one *papier collé*. But he did not have much longer to wait. In March 1917 Braque's request to be released from active service on health grounds was finally granted. He was free. He decamped to Sorgues and fired off an elated postcard to Picasso: 'I'm delighted to tell you that I've been discharged. I'm longing to pick up my brushes again. By the end of the month I think I'll be on the way.'[38]

So it proved. Braque worked all summer long in the haven of his studio at Sorgues. He was out of condition – he realized that – but he had already begun to consider the possibility of an exhibition at the Galerie de l'Effort Moderne, followed by a timely return to the Salon d'Automne. 'I believe that would be a good thing especially after my exhibition since the public forget the absent too easily.'[39] None of this could be done in a day. First he had to paint

21. In his Sorgues studio, 1917

some pictures. Then he had to satisfy himself that they would stand scrutiny. 'It is the precariousness of the work that casts the artist in a heroic light.'[40] The way back from the war was a struggle against many things, above all against precariousness. His staunch ally in that struggle was Pierre Reverdy, who escaped from the hurly-burly of the metropolis and installed himself and his wife Henriette in a neighbouring hamlet. Braque and Reverdy were profoundly in sympathy. Reminiscing with the trusty Jean Leymarie after the poet's death, Braque recalled fondly 'his touchy disposition, his nerves always on edge, his hasty prizefighter's attitude, sometimes ill-advised, his hatred of literary posers, his sure knowledge of the plastic arts, as opposed to Apollinaire who understood hardly anything, his love and nostalgia for the métier, for manual mastery' – high praise. Braque was rarely so self-revealing. Reverdy was a fellow-traveller of Cubism, and Cubists. 'He only liked the company of painters,' Braque continued. 'He would come to the house

22. Braque and
Marcelle (and Turc)
with Pierre and
Henriette Reverdy,
Sorgues, 1917

every day. He couldn't control his manias. One day when we were
talking about one of his *bêtes noires* he grabbed the telephone, found
the person concerned, and abused him for an hour. After an
unexpected cooling-off, he stayed away for seven years. We met
only outside. And yet he adored me and suffered by it. What
astounded him most in me was my calm.'[41] Melancholic and tender,
Reverdy was not always loquacious. Asked why he preferred the
company of painters, he replied: 'They lie less.' Asked what it was
about Braque, he responded simply, 'What he has, Braque, is
poetry.'[42]

The two men were accustomed to walking together over the
fields between their quarters. One fine day the artist appeared with
a stick over his shoulder, toting one of his canvases. He was in
search of reassurance. They walked for a while and then halted.
Braque unwrapped the painting and laid it flat on the ground.

Reverdy looked on in astonishment. He burst out: 'It's amazing that it holds up against the actual colour and the stones.'[43] The painting was *Glass and Ace of Diamonds* (1917), fresh off the easel, a work still little known but much discussed.

The proving of *Glass and Ace of Diamonds* in unison with nature, as Braque liked to say, was not a stunt. But it did become a legend: a tale told throughout the twentieth century, told with reverence and relish by the poet, and readily admitted by the painter himself. 'They say you used to take one of your canvases out into a field,' Paulhan suggested to him once. 'Yes,' replied Braque, 'I had the habit of lugging them around, introducing them to things. To see if they would hold up.'[44] It was a treatment he recommended all his life. Douglas Cooper became so worried about the wizened, darkened state of a middle-aged canvas of 1913 that he consulted its creator. Braque was unconcerned. 'Put it outside, in the sun,' he advised, 'and you'll see that it will regain its freshness.'[45] The legend of the field was repeated, and the stakes raised, by none other than André Breton, the Pope of Surrealism, who issued a strenuous, intriguing, ambivalent encyclical on Georges Braque in 1926. He began magnanimously enough but soon turned a good deal sterner:

I cannot help being moved by the destiny of Georges Braque. This man has taken infinite precautions. Between his head and his hands I seem to see a great hour-glass whose grains of sand are in no greater a hurry than the grains of dust dancing in a ray of sunlight. Sometimes the hour-glass sinks, horizontally, on the horizon and then the sand flows no longer. That is because Braque *'loves the rule that corrects the emotion'* whereas my sole concern is to deny this rule violently. Where does he get this rule from, I wonder? There must be some vague notion of God behind it . . . Braque is at present a great refugee. I greatly fear that in a few years' time I shall no longer be able to mention his name. . . .

I know that not long ago Braque had the idea of taking two or three of his pictures out into the heart of a cornfield to see if they 'held up'. A splendid idea, so long as one refrains from asking oneself in relation to what, compared with what, the *cornfield* 'holds up'. As for me, the only pictures I like, including Braque's, are those that hold up in the face of famine.[46]

A gauntlet had been thrown down. Many years later it was picked up by Pierre Reverdy. Reverdy also knew something of slowness. Eventually, in 1950, he published a long thesis on his friend Georges Braque. 'A Methodical Adventure' is a moving act of witness, an attestation of his belief in the congruent Braque – *l'homme intégral* in the words of another poet – 'a man who has thrown so much of himself into his work that the look of the work differs hardly at all from the look of his face'.[47] What is immanent in the work, for Reverdy, is the spirit of its maker. Look, he says, regarding the unregarded jug or glass or fruit, *there's* Braque! Braque embodies Braques. There is an inalienable congruence, a congruence that cannot be faked or manufactured, between the painter and the painted. Braque dredges deep inside himself to produce the work. The matter inscribes the man. Worker and worked are one.

From these considerations Reverdy delivered his verdict. 'I have heard since,' he wrote with magisterial restraint, 'that it is above all a matter of whether the painting would hold even against famine. Here is my response. Yes, it has held and against a lot of other things too, because the canvases are not afraid of anything.'[48]

Something else germinated during that refugee summer in Sorgues. Deprived of painting, Braque had been cogitating. The war was packed away inside him, almost never mentioned or directly acknowledged. 'Was it not noticeable at the end of the war that men returned from the battlefield grown silent,' mused Walter Benjamin, 'not richer but poorer in communicable experience.'[49] In the 1920s he joined a collective known as the Beavers of Montsouris, a group of artists building houses and studios near the Parc Montsouris on the fringe of Montparnasse. Another Beaver, Louis Latapie, a veteran of eight years' military service, was one of the very few to hear from Braque's lips an '*Oh! là! là!* that reminds me of the trenches!' after a day's hard pounding with their architect. Latapie, a younger man despite his service, revered Braque not least for his punctilious treatment of a much junior artist as an equal.

Latapie thought the shared history made a difference. 'Braque had done a year of war and that had been enough to give him that sort of painful maturity that only the veterans of [19]14 can recognize in each other.'[50]

Braque did not need to be reminded. 'Survival does not erase the memory,' he recorded poignantly. In the aftermath of a second war Jean Paulhan prompted him to say something about his experience of the first. He replied: 'Well! My memories of war remain in "no-man's-land" recalling that it's there that the bravest are to be seen.'[51] Was there a hint of survivor guilt in such reflections? His memories were buried where his bones were not. The bravest did die out there. The best did not return, as Primo Levi said of another holocaust. There were some who found this unbearable. Georges Braque was not one of them. If he was in some sense an escapee, his experience was as near-death as it is possible to imagine. His life had been saved. Rather, his death had been held in abeyance. From then on, for Braque the two states were never so distinct. The master of metamorphosis had been given a great endowment. His only war story was a common-or-garden transfiguration. 'I was at the Front. I said to my batman: "God, it's cold!" My batman gets an old petrol can, pokes holes in it with his bayonet, hangs it on a wire, making a stove. There's poetry for you!' Nothing could be tied down to one sort of reality, as he put it.[52] Things were mutant. The living were revenant. The dead were ever-present. When Jean Leymarie expressed sadness at the loss of Reverdy, Braque immediately contradicted him. 'He is here, always present, what else is there to say, and of how many others, still living, can one say the same?'[53]

The persistent irony of war is that it is worse than expected. Braque had not forgotten the ironies of this one: 'Our soldiers, in 1914, charged in red trousers! They came back from the war with pigs' snouts [gas masks].' The generals, too, learned to do differently. 'At first it was nothing more than a vaguely Impressionist illusion.'[54] After the brightly lit battle pictures came a drab contest of restricted palettes, in which colour was deliberately used to disrupt form – the word they used was *denature* – painting familiar objects in strange ways until they became unrecognizable. Camouflage was the Cubists' revenge, as Jean Paulhan pointed out. The very art that resembled nothing and deformed everything, the bizarrerie in all its glory, was precisely what was now required. *L'art boche* was the best defence. 'We did that,' said Picasso proudly as camouflaged guns trundled by, and troops mustered as Braque landscapes.[55]

He had not forgotten, either, the shirkers like Delaunay, who waited out the war in Spain making cheap cracks about cube roots and chilling remarks about the need to 'cleanse' Paris of 'certain mystifiers' of a Cubist persuasion; or Duchamp, who fled to the United States and professed to admire the attitude of combating invasion with folded arms; or Gleizes and Picabia, who joined up but thought better of it – men with convenient medical conditions or well-placed fathers-in-law.[56] 'That bastard Gleizes.'[57] Léger's verdict from the depths of the Argonne captures Braque's feelings nicely. The non-French were exempt from this despicable category – though Apollinaire, born Kostrowitzky, offered an alternative mode – but not from a baleful scrutiny of the way in which they had comported themselves in the meantime. Braque summarized his impressions for the exiled Kahnweiler. 'I found Gris in the process of making patriotic paintings, "Our Little 75", heads of soldiers, all that in Cubism (sic).' 'Our Little 75' was a shell. (Blaise Cendrars, who was there, wrote of 'the insane meow of the 75s'.)[58] If it was not for Gris to do the fighting, he considered, it was not for Gris to play at patriotism. 'As for Picasso,' he went on, 'he's apparently creating a new style called the Ingres style. You ask me what I think of his progress. In him, I find it absolutely natural. What is truly constant in the artist is his temperament. Apart from that Picasso remains for me what he has always been: a virtuoso full of talent. Fortunately, France has never been a country of virtuosos.'[59] Coming from Braque, this was a scathing assessment. In his language 'virtuoso' was close to 'dabbler' and in any event fundamentally unserious. 'Talent' was suspect. Talent could betray a man on a dark night. Like intelligence, it was a dubious quotient. Many fine artists have talent. To rely upon it was close to fraudulent. To flaunt it was unforgivable. For Braque, who did not have talent, this went to the heart of how to be. His position is encapsulated in one of his most characteristic maxims: 'There are some works that make one think of the artist and others of the man. I have often heard tell of Manet's talent, never Cézanne's.'[60]

What had Picasso done to deserve this? Doubtless he had prospered. More importantly, as Braque saw it he had betrayed his past, a past in which Braque himself had a large stake. Picasso had gone up in the world. Eva had died after a long illness in December 1915. After trying on several others for size and more than once being spurned, Picasso fell for the well-born Olga Khokhlova, a dancer in the Ballets Russes, the company of the great Serge Diaghilev. They met when Diaghilev engaged Picasso to design sets and costumes for *Parade*, the epitome of confectionery chic, with a libretto by Jean Cocteau, typewriter music (or *trompe-l'oreille*) by Erik Satie, and choreography by Léonide Massine. In July 1918 they were married. Soon they moved into a grand apartment in the refined quarters of the rue de la Boëtie, north of the Élysée palace. In January 1919 Picasso started to collect his own press cuttings. His 'duchess period' had begun. The conductor Ernest Ansermet arrived at Picasso's hotel room in Barcelona one evening to find him dressing for the ballet. The painter completed his toilet, put on his top hat, looked at himself in the mirror, and murmured: 'Monsieur Ingres.'[61]

Braque was deeply affronted by Picasso's worldliness.[62] He saw the socializing and the dressing-up as a kind of abandonment, a dereliction of duty: duty to the métier – the long caress – and perhaps also to the partnership as it used to be. Gertrude Stein told of an evening when Man Ray brought with him a photograph he had taken of Picasso, dressed as a toreador, at one of Count Étienne de Beaumont's talked-about balls. 'The photograph was being passed around and when it came to Braque he looked at it and said, I ought to know who that gentleman is, *je dois connaître ce monsieur*.'[63]

Braque was not the only one to have such a reaction. 'Picasso still produces some fine things,' Gris reported to Kahnweiler, 'when he has the time between a Russian ballet and a society portrait.' The duchess period was itself a coinage of Max Jacob. Even Roché, who knew everyone, noted *le snobisme* that attended 'Notre Tor-éro'.[64] But it was Braque who experienced the greatest difficulty of adjustment, to this and to the various other artistic currents he deplored. His response could not have been more unexpected. In collaboration with Pierre Reverdy, he published a distillation of his 'Thoughts and Reflections on Painting' in the influential journal *Nord-Sud* (see Appendix B). Throughout the dry period of his convalescence, thinking was one activity that was not denied him. These first thoughts were scribbled on the margins of his drawings. It was Reverdy who spotted them and ushered him into print. Braque was a Sunday writer. Some of his thoughts were well formulated, even aphoristic; others were not. Reverdy retouched them.[65] They came out as a batch of twenty, culminating in the much-parroted rule that corrects the emotion. The most effective, and the most typical (Reverdy notwithstanding), were the simplest. 'One must not imitate what one wishes to create.' 'New means, new subjects.' 'The painter thinks in forms and colours.' Several were plainly seen as maxims to live by. They could also be inter-preted as countermanding recent drift – a sort of call to order of his own.[66] In Braque's view, for example, Gris tended to think not in form and colour but in constituent parts – he spoke privately of Gris arranging still life like a head waiter – whereas Léger thought in finished paintings: both approaches too schematic, Braque main-tained, to seal the poetry in. 'The mistake of artists in general is to have subjected art to science, in other words to analysis, for in my view art begins only with the synthesis.'[67]

The maxims took wing. They were read with attention by intellectuals of every stripe, French and non-French alike (Jean Grenier, Henri Maldiney, André Malraux, Maurice Merleau-Ponty, Paul Ricœur, Carl Einstein, Meyer Schapiro, Martin Heid-egger, among others); though not across the Channel.[68] They had a powerful influence on younger painters such as Roger Bissière and Jean Bazaine. They also had an influence on their author, who had discovered an addictive sideline, and who began to keep a notebook from that day on.[69] In due course the notebook itself took its place in the life of the paintings. 'Braque-Rochefoucauld', however, *le moraliste cubiste*, was not to everybody's taste. Gunner Derain, still resentfully serving, was unimpressed. 'I'm staggered by the aphorisms of Lieutenant Braque,' he wrote to his wife,

I even feel sorry for him, I have to say. What a filthy journal! He doesn't see that the others are using him. I'd like to know what the General of Cubism [Picasso] thinks of it. As a reflection, he doesn't exactly strain himself . . . I can't help thinking about Braque's nonsense. It's so appallingly dry and insensitive. It manages to combine fanaticism with some initial omissions. One needs centuries of painting, good and bad, for or against, in order to have an idea about art. It regulates the imagination. In the end, it's not worth the trouble of talking about it so much, and yet it's what everyone thinks.[70]

General Picasso did not comment, but it is safe to say he did not rate Braque as a philosopher.

The polished maxims still outnumbered the finished paintings. By the end of the year 1917 Braque had despatched eight canvases of varying size to Léonce Rosenberg, including a *Musician* of skyscraper proportions, over 7 feet high, a work literally off the scale of their agreement, for which brazenry the dealer paid 3,675 francs. This ambitious painting was clearly intended to match or overmatch Picasso's *Seated Man* (1916), to whom the woman musician bears a striking resemblance, weighing in a little lighter but towering some 8 inches taller. *Seated Man*, originally *Man Seated in Shrubbery*, was itself a work of high ambition, a long time in the making (and sporting a Braquian pipe). Against such opposition Braque's effort was good, but not good enough. The Amazonian *Musician* was *Large Nude* in late Cubist clothing. It strained but it did not sing. Yet it is more interestingly derivative than at first appears. Like several other transitional canvases of this period, it derived as much from his own earlier practice as from his convalescent observation of Picasso or Gris or Laurens. In order to jump-start his work, to use John Richardson's apt expression, Braque consulted all of them. He also consulted Braque. *Musician* had ancestors, most notably the disputed masterpiece of 1914, *Man with a Guitar*.

Trying out different things over the next two years, Braque relied heavily on 'the new seeing machine' of which he was so proud, the *papier collé*. 'You know,' he wrote to Kahnweiler, who was plotting a comeback of his own, 'or rather you don't know that I'm now doing my canvases on a black background. It's a colour that we've been deprived of for so long by Impressionism and is so beautiful. It's a little like the pasted white of my *papiers collés* in reverse. I'm pleased with the results and it served me well. Working every day you acquire surer means and for me, the means, that's a lot.'[71] These *papiers collés* in reverse led him back to still life and musical instruments, indeed to a new interpretation of the attributes of music, camouflaged on a pedestal table, a strategy of which Joffre himself might have been proud.[72] The pedestal table was no doubt an unlikely platform for a surprise attack, but that was Braque. *Musician* had been a defensive construction, a bulwark against frailty. (Anything less precarious would be hard to imagine.) The work that followed caught observers unawares. It was plush, supple, undulant – 'vague allusions to familiar produce', as one critic put it.[73] In a telling line of his maxims Braque had declared that the *papiers collés* had given him certainty, a point to which Louis Aragon would return with keen insight many years later.[74] In his post-convalescent painting he found the nerve to shed that certainty. 'Made-to-measure Braques are not for me,' said Braque.[75] The regulated imagination was tuning up and turning loose. Klee famously took the line for a walk. With Braque it was more of a meander. Liberated from the deathly chatter of the coffee mill, he discovered a renewed interest in the grounds, exploring what he called the amplitude of colour. 'The Impressionists used to say: colour changes. One of their projects was to investigate all the causes of that change, open air, atmosphere, sun. Me, I say colour absorbs or is absorbed, which allows me to keep my local colour [*ton local*], varying it only in extent.'[76] His art was afloat again, rich in ambiguity and remembrance of still life past.

The second individual exhibition of his career took place at the Galerie de L'Effort Moderne in March 1919. Max Jacob assured Picasso that it was monotonous compared to his own, André Lhote was stuffily unconvinced, but the rest of the world was not fooled.[77] The exhibition was a *succès d'estime et morale*. Gris was not alone in admiring the artistic authority on display.[78] There was no song of praise, however, from Apollinaire. The poet-in-chief had died on 9 November 1918, two wretched days before the armistice. He was an absent presence.

Apollinaire's place was taken by Blaise Cendrars, one-armed and sharp-witted, who dedicated his appreciation, unsolicited, to Madame Braque.

Monsieur Georges Braque is a pure man. He has only one thing in mind: quality. M. Georges Braque is the quality Cubist painter. He is the artist who reviewed all the Cubist theories and who chastised each of them for their excesses. He has questioned, interrogated, heard confession. Each Cubist painter has been led, in turn, before this austere figure, and has received from him a strict sermon. Through his authority and his insistence, he has succeeded in subduing these over-enthusiastic painters. He has arrested their growth, breaking off any tendentious branches and pruning the youngest shoots, which he called parasites. This puritan is a hard man who has ended up imposing his own laws, who has kept the entire order subjected to his will. What, then, is his discipline? The doctrine of quality.

Thus, M. Georges Braque is closer to Versailles than to Paris, and as his 'quality' becomes more and more synonymous with virtue, M. Georges Braque resembles even more closely the mentality of Port-Royal. Thanks to him, the Cubist painters can be situated fully within the venerable French traditions of cold reason, unswerving stubbornness, and ceremonial pomp. (A Jansenism of which Picasso could be called the feverish and often plaintive Pascal and M. Braque the rigid and didactic logician, the Arnauld, the Grand Arnauld.) Useless to push this analogy further. M. Georges Braque's art is the painting of quality, but before it is pure painting, it is the manifestation of M. Braque's quality. Which he is able to demonstrate by embodying all the Cubist painters' investigations.

M. Braque is, then, a painter of quality. He is dry and precise in his distinguished manner, with suddenly a slight thickening which is a sort of tribute to the thing he has undertaken: the defence of his painting, the patent proof of his quality. (It is also a tiny outlet of the emotion that stirs this painter, and that is so willingly repressed.) Every one of M. Braque's canvases is at once a discourse, a panegyric, and an oration.[79]

Braque returned to exhibiting, one might say, with a vengeance. At the 1920 Salon des Indépendants he refused, hurtfully, to appear in the same room as Gris: the penance for his presumption.[80] The problem did not recur. At the 1922 Salon d'Automne, fourteen years after the contretemps over the little cubes, Georges Braque was given the accolade of the Salle d'Honneur.

7. 'Tous les conforts, pas de téléphone':
Braque–Chardin

In 1921 the Dadaist house journal, *Littérature*, published approval ratings of the high and mighty throughout history – not to classify but to declassify, as they said – on a scale from 20 to −25, where 20 indicated complete approbation, −25 extreme aversion, and 0 absolute indifference. Against expectation, Braque emerged with a creditable 2.77, on a par with Kant (2.90) and Alcibiades (2.72). This was far behind Baudelaire (9.00) and Freud (8.60), but far ahead of Delacroix (−8.54) and Debussy (−9.18), or for that matter Cézanne (−3.36) and Corot (−4.90). The average concealed a startling 14 from the editor, André Breton, an annihilating 0 from the writer Tristan Tzara, and a whimsical −10 from the poet Paul Éluard.[1]

These men soon had Braques of their own. *Le tout Paris* bought a Braque in the early 1920s – supporters, detractors, rivals, aspirants; the curious, the greedy, the timid, and the shrewd – even Louis Vauxcelles. They came to the liquidation of Kahnweiler's sequestered stock at the Hôtel Drouot – four sales, spread over two years (1921–3). Uhde had suffered the same fate, and his sale served as a curtain-raiser. The two victims spoke of being present at their own executions. In all, the authorities disposed of 135 Braques, 132 Picassos, 111 Derains, 56 Grises, 43 Légers, 33 Van Dongens, and no fewer than 215 Vlamincks. The inventory was sufficient to provision several museums of modern art, with plenty of major works left over. As a conspectus of Cubism, it was the sale of the century. This stupendous haul went for less than 900,000 francs. Of that, almost a third was accounted for by the Derains, an accomplished and eclectic œuvre which comfortably outperformed everything else. (One bitter pill, a *Portrait of Madame Kahnweiler*, fetched a record 18,000 francs – bid up deliberately, it seems, to put it out of reach of a syndicate representing her

anonymous husband, doing his desperate best to buy back some of
his own stock.) The Braques might have held up out of doors but
they did not do well in the sale room. They made little more than
60,000 francs.[2] What these aggregate figures indicate is that, Derains
apart, hundreds of works were sold at knock-down prices. If ever
a market was flooded, this was it.

Braque was sore about these proceedings before ever the auc-
tioneer raised his gavel. Slowness lends its own perspective. Braque's
catalogue raisonné for 1907–14 has a total of 247 entries. Picasso
produced more than three times as many Cubist works as his partner
in that period. For Braque, 135 was several years' work. The sales
represented a substantial tranche of his output, officially despoiled
and compulsorily discounted. Adding insult to injury, the 'expert'
retained to do the discounting was none other than his own former
dealer, Léonce Rosenberg. Braque had left Rosenberg for
Kahnweiler when the latter resumed trading in Paris (under a
different name) the previous year. At that juncture Braques were
buoyant. His new contract of May 1920 with Kahnweiler stipulated
prices by the number, in this instance 130 francs per number, so
that the dealer paid 780 francs for a small number 6 canvas and
6,500 francs for a larger number 50, as compared to 150 and 1,100
francs respectively in 1916 (see Appendix A). These prices were
broadly in line with those of Matisse and Picasso. (Though they do
not necessarily say anything about income in a given period. The
hyperactive Picasso is estimated to have earned over 100,000 francs
in 1920. Braque may not have earned more than half that.)[3] The
prices of all three then accelerated sharply. On the open market the
price of Braques doubled over the next few months: something to
do with Kahnweiler, no doubt, but also a result of the Chardin
effect. Braque–Chardin, like Braque–Rochefoucauld, proved con-
tentious in some quarters, but it was increasingly the equation on
every critic's lips; and 'our Chardin' was a selling proposition.[4]
Roché, now scouting for the venturesome American collector John
Quinn, had his practised ear to the ground. What he heard in
October 1920 was that Braques were selling for no less than 300

francs per number, and he had it from the artist himself that almost everything had gone.[5]

Egged on by Kahnweiler himself, Braque, Derain and Vlaminck turned up at the viewing session before the first sale, in June 1921, to protest against the liquidation. Braque had not returned to Kahnweiler purely for old times' sake. He lost faith in Rosenberg well before the sales. They had quarrelled over the dealer's sharp practices: Braque accused Rosenberg of reneging on their contract by refusing to pay agreed prices; Rosenberg accused Braque of falsifying the measurements of the works coming out of his studio. After the break, the dealer's vituperative tongue was unrestrained. 'Braque's works are . . . dead, and have never really lived,' he wrote to Léger; 'they're well-named *natures mortes*.'[6] In this context Rosenberg's appearance in the guise of expert was a joke in poor taste. The expert did not disappoint. He failed to send the catalogue of sale to interested parties notified to him by Braque – an omission described by the latter as 'an act of sabotage' – and produced estimates so low as to remove any shadow of doubt about official expectations of the exercise in which they were engaged.[7]

The three protesters arrived at the Hôtel Drouot to find the viewing area packed. All of a sudden Braque spotted Rosenberg in the crush, grabbed him by the scruff of the neck, and shook him like a bad dog, berating him the while for his turpitude.[8] The expert was heard to call the artist a Norman pig. Braque spun him round and hit him. At this point Amédée Ozenfant stepped between them. 'How can you defend this bastard?' spat Braque, sending Ozenfant reeling with a jab to the solar plexus, before getting back to his work. 'He's mad, he's mad!' expostulated Rosenberg. No one else came to his rescue. At length Braque calmed down and unhanded the mewling expert. Order was restored. Matisse arrived, too late to see the action but in time to hear all about it from Gertrude Stein. 'Braque is right,' he said, 'that man [Rosenberg] has robbed France, and we know very well what it is to rob France.'[9]

The case was heard, impromptu, by the local *commissaire de police*. As the sorry tale was unfolded, Rosenberg in his turn lost his temper when addressed by Braque in the familiar 'tu', and was publicly rebuked for so maligning an officer and a recipient of the Croix de Guerre. Both men were released from police custody. No charges were pressed. Braque apologized to Ozenfant and departed for Sorgues, abstaining from any further part in the proceedings – forgoing the pleasure, as he wrote to Kahnweiler, of seeing his old canvases again.[10] Rosenberg took up boxing. 'Braque,' noted Paulhan admiringly, 'is reflective, but violent.'[11]

From the painter's point of view the outcome of the sales was, on the face of it, every bit as bad as he feared. Braques opened low and plunged lower as more and more were unloaded on to the market. Expressed in terms of average price per number, at the first Kahnweiler sale in 1921 it was 66 francs, a figure sustained only by the purchases of the Kahnweiler syndicate, which managed to acquire eleven of the twenty-two on offer that day. *Violin and Pitcher* (a number 50), one of Clement Greenberg's all-time great paintings, reached the dizzy height of 3,200 francs – perhaps a fifth of its previous value – whilst the remainder went for less than 1,800. At the fourth and last sale in 1923 the average price per number was down to a derisory 19 francs (see Appendix C). At these prices, a small Braque could be had for some 200 francs, a *papier collé* for as little as 50.

Yet, not by design, the sales also developed into an exercise in redistribution. Many of those who bought could not otherwise have dipped a toe into such expensive waters; and some of those who bought big would not otherwise have been tempted. The constituency of Braque-owners was broadened and deepened in interesting ways: new adepts emerged. In sharp contrast, more traditional brethren sat on their hands. Despite a right of pre-emption, official purchases were negligible.[12] France paid dearly for its dilatoriness. The *Man with a Guitar* (1914), repossessed by the Kahnweiler syndicate for 2,820 francs in 1921, entered the collection of the Musée national d'art moderne in Paris sixty years later at a cost of some 9 million francs. Dealers, also, bought less than Kahnweiler himself expected, swearing off Cubism in favour of neoclassicism, syncretism, or archaism – a mood caught by the

Derains. The Braques went instead to the opinionated poor, the artists and writers who found Braque in the 1920s, converted, testified according to their means, and remained spellbound to the end of their days. As the works changed hands, so the word spread.[13]

Léonce Rosenberg bought the first *papier collé*, *Fruit Dish and Glass* (235 francs) (col. pl. 9), fencing it quickly to André Breton, from whom it passed into the hands of Douglas Cooper, who coddled it with pride.[14] His brother, Paul Rosenberg, another and better dealer, bought its painted counterpart, a more cluttered and less successful work, *Fruit Dish, Grapes, Newspaper and Playing Cards on a Table* (780 francs). The expert's expertise was torpedoed by the poet Robert Desnos, who paid 37 francs for an unsigned Braque charcoal drawing measuring 37 × 46 cm, according to the catalogue, only to find that it was in fact a signed Picasso measuring 24 × 31 cm.[15] André Breton bought a dozen paintings for himself, among them the *Large Nude* of blessed memory (240 francs) (b/w pl. 4) and a delicately clawed *Woman Playing a Mandolin* (550 francs). Paul Éluard bought three, including *The Bottle of Rum* (210 francs). At the same time he composed a poetic tribute to the painter.[16] 'Monsieur Silichpitz', alias Lipchitz, bought one and sold it on to his friend H. P. Roché. Louis Aragon bought another and off-loaded it six years later for a hundred times what he had paid.[17] Ozenfant, who bore no grudges, acquired an outstanding *papier collé* of doubtful title, *Clarinet*, for 430 francs, selling it 'in a moment of difficulty' thirty years later for $8,000 to Nelson Rockefeller, who generously bequeathed it to the Museum of Modern Art in New York in 1979.[18] With pleasing symmetry, Ozenfant's partner in crime, Jeanneret (Le Corbusier), bought *Clarinet and Bottle of Rum on a Mantelpiece* (400 francs), which passed through the hands of the Galerie Beyeler in Basle (1,260,000 francs in 1970), a private collector in Portugal, and an enterprise named Cofinarte in Switzerland (£240,000 in 1974), before entering the Tate Gallery in London in 1978 (£620,000 or $1.25 million). In a way that Braque might have appreciated, slowness of execution found an echo in slowness of appreciation: a lag of fifty to sixty years was about the norm. On rare occasions it was anticipated. Shrewdly advised by Ozenfant

23. Jean Paulhan in the débris of his room, Braque's *papier collé*, *Violin* (1914), on the wall behind him (compare col. pl. 10)

and Jeanneret, the Swiss banker Raoul La Roche made a down payment of 50,000 francs on a world-class collection of modern art, beginning with some bargain-basement Braques, *Violin on a Table* (1,750 francs), *Mozart/Kubelick* (an astonishing 160 francs), and over forty *papiers collés* and other works on paper.

Sometimes the smallest purchases caused the biggest ripples. Jean Paulhan, fast becoming indispensable in the editorial circles of the *Nouvelle Revue Française*, plucked up courage to part with 170 francs for a *papier collé*, *Violin* (1914). Paulhan loved his *papier collé* and put it up wherever he went. In due course he acquired others; and in 1935 he finally encountered their creator. Jean Paulhan was a man of immense personal and intellectual sophistication. *Savoir-faire*, an expression he enjoyed, might have been minted for him. The doyen of the *NRF* was not given to hero worship. This one, however, was different. 'There is a certain indefinable *autonomy*. By all accounts Braque operates entirely alone, never tampering with any of his reflections – his canvases – to make them more acceptable (or, like Picasso, more unacceptable).'[19] Paulhan held him in semi-superstitious awe. Braque *knew* something – and not only about painting – something that was perceptible in the man and instinct in the work. Of that Paulhan was convinced. He spent half a lifetime trying to explain to himself and others what it was.

Because of his position, his authority, his subtlety, his skill at friendship, his unquenchable correspondence, and his devil-may-care literary style, he became Braque's greatest tribune and celebrant.

I am only trying to be faithful, too bad if I appear to be silly. No doubt there is a secret in Braque – as there is in van Gogh or Vermeer – it is without doubt that his work is at all times strangely complete and sufficient: fluid (without needing more air); radiant (without any source of light); dramatic (without pretext); at once alert and tranquil: reflecting such that it gives the sensation of a mirage of its own reality. Yet as soon as I try to pin down the secret, or the feeling it inspires in me, this is all I find: it is that Braque offers to the lemon, to the grilled fish, to the tablecloth, exactly what they have been waiting for – yearning for – their familiar. There is something inexpressibly sad about an obligation; bitter about a delay: we are afraid of being disappointed. But each of Braque's paintings conveys the feeling of a delay enjoyed, and an obligation fulfilled.

Of course, one must furnish the proof. And I will furnish it. As it happens, I am only stating the banal. (It would be no bad thing here to use another word – to speak of the *ideal*, for example.) So much the better. What I would also like to say is that Braque's painting is banal. Fantastic, without doubt, but common. Fantastic, as it is fantastic, if you think about it, to have a nose and two eyes; and the nose exactly between the two eyes.[20]

Before they ever met, Paulhan wrote to a friend: 'Picasso makes so much noise that one loves Braque first for his discretion, then for his silence, and finally because one imagines that he knows so much more than the other.' After getting to know him a little, Paulhan reflected: 'I think I like in him . . . a patience, a meticulous French artisanship. One is never so aware of the Cocteau-side of Picasso than in front of Braque.'[21] He addressed the same question in the concluding flourish to his scintillating, eyebrow-raising *Braque le patron*, first published in 1945, against the grain of Picassian adulation and Braquian mortification, in a deluxe edition with a lithograph frontispiece and cover by the artist, available direct from the printer Mourlot at 7,000 francs a copy, and quickly sold out; republished, enlarged but shorn of illustrations, by Gallimard in 1952, and still in print. Denigrated by Kahnweiler among others as so much 'literature', or verbiage, *Braque le patron* was the single most effective literary intervention on Braque's behalf in the artist's lifetime.

And why Braque, I will be asked, rather than . . . ? Here I can make only one reply: it is Braque (as I said) who came to find me. Besides, these questions of precedence are wearying. I would find it hard to say whether Braque is the most inventive or the most versatile artist of our time. But if the great painter is the one who gives at once the most acute and the most nourishing idea of painting, then without hesitation it is Braque who I take as master.[22]

Paulhan intended *le patron* in the religious sense, as he put it to Braque, like a guru. His original conclusion was wordier and perhaps a shade more didactic. 'If the greatest painter is the one who gives the most measured but insistent, the most precise but radiant idea of painting, well, it is Braque who we will take for master, professor and secret law.' The signature of the old craft guilds tickled his fancy: 'Braque-le-patron, Anatole-la-justice, Montauban-tu-ne-le-saurais-pas [Montauban-you-wouldn't-know-it], etc. Why not: Braque-the-joyful-conscience? (I'm thinking of Hegel's "unhappy conscience".)'[23] Braque's response to this is not recorded, but may be guessed.

Paulhan had the knack of identifying other Braque people (though they might not know it yet) and introducing them. One of these was Francis Ponge, whose extraordinary affinity with the painter made him almost a verbal *doppelgänger*. In a posthumous tribute, the writer himself affirmed his 're-co-naissance' with Braque. Ponge made free with him in a way that no one else did – or no one else dared – made free with his maxims, his spirit, his things, even his name. Paulhan took him unhesitatingly for master; Ponge took him 'completely for my own'. For the man who wrote a hymn to soap (something else that comes alive to the touch), the

Braquian maxim 'the object is the poetry' made a kind of motto; and in the impasto of his own distinctive œuvre, 'thickened with my own colours', Francis Ponge broached Braque afresh, oblique, various, savoury.[24]

You won't find here what I do best; I mean I'm not going to lay a serious basis in reality (in words) for the magma of my real opinions, according to which, for example, for me, well, Braque stands more or less equidistant from *Bach*, as pronounced in French, and *Baroque* – with a slight pull towards the second because of the common adjective *braque* [madcap, hare-brained], which also really exists, not that I can do anything about it, and offers some connection with Baroque; or again according to which the good dog that bears the same name [*un braque*, a pointer], unsophisticated, rather serious and very loyal, soon appears nearby, like those *barques* [boats] (turned over for the purpose on the sand) that can very well be painted all sorts of bright colours; they are no less likely to be chestnut, like wood in general, than sheds or barns in the green countryside, or panelling in the dining room, or lecterns, or organ loft, or simply violins or guitars whose right (i.e. left) half looks a lot like the initial B of the name of our great man, while the Q with its handle irresistibly suggests either an earthenware saucepan, or a ladle, or a hand mirror – and the A with its single syllable makes a deep, open sound, like the roar of a train . . . No! I do not need here to base all that in reality.[25]

In fact someone else did venture a play on Braque's name and was slapped down, not by the artist, but by his post-Second World War dealer, Aimé Maeght, who boasted a gallery, a press, and ultimately a foundation. The critic Michel Seuphor had been asked to fill some space in the upmarket review published by the press, *Derrière le miroir* (*Behind the Mirror*). Seuphor submitted some little poems, rather like haiku, one of which ran:

Braque mad dog,
with his muscles and his fangs,
Braque very fine.

The next thing he knew he was confronted by Maeght himself, aghast. 'Seuphor, what have you done? You have written that Braque is a dog! Do you want to ruin the gallery? Everything rests on Braque, without Braque we can do nothing!'[26]

In the early days Braque's Cubist work had prompted hostile commentators to suggest caustically that he was aptly named ('Braque le Bien-Nommé'). The natural affiliation of Braque and *broc* (a pitcher) did not escape students of still life, and the artist himself seems to have enjoyed the euphony: *Violin and Pitcher* (1910), identified by one expert as a closet self-portrait, was originally *Broc et Violon* (col. pl. 11). Antoine Tudal's verse homage was much praised:

> I thought I knew what a pitcher was
> I thought I knew what a man Braque was
> But when I saw the pitcher in Braque
> Then I understood the thing
> Then I understood the man.[27]

André Salmon kept up a running gag over misspelling (Bracque, Bruque).[28] Gertrude Stein misspelled it Brack, which in a Pongean age irresistibly suggests brackish, rather salt, and not entirely healthy. Notwithstanding her famously inadequate command of French, it has been suggested that she too played with multiple meanings of the name in her experimental and often incomprehensible word-portrait of Braque, usually dated 1913, and first published in 1922:

Cap and corn, auditor, interest and exertion, aim and audience, interest and earnest and outset, inside in inside. Alarm no sun, alarm is thinking, alarming is determination an earth wide moth is something. Price in curving is weeding. There is an undetermined super division. There is the percolating bread stuff, the window is thickening . . . Brack and neuresthenia [*sic*] and lean talk with a marvel and make a spittoon clear with a mixing in a mustache. The sense is in that. Pie is not peeling and the date and the poison and the cake when the pan is a shape is not minus all the practice. The time is not filling. Brack, Brack is the one who put up the hooks and held the things up and ate his dinner. He is the one who did more. He used his time and felt more much more and came before when he came after. He did not resemble anything more.[29]

Braque remained silent on this, but not on *The Autobiography of Alice B. Toklas* (1933), as ghosted by Gertrude Stein. In a contribution to the 'Testimony against Gertrude Stein' gathered by the advanced literary journal *Transition*, Braque concluded, witheringly,

Miss Stein obviously saw everything from the outside and never the real struggle we were engaged in. For one who poses as an authority on the epoch it is safe to say that she never went beyond the stage of the tourist . . . We in Paris always heard that Miss Stein was a writer, but I don't think any of us had ever read her work until *Transition* began to make her known in France. Now that we have seen her book, *nous sommes fixés*.[30]

Publicly, at least, any more play of the brackish sort would have to wait for Jacques Prévert's posthumous hymn to Braque and the sea, 'Varengeville', or Jacques Derrida's warmed-over Ponge ('Bracket the range . . .'), or the ungovernable Vladimir Nabokov. 'Braques,' runs a cod footnote in one of Nabokov's novels: 'allusion to a bric-à-brac painter'.[31] The bric-à-brac side of Braque was part of the appeal for Francis Ponge, for whom it was love at first sight, in 1923, when Paulhan's *papier collé* was originally revealed to him:

The first picture that I saw of his, that I truly frequented, was in the studio then occupied by Jean Paulhan, 9 rue Campagne-Première, a *papier collé* of 1912 or 1913, representing vaguely (vaguely is not the word) a violin. On the only big wall of the studio, this modestly-proportioned picture was next to one other painting, much more grandiose in scale, in 'subject', in ambition: one of de Chirico's big 'metaphysical landscapes'. Which of them had the grandeur, I leave to your imagination.[32]

Half a century later Ponge recalled how that picture had haunted him ever since. He was enchanted by its 'poverty', its deliberate lack of means, the voluntary simplicity of its situation. In 1945, nearly twenty years after he first made its acquaintance, it became his familiar in his own home. Paulhan lent it to him whilst he worked at the first of his texts or excavations on Braque, 'Braque the reconciler', the beginning of a wonderfully idiosyncratic series, one of which was translated into English by Samuel Beckett.[33] Ponge's argument for the 'reconciliation' of Braque's art was very similar to Seamus Heaney's argument for the 'redress' of poetry, with peculiarly appropriate imagery: both attest to the art functioning as a kind of moral spirit level, an agent of equilibration, 'an upright, resistant, and self-bracing entity within the general flux and flex'. This has an ethical foundation or premeditation – Ponge states exactly that Braque has been good for him – but it is also founded in surprise, in ambush, in what Heaney calls the unforeseeable thereness of the work,

the way it enters our field of vision and animates our physical and intelligent being in much the same way as those bird-shapes stencilled on the transparent surfaces of glass walls or windows must suddenly enter the vision and change the direction of real birds' flight. In a flash the shapes register and transmit their unmistakable presence, so the birds veer off instinctively. An image of the living creatures has induced a totally salubrious swerve in the creatures themselves.[34]

Ponge frequented the work long before he frequented the man, a not uncommon experience with Braque. Paulhan took him into the inner sanctum, Braque's studio, during the Second World War. Ponge thought of the studio as a workshop, and the painter as a mechanic, repairing car after car, steadily and inventively, without pretence or exclamation. 'Of course it is not about virtuosity, or delectation,' he wrote, selecting two of Braque's pet hates. 'It is solely about getting them back on the road, making do, often in reduced circumstances.' The car theme also had punning potential for his own work. 'Braquez à fond,' one of the series begins instructively, 'pour vous dégager du créneau': 'turn full lock, to get out of the parking slot'. (b/w pl. 8)[35]

Ponge's intuition did not fail him. Cars were a favourite mode of conspicuous consumption among artists in the 1920s. 'Modern painting fuels the man, and also the motor,' reported *Le Crapouillot* waggishly.[36] Derain bought a Bugatti. Matisse had a Buick. Picasso, who used to say that he wanted to live like a poor man with lots of money, had a highly polished Hispano-Suiza, complete with liveried chauffeur. He always refused to drive for fear of spoiling the suppleness of his hands and wrists. In accordance with his general principle he held that a painter should be either too poor to have a car or rich enough to have a chauffeur. Picasso used to reprove Braque for driving fast cars himself, something he enjoyed doing, at breakneck speed, until well beyond the rally drivers' age of retirement. 'I know painters who like driving,' recorded Geoffrey Grigson, 'and who walk round their expensive cars and wipe them with a chamois. One of them says a car still goes as fast now he is seventy. When he is driving, his car inscribes not entirely predetermined lines and curves, without hesitation or tremble.'[37]

'Like everyone else, I would refuse only, politely, to join him in his little sports car,' remembered Jean Bazaine, 'which he drove, at seventy years of age, like a madman.'[38] With one eye on the rarity and another on the Bugatti – he was competitive in cars – Braque acquired an Alfa Romeo, which he customized and painted red. After a while he sold this souped-up Braque to an excited Blaise Cendrars for 1,000 francs (more than the sedate models at the Kahnweiler sales) and promptly bought another.[39] So began a lifelong affair with motor cars: a Rolls or a Bentley for more stately passage, with Marcelle, and a pedigree roadster with the necessary pep – a Simca 8 perhaps – for road-hugging, accelerating *gran turismo*, without Marcelle. And, in the fullness of time, a liveried chauffeur.

Braque, too, was going up in the world, and not simply in Picasso's slipstream. He moved from Montmartre to Montparnasse, bought a plot of land, joined the Beavers of Montsouris, and commissioned the architect Auguste Perret to build him a house topped with a studio at 6 Villa Nansouty, later rue du Douanier, later still rue Georges Braque. For Braque the light was crucial;

24. Braque's *maison-atelier* near the Parc Montsouris in Paris, built by Auguste Perret, newly completed in 1930, the studio occupying the whole of the top floor

25. Georges Braque by Man Ray, 1922, a portrait that appeared in magazines all over Europe

the windows were designed to his own specification. So too the orientation. In defiance of tradition, the studio faced resolutely south. He was photographed by Man Ray, who caught something of his physicality and his allure: a portrait widely admired at the time, and regarded with favour even by its subject, who insisted on recompensing the photographer with a small Braque. He was requisitioned by Diaghilev to design *Les Fâcheux* (1924), with music by Georges Auric; *Zéphyr et Flore* (1925), with music by Vladimir Dukelsky; and *Quadrille*, with music by Erik Satie, an adaptation of Chabrier's *Souvenirs de Munich* and Fauré and Messager's *Souvenirs de Bayreuth*, both Wagnerian pastiches – a tantalizing project never realized.

Braque's designs were lauded by Cocteau and badmouthed by Poulenc, who had a habit of telling Picasso what he thought he wanted to hear.[40] Praised or blamed, his experience of commissioned work for Diaghilev was not a happy one. In the Ballets Russes artistic differences were resolved by Diaghilev, in favour of Diaghilev. Braque's ideas were not always welcome. The dancers in *Les Fâcheux* did not care for his trick of camouflaging them against the scenery, if they turned away from the audience, by blending the back of the costume with the décor; nor did they want to be the naked nymph dancing a prologue in front of his verdant curtain, so he painted one in himself. No doubt the circumstances were difficult and strange. But collaboration was not his forte. 'Only the other day,' recorded Poulenc, 'Braque said to me: "Isn't it already a great deal to have to take three people into account, namely the choreographer, the painter and the musician; if you have to include a writer as well, then all unity is sacrificed." Quite so . . .'[41] Braque was ill at ease in his bowler hat and bow tie in the exotic gardens of the casino in Monte Carlo, where Serge Diaghilev and Boris Kochno took their ease whilst the sets were being prepared. A falling-out was predictable. It came over a project for *Les Sylphides*. At Diaghilev's request, Braque had made some sketches of the décor for a new production, enjoining the director not to use them until the work was finished. When Diaghilev went ahead regardless, Braque instructed the authorities to seize the sets.

This called for another visit to the *commissaire de police*. 'One might say that you are difficult to deal with,' observed Diaghilev gratuitously. 'And besides, you have no business sense.' 'Sadly, it was true,' recalled Braque.[42] He did no more designing for twenty years, until tempted out by his friend René Char for *La Conjuration* (1947), a work of the poet's own composition, staged by Pierre Boulez; and a little later by request of the celebrated Louis Jouvet, who wanted something 'untraditional' for Molière's *Tartuffe* (1950).[43]

Braque certainly enjoyed the things that money could buy. He revelled in the Alfa ('a wonderful machine'). He no longer painted houses, he built them. He was proud of that.[44] As Gertrude Stein had remarked, he liked to eat. The Steins had a cook who made excellent soufflé. 'It was Braque who said . . . later when they were all beginning to be known, with a sigh and smile, how life has changed we all now have cooks who make soufflé.' It was difficult to get over this feeling of surprise. 'Do you realize,' he exclaimed to Picasso in later life, 'we each have a car, and a chauffeur!'[45] He ate well, and *fast*. His friends said he was a gourmand rather than a gourmet. Braque was in sympathy with the *Guide du Gourmand à Paris*, whose author addressed himself to the gourmand, not the gourmet, on the grounds that it was impossible to like food if you did not like a lot of it. When Roché sought his advice on restaurants, Braque had detailed recommendations for the best dishes, wines, beers, and stouts; but when he and the painter Humberto Stragiotti went on a gastronomic tour of Paris after the Second World War – nothing but three-star restaurants – he spoiled it for Stragiotti by eating too quickly.[46] He kept a good cellar but tended to reserve the best bottles for those who would really appreciate them – his barber, Bernard Lachaud; Dominican monks like Jacques Laval; portionless poets. Yet he was never entirely comfortable in the lap of luxury. All forms of central heating were regarded with grave suspicion. There was an almost peasant feeling that the way to keep warm was to stay as close as possible to the fire or the stove, or, failing these, the boiler. On a tour of the new Braque house, Gertrude Stein was surprised to find the bathroom in the basement,

16. With chauffeur Jean Ferrand and Simca, *c.* 1955. A pit stop en route from Paris to Nice.

under the living room. 'When we said, but why, they said because being nearer the furnace it would be warmer.'[47] Other appurtenances were even more unwelcome. When Braque visited the curator Jim Ede in London in the early 1930s he noticed that Ede did not have a phone and remarked with the pleasurable recognition of a kindred spirit that he, too, had 'tous les conforts, pas de téléphone'. The phone was an unconscionable instrument to be avoided if at all possible. If there was absolutely no alternative, then a certain ceremony had to be observed; before taking his first transatlantic call, he carefully combed his hair.[48]

In 1924 he changed dealers again, leaving Kahnweiler (amicably) for the Galerie Paul Rosenberg, described by Jacques-Émile Blanche as 'a facade entirely of marble, a vestibule of marble, a staircase of onyx . . . vast rooms hung with watered silk receiving torrents of light thanks to ingenious lozenge-shaped ceiling fixtures in which a dozen bulbs cluster like grapes on a vine'.[49] In these seductive trappings, small Braques were set out like sweetmeats. Two individual exhibitions, a taster in May 1924 and a feast in March 1926, were picked clean. Louis Vauxcelles gave these new, no-longer-dilapidated Braques his seigneurial seal of approval. But he could not resist a sly dig. Georges Braque, he announced mischievously, is a pedigree painter – best in show.[50] His old *accompagnatrice* Marie Laurencin kept a coquettish eye on the latest trends. After a few more Braque shows at Paul Rosenberg's, she told a friend: 'He's a greater painter than Picasso; more paint, less experience, more French, less toreador.'[51]

Paul Rosenberg had effectively supplanted his brother. The younger of the two was also the steadier – the realist as opposed to the fantasist, in Heinz Berggruen's terminology.[52] He had made his mark rediscovering the nineteenth century. He used this astutely as a springboard into the twentieth. *Chez* Paul, Braque and brothers joined a ready-made family of quality: Courbet, Corot, Daumier, Cézanne. Braque himself hung a Corot exhibition there in 1930. The lustre of the past master rubbed off – 'the discretion and propriety of the French temperament!'[53] As it did on their dealer: Paul Rosenberg was suave, smart, discreet when necessary; too haughty for some, too pressing for others; above all, rich. The manner of the man rings through his jousting with Tériade in an interview for *Cahiers d'Art*:

– What devices . . . do you use to sell paintings?
– Very simple. I never sell paintings. The clients buy them from me. Besides, different clients, different temperaments. You never know the reason why such and such a canvas is bought, it depends too much on the mood and state of mind of the buyer. Painting is intrinsically a market of love; it is difficult to reason when one is struck by that disease.
– What is the role of the dealer?

– No role. He cannot and should not usurp the glory of the artist. It is not he who paints the canvases. In my opinion, he should offer his clients the best painting, that best corresponds to his own temperament. . . .
– What do you think of your peers?
– I hold each one in particular in the same esteem as he holds me.[54]

Paul Rosenberg had panache.

The agreement he had with Braque was a right of first refusal. Rosenberg's winning combination of purse and perspicacity ensured that this arrangement lasted until another war and another invasion threw everything into confusion.[55] During this period artist and dealer both prospered exceedingly. They had a certain mutual respect for each other's professional judgement. Rosenberg was mightily impressed that Braque made so bold as to buy a Cézanne watercolour. Braque had at last found a dealer who would market him vigorously (unlike Kahnweiler) and judiciously (unlike Léonce). Under Paul Rosenberg's aegis Braque was catapulted into the popular arena. He bankrolled Braque's on-going investigations into colours and grounds, encouraging the production of opulent still life in a variety of forms and a diversity of formats, large and small, from the chimney piece to the decorative panel. Different clients, different pockets. He even commissioned work for his own apartment.[56]

Some of these paintings are so luscious they might be licked; indeed, the impulsive Reverdy kissed one passionately before handing it over to a new owner.[57] On others there is a deposit of thought, in Robert Hughes's phrase, quietly coating the objects. André Malraux fancied that a certain painting of Chardin's 'might be a first-class Braque, dressed-up just enough to take in the spectator'.[58] Braque said that Chardin had revealed to him the emotional connections between the objects in a painting.[59] His own works are ripe Chardins, from the same grower, out of the same kitchen. The objects in them live fuller lives than they ever dared hope. Diderot, Chardin's Paulhan (and Paulhan's model, it may be), celebrated the great man and his exquisite *Jar of Olives* at the Salon of 1763 in terms redolent of a later painter:

[The painting] to be seen as you climb the stairs is particularly worthy of attention. The artist has placed on a table an old Chinese porcelain vase, two biscuits, a jar filled with olives, a basket of fruit, two glasses half-filled with wine, a Seville orange and some pâté. To look at the paintings by other people I have the impression of needing different eyes; to look at Chardin's paintings I need only make good use of the eyes given me by nature. If I was hoping to steer my child towards a career in painting, this is the painting I would buy. 'Copy that for me,' I would tell him, and 'copy that for me again'. But perhaps nature itself is not more difficult to copy. This porcelain vase is really made of porcelain; these olives are separated from the eye by the water in which they float; these biscuits need only to be picked up and eaten, this Seville orange opened and squeezed, this glass of wine drunk, this fruit peeled and this pâté sliced.

Here is a man who understands the harmony of colours and reflected light. Oh Chardin! The colours crushed on your palette are not white, red or black pigment; they are the very substance of the objects. They are the air and the light that you take up with the tip of your brush and apply to the canvas . . . This magic defies understanding. The thick layers of colour are applied one on top of the other and the effect breathes out from below. At other times the effect is like a vapour breathed lightly on to the canvas; elsewhere a delicate foam has been scattered on to it . . . Approach the painting and everything blurs, flattens out and vanishes; step back and everything comes together again and reappears.

I have been told that, as Greuze walked upstairs to the Salon, he noticed the painting by Chardin which I have just described, looked at it and went on, heaving a deep sigh. His paean of praise was much shorter than mine, but worth much more.[60]

The unknown quantity in Braque's art has always been much appealed to, even by the most discerning. Giacometti's anguished cry: 'But how to describe his paintings? How to speak about the sensation provoked in me by the vertical, slightly out of kilter, of vase and flowers on grey ground? . . . But why, why do his flowers seem to us so marvellous?' The ineffable may be a last resort, but it comes on good authority. 'The only thing that matters in art,' declared Braque, 'is what cannot be explained.'[61]

Rosenberg was good at selling, or letting clients buy. In 1925 he sold an appetizing flowerpiece (a new speciality) for a very satisfactory 18,000 francs: *Anemones and Two Lemons*, a classic example of the mechanic's job of work, where the flowers well up from the Braque-brown backdrop, while the fruit vibrates sympathetically on the ocean wave below – a picture of enlarged lives in reduced circumstances.

The strategy paid off the following year, when Dr G. F. Reber snapped up the most startling works in Rosenberg's posession, a pair of life-size basket-bearers or canephors (the Greek name given to them by Braque) – said to be modelled on Marcelle – whose unheralded appearance in the place of honour at the 1922 Salon d'Automne had sent the critics into howling disarray. Fourteen more Braques went the same way. Dr Reber was a pocket battleship of a collector, ransacking dealers and raiding auction houses with brilliant success. As early as 1910, by the time he was thirty, he had built up a collection of twenty-seven Cézannes, not to mention a sprinkling of van Gogh, Gauguin, Degas, Renoir and Manet. In the 1920s, installed in the grand eighteenth-century Château de Béthusy in Lausanne, he changed direction. Impressionists and post-Impressionists went out; Cubists and post-Cubists came in. Overnight he amassed the finest private collection in the world. Reber rose and fell like an empire, but speeded up, as if shown in silent film. Huge losses on the Paris Bourse in 1929 put a sudden end to his profligacy. Dispossession and dispersal set in, the steep descent marked by a brief but ignominious accommodation with the cultural scavengers in the pay of Hermann Goering. The bottom dropped out of Reber's world and he disappeared from view. An heroic legend dwindled into an academic footnote. Yet Reber was a man of consequence. His networks mapped the transmission of Braque's art across borders of every kind. He had direct channels to dealers like Kahnweiler and Rosenberg. In the 1920s he formed an alliance with a brilliant intellectual agent of influence by the name of Carl Einstein, who developed a close relationship with Georges Braque, and became one of his most devoted interpreters. In the 1930s some of the contents of the Château de Béthusy were bought by the young Douglas Cooper, who came into his inheritance in 1932; the finest Picasso he ever owned was redeemed from the municipal pawnshop in Geneva for £10,000.[62]

As Carl Einstein underlined, Reber's collection was not confined to the moderns. 'Reber created an ensemble of pre-Hellenic and archaic antiquities. He saw that Greek art is not this miracle confined to philologists, but part of a vast Mediterranean culture. That sort of intuition opened up strong connections with the East, and placed these Greeks beside their Asian forebears. Thus Reber uses a piece like a springboard to jump on to a still hidden trail which he then follows with the passion of a hunter obsessed.' The conclusion drawn by Einstein was an interesting one. 'Reber,' he argued, 'has recognized that the point of departure for the whole history of art rests on the present, that is to say, historical emphases are determined by modern art.'[63] The argument was picked up and popularized by André Malraux.

Manet and Braque [have] acted as interpreters of the language in which the Sumerians, the pre-Columbians and the great Buddhist arts address us. Perhaps I was wrong to use the word 'interpreters'; what Manet and Braque have done is to teach us to 'hear' that language. The surgeon who removes a cataract does not interpret the world to his patient but gives it, or restores it, to him. Before the coming of modern art no one *saw* a Khmer head, still less a Polynesian sculpture, for the good reason that no one looked at them.

This became one of Malraux's best tricks: filtering new art through old, such that the former could be said to anticipate the latter; or resuscitate, miraculously, as good as new. Malraux invoked Braque's work as a touchstone of artistic worth. 'All our art, even the least denunciatory, Renoir's or Braque's for instance, contains a challenge to the world it disowns.'[64] Braque's art was virtue-proof. For Malraux himself it had something approaching talismanic significance. He too had his Braque. Into his bag, on his ceaseless questing, went his entourage of fetishes – two or three of the usual kind and a small Braque, a beachscape, with an empty boat, an uncanny blue, and the night drawing in.

Unlike Malraux, Carl Einstein was an original thinker. It was his fate to sow ideas without getting credit for them. A quintessential European of the twentieth century, his life remains almost as deeply shrouded as his death.[65] Like Walter Benjamin, he committed suicide in 1940, haunted by the Gestapo. His natural habitat was the frontier. In 1906–9, during the years of ferment in Paris, he wrote a pro-Cubist, pre-Expressionist fantasy, dedicated to André Gide, and published in 1912 under the title of *Bébuquin or the dilettantes of the miracle*. In 1915 he produced the first serious treatment of *art nègre* in the West. In 1917 he was with the Bolsheviks in spirit. In 1918 he was on the barricades with the Spartakists, Germany's homegrown communist revolutionaries. In 1926 he illustrated the Cubist section of his anatomy of modern art with Braques and Picassos from Reber's collection, in a work that laid special emphasis on Braque's recent contributions.[66] In 1930 his good friend 'Heini' Kahnweiler published his first book of poetry, dedicated to Erna Reber. In 1933 he masterminded the first Braque retrospective (at the Basle Kunsthalle).[67] In 1934 he and Jean Renoir wrote the screenplay for the latter's film *Toni*. That same year he delivered *Georges Braque*, the most substantial monograph yet written, and also the most important. It had been announced twelve years earlier, following discussion with Braque, as 'the pure quest for space by a painter', or 'the morality of purity', or even 'direct painting', with its premonitory hint of action painting.[68] Einstein was an inveterate expositor, but he was also an enthusiast. 'In the works of Braque there is such serenity, such completeness that one cannot add anything to it with words. Instead these works would be veiled by metaphors or lyric allegories; and delirious enthusiasm does not consort with the aristocratic composure of this painter.'[69]

'I think ... it's Braque who is developing in a fairly logical fashion,' Einstein wrote to his friend Moïse Kisling in 1923. 'The hands of the others tremble with nerves or stupidity. I see Braque's limitations; but all the same, he is a fine, strong person.'[70] It seems they met as early as 1907, on Einstein's first visits to Paris. After the war they became fast friends, a friendship cemented by common experience on opposite sides. Einstein too was wounded in the head and invalided out of the fighting; he was operated on in 1919. 'It's a fine thing to get your head blown off for the grand strategists.' They both loved 'the old Chinese', Lao Tzu in particular. They may have indulged in a little private banter concerning 'Pipasso', otherwise known as La Pablotte, 'a mad professor who scrapes a cathedral'.[71] They were especially close during the very period of comparative *froideur* between the two former partners: perhaps Einstein more nearly met the requirements. He often came to stay during the 1920s; and Braque acted as witness at his wedding to Lyda Guévrékian in 1932. It was Braque who was entrusted with Einstein's papers after his suicide, Braque who safeguarded them during the Occupation (when possession of Jewish goods was itself incriminating), Braque who supported Lyda, discreetly, throughout the years that followed, until she returned to her Iranian homeland.

The two men learned from each other. Einstein's view of the possibilities of painting was decisively influenced by his early encounters with Cubism; as with Pierre Reverdy, it was refined in his continuing dialogue with Braque.[72] Many of his *obiter dicta* sound like Braque's first batch of thoughts and reflections. 'To paint, that is to create space.' 'Paintings should not represent, but be.' 'No longer an *interpretation* but a *fact*.' 'The painting is completed when the emotion is entirely concealed.'[73] Some of these went into the laboratory for further development. Others surely provided the painter with seeds for the next crop. 'Technique is the excuse of the idiot who lacks ideas' is Einstein. 'Where talent is called upon, there imagination gives out' is Braque.[74] When Einstein made due acknowledgement of the revolutionary significance (and parentage) of the *papiers collés* as 'the most violent purification of reality' of the Cubist era, he took his cue from Braque.[75] But his writing cascaded with ideas of his own.

Einstein conceived of Braque operating in 'a dimension of hallucination' far removed from tepid naturalism, a zone where convention is abolished, memory is extinguished, and no element of the existing order is sacred. He paints not with the brush but with the soul. In consequence, his reality is no longer determinate but labile, unstable, prone to slip and change. Einstein's word for this condition was *metamorphosis*. The extraordinary thing about Georges Braque, according to Carl Einstein, was the metamorphic dynamism of his life and art. What Braque knew – what Braque lived – was 'the drama of metamorphosis'. There could be no higher praise.[76] 'The copiable he does not see,' as Beckett put it in his contemporaneous observations on Proust. 'He searches for . . . substrata.' He considers his output as a series of 'inspired omissions', and the work of art 'as neither created nor chosen, but discovered, uncovered, excavated, pre-existing within the artist, a law of his nature. The only reality is provided by the hieroglyphics traced by inspired perception.'[77]

As well as consolidating Braque's reputation, this theorizing was directly helpful to the artist wrestling with his inspiration. Braque worked experientially. Intellectually, he knew rather less than Einstein. *Georges Braque* served to articulate and codify for Georges Braque what it was that he had been doing, or reacting against, or feeling his way towards. Einstein had him rejecting 'the given', 'the prejudice' of traditional perspective or 'mechanized reality' in favour of 'a new conception of space'. Braque's subsequent self-explanations correspond well with these propositions.[78] As Einstein adopted Braque, so Braque adopted Einstein. Out of the massed abstractions of their talk he forged his mature idiolect, encapsulated in his notebook:

Impregnation
Obsession
Hallucination[79]

In terms of Braque's global reach, a zone still low on hallucination was the United States. Paul Rosenberg set himself to correct this deficiency. The connection he made was not with the Museum of Modern Art in New York (founded in 1929), whose director Alfred H. Barr had his monocular gaze fixed on Picasso, but with the

Phillips Collection in Washington (founded in 1918): an ashram rather than a pantheon.[80] Duncan Phillips was a passionate pilgrim, to borrow an expression of his own, and a natural evangelist. He had always been averse to Cubism, but in the mid-1920s he began to see the point of Georges Braque. In 1928 he succumbed to a brace of still lifes, *Plums, Pears, Nuts and Knife* ($2,000) and *Lemons, Peaches and Compotier* ($2,600), which he would borrow from his own gallery to hang in the dining room at home, and debate with dinner guests. (Debates usually won by his friend Henri Focillon, whose position on *Plums, Pears, Nuts and Knife*, that it was 'too Cartesian', proved impossible either to explain or to shift.)[81] By the end of the decade Duncan Phillips was hooked, and wanted fervently to share his illumination. In 1930 he went to some lengths to acquire *Still Life with Grapes and Clarinet* ($5,400), which became his favourite, and which he later made available to every American in a handsome colour print, together with an encomium to the master builder:

In 1914 Braque was interrupted by the outbreak of the First World War just as he was arriving at the real starting point of his personal style. After being severely wounded and restored by surgery he returned to his easel and revealed at once the same creative purpose as before the war, but now clarified and with craftsmanship almost instantly at concert pitch.

From 1918 to 1930 Braque painted the outstanding decorations of his age. His influence on applied design spread from France around the world. He had evolved a curvilinear rhythm sometimes simple, often more complex. No longer restrained from rich sensuous painting he stylized bowls, and goblets, mandolins and guitars, fruits and flowers, and a few monumental nudes, and 'décors de ballet'. It was the best style in Europe during that interval between the wars when epicureanism flourished for a little while and when cubism finally justified itself by producing works of art at once architectural and lyrical. There has seldom been more subtle colour in painting and certainly never logic more charming.[82]

Phillips soon passed another milestone. In 1934 Paul Rosenberg organized an exhibition at the Durand-Ruel Galleries in New York, hailed as 'the finest collection of modern art yet to be seen in

America'. It comprised 23 paintings by Picasso, 13 by Braque, and 10 by Matisse. Braque had not been seen in strength in New York for some twenty years. On this occasion Rosenberg presented a choice selection from the period 1927 to 1931. The work that stood out immediately was a freewheeling *Pedestal Table* (1929), blazoned on the cover of *Art News*, the art magazine with the largest circulation in the United States.[83] Rosenberg conducted Duncan and Marjorie Phillips round the exhibition personally. Phillips was bowled over by *The Round Table*, as it came to be known (col. pl. 12). He had to have it. He could not afford it. His first thought was to swap two of the smaller Braques from his existing collection, but he quickly decided that he could not bear to part with them. He would have to offer up something else. Within weeks he and Rosenberg agreed 'an even exchange' of Daumier's *The Reader* and Sisley's *Banks of the Seine* (together valued at $20,000) for *The Round Table*.[84] Phillips was as euphoric as the still life in the painting.

As El Greco fulfilled himself in his *Coronation of the Virgin* and Cézanne in his *Still Life with Clock*, . . . so Braque has accomplished his mission in such a consummation of his best powers as *The Round Table*. It sums up all that was hoped for in founding a school on Cézanne's cubes and cones. In this large decoration the familiar and intimately characterized objects such as the red apple, the clay pipe, and the short thick kitchen knife are 'the visible medium of exchange' between Braque and his public. The rest is architecture – and music. It is functional and majestic in its forms, and in its chromatic range it is exultant. It seems to open like a huge, strange flower and to absorb the light over its rough surfaces with an ecstatic life of its own.[85]

Not everyone was charmed by Paul Rosenberg. He met his match in Lady Cunard, who presented a textbook case of the dealer's theory of temperaments. Roger Fry was on hand to witness their unprofitable encounter:

At Rosenberg's heard a lady with a parrot voice screaming that she wanted a Picasso of the blue period and violently refusing a very ugly head and a silly little landscape by Picasso which were being pressed on her. Then she was shown (*faute du période bleu*) a *période rose* two nude boys. 'No, I can't bear people on my walls. I want trees, but you have nothing here to show me. I want a blue Picasso and you haven't one and a Matisse and you show me a silly fish on a plate!' (A stunning thing this, by the by, but undeniably a fish on a plate.) I meanwhile had made myself known to her and listened to her endless plaints and screams and Rosenberg's deferential murmurs. At last, the whole thing was becoming so pathetic that I pointed to two exquisite Braque panels [the canephors]: two caryatids holding baskets of fruit and I said 'Now you want something beautiful and decorative for your rooms: if you get these all London will envy you' (foreseeing them as part of a Duncan [Grant] decoration). To show them better they were borne off to an inner room and arranged against a Wedgwood blue silk brocade and looked incredibly precious and aristocratic. 'Yes, but I can't make out what they are.' I pointed out the figures and to help her said they are rather like those early Chinese paintings where you half guess the figure against the ground. Whereupon Maud uttered one of the great sayings of the century. 'Well, if you call them Chinese' (and she hisses this) 'I think they're very beautiful, but if you call them French I think they're quite stupid!'[86]

Happily, Lady Cunard was an anachronism. The paintings may have been difficult to decipher, but the prices were plain enough. For the latest big canvas in Rosenberg's sweetshop, H. P. Roché noted in 1930, they were asking 40,000 francs.[87]

Roché himself coveted one a little cheaper: *Homage to J. S. Bach* (b/w pl. 10). He had seen it before, in 1912, soon after it was painted (400 francs); ten years later it had slipped through his fingers at the Kahnweiler sales (330 francs); now it had resurfaced again (28,000 francs). Roché wanted it desperately. But he also wanted Braque's benediction. He arranged to borrow it for twenty-four hours, wrapped it up, took it hot-foot to the painter's house, and silkily explained his purpose. 'I want to buy a Braque I like, but I'm keen for you to like it too.' 'Let's have a look at it,' said the painter without ceremony.

Braque unwrapped the work and balanced it on an armchair in

the living room. He positioned another armchair directly in front of it, about five feet away. 'I haven't seen this one in ages,' he remarked, and settled down to stare it out.

Silence reigned. Nothing stirred. Braque sat completely still, rapt in concentration. Roché stood, hushed, behind him. Frozen minutes passed. The painter voyaged in the painting, gradually squeezing this Brach of its secrets: the architectural panelling; the pleating and layering; the lightness and airiness; the distributed violin with its remnant strings and scrolls; the organ pipes doubling as the pan-pipes he had seen that summer in Céret; the signature cord, the stencilled letters, the first mock wood . . . the call and response with Picasso . . . the painting and decorating learned at his father's knee . . .

'It's OK,' he said. 'Buy it.'[88]

8. 'The hand that ponders and the eye that fashions': The Studio

Roland Penrose, the future impresario of modern art in Britain, was a well-connected Cambridge graduate on his first visit to Paris, in 1922, when he encountered Georges Braque poring over a book at the house of a friend, the printer and engraver Demetrios Galanis. Penrose was thunderstruck.

I was at once captivated by the imposing presence of a man who could spend a good half hour completely absorbed in contemplation of a mere photo of Goya's *Naked Maja*. Never before had such concentration on a painting seemed possible and Braque's example alone did much to encourage superficial good taste and academic standards to float rapidly away and to be replaced by a passionate dedication to the arts.

This epiphany was a turning-point, as his son Antony has confirmed.[1]

Everyone remarked on the eye of Braque.[2] On one occasion, at the house of Pierre Gaut, the colour merchant, after silent contemplation of a work of his own, he said firmly, 'I didn't paint that.' He proved to be right. He had identified a tiny patch of canvas, a few brushstrokes, retouched by the luckless Gaut after the original had flaked off. ('In each brushstroke is there not something distinctly individual?')[3] In 1951 he caused a minor sensation at the Galerie Maeght – he who was seldom seen in galleries – by pausing for twenty minutes in front of an abstract work by an as-yet-unknown American artist called Ellsworth Kelly, confiding later to Marguerite Maeght that it had suggested to him a solution to a problem he faced in a painting of his own: what to do with the bird in one of his giant *Studio* series, a problem solved by fracturing the form in a manner reminiscent of a stained-glass window – or an Ellsworth Kelly.

1. *Landscape near Antwerp*, 1906. When Robert Lebel bought this painting in 1935 unsigned, and took it to Braque, 'he signed it right away and nearly cried when he recalled the hard time he had at the period this work was painted.'

2. *The Little Bay of La Ciotat*, 1907

3. Picasso, *Les Demoiselles d'Avignon*, 1907

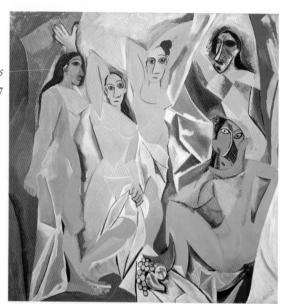

4. *Houses at L'Estaque*, 1908

5. *Girl with a Cross*, 1911

6. *Still Life with Musical Instruments*, 1908

7. *Man with a Guitar*, 1911

8. Picasso, *The Accordionist*, 1911

9. *Fruit Dish and Glass,* 1912

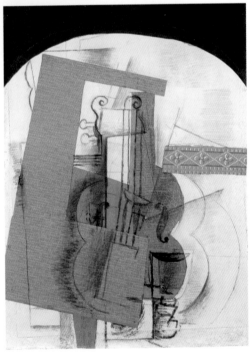

10. *Violin,* 1914

12. *The Round Table*, 1929

11. *Violin and Pitcher*, 1910

13. *The Black Fish*, 1942

14. The Braque ceiling
in the Louvre, 1953

15. *The Bird and Its Nest*, 1955

16. *Studio VIII*, 1954–5

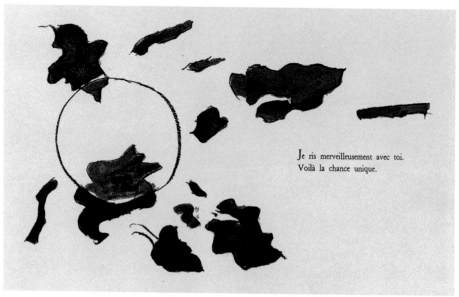

Je ris merveilleusement avec toi.
Voilà la chance unique.

17. A seven-colour lithograph from *Lettera Amorosa*, 1963

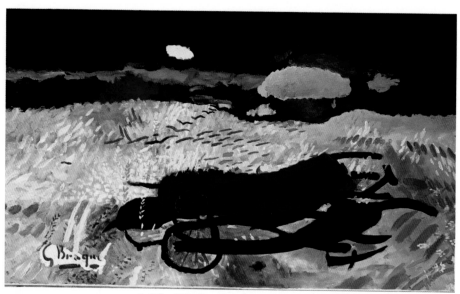

18. *The Weeding Machine*, 1961–3

His eye was not infallible. There is little doubt that both Braque and Picasso had difficulty telling apart the work they produced in their Cubist heyday. 'Is that you or me?' Ede heard Picasso ask Braque. 'It's mine – no, no I'm wrong . . .' In the well-stocked residence of one patron of the arts, Picasso was seen staring at a painting in puzzlement; he was sure it was one of his, he said, but he could not identify it. Suddenly he turned it over and looked at the back. It was signed, inconspicuously, by Braque.[4] This twinning was a mild form of confusion. Worse, much worse, Braque had been known to acknowledge a 'Braque' of doubtful authenticity from the same polymorphous period, though he did have second thoughts.

Counterfeit work was a perennial vexation. Once bitten, Braque was more cautious. Around 1960, the dealer and collector Heinz Berggruen, a respected figure in the international art world, was asked by Sotheby's in London if he could help them authenticate a Cubist drawing by Braque; specifically, if he could gain entrance for their representative to the artist's studio. Their representative turned out to be a blue-eyed blond, all of twenty years old, by the name of Bruce Chatwin. Berggruen escorted him to the Braque house, up the Auguste Perret staircase to the hallowed top floor, through the vast studio, and into the presence. Chatwin proffered a photograph of the drawing. Braque sank into deep contemplation. Eventually he took up a piece of paper and a pencil and tried to make a copy; and then, evidently dissatisfied, tried again. Finally he looked up. 'Frankly, I don't know. It could have been . . . I'm not sure.' The audience was over. No signature was forthcoming. The visitors took their leave. Berggruen was amazed; such frankness was unique in his experience.[5] Chatwin was elated; he had a great story for his diary ('Gide with the bits left in'), and an even better one for his friends. There are many versions of the Chatwin story, almost as many as there are friends. Perhaps the best is the one he told Colin Thubron. At Sotheby's, Chatwin's nominal brief was Impressionism:

Each Impressionist artist had spawned an 'expert' who gave out certificates of authenticity: Paul Brame in Paris for a Degas, John Rewald in New

York for a Gauguin. In Paris, Bruce met Braque, dressed in a lilac tracksuit. 'I had a marvellous morning sitting in Braque's studio while he painted one of those great birds, which actually was his soul going out through the studio roof.' Braque looked at Bruce's photograph. 'I've got very feeble eyes, can you tell me whether it's fake or not?' Bruce told him it was. 'He said "*Bon*". He signed the photograph. "That this is not by me."[6]

The local colour here is all highly suspect. Not the least implausible embellishment is the lilac tracksuit – elsewhere a white leather jacket, a white tweed cap, and a lilac chiffon scarf. Lilac may have been in that year, but it was definitely not Braque's colour. As for his apparel, whatever is connoted by the term 'tracksuit', circa 1960, it is most unlikely that the painter (then nearly eighty) ever possessed one. Braque had style. Fluorescent kitsch was no part of it.

The impact of his appearance, however, places the story in a tradition extending back sixty years. Roland Penrose's testimony was symptomatic, and his reaction was not confined to the young. To encounter Braque for the first time was to be profoundly stirred. It was the figure he cut, his look, his carriage, his tone. 'He isn't like anyone else,' reflected Paulhan, awed, after his first visit.[7] Visibly, he had lived. It was not his garb but his physiognomy that dazzled. The creases were fascinating, the crags breathtaking. The lines that ran from his nose to the corners of his mouth were particularly marked; even in poor light, they cast deep shadows. It was as if he had come to embody a fantasy of Borges: 'A man sets himself the task of drawing the world. As the years go by, he peoples a space with the images of provinces, kingdoms, mountains, boys, ships, islands, fishes, rooms, instruments, stars, horses, and people. Shortly before his death, he discovers that this patient labyrinth of lines charts the image of his face.'[8] With age the spiritual smile grew more expressive. As an etching, he was magnificent. In flesh and bone he was beautiful. Brassaï registered the eyes, Doisneau the hands. 'Georges Braque, the alliance of the hand that ponders and the eye that fashions.'[9] Add movement, and the total effect was

27. In his Paris studio,
c. 1935–6, by Brassaï

apt to be overwhelming. He combined the wary animality of an
experienced stuntman with the aura of a matinée idol. Gary Cooper
took after Braque, Roché thought, as the epitome of the detached
hero, the Westerner, a man with a code, laconic, solitary, durable,
loyal.[10]

Braque's sartorial elegance had impressed observers from the
start. At the Académie Humbert, Georges Lepape rhapsodized over
the immaculate turnout of his mentor: 'How I used to envy Georges
Braque, powerful, olympian, sporting tweed suit, flannel shirt with
detachable collar cut extremely low, brilliant white, stiff. His tie is
black silk, one centimetre wide, tied in a tight bow. Mahogany
leather shoes with thick soles, black bowler hat, and a little Javanese
bamboo cane, thin and flexible . . . that I rediscovered fifteen years
later, in the first appearances of Charlie Chaplin on the cinema
screen.' A few years later, the ensemble was a little more restrained
but the effect was no less compelling. The fastidious Kahnweiler
considered Braque a dandy, albeit a discreet one. 'He's still extraordinarily elegant. In those days he used to wear very simple blue
suits, of a wholly distinctive cut, the like of which I've never seen.
He also had black shoes with square tips but not huge soles which
he said came from Abbéville. Like Max Jacob, he had a black ribbon

28. Portrait of Georges
Braque by Picasso, 1909

tie. He looked really stylish in all that.'[11] In the first known portrait photograph taken by Picasso in his boulevard de Clichy studio, in 1909, Braque models such an outfit. He stands between an engraving of Cézanne's *Bathers at Rest* (1875–6) and Picasso's *Nude with Raised Arms* (1908). He has everything to hand. This *Portrait of Georges Braque* might have been entitled *The Attributes of Cubism*.

The most significant attribute was the hat. Cézanne had worn a Kronstadt hat (a big flat-topped bowler with a curly brim). Famously, Braque did the same, in homage. The hat was immortalized in another portrait by Picasso. With a whiff of controversy, so was its wearer. Over the winter of 1909–10, Picasso painted a riotous Cubist portrait of a man in a hat that has come to be known as a portrait of Braque (on the front cover of this book), notwithstanding Picasso's claim that it was painted without a model, and that the two of them only pretended it was Braque, afterwards, to make mischief. Braque for his part affected to recognize only the hat, and passed the whole thing off as a jape of Picasso's. It is what André Breton called a riddle-image, ostentatiously denied by both parties.[12] Picasso, as usual, said different things to different people. Asked who it was, he would say he didn't know. Asked by inquisitive persons if it was Braque, he would say, 'If you like.' Asked point-blank by Heinz Berggruen, who waited forty years to buy it and finally succeeded, he said, 'Of course it's Braque.'[13] No other candidate comes to mind, as John Richardson has remarked. Whether it was painted with or without a model is irrelevant. Picasso's own photograph may have served. We now know that there was a good deal of cross-pollination between his photography and his painting; and in this instance there are strong affinities between the two images. The face in the painting is a kind of split-level tribal mask, not easy to read, but the schematic shape of the nose is right, and the volume of the face. The horizontal over the shoulder agrees with the furnishings in the photograph. The crook of the left arm seems familiar. The clay pipe is in character, an essential component of the bric-à-Braque. In the final analysis the painting is perhaps more a *tableau-objet-Braque* than a caricatural portrait of the kind Picasso conferred on his dealers; more an emanation or vibration; more a thereness than a likeness.[14]

As a riddle-image that playful portrait is trumped by another, painted some ten years later, in completely different style and mood. *The Reading of the Letter* presents two young men, obviously very close, doing just that (b/w pl. 11). They wear contrasting suits, and each has his hat. The symbolic Kronstadt sits on a book by the side of the darker suit; a more conventional trilby is held in the hand of the lighter one. This painting was discovered only after Picasso's death in 1973. He had kept it, and kept it hidden, all his days. *The Reading of the Letter* is a hermetic work, as yet unexplained. Conceivably, it is an allegory of amity – and a lament for amity sundered – cast as a meditation on hats. Hats were to Picasso and Braque what apples were to Cézanne and Zola. When they were at school together, in Aix, Zola was ostracized by the other boys. Cézanne broke this embargo and took a beating for his pains. The following day Zola gave him a basket of apples. The gift sealed the friendship. For several years in the 1850s and 1860s it was as close as could be. For several more it endured at a distance. In 1886 it was ruptured, fatally, by the shocking revelation of Zola's novel *L'Œuvre*. The novel's painter-protagonist, Claude Lantier, modelled unmistakably on Paul Cézanne, is shown to have failed in his life's work. Afterwards, it was Cézanne himself who told the story of the boyhood gift, a story published for the first time in Joachim Gasquet's reminiscences of their encounters, in 1921, the same year that Picasso was working on *The Reading of the Letter*. Apples were not only Cézanne's capital subject, the subject he succeeded in knowing fully, *all round*, as D. H. Lawrence aptly said; they were freighted with personal meaning, and complicated emotion. 'Ah, Cézanne's apples!' exclaimed the painter. 'They go far back.' They also go bad.[15]

During the exuberant phase of their relationship, in 1911, Braque gave Picasso a box of hats. He had bought a job lot of 100 for a pittance at a public sale in Le Havre. According to André Salmon, they were cloche hats, bell-shaped, more curiosity than accessory – 'the envy of Second Empire bookmakers'. Picasso had great fun dressing up with them that summer in Céret. 'What a surprise, you have no idea how much I laughed, especially in the nude . . . With Manolo we put them on last night to go to the café but with false moustaches and sideburns applied with cork.' As he set off from Paris to join his friend, Braque was expecting Picasso to meet him off the train, hat in hand.[16] When they were both in Paris they sometimes went shopping for clothes together. At Picasso's request, Braque found him one of the distinctive blue suits, 'Singapores' as they called them, much fancied for their 'American' style.[17]

Braque and Picasso spoke in tongues – and also in clothes, hats in particular. Costume was another private language, another of those things that would be incomprehensible to others and which gave them such joy, as Braque would recall, not without emotion.[18] Beyond the ravelling and unravelling of a relationship, style mattered. For the mature Braque, the right clothes had a significance transcending both fashion and tradition. The right clothes were right for the purpose and right for him. He loathed the traditional white painting smocks favoured by Matisse and Rouault. 'I hate those smocks,' he told Brassaï, 'because they're too confining. I much prefer mechanics' overalls.'[19] He gave his attention to dressing as he gave his attention to everything he did, engrossed in the moment. 'When he drank a half of beer,' marvelled Roché, 'it was like a dialogue between him and the beer; in that instant he would think of nothing else. *He does only one thing at a time!* He does only what he *chooses* to do.'[20] The simplest things called for the greatest concentration. 'Keep a clear head,' said Braque. 'Be present.'[21]

Fernand Mourlot, who printed *Braque le patron*, and who persuaded Braque to try 'un peu de litho' (lithography) in his workshops, found himself a little overawed on first acquaintance, not on account of any finery, but because the artist's presentation was so perfectly judged. For the studio, Braque's regular attire was a blue cotton tunic and corduroy trousers, later a corduroy suit, set off by an ample yellow cravat (wool or silk, not chiffon), the occasional tartan tie, and headgear appropriate to the season. The colour scheme might vary, within a carefully coordinated and curiously familiar range: blacks, browns, yellows, greens, taupe, white and off-white verging on putty. The sense of familiarity had to do with the congruence between outfit and output. To the young Dora Vallier, 'he seemed to have stepped straight out of his own painting'.[22] As he grew older, he diversified: Doisneau, not invited to the table, remembered less than fondly, 'Braque, in carpet slippers, with his lordly ways'. Brassaï, who fared better, discovered him tending the stove in the studio, looking every inch the elegant stoker, with a fur-lined jacket and a wool cap against the cold. Braque had a fine white mane, but his head was sensitive, he said, after the trepanation. He had a cap for every occasion, among them a white one of his own design, spotlighted by the celebrated Karsh of Ottawa.

For beachcombing, for marine contemplation, for promenades along the shore, it was the corduroy suit – with occasional deviations.

In 1928 Braque and Marcelle began to think about making their second home in Varengeville, near Dieppe, on the Normandy coast. They had quit Sorgues for good the previous year. In one of the long cycles so typical of Braque's life, he returned to his roots, after an interval of nearly thirty years.

The catalyst for this reorientation was Paul Nelson, a bonhomous Chicagoan who had come to Paris to study with Perret, receiving his diploma in 1927. Nelson had married a Frenchwoman, Francine Lecœur, and speedily established himself as a social force among the avant-garde. As an architect he was well qualified, futuristically inclined, and despondent about his practice. He wanted to do differently, like his friends, but he did not know how. He was out of sympathy with 'the schools' and not at all satisfied with his own designs. He and Braque had known each other for some time; Nelson thought he had learned more from the painter than from any of his teachers, despite the fact that they never talked about art. One day Braque took a look at his drawings. Nelson said they were ugly. After further study Braque gave him the benefit of some characteristic wisdom. 'Throughout your drawings there is some continuity in what you find ugly. It is that continuity that is most often lacking in what you find good. First of all, you must retain what is constant: that is what marks you out. Then you must make use of your defects as your virtues: that is what will distinguish Paul Nelson.' Nelson took heart. Braque, he noted, had the gift of simplification.[23]

The Nelsons had a house in Varengeville. They invited the Braques to stay for the summer. Paul Nelson was a great introducer. 'I've lived in Varengeville for forty-four years now,' he wrote, looking back on a life of it,

and I've taken great pleasure in sharing its sights with lots of artist friends, not only Georges Braque . . . but also Miró, Derain, [Alexander] Calder, [Georges] Duthuit [son-in-law of Matisse], Paul Matisse [a grandson], Raymond Queneau, Michel Leiris, to say nothing of the regulars at our table: the Kandinskys, Fernand Léger, Arp, Zervos, Laurens and many others . . . If I list so many famous names, it's to demonstrate to you the pricelessness of this place and how precious it is in the eyes of creators. My own studio, for example, opposite the house, was built 125 years ago and rented by Claude Monet, Corot and [Eugène] Isabey before I bought it.[24]

In 1928 he took it upon himself to introduce his artist-friend Braque to the place Marcel Proust had called divine. They marched across muddy fields to the little church of St Valery, perched on the cliff top, with the *cimetière marin* that had unloosed Proust's lyricism: 'the sweet little cemetery, where the prelude to eternal silence (savoured by its dead, that our living ears cannot hear) is the relative silence that gives more depth to the regular and repeated coming of the waves, so far below'.[25] They explored the splendid sixteenth-century Manoir d'Ango, where Breton had taken up residence the previous year to write *Nadja*. They marched along the lanes. They skirmished in the bocage. They wandered on the cliffs, with their Jack tar names. They slipped past the Fat Woman to the pebbled shore. They foraged there, in time-honoured fashion.[26] They inspected the boats, the nets, the bones. They saw the sea in its triple harmony, as Braque's poet-ally René Char wrote, 'the crescent blade cutting off the dynasty of absurd griefs, the great wild bird preserve, the sea as credulous as bindweed'.[27] They watched the wheeling gulls, and the crows in the cornfields. They watched the light change – one of Braque's special pleasures.

He was back the following summer, renting first in Dieppe, and then in Varengeville itself. In 1930 he bought a plot of land and asked Nelson to build him a house. Nelson felt very proud. Pride soon turned to anxiety. Like Perret before him, Nelson discovered that Braque had ideas of his own about building. The right construction was as important as the right clothes. The architect had imagined a wall of glass bricks as a shield against the west wind. This conception was uncompromisingly rejected. 'No, that is Nelson's house. What is wanted is Braque's house, a house that I can master.' Braque had firm views on glass in general. 'Above all, I don't want top-quality glass! None of those panes that are too clear and too perfect. When I open the window, I want to see nature in a different way, and differently again when I go out.'[28] What was wanted, it transpired, was a Norman peasant's hut, long, low-slung, snug under the eaves, customized for *le patron*. That was what he got. It was completed in 1931, with the studio incorporated in a dacha-like outbuilding some 50 metres from the house. A second, larger, studio was added in 1949, under Nelson's supervision. The architect had learned his lesson. 'Le Corbusier imposed a style on man. I understood that one needed a structure appropriate to the man he was.' The artist had found his place. Varengeville was at the same time a sanctuary and a community (an imagined community) of artists past and present. 'We are born, so to speak, provisionally, it doesn't matter where,' says Rilke; 'it is only gradually that we compose, within ourselves, our true place of origin.'[29] Georges Braque was born, provisionally, in Argenteuil. His true place of origin was Varengeville.

The rhythm of the day, and the year, was important to him. His usual routine was to spend roughly February to July in Paris and August to January in Varengeville. Braque and Marcelle would drive to and fro in the big car, attended by Mariette Lachaud, furled canvases on the roof. En route Braque would absorb the countryside. On arrival he would relax: Varengeville was nothing if not restorative. There were no walls between the artistic departments of life. Braque spent time at each of them. First of all he made himself some tools. Then he made a magnificent pear-wood armchair, the back decorated with a strangely knotted bark that appealed to him because 'you can see in it anything you choose, can't you?'[30] As an interior decorator he mixed intimacy and austerity, with some striking juxtapositions. The walls of the living room were covered in whitewash stained different shades of ochre. The effect was a warm orange-yellow force field containing some massive pieces of waxed dark-wood furniture. The room was lit by lamps with yellow silk shades (the only colour that did not tire his eyes, according to Marcelle), curtained in the same fabric, and heated by a huge open fire, well fed with logs. There were pewter teapots, copper platters, occasional pieces of *art nègre*, a few home-made sculptures. Under a French naïve painting was an Eames chair. Braque was not timebound. 'The present is perpetual,' he wrote; and that is where he lived. Bold use of still life created an intense vibration of colour – not only flower arrangements but fruit and vegetable arrangements, by Mariette – asparagus ferns, marigolds, beetroot leaves, shoots of ivy, dandelions, moss. Braque

29. In his Varengeville dining room, 1953, by Doisneau

himself contributed found objects from beach promenades: ancient ironmongery, stones, starfish, a crab shell, a tatter of blue fishing net. 'Nature does not give a taste for perfection. One cannot conceive it as better or worse.'[31]

His bedroom was a cell with one small east-facing window. First light was precious.

The studio walls were painted grey. No ordinary grey, but grey made from crushed pigments, black, white, a dash of ultramarine, and a touch of ochre. A paper folding screen (pale coral) might be positioned behind the easel at which he was working. There were palette trees and lecterns, also home-made. The floor was made of teak boards, the kind used for fishing boats, over which Braque would trundle on his wheeled stool, the charioteer in the coliseum. The curtaining here was a complicated system of painted hessian, infinitely variable, designed to convert natural light into personal illumination. It was this aspect of Braque's mastering of his environment that fascinated the photographer Alexander Liberman:

30. Homemade palette, palette tree, lectern, and small beachscape in his Varengeville studio

I have always felt that this light is softened as if silenced; and, in the hushed luminosity, the contrast between objects ceases as they lose their individuality and fuse into their environment. This knowing manipulation of perception creates a unique universe. Air, space between things, acquire tangible substance; all matter seems unified; all things in the room exchange substance – reality becomes purposely de-intensified. As a scientist needs to dilute a rich substance to study it better, so Braque reduces jarring reality in order to live with it . . . This process of possession, the absorption and digestion of visual phenomena through the use of light, is one by which Braque's rendition of reality acquires mystery. The miracle of plant life is based on the transformation of light into energy; maybe photosynthesis is the image of Braque's creative process. First, slow contemplative assimilation is made possible by the manipulation of light; then inspiration, like chlorophyll in a plant, makes growth and expansion possible. Light is the energy behind the creative restitution that is the act of painting.[32]

The garden looked like an outdoor Braque. It had brambles and gorse, pruned by other hands. Braque did his pruning in the studio (the École des Beaux-Arbres, as Jacques Prévert had it). The garden was the province of the gardener, Paul Lavenu. He too was struck by his master's eye. 'The rest of us, we would see things straight, he would see things all odd. Afterwards, though, well, you would find that he was right. It was lovely.'[33]

Walking or cycling every day, whatever the weather, Braque rediscovered live nature – no better or worse than dead, perhaps, but almost completely absent from his work since the disappearance of the sky, circa 1908. Twenty years on, he returned to the landscape, or seascape, painting a flurry of crepuscular beach scenes conceived as still lifes, with boats but without people, featuring characterful cliffs hewn from those at Varengeville and Dieppe. The *barque* joined the *guéridon* in the repertoire. Increasingly, it was his habit to work on a variety of different paintings at the same time. Small, fast-painted landscapes jostled big, other-worldly interiors that might take years to bring to a resolution – or might never see the light of day. Braque continued to destroy canvases with which he was not content, sparing only those for which he had a soft spot, or which might still mature with time and a dab of burnt sienna. Braque knew what the philosopher R. G. Collingwood apprehended from his own artistic upbringing: 'I learned to think of a picture not as a finished product exposed for the admiration of virtuosi, but as the visible record, lying about the house, of an attempt to solve a definite problem in painting, so far as the attempt had gone.'[34] The finished work was in this sense a misnomer, and a misconception. Rather, the work was perpetually in progress. Canvases were experiments with a view to improvements, as Mallarmé said of his poems. Nonetheless it was clear that some canvases improved faster than others; and there were plainly enormous disparities in scale and register. When Patrick Heron commented on this, Braque replied that it was only natural. The small ones were there 'to express direct emotion'. Small *barques* were visceral Braques, 'breakaways into the outside world,' as he said, 'forays into immediate reality, contacts with the elements –

flute and oboe solos necessary for swelling to a full orchestral composition'.[35]

'The dangerous age for the artist is the pride of achieving mastery of his means, towards fifty,' Braque told Nelson. 'If he doesn't look back to regain contact with his youth, and enrich himself from it, then he becomes impoverished and sterile in his own formulas.'[36] This was a warning to himself. Braque turned fifty in 1932.

There were more forays at that dangerous age. Braque very rarely travelled abroad, even for his own exhibitions. Abroad was a distraction; travelling an interruption. Nevertheless, he did lay in a few sensations. He had made a fleeting visit to Rome in 1925, in the company of Walter Halvorsen. In 1931, as part of the programme of self-enrichment, he packed his bags again and pushed on to Venice and Florence. In 1949 he recollected:

Clearly it's pointless to set out for Italy with all one's ideas neatly packed, like a great many travellers. Quite the contrary, I use it as a change to gain a fresh view, to arrive unencumbered, which is the only way to cleanse oneself, if a little, to renew oneself.

So, with regard to the paintings, I had no prejudice. Though after a few days in front of that Renaissance art, I had had it up to here. As I went along the feeling grew in me that we're over that; there's nothing more to be extracted from it for us. *The Marriage Feast of Cana*, if you like, reeks of squared paper.

Today we ask the artist for the real thing, not merely the representation. Actually all those works were destined to decorate the walls of palaces, to offer a kind of spectacle, but one didn't live with them. Wouldn't there be something inappropriate, completely out-of-place, about van Gogh's canvases in those palaces? All that is set in an age so different from ours. So they shouldn't keep going on about it.

However I confess to have taken great pleasure in contemplating the Carpaccios, and I rediscovered them last year [1948] with the same satisfaction. It's true that Venice is an exceptional city. Say what you will, its heterogeneous architecture is horrible and its houses are like cakes, but there is the light that arranges everything and that is so captivating.[37]

He thought that Veronese's *Marriage Feast of Cana* was something akin to painting by numbers. In Braque's terms, for all its surface brilliance, it was an unfinished work. 'The painting is finished when it has erased the idea.'[38] Perhaps indicatively, Veronese's squared paper was to be found in the Louvre. Braque abroad was notoriously reluctant to enter museums, unless it was to see particular works. The story goes that the car would pull up at the door, and Marcelle would be despatched inside to establish whether there was anything worth contemplating. The story was apocryphal, no doubt, but not very. Braque rediscovered the Carpaccios on the occasion of the 1948 Venice Biennale (when he was awarded the coveted first prize for a foreign painter) only after Aimé Maeght and Louis Clayeux, Maeght's right-hand man, virtually compelled him to go and see them.[39] Still he did not go to the Accademia, but rather to the Scuola di San Giorgio degli Schiavoni (the Society of St George of the Slavs), a kind of seamen's institute for the benefit of the indigent and miscreant from Dalmatia, which housed a cycle of Carpaccio's paintings illustrating the lives of the Dalmatian patron saints: the valiant George, the obscure Tryphonius (who had a gift for casting out devils), and the studious Jerome. By cunning indirection, the masterpiece of the cycle is in fact St Augustine, experiencing a vision following Jerome's death; his meticulously arrayed study bears a passing resemblance to the artist's studio. At last there was a twinge of recognition. Braque could imagine plying his trade as a hired hand in Carpaccio's workshop, contributing the detail that made him famous – the music, the books, the objects, the faithful cat-turned-dog. If Renaissance painters were either demi-gods or manual workers, as Sartre said, Braque's preference was plain enough. As if to prove the point, Paulhan had him wearing artificer's tunic, carpenter's trousers, and fishmonger's cap.[40]

Beyond Carpaccio, it was the international trends in illumination that remained with him. 'Impressionism is French. A portrait by Ingres has an atmospheric quality found in almost all French paintings. In Cranach [a personal favourite], nothing of the sort: he is Expressionist. The Italians are influenced by the light of their country: when I went to Italy, I was struck by the golden light, whereas here [in France] it is silver.'[41] England did not figure in the lists of light, but Braque slipped across the Channel, briefly, in 1933 and 1934. He and Marcelle were chauffeured around by Ben Nicholson, squeezing with some difficulty into the British painter's elderly Austin – in motoring terms, rather a comedown – the little car fit to burst with its foreign dignitaries. On these raids he scarcely seems to have ventured beyond Hampstead and St James's. Nicholson showed them Keats Grove; they visited Jim Ede, then an assistant curator with suspiciously advanced tastes at the Tate, later the inspiration behind Kettle's Yard in Cambridge, supping at Ede's with Nicholson, Barbara Hepworth, John Piper and Jean Hélion, among others; they made a few strategic purchases (shoes from John Lobb), and withdrew.[42]

In Germany – a whistle-stop tour in 1936 – the light had already begun to fail. Braque was followed all the time by the police; the oppressive atmosphere lived in his memory.[43] There was nothing to detain him here but the Cranachs, and on his way through the Rhineland, the wondrous Isenheim altarpiece in the Musée d'Unterlinden, Colmar, the very name of the museum a sharp reminder of the contested ground on which it stood and to which it bore witness. According to Mariette Lachaud, Mathias Grüne-wald was Braque's favourite painter. The altarpiece was his *magnum opus*, a magnet for all the great cultural pilgrims of the twentieth century.[44] A few years before Braque, the young Elias Canetti spent an entire day circling it, reluctant to leave. 'When the museum closed,' he recalled, 'I wished for invisibility, so that I might spend the night there.'

I saw Christ's corpse without plaintiveness; the dreadful state of his body struck me as true. Faced with this truth, I realized what had bewildered me about crucifixions: their beauty, their transfiguration. Transfiguration belonged to an angelic concert, not on the cross. The thing that people had turned away from, horrified, in real life, could still be grasped in the painting: a memory of the dreadful things people do to one another. Back then, in February 1927, war and gassings were still close enough to make the painting more credible. Perhaps the most indispensable task of art has been forgotten too often: not catharsis, not solace, not disposing of everything as if it would end well, for it does not end well. Plague and boils and torment and horror – and for the plague that is overcome, we invent even worse horror. What can the comforting deceptions signify in the face of this truth, which is always the same and should remain visible to our eyes? All horror to come is anticipated here. St John's finger, enormous, points it out: this is it, this is what will be again.[45]

The year of Braque's visit, Hitler reoccupied the Rhineland.

Braque did no more touring. There was a muscle-stretching excursion to Belgium after the war was over, when he bought himself a celebratory sailor's cap; a Channel-hop to visit the Braque–Rouault exhibition at the Tate in 1946 (typically, he attended the closing rather than the opening); and the prize-winning appearance at the Venice Biennale. Other than that, he never again left France. 'After Italy, Provence, which I prefer.'[46] Already it was clear that the English and German journeys had a different flavour to the Italian one: more exhalation than exploration, more dash than stroll. But he was far from giving up on discovery. Reaching a half-century, he was just getting started. He believed with Heraclitus that 'you will not find out the limits of the human soul by going, even if you travel over every way'.[47] And yet he also spoke eloquently of the artist's need to deepen his experience of the world. 'For that, it is indispensable that he freshens his vision, that he raps his sensibility very hard, to shake out everything that is caught inside by repetition, and to give it renewed efficacy.' As Beckett put it in his disquisition on Proust, 'the only fertile research is excavatory, immersive, a contraction of the spirit, a descent. The artist is active, but negatively, shrinking from the nullity of extra-circumferential phenomena, drawn in to the core of the eddy . . . "Man," writes Proust, is not a building that can receive additions to its superficies, but a tree whose stem and leafage are an expression of inward sap.' For Braque, deepening his experience meant tapping the inward sap. It was not the world that waited to be explored, but what he called the sensory faculties.

What counted in the end was not fuel consumption but spiritual activity.[48]

So his voyage of discovery sailed inwards. From his desk or his bed – he was a night reader – Braque fed the inner man. This one was the gourmet. The past is a hypothesis, he said, but it was the ancient world, more hypothetical than most, that held his attention.[49] When Ambroise Vollard wanted to commission a suite of etchings for a superfine 'artist's book', in 1931, and offered Braque his choice of author, he immediately proposed Hesiod. This was a recherché selection. Braque was deeply attached to Hesiod's *Theogony*, an epic from the very beginning of Greek literature, something in the nature of a *catalogue raisonné* of the gods in verse form. Then as now, the *Theogony* was overshadowed by the *Iliad* and the *Odyssey*; but Hesiod used to be mentioned in the same breath as Homer (his approximate contemporary). Three centuries after their works became known, the philosopher–poet Xenophanes noted tartly that 'Homer and Hesiod have attributed to the gods everything that is held discreditable among men – thieving, adultery, deceiving one another'; less judgemental, the historian Herodotus recorded that 'they were the ones who created the gods' family trees for the Greek world, gave them their names, assigned them their honours and areas of expertise, and told us what they looked like.'[50]

Braque for his part mentioned Hesiod in the same breath as Aeschylus and Sophocles, finding him more interesting than either. According to the well-informed Christian Zervos, editor of *Cahiers d'Art*, Braque began with Pindar (in the fifth century BC) and worked back to Hesiod (in the eighth). Pindar wrote triumphal odes to the victors of the Panhellenic games. He was moved by the tremendous gulf between the flimsy, transitory world of men and 'the brazen sky', the everlasting home of the gods, where order and harmony glowingly prevail.[51]

> Creatures of a day! What is a man?
> What is he not? A dream of a shadow
> Is our mortal being.[52]

Pindar composes a poetry of nobility. Insubstantial things are subject to flashes of illumination from above, by which they are transfigured and redeemed. Zervos thought that Braque was much affected by his reading of these poems. It may well be so; not necessarily for the uplifting sentiment, but for the arresting images – ploughing a garland, snowflakes of gold, cold fire, storm-footed horses – and the exhilarating liquid forms. Zervos cites Braque's representation of horses, and it is easy to imagine certain passages appealing to the hand that pondered and the eye that fashioned.[53]

A former merchant seaman turned temporary shepherd, Hesiod became a poet, he claims, following a visitation from the Muses themselves while he was tending his sheep. His poem opens with that epiphany, conveniently placed on the local mountain top, in Boeotia. 'From the Muses of Helicon let us begin our singing, that haunt Helicon's great and lofty mountain, and dance on their soft feet round the violet-dark spring and the altar of the mighty son of Kronos.'[54] The son of Kronos is Zeus, the father of the Muses. A theogony is properly speaking an account of the birth and genealogy of the gods. The *Theogony* that Hesiod compiled not only named the Muses but defined them for Western mythology.[55] Our very conception of a *Mousa*, an inspiring goddess incarnate or more vaguely imagined, is Hesiod's. Braque knew an artist who could hardly do without them. Their dwelling place is also Hesiod's creation. Mount Helicon is the original *mouseion*, a notion to tickle the fancy of one who filled museums and at the same time fought shy of visiting them.

Hesiod is obsessed with genealogy; the *Theogony* is crammed with names. Braque could not get enough of them. He revelled in the personifications.

Night bore hateful Doom and dark Fate and Death, she bore Sleep, she bore the tribe of Dreams. And gloomy Night bore Cavil and painful misery, bedded with none of the gods; and the Hesperides, who mind fair golden apples beyond the famed Oceanus . . . And baleful Night gave birth to Resentment also, an affliction for mortal men; and after her she bore Deceit and Intimacy, and accursed Old Age, and she bore hard-hearted Strife.

He was enchanted by the *nereids* or sea-nymphs, the goddess-children of Nereus in the undraining sea:

> Protho, Eucrante, Sao, and Amphitrite,
> Eudora, Thetis, Galene, and Glauce,
> Cymothoe, swift Speo, and lovely Thalia,
> Pasithea, Erato, and rosy Eunice,
> delightful Melite, Eulimene and Agaue,
> Doto and Proto, Pherosa, Dynamene,
> Nesaea and Actaea and Protomedea,
> Doris, Panope, and beautiful Galatea,
> Lovely Hippothoe and rosy-armed Hipponoe,
> Cymodoce, who stills with ease the waves,
> in the misty sea and the gusts of strong-blowing winds
> with Cymatolege and fair-ankled Amphitrite . . .[56]

Of necessity, Braque read Hesiod in French, but he liked the look of the Greek letters. One interviewer speaks of him, 'seduced by the name, tracing the ancient letters like a magic spell' on to his etchings.[57] Hesiod gave Braque freedom of manœuvre (a freedom greater than the tightly plotted tragedies of Aeschylus and Sophocles). Not understanding the language may actually have helped. Braque inverted the letters and switched the identities of the characters as it pleased him (b/w pl. 12).

He also liked the cross-cultural conversation. 'As for me, at the moment I'm illustrating a Greek text, and why not!' he announced to the visiting René Gimpel. 'Isn't the art of today allowed to offer a vision of earlier times?'[58] Here he was stimulated by Carl Einstein. The omnivorous Einstein knew his Hesiod. In fact he saw a stylistic connection between the ancient and the modern, that is, the pre-Classical and the Cubist. He described both as 'tectonic', evoking the art of structural change. Certain Cubist heads reminded him of archaic ones (and their colloquy in Reber's castle). The tectonic-poetic made an apt synthesis. Einstein wrote suggestively of the 'mythic realism' of Braque's work.[59]

There were other considerations. Braque cannot but have been aware that Picasso had recently illustrated Ovid's *Metamorphoses* with a series of thirty etchings in a pure linear style reminiscent of ancient Greek vase painting.[60] The circumstances seemed favourable. Vollard's association with the project was not to be taken lightly. Vollard had been Cézanne's dealer. On Mont Parnasse he was a minor deity in his own right. His terms were acceptable: initially 150,000 francs for twenty original, printable, woodcuts. More to the point, he did not skimp. 'It's Vollard who has commissioned these drawings,' Braque explained to Gimpel in the studio, 'and it's nice to be working with someone who doesn't count the cost. He has never done a book for profit. No matter what the text, he'll tear it up if there's one letter missing, and his editions have cost him a fortune.'[61] Thematically and aesthetically, Hesiod was a rare treat.[62] The order of things, darkness and light, apparitions of every sort, the origins of forms . . . all of this was not so foreign to Georges Braque.

Braque's illustrations for the *Theogony* were part and parcel of his programme of self-enrichment. The project generated over 100 recipe drawings, scribbled vigorously with a fat, soft 6B pencil, in his cookery-book *carnets*.[63] The task of printing the finished etchings as they emerged was entrusted to his friend Demetrios Galanis, very likely at Braque's instigation.[64] Galanis undertook the work on his own press, which had belonged to Degas. The mingling of individuality and continuity appealed to Braque. The two of them would have been able to talk it over on the painter's regular Sunday visits to the printer's house in the rue Cortot; Galanis could instruct Braque in the procedure and if need be in the language. But Galanis was not the only one from whom he sought instruction. He also approached Diego Giacometti, brother of the sculptor, himself a skilled craftsman and designer. For Paul Rosenberg's apartment, Braque had the idea of making engraved plaster panels, a stratagem he repeated in another apartment for another wealthy patron. The plaster was coated in black paint and incised to expose the white beneath. The technique was Braque's own invention; the preparation he worked out with the help of Diego, who promptly joined the ranks of those accomplices who dignified the man and the artist above other men, as their mutual friend Jean Leymarie expressed it.[65] In subject and style the panels mirrored the illustrations: the *nereid* Sao and her ilk, executed in a rhythmic, cursive hand, patterned on the ornamentation of the ancient Greek and Etruscan pieces he had studied in the Louvre thirty years earlier, with a nod to Cubism and Surrealism, a wink to Picasso, and a palpable debt to pleasure.[66]

'I have a heavy hand for drawing,' Braque said of himself. 'Whenever I start to do a drawing, it turns into a painting, with crosshatching, shadows and ornamentation.'[67] The heavy hand had found the means of adaptation. Some of the drawings did turn into paintings – a limpid *Large Brown Still Life* bearing a surprising resemblance to a *Reclining Nude* communed serenely with a Rothko in a corner of the Musée national d'art moderne in Paris for several years – the slippage of genre testimony to *the climate*, as Braque called it, the cherished state of things in flux, malleable, a notion dear to Heraclitus; Braque's expression of it much discussed among modern painters.[68] Contemplating the *Theogony*, Braque approached that climate as never before. 'For me, it's no longer a question of metaphor but metamorphosis.'[69] The mysterious Etruscan character of his later work, as perceived by Antonin Artaud, was a case of the artist looking back to regain contact with his youth and enriching himself in the process, according to his own prescription. Braque's pronouncements on this subject are chronically immersive, almost mystic. 'Impregnation is everything that penetrates us unconsciously, that is developed and conserved by obsession, and that is freed one day by the hallucination of creativity. Hallucination is the definitive realization of a long impregnation whose origins go back to our youth.'[70] His poetic engagement with Hesiod parallels Hölderlin's with Pindar two centuries earlier, in its unfeigned ardour and its conscious application, as if to echo Hölderlin's belief in the indispensability of an apprenticeship 'abroad'.

That engagement had a lasting impression on his work. Braque–Hesiod took an inordinately long time to appear. Braque had completed his part by the end of 1935 (sixteen etchings, in the

event, on copperplate). At that stage Galanis was still requesting
more paper to complete the printing, and reminding Vollard to
collect the work already done.[71] The requests went unanswered.
Vollard died in 1939 with twenty-four artists' books unpublished,
the *Theogony* among them. Small editions of loose etchings were
printed and circulated, signed and unsigned, numbered and un-
numbered, with and without *remarques* – the marks made on the
edges of the plates, normally to test the strength of the acid used in
the etching process, in Braque's case to indulge in a pyrotechnic
display of semi-automatic doodling, introducing the doodle birds
that became an increasingly important motif in his work.[72] As time
went on the plates themselves were scattered, and at some point in
the 1930s cropped, eliminating the *remarques*, allegedly at Braque's
behest.[73] Eventually, in 1954, Aimé Maeght took the initiative to
publish the series complete in book form, with text in Greek (and
without *remarques*). Maeght's deluxe edition of 150 on handmade
paper, signed by the artist, came out the following year. The
Greek text was not much appreciated, but the illustrations were
immediately recognized as a milestone in printmaking. In truth the
artist's work was less illustration than translation into his own idiom,
at once faithful and inspired.[74] For Braque it was in every sense a
personal triumph. Eclipsed for twenty years, his work on the
Theogony was immensely fruitful for his private rituals. 'If he etched
for Vollard, he painted for himself,' as Dora Vallier succinctly put
it. Muses, like birds, stole into the studio. Braque's world was a
world of its own. Alexander Liberman imagined himself standing
in a luminous womb.[75] It also made a fine *museion*.

> And look at the half-assurance of the bird,
> from the manner of its birth almost knowing both worlds –
> as if it were the soul of an Etruscan, released
> from a dead man sealed in space
> that has his reclining figure for a lid.
> And how confused is any womb-born creature
> that has to fly! As if frightened
> of its own self, it zig-zags through the air

Like a crack through a teacup. The way a bat's trace
crazes the porcelain of evening.[76]

After publication darkness overtook Braque's *Theogony* once
more, until a magnificent commemorative exhibition at the Galerie
Leiris in 1982. And yet it continued to provoke. As late as 1978,
Roy Lichtenstein produced a pop *Cosmology*.[77] Most provoked,
however, was an old devil called Pablo, whose œuvre still lacked
something Greek. In 1960 he tried to get his own back. His eye fell
on Pindar's eighth pythian. The eighth pythian is an ode to the
winner of a Boys' Wrestling Contest.[78]

9. 'Stricken by and seeking reality': The Occupation

War crept up again, with almost Braquian slowness, during the winter of 1939–40. This was the *drôle de guerre* – the Phoney War. Seasoned Parisians carried their pigs' snouts with soldierly resignation, and expected the worst. They were not disappointed.

At the declaration, in September 1939, Braque was in Varenge-ville, coaching Joan Miró in poker-work and life. Prompted by Paul Nelson, Miró took refuge there throughout the Phoney War, renting a house in the village and seeking his own version of renewal. Down the lane was Georges Braque. The newcomer went to call on him regularly. Miró's working notes give glimpses of what passed between them.

The preparation of the series of large canvases for Daphnis and Chloe is very unsatisfactory; if you press on the back of them with your finger the preparatory coat comes off. Use a solvent to remove that preparation and then give the canvas a coat of white lead or casein, the preparation Braque and Balthus use . . . Using the lost wax process – which Braque taught me – I could make some designs that could later be made in gold, like the primitive Mexicans used to . . . I could start out by taking red-hot irons and applying them to the wood the way Braque and Mariette did . . .'[1]

In spite of the times, Miró profited in both creation and reflection. Encouraged by Braque, he began an experimental series of works on paper, 'Constellations', in which he played with surface texture, natural phenomena, Biblical allusion, and contemporary reference – the second in the series is called *The Escape Ladder* (1940) or 'On the 13th the Ladder Brushed the Firmament' – producing some of his strongest images and refreshing himself in the process.[2] Propinquity paid dividends. Miró was inspired by Braque's example. 'Look to Braque,' he reminded himself, 'as a model for everything that is skill, serenity, and reflection.'[3] After a few months in Varengeville he was already talking about attaining 'a high degree of poetry' from the contemplative life he was leading. Twenty years later, when he spoke of his working methods, he sounded exactly like his exemplar. 'I work like a gardener or a wine-grower. Things come slowly. I didn't find my vocabulary of forms, for example, all of a sudden. It developed almost in spite of me.'[4]

Braque may have appeared serene, but he was not. Earlier that year, *Cahiers d'Art* published the responses to one of its periodic surveys, on the influence of events in the outside world on the creative artist – in the circumstances, a matter of some delicacy. Creative artists of every colouration were asking themselves the same question. 'Oh heavens, yes, I am well aware in what sense I could say with Valéry that "events do not interest me",' mused André Gide in his journal. 'None of the things I cherish spiritually is dependent on this war, to be sure; but the future of France, our future, is at stake. Everything that still concerns our thought may disappear, sink into the past, cease to have for the men of tomorrow anything but an archaic meaning. Other problems, unsuspected yesterday, may trouble those to come, who will not even understand our reason for existing . . .'[5] Braque could have said the same. He was more unsettled by the gathering storm than might have been supposed. His response to *Cahiers d'Art* constituted perhaps the most important unmediated written evidence he was ever persuaded to give.

Contemporary events influence the painter, that goes without saying, but to what extent and in what form they mingle in his work, that cannot be determined. In any case, the artist should not be expected to deliver a rounded verdict on the future of civilization. His role is not to prophesy. For all that, he still belongs to his time, even if he refuses to acknowledge certain *a priori* facts concerning either external events or the inner life. Ideas only ever enter his work as a driving force. They bear only a very indirect relationship to the expression of quality, and may disappear when the painter looks at his canvas. Quality itself is innate, and we can see it persist, standing the test of time. In art, it is fate of a kind that leads to valid decisions. For the rest, everything that does not assert itself irresistibly, irrefutably, engaging one's whole being beyond all discussion, can only promise failure and destruction. Whether the end result conveys serenity or anxiety is something we cannot know. Do we need to repeat, here, [his maxim] that we are concerned with establishing not an anecdotal fact but a pictorial fact?

The artist is always under threat . . . One cannot separate him from other men. He lives on the same level as everyone else. His role is much too serious for what he wishes to contribute to be called 'escapism' or 'happy holidays' [terms used in the inquiry]. I have never thought for one moment that art is an illusion. Whatever is viable in the creative process develops almost involuntarily. We do not give enough credit to the dark forces that drive us, that many – in their optimistic approach to the universe – seek to ignore, but that must be controlled, advancing slowly and continually rediscovering before us the mystery we are striving to repel.

Changes of régime necessarily affect the life of the painter since, like everyone else, he endures his age. But his work depends too much on the past for him to accommodate to the changes of the hour with a clear conscience. Who said: 'We have to live out our previous life'? Fulfilment requires physical time; if it takes ten years to conceive and execute a canvas, how is the painter supposed to stay abreast of events? A painting is not a snapshot. Once again, this does not mean that the painter is not influenced, concerned and more by history; he can suffer without being militant. Only let us distinguish, categorically, between art and current affairs.[6]

Braque had been troubled by the march of events for some time. According to his own precept, he suffered without being militant. 'The militant is a man behind a mask.'[7] *Guernica*s were not his style. What mattered was staunchness: whether the work (and the worker) would hold. In this as in other matters he stood four-square with Paul Celan. The poet of the death fugue and the painter of the dustbin shared an unexpected sense of humour. 'What a game!' said Celan, of the poet-life and his own struggle. 'What a joke!' said Braque, of the famous northern light and his carefully designed south-facing studios.[8] Both men loved puns. 'Something is rotten in the state of D-mark,' quipped Celan, in a manner reminiscent of the crypto-grams in Braque's *papiers collés*.[9] Both appropriated Apollinaire to their own concerns. Both felt a spiritual affinity with Hölderlin.

> But it is the sea
> That takes and gives remembrance,
> And love no less keeps eyes attentively fixed,
> But what is lasting the poets provide.[10]

Celan's characterization of poetry as 'a message in a bottle' might well have appealed to Braque, for the element and the method of delivery, for the undertow of the work in motion, making towards the unknown; and above all for the idea of art as a realm not subject to prediction or legislation, the bedrock faith of both practitioners. Celan also subscribed to slowness. His apothegm, 'poetry no longer imposes itself, it exposes itself', could have come straight out of Braque's notebook. His statement of purpose, 'to sketch out reality for myself', is pure Braque. So too his predicament, 'stricken by and seeking reality', and his immersive calling: 'With art you go into your very selfmost straits. And set yourself free.'[11]

Both eschewed direct social comment and were criticized for it. Celan considered Brecht's hammer-blow agitprop too 'explicit'. Braque felt similarly about Picasso's communist capers and the famous dove of peace. Braque was not so much grower as *remueur*, turning the bottles over the years as the wine slowly ages. Impregna-tion could not be rushed or forced; hence the sharp distinction between art and 'current affairs'. 'I call "journalism" everything that will be less interesting tomorrow than today,' wrote Gide. 'How many great artists win their cases only on appeal!'[12]

There too Braque and Celan stand together. Yet both dwelt in the world, and on it. Braque did not go in for history painting. He had no wish to tell stories.[13] His drum and trumpet played in private, quietly. There is no scream in Braque, no ecstatic ululation. There is the murmur of moral scruple. Ecstasy is easy: talent will see you through. Constancy is the lonelier furrow. 'One is so alone in life that from time to time one feels the need to make something people like,' Braque confided once to Louis Clayeux. His dealer played on that all too human feeling.[14] The chequebook Braque was a sore temptation. 'In art the temptation to please too easily is ever-present,' John Berger has observed: 'it comes with mastery.' This called for constant vigilance and self-scrutiny. Braque's testamentary emphasis came from the heart: 'It is very important for an artist to combat routine.'[15]

In his own fashion he was attentive to the times. Apart from the utterances in his notebook ('the democracies have replaced pomp with luxury'), he did not make statements.[16] He offered quiverings and intimations.[17] Skulls began to appear on his tables in 1937. By the time of the Munich Agreement (September 1938), in which Britain and France accommodated to the changes of the hour by conniving at the dismemberment of Czechoslovakia, he was at work on a series of *Vanitas* culminating in a macabre *Death's Head*, at once mask and ghost (b/w pl. 14). In the same period a skull invaded other compositions, doubling as a palette (a duality he relished), and floating eerily in space as if obeying a different law of gravity (b/w pl. 15). Skulls are otherwise absent from his *œuvre*, but Braque made no concession to coincidence. He claimed that his interest was purely technical. 'I was fascinated by the tactile quality of the rosary and the formal problems of mass and composition posed by the skull.'[18] Skulls were like musical instruments. He kept one in his studio in Varengeville, as part of his stock company. It too came alive to the touch. Braque remembered his disturbing encounter with the mummy forty years earlier in the museum at Le Havre. 'No external event, no matter how overwhelming its scope, engenders a work of art unless it becomes an inward occasion,' as Leo Steinberg has said; and great artists have long memories.[19] It is difficult to believe that he did not also remember a subsequent disturbance in no-man's-land, and other cadaverous encounters. Georges Braque had a richer store of *memento mori* than most of humankind.

The skulls evoked a mixed response. Braque savoured the

untutored one. 'How awful!' He overheard the outburst of a shocked spectator. 'At last a person who said something with feeling. For me it was a eulogy,' Braque told his friend Stanislas Fumet. 'Others would not have stinted in praising the arrangement of the composition, in admiring the harmony of the forms, the quality of a white that further highlighted a grey, the *rapports* between a green and a yellow, the quality of the matter, etc. Ah! Fumet old man, I was content. What!' Art required, not elucidation, but submitting-to.[20]

The intimations intensified. In 1939, a beached boat hoisted a tricolour.

War imminent, Braque wavered. In August 1939 he and Marcelle seriously considered making a dash for Geneva, and neutrality, before the borders closed. They were loath to go alone, and asked another couple to join them.[21] Braque was careful not to reveal the identity of this couple, but it was almost certainly Henri and Marthe Laurens, their closest friends. In the event nothing came of it. The idea may not have found favour with Laurens; or Braque may have thought better of it; or the phoniness of the war in its initial stages may have encouraged them to stay put: it is impossible to be sure. Only one thing seems certain. Braque remained profoundly unsettled. For the first time since 1917, he stopped painting.

'Before the war . . . I'd started quite a few canvases,' he wrote to Rosenberg in October 1939, 'but the turbulence that's arisen put a stop to all that. I haven't gone back to painting and for about a month now I've been making sculptures, which I am greatly enjoying. It's athletic work because I've got to bring stones up from the beach that sometimes weigh more than 20 kilos.'[22] Pleasure leached away with the winter rains. Braque was dogged by influenza. For the next few months he toiled at not painting. Mariette Lachaud watched over him in distress. 'He was so shocked by the disaster that was looming . . . His sensitive soul couldn't bear what he had already lived through personally during the First World War. It's that above all that traumatized him for over a year.'[23]

On 10 May 1940 the weather turned vicious. The German armies overran Luxembourg, slashed through the Ardennes, cuffed the British, French and Belgian forces into the pocket of Dunkirk, abandoned them to their fate, overwhelmed General Gamelin, imposed an armistice on Marshal Pétain, occupied Paris, and staged a victory parade for the Führer on the Champs-Élysées. Hitler had achieved in seven weeks what the Germans had dreamt of for seventy years. The French counted 124,000 dead, a further 200,000 wounded, a field force shattered and a people humiliated. Rarely has a major power been so cruelly exposed. Luxury curdled into ignominy. Three days before the Panzers rolled, normal leave was restored for the French army. Of the cyclone that was about to hit them, the general staff had fewer intimations than Georges Braque. 'Personally, I envisaged a group of four tank divisions around Châlons,' testified Gamelin after the fact. 'How was I to know it would get broken up? We had no advance knowledge of where and how the Germans would attack.'[24] Tactically and psychologically, they were absolutely unready. So deeply were they committed to a cut-price cat-fight on someone else's territory that they had nothing to offer when lightning war exploded in their faces. At one stage in the débâcle the invaders took 10,000 prisoners, in a day, for the loss of one officer and forty men. Churchill dignified it as the Battle of France. For the Germans it was a walkover. For the French it was not so much a military defeat as a national catastrophe. France had been eviscerated.

In Paris, as the Panzers bore down, Matisse bumped into Picasso. 'Where are you going like that?' asked Picasso. 'To my tailor,' replied Matisse. The other was astounded. 'What, don't you know that the Front is completely broken through, the army's turning somersaults, it's a stampede, the Germans are approaching Soissons, tomorrow they might be in Paris?' 'But, our generals,' Matisse inquired, 'what are they doing?' Picasso looked at him seriously. 'Our generals – are the École des Beaux-Arts.'[25]

Open war restored Braque's equilibrium.[26] Methodically he cleaned his brushes and made his dispositions. Better prepared than Kahnweiler, Paul Rosenberg had decamped to a rented château on the outskirts of Bordeaux, poised to ship out if the moment came. Braque and Marcelle visited him there in late May. They brought with them what little gold they possessed, and the canvases from Varengeville. These were left in the strongrooms of the National Bank for Commerce and Industry at Libourne, a few kilometres away, where Rosenberg had already deposited fourteen Braques, twenty-one Matisses and thirty-three Picassos, together with a choice selection from his fabulous inventory. Mariette meanwhile had been left in the house in Paris with her mother Amélie. As German forces closed on the capital her friends tried to persuade her to leave. She refused. Amélie for her part would not be separated from her daughter, so they both stayed. Mariette was afraid. But she was the guardian of the studio; Hitler himself could not have induced her to abandon her post. She had instructions from Braque to destroy all his paintings if the Germans came. She refused that too. Instead she set about undoing the canvases from their stretchers – 120 of them. Her work done, she occupied her time in defiantly watering a row of newly planted fir trees in the garden. Asked by their neighbour, a sceptical communist, 'Who are you doing this for?', she replied heroically, 'For my pleasure'.[27] She was certain that *le maître* would be back, if not for her, then for the paintings.

Braque returned a few days later. He was surprised to find his canvases rolled up and ready to go. He wept, but he did not linger. They packed the canvases, the fine linen and the silver in the car and set off together for Pacy, near Evreux, north-west of Paris, where Braque's elderly mother was staying with his sister Henriette.[28] Braque gave Henriette money – a lot of money – and drove on to Varengeville to regroup. From there the four of them, Braque, Marcelle, Mariette and Amélie, headed south to La Valade in the Limousin, where Mariette's family came from, and where her aunt still lived. The Lachauds had invited the Braques to stay, for as long as they wished or felt the need. In the wreckage of international agreements, a domestic alliance held fast.

Their journey was disorderly. Bridges were blown; the roads were chaotic and uncertain. Those who had the means, and many who did not, were on the move, trailing west and south, out of Paris, out of the path of the German juggernaut, a combination of forced migration and mass flight known to the French as the Exodus. In between arrests as a suspicious alien, Arthur Koestler logged the loss of hope. 'The onslaught on the railway stations. The disappearance of the buses and taxis from the streets. The melting away of the town, as if infected with consumption. The tommy-guns of the "flics" [police] at the street corners. The peculiar glance of the people in the Underground, with the dim candles of fear lit behind their eyeballs. The parachutist scare. The Fifth Column psychosis.'[29] In certain cases the loss of hope was irreparable. After the *Blitzkrieg*, Carl Einstein took his own life.

The Braques and the Lachauds and their precious cargo were safely established in La Valade by the end of May. 'Morale is good,' reported the old soldier.[30] For about three weeks the barnhouse became their southern headquarters. They lived higgledy-piggledy with everyone else, sleeping on straw, Braque presiding calmly at the huge table like a minister. The local residents cordially approved of their distinguished visitor. He seemed unruffled by all the turbulence, pleased to be among these good people, curious about their lives, observant, unaffected, impeccable. He displayed a keen interest in their jars of pickled snails and mushrooms, and fed a hearty appetite. He was obviously a fine man.[31] But he could not stay there for ever. They buried the canvases, stashed goods and chattels in the roof, and moved on.

In Barbézieux, not far away, they teamed up with the Derains. The caravan rolled on to Gaujac, south of Toulouse, where they stayed with Derain's cousin, within sight of the Pyrenees.[32] Their odyssey seemed to be tending in that direction. Braque and Derain would have been familiar with the Mediterranean end of the border, near Port Bou, from their youthful sojourns in Céret and Collioure; but they would also have heard that the crossing was dangerous and the reception on the other side at best unpredictable. Other questions pressed in. If the art was degenerate, according to Nazi aesthetics, what of the artist under that dispensation? How should he live? Where should he go? Braque had not given up the idea of returning to his house and his studio if conditions allowed.[33] Could he exist unmolested in Occupied Paris? Could he paint? Could he sit it out, in splendid isolation, as Matisse did in Nice, or Bonnard in nearby Le Cannet, above the fray, out of reach? Could he leave France, if it came to it? Could he bolt?

Bolting, now, was almost inconceivable. Braque visited Bordeaux again from La Valade in June. He was still conducting business with the bank; he may have made some more deposits. If he discussed emigration with Paul Rosenberg, it was only to rule it out for the foreseeable future.[34] In July 1940, after a month of watching and waiting, he decided to take his chances in Paris. The caravan divided. The Derains remained for the time being in Gaujac. The Braques and the Lachauds made their way back to a city under siege. Luck was with them. The house opposite had been commandeered as German officers' quarters. The Braque house was empty and virtually unscathed. The Germans had entered the studio and stolen his accordion, but nothing else had been disturbed. In the garden a row of fir trees had taken.

Braque dug in for the duration. Deep in his selfmost straits he found new resources. His battle pieces were still lifes and his landscapes interiors. 'One can't be painting apples while heads are rolling,' declared Jean Fautrier. There were precedents – Cézanne painted apples during the Franco-Prussian War of 1870.[35] The strategy of still life was too indirect an approach for some, but for others it made all the difference. Jean Paulhan was now the editor of the *Nouvelle Revue Française*. The Occupation tested his *savoir-faire* to the limit. 'I love the poetry that admits defeat and the politics that offers its resignation,' he scribbled to himself, half-seriously, echoing Braque's love of the rule that corrects emotion. 'I am too modest to commit suicide, too proud to live.' In spite of all, he was committed to a cause. 'I am committed, partly by shyness, basically by love of my country.'[36] By day he accommodated imperturbably to the exigencies of the moment: the suspension of a 'free' *NRF* and the imposition of a new editor, the doubly dangerous Pierre Drieu la Rochelle, a literate fascist, bent on shaking up this collection of 'Jews, pederasts, timid surrealists and agents of freemasonry'.[37] By night he roneoed for the Resistance, a one-man commissioning agency and clearing house. In every circle in which he moved he became a kind of plenipotentiary. He was an antidote to demoralization. It was perhaps for this reason above all that a young firebrand by the name of Claude Roy made an appointment to see him in the little office to which he had been relegated at the *NRF*. Claude Roy was a socialist, an intellectual and a patriot – not necessarily in that order – and an eager anti-fascist. He had come as if on a pilgrimage to seek Paulhan's advice: what could he do?

Paulhan sat him down and made him welcome, and began to speak. 'Defeat is certain. One cannot make war with excessive regard for humanity. Some had no wish to fight for the King of England. Others had no wish to fight for the Committee of Ironworks. In fact no one wished to fight for anyone.' Roy interjected feebly and in vain. Paulhan was reaching his peroration. 'Who knows which is worse? To be convinced that one is right, or (too quickly) that one is wrong? Victory and defeat whisper the same thing: what is done, is well done.'[38] Roy's head was spinning. Naïvely, as he remembers, he asked what he should do. Without a word, Paulhan steered him gently towards a painting on the wall – a Braque – *The Kitchen Table*. The two men looked at it in silence. After a while Paulhan spoke again, of a lemon whose yellow was exactly what it wanted.

Roy took his leave. That evening he received a characteristic note from Paulhan. It read: 'I can scarcely see how we can avoid a long war. All the same, one would wish it short. I feel one should set aside a few acres, a small corner where the air is free, where no one lies (even with the very best of intentions). I don't ask for a big corner, by any means.'[39]

The strategy of still life was a strategy of preservation – self-preservation, to be sure, but in an ideal sense – 'to make the best selves for ourselves that we can', freely, in solidarity, against the grain.[40]

Later in the war, Paulhan took Francis Ponge on his first visit to Braque's studio. Ponge was transported. Most of the time was spent in wordless communion. On their way out, at Paulhan's behest, Braque opened the door to the living room. Ponge immediately recognized a painting he had never seen before, as he put it, a plate of fish beside an iron stove. 'I was seized by an irrepressible sob . . . a sort of spasm between the pharynx and the oesophagus.' His eyes filled with tears. 'No doubt a certain nervous disorder had something to do with it: we were all still rather under-nourished at that time. But painting has hardly ever affected me like that.'[41] Ponge thought Paulhan less affected by the glimpse of the fish; Braque had already given him one of his own. 'The fish prompts me to ponder your personal blend of extreme violence and serenity. I have it near me; we are inseparable,' Paulhan wrote to him beguilingly. 'You remember the words of Vasari: "Mindful of the most important thing in art, this painter left to others the play of fancy, whims, novel ideas. In his paintings you will find neither houses nor trees nor factories. You would search in vain for some of the niceties of art, to which his genius would make no concession." '[42]

Braque's studio turned aquarium throughout the war. Paulhan noticed two little fish in bronze, swimmingly contentedly on the floor near the stove, apparently in their element. 'See what I sculpted from water,' said Braque.[43] On canvas, the striking thing about these creatures was their colour. They were black – black as the market and the years. (col. pl. 13)[44] For those with the right eyes, they were invested with meaning. On one of their earliest appearances they were accompanied by a nondescript vegetable that might have been a spring onion or a leek. In French slang, 'a leek' is someone, in particular someone official, who keeps an eye on things (or people).[45] Perhaps the fish were under surveillance. In spirit, however, they were free. As Francis Ponge dreamed of dinner, so 'the heavy black fish dream of the open sea', in the lullaby of liberation written during these years by Louis Aragon.[46] Goya's golden bream defied war and tyranny in Napoleon's time; Braque's black fish did something similar in Hitler's. As Pierre Reverdy wrote:

Do you demand of the painter that he display on this plate, on this white tablecloth, fish cooked just so? Well, these fish are black, inedible. Already you are bristling with disgust, anger perhaps, because fish of such a beautiful black are not to be found in nature, but only in the privileged human species. But did no one ever tell you that Braque's canvases trailed like fishing nets over the sea floor? . . . And that for me those black fish are a strong and stirring image that I could not have invented or brought to light myself, and that the wholly unpredictable *rapports* that I find in the picture between the dish, the table, the wall panelling and the apples contrive to make a new living being of such towering free will, such determination and authority, that it overwhelms my senses and delights my soul! Black fish that were still not at rock bottom filled my dreams. Black fish confronted with their apples for evermore, beyond the vicissitudes of time, in infinity.[47]

Reverdy's talk of *rapports* was an acute perception. 'The object is everything,' Braque used to say. But this was just the beginning of wisdom, to be inculcated, appreciated and transcended. Let us forget *things*, he counselled later, and consider only *rapports*, a proposition very close to Mallarmé's aspiration 'to paint, not the thing, but the effect it produces'.[48] Braque illustrated this proposition with a variety of examples. 'It is not the boxers that are interesting, but the fight they engage in.' He did not paint things, he explained, he painted space, and then furnished it. 'People are extraordinary! They say to me: "You have painted this tobacco jar and this bowl." And what there is between the two? That is more important.' The same thought was piquantly expressed in his notebook: 'Some would die of thirst between a carafe of water and a cup of coffee.'[49] In due course he arrived at a stronger formulation. 'Objects! For me, they don't exist! What counts is *rapports*. They are infinite.' In more measured terms, 'objects don't exist for me except in so far as a *rapport* exists between them, and between them and myself' – 'between the thing presented and the thing seen'.[50]

Often in his Cubist work, the still life resembled a landscape. The war fish were different. Their blackness was a revelation, stunning still in 1946–7, when they stole the show at the Galerie Maeght and were offered by the artist to the nation, through the good offices of Jean Cassou, founding director of the Musée national d'art moderne and courageous *résistant*, a man always welcome in

Georges Braque's studio. ('Voilà Cassou. Montez, Cassou.')[51] The show was entitled *Black Is a Colour*, a clever presentation, but in truth – or rather in lived experience – black was more of a condition than a colour. The black fish bore witness. Still life may be silent, but the silence in Braque is loud.

There were other images of resilience in adversity: Braque's portrait of his stove – the improvised brazier of the first war metamorphosed into the studio stove of the second – 'that God-stove with its black belly crammed full of fire, that warmed us with its embers during the Occupation, when we were frozen to the marrow with cold.' When he was reminded of it in these terms after the war, Braque smiled his spiritual smile. 'It was a God,' he replied.[52] The painter had his own *rapport* with the pot-bellied beast. He was fascinated by the ash it produced. He added some to his paint, to give it more body. 'Start with ash, the humblest thing, the most useless,' he would repeat, 'and bring that to light and life.'[53]

Francis Ponge for his part was sustained for most of the Second World War by *The Banjo*, also known as *Mandolin and Score* (1941). Wherever he laid his head during the Occupation – Ponge was an active *résistant* – he pinned up a small illustration of that painting, torn out of a cheap picture book, 'a little like my flags, or my reasons for living (and fighting)'. It was the colours he remembered, and their application, 'very bold but properly arranged in all their variety, with an especially violent mauve'. It furnished Ponge's small corner. '*That's* why I could live. Happily. That's the society (of friends) for which I fought . . . In sight of that, during my rare moments of leisure, guided by the Latin alphabet and the roots of our French words, I wrote.'[54]

Tattered reproductions apart, the only way to see new Braques in the period 1940–43 was to secure a visit to the artist's studio. Old Braques were hardly more visible. One or two strays were sold at auction, at modest prices (a *Cubist Composition* for 126,000 francs, a *Pipe and Tobacco* for 96,000 francs).[55] The right customer might just be able to find something suitable in the inner recesses of the Galerie Simon (formerly Kahnweiler). Braque was represented in the Fauvist exhibition at the Galerie de France in 1942, and in the hastily assembled opening exhibition of the Musée national d'art moderne at the Salon des Tuileries the same year. That was all. The Galerie Rosenberg was defunct. 'The Jew Paul Rosenberg', as he was known to his persecutors, had sailed for New York. Unfortunately the precautions he had taken before his departure were not equal to the depredations of the New Order. As a Jew, under Nazi law, he was declared stateless. His possessions could be expropriated with impunity. That was the fate of the works in the bank, 100 more in the château, and the remainder in Paris: some 400 in all. In another damaging blow to the French artistic community, his business records were confiscated by the Einsatzstab Reichsleiter Rosenberg (ERR), the agency headed by the fanatical Alfred Rosenberg, founder of the Combat League for German Culture, whose *Myth of the Twentieth Century* (1930) characterized art falling under the loose category of Expressionism as 'syphilitic, infantile and mestizo'.[56] The mission of the ERR was ruthlessly to 'safeguard' cultural property for the good of the Reich, not to mention the greed of the Reichsmarschall, Hermann Goering, who wolfed down old masters like oysters. Goering did not covet Paul Rosenberg's stock for itself. There was nothing there to appeal to him; it was too much contaminated by the *wild expressionistisch* work of Braque and Picasso. But he did have a use for it, as for other plunder, as currency for the classical works he really wanted. In the twisted economy of aggrandizement that ran rampant under Hitler's imperium, Braques changed hands as a kind of illegal tender.

As an Aryan, albeit a degenerate, the artist himself was in a much stronger position. Even so he remained subject to the vagaries and rapacities of the Nazi régime, at the same time a dictatorship and an organized competition. ('I prefer the English system to the German,' he remarked to the philosopher Jean Grenier. 'In England, no more unemployed, nothing but rentiers; in Germany, nothing but soldiers.')[57] His own deposits at Libourne were discovered during the pillaging of his dealer's. In September 1941 they came to the notice of Goering's personal art adviser, Walter Andreas

Hofer, a former assistant to the hapless Reber. Hofer apprised his master:

Braque is an Aryan and lives in Paris as a painter. His collection is in Bordeaux, put into security by the Devisenschutzkommando [Currency Control Unit], must therefore be unblocked. I negotiated with him personally about his Cranach *Portrait of a Girl*, and held out to him the prospect of an early release of his collection if he were ready to sell his Cranach!!! He is reserving the picture for me, which he intended never to sell, and will notify me of his decision on my next visit to Paris. His other pictures are of no interest to us.[58]

Clearly Braque was temporizing. He may have been successful. No further dealings with Hofer have come to light. Goering is said to have acquired fifty-two Cranachs by the end of the war, but *Portrait of a Girl* was not among them.

The Nazis specialized in corruptions large and small, public and private. The opportunities they offered were legion. Hofer's unwelcome attentions coincided with a broader solicitation. The aristocracy of French artists were invited to go on a guided tour of Germany, to see for themselves how seriously Hitler and his henchmen were taking their artistic responsibilities, to repair Franco-German cultural relations, to generate some propaganda – similar tours were laid on for actors and writers – and to compromise, if not suborn, the tourists. A variety of sweeteners were put before them if they accepted, from the release of French prisoners to the promise of more fuel. The organizers were the German Ambassador, Otto Abetz, whose wife had been friendly with Derain before the war, and the Führer's favourite sculptor, Arno Breker, whose wife had modelled for Derain. Breker himself had spent many years in Paris and knew most of the artists personally. 'They asked me what I thought of Breker,' Braque told Grenier. 'I said: "I think that's amazing." You understand: they ask you that with guns in their pockets!'[59] The caravan divided for the second time. Derain duly went to Germany, as did other veterans of the avant-garde, including Friesz, Van Dongen and Vlaminck. On their

31. The French tourists at the Gare de l'Est, Paris, before their departure for Germany in 1941. Left to right: Despiau, Friesz, Dunoyer de Segonzac, Vlaminck, Van Dongen, Derain. The other members of the party were the painters Legueult and Oudot, and the sculptors Belmondo, Bouchard, Landowski and Lejeune. Denis and Chapelain-Midy are known to have declined the invitation. The trip was announced on the front page of *Paris-Soir*, 1 November 1941.

return, stooge-like, several pronounced themselves favourably impressed.[60]

Braque was not invited. His only recorded comment on the subject was a conciliatory one, tinged with relief. 'Fortunately my painting didn't please; I wasn't invited; otherwise, perhaps I would have gone, on account of the promised releases [of prisoners].'[61] He may well have felt relieved. Nevertheless his comment concealed more than it revealed. It was made to Mourlot, the printer, whose prime concern was to exonerate Derain from the charge of collaboration. In the circumstances Braque was not about to disavow his old friend. He was a *moraliste*; he was not a moralizer. Like Tarrou, Camus' spokesman in *The Plague*, he distanced himself from the thirst for *épuration*, a 'purge' of the guilty. 'Other men will make history . . . I clearly cannot judge those others. There is a quality which is lacking in me to make a reasonable murderer.'[62] But the tie had been broken. Braque and Derain were never reconciled. His relationships with the others went the same way.[63] Braque sometimes happened on Van Dongen in Deauville after the war: not a word was exchanged between them. He had no more dealings with Friesz. Vlaminck was beyond the pale after a poisonous tirade against Picasso and the past, complete with racial overtones ('this Catalan, with the look of a monk and the eyes of an inquisitor'), trumpeted in the periodical *Comœdia* in June 1942. 'Cubism! Perversity of spirit, inadequacy, amoralism, as far from painting as pederasty is from love.'[64]

In fact Braque's painting pleased an influential and surprisingly vocal constituency, given the official promulgations. *Comœdia* also carried an extraordinary tribute from Drieu La Rochelle:

Ah yes, Monsieur, you stand in front of a Braque and you say to yourself: 'What is that?' You can see only a mass of green porridge? . . . Well, from the moment you concede that Braque depicts nothing on his canvas – nothing you have been expecting – that is to say neither a human figure, nor a landscape, but that he uses colours as a musician cherishes sounds, perhaps in due course you will perceive that Braque is a great architect, a great composer, that he builds and harmonizes unlike any of your safe painters, that he is so much more fond of severity and order, science and reason, than such and such a fabricator of nudes, that buttock-dauber you admire in the confectioners of the Champs-Élysées.

Come on, Monsieur, make an effort, hurry up and admire Braque before you go, and before he goes. Otherwise posterity will mock you, as it mocks your esteemed grandfather who became indignant in front of a Degas or a Renoir.

That makes me think that it would be good to prepare an exhibition on Braque or on another of those 'Cubists' of yesterday. That would be a small consolation for the exile of the canvases of the Louvre.[65]

More surprising still, this wish was granted by the authorities. There was a small Braque exhibition at the Galerie de France in May–June 1943 (twelve paintings from 1908–10). And in another of the long cycles of the artist's life, the centre of attention at the 1943 Salon d'Automne was the room devoted to Georges Braque, where twenty-six paintings and nine sculptures were on show for the first time, *memento mori*, kitchen tables and black fish, together with some startling new interiors – a concertina table-top in reverse perspective, a levitating jug, and funnelling up through open windows, smoke-signal clouds, a memory of childhood.

In Occupied Paris the contents of the Braque room caused a suppressed sensation. For French citizens, Braque embodied what French painting could be. For French painters, Braque embodied what painting could be.[66] Jean Bazaine, a combative intellectual partisan of the avant-garde (and an ardent anti-fascist), fulfilled Drieu La Rochelle's best hopes and published an admiring profile. Braque emerged in his own words as a mixture of seer and under-labourer. 'I am among my canvases like a gardener among his trees: I trim, I prune, I train . . . I've finally found my climate.' There was an encomium from Paulhan, replete with the sayings of the master. 'I've always liked to look at rubbish dumps. Events take place in them, just like in a painting. Bodies change their nature. They lose their way, their taste. (A painting should also be distasteful.) One day, I saw this amazing thing: a cyclist stopped in front of a rubbish bin. He pulled out an umbrella handle. The handle was all that remained of the umbrella. He pushed it on to his pump, forcing it a little. That made a pump handle. Painting is just that. It is objects removed from their usual function.'[67] As for the works themselves, their gravity and their humanity were an inspiration. The younger generation – Louttre Bissière, Jean Deyrolle, Nicolas de Staël, many others – needed no instruction from Jean Paulhan. Braque was their *patron*, naturally.[68]

Paulhan's exact verdict, that Braque's painting was at once *acute* and *nourishing*, was loaded with meaning for a public starved of everything from sausages to self-respect.[69] But the adulation was not confined to the *résistant*. Collaborationist critics fell over themselves to praise his work. André Fraigneau was 'enraptured' by the almost funerary colours of the recent still lifes; Braque, he wrote, was 'the Chardin of the ashes'.[70] Nazi functionaries with cultural pretensions came to call. Gerhard Heller swooned. 'He speaks to us and listens to us with great patience and gentleness. He says to me: "Don't call me 'Maître', or 'Monsieur Braque', but quite simply 'Braque', and I shall call you 'Heller'!" '[71] A more substantial figure, the aesthete Ernst Jünger, went first to see the paintings – 'for me, they represent the moment when we emerge from nihilism and gather within us the material for new creations' – and then the painter, whose presentation intrigued him.

Braque, who detests having the model or the object in front of him, always paints from memory, and it is that which gives his paintings the most profound reality, that of dream. On this subject, he related how he had recently put a lobster in one of his paintings, without knowing how many legs that animal had. Later, at the dinner table, once he had been able to check, he had realized that he had given it exactly the right number – he posited a relationship between this fact and Aristotle's conception, according to which each species has its own characteristic number.

As I do whenever I meet creators, I asked him what he had learned as he grew older. He replied that one of the charms of growing old was that one should reach the point at which one no longer had to choose – which I interpret thus: with age, life gains in necessity and loses contingency; it follows a set course.

He added: 'Thus one reaches a point at which creation comes not from *there*, but from *here*.' Saying this, he pointed first to his head, then to his chest. The order of the gestures surprised me, for in general one assumes that work becomes more conscious – and when work is simplified by exercise, by routine, by experience, these remain conscious short-cuts in the creative process. Nevertheless, the gesture made me understand better the path that has led him from Cubism to a more profound realism. There is also progress towards naïveté. In the realms of the mind, there are climbers and there are miners: climbers are driven by the instinct of fatherhood, miners by a taste for matter. Climbers scale the summits, gaining a clear view. Miners fathom ever deeper wells, where the idea is revealed to the mind in its drowsiness, all its fertility and crystalline splendour . . . But the greatest men are driven by both forces – they use a double measure, like the Andes, whose topmost crests seem to cleave the mirror of the seas. Their kingdom, however, extends from the pure air where the condor glides to the monsters of the deep.[72]

Jean Cocteau, however, who had publicly saluted Breker, privately condescended to Braque, 'with his perfect taste of a poor milliner'. Cocteau hesitated to go any further.[73] The notorious Lucien Rebatet, a foaming anti-semite, detected a plot to promote the 'decadent ornamentation' he saw on the walls of the Salon. Disappointingly, he could not find a Jewish conspiracy, however hard he tried. 'This murky business is conducted by Aryans, Aryans deeply ashamed of their foreskin and baptism, but Aryans nonetheless . . . The Jews would have been too cunning to go and hunt out, among M. Gallimard's pen-pushers . . . a ceremonious simpleton amidst all the blunders and nonsenses of the inter-war period, the wretched Jean Paulhan, who analyses the subconscious of that old fox, that crafty schemer, Georges Braque.'[74]

One winter evening a couple of German officers marched into Braque's glacial studio. 'How can a great painter like you work in the cold!' was their cocksure refrain. '*We* will provide you with two lorry-loads of coal.' 'No, thank you,' he replied, with a finesse much toasted among his friends, 'for if I accepted, I should no longer be able to speak well of you.'[75] More exclusive offers met the same response: Braque also refused a commission to make an emblem for the Vichy government. Other invitations he accepted. In March 1944 he attended a star-studded reading of Picasso's Surrealist farce, *Desire Caught by the Tail*, in the apartment of Michel and Louise Leiris. Among the readers were Simone de Beauvoir, Dora Maar, Jean-Paul Sartre and Raymond Queneau, with Albert Camus as stage-hand – a nest of free-thinkers whose very assembly was a conscious act of intellectual resistance. The same month he attended another discreet gathering, at the parish church of St Roch: a funeral mass for Max Jacob, who perished in the transit camp at

Drancy, on the outskirts of Paris, before Treblinka or Auschwitz could claim him. Jacob had been arrested a few days earlier. A direct appeal to Gerhard Heller to intercede, from the wife of another detainee, had been perfunctorily dismissed. 'Max Jacob is a Jew, madame, these people, they're vermin.'[76]

Those without compunction did not like to be refused. It is still not known precisely who in the artistic community was courted by the Nazis. (Or who needed no courting. Gertrude Stein foolishly volunteered to translate Pétain's speeches. Le Corbusier tried to interest his government in some building projects. Gleizes spoke favourably of the Nazi 'revolution'.)[77] According to Breker, Derain and Maillol received lucrative commissions from Berlin. Derain's loyal sidekick Papazoff claimed that the great man received many seductive offers – a castle at his disposal if he would paint the family Ribbentrop – and that he declined.[78] Whatever the truth of such claims, it seems that 'Maître Derain', as General Stulpnagel called him, was not immune to a little fawning from the well-bred German general staff. Braque had the opposite failing: he was not biddable. In Jean Hélion's cool estimation, 'he is a patriot, even a jingoist, but too sensible to have gone in for being servile and licking the boots of the Nazis, like Derain in his senility'.[79] The rejectionist stance of no commissions and no concessions cannot have gone unnoticed. Georges Braque's presence on the artists' tour of the Fatherland would have been a major propaganda coup for the Germans. It was not his painting that deterred them – Vlaminck's painting was equally unacceptable, in theory, but examples of it could be seen in gallery windows all over Paris – it was his disposition. Braque's friend Laurens was not invited either; his opinions were well known.[80] Henri Laurens was a man of principle. Kahnweiler remembered him fondly as a modest anarchist, one of the very few people to turn down the Legion of Honour ('Oh no, that would make Marthon [Marthe] laugh too much.')[81] His fellow sculptor Lobo, who had fought against Franco in the Spanish Civil War, found refuge in the Laurenses' home throughout the war – courageous hospitality. Anti-fascists, they felt, had to make common cause.[82]

Braque's posture is perhaps best encapsulated in Jean Grenier's expression *active passivity*. 'True wisdom is not of a rational order, nor yet in belonging to a faith, it lies in a special quality of being, an "active passivity" that is rooted in living sensation, feeling, palpitation.' It was echoed in Braque's reflection on fatalism: 'Contrary to belief, fatalism is not a passive state.'[83] If these formulations suggest a family resemblance to the quietism of the *Tao Te Ching*, it was not an accidental one. Grenier was Camus' teacher; he spent an ethical lifetime working on the problem of moral choice and the limits of commitment. He too was steeped in the old Chinese. The Taoist requirement to practise a certain measure of asceticism was no more of a burden to him than it was to Braque. Principled non-engagement had a strong appeal for both of them.

> Therefore the sage is square-edged but does not scrape,
> Has corners but does not jab,
> Extends himself but not at the expense of others,
> Shines but does not dazzle.[84]

Georges Braque in being, in Paris, was already important, as a kind of existential reassurance and symbol of hope. 'He who does not lose his station,' says Lao Tzu, 'will endure.' Braque endured. He was a believer in absolute truths who acknowledged human frailties. 'Now I accept being what I am, I have learned modesty. All I say is that on this earth there are pestilences and there are victims – and as far as possible one must refuse to be on the side of the pestilence.'[85]

Braque did not comment on current affairs. He said as little about this war as he did about the last one. His only war story, as told to friends: at the time of the abortive raid on Dieppe, in August 1942, he was in Varengeville. Planes flew over the house; there was a prolonged bombardment; in the village a German battery was put out of action by British commandos, who were rewarded by the proprietor of the Hôtel de la Terrasse with the pick of his cellar. Wisely the commandos did not loiter, but invited the hotelier to come back with them. In the evening Braque went out see what had happened. He found a discarded parachute and made off with some of it. Stopped by the Germans, he said he was a painter, short of materials; they let him go. The parachute silk made several fine cravats.[86]

Other stories went stubbornly untold. A fleeting reference in one of Braque's letters to Paulhan indicates that the Germans felt it necessary to have a number of conversations with him on the subject of 'Jewish goods' in his possession (possibly an allusion to Carl Einstein's papers), which Braque nonetheless managed to retain.[87] For the rest, he meditated on fate. 'To explore fate is to discover oneself.'[88]

Braque held. In the historical reckoning, however, one indignity has been visited upon him. John Richardson has proposed that he lurched so far to the right in the period between the wars as to become an adherent of the ultra-nationalist Croix de Feu (Cross of Fire), a body whose programme and ethos lead some commentators to describe it as fascist or quasi-fascist.[89] Founded in 1927, the Croix de Feu began as an old comrades' association, originally restricted to holders of the Croix de Guerre. In the early 1930s, under the sway of Colonel François de La Rocque, it became more of a social movement and a political force. It was dissolved into the Parti Social Français in 1936. These organizations addressed themselves to 'the true France'. Their god was Order. They were virulently anti-communist ('muscovite and cosmopolite slime'), but their appeal extended far beyond the lunatic fringe.[90] The Croix de Feu/ PSF attracted more supporters than any other party of the day, boasting as many as 1.2 million members. There is no evidence that Braque was one of them.[91] His name does not figure in their membership lists, nor in their propaganda literature, nor in their leaders' correspondence. Nor is there any indication in the file kept on Braque as he advanced through the grades of the Legion of Honour, a file in which questions of that sort are routinely asked and answered.[92] No doubt the records are incomplete; and in the nature of the case, there must be some whose allegiance was never recorded in the first place. But Georges Braque was not an island, however much he might have wished it. Especially during the Occupation, his allegiance was a matter of moment. His sympathies were under scrutiny, as never before. And if the Croix de Feu or its successors had had the slightest inkling that he was in their camp they would surely have tried to make use of it.

Movements of any stripe, political, social, or cultural, were not for Braque. To his dying day he defended his own revolutionary practice, and his partnership with Picasso, but always fought shy of Cubism as a denomination. The 'ism' was too doctrinaire, too programmatic, too collective. Ideas were there to be effaced. Systems were the enemies of creation. Associations were for followers. Georges Braque followed no one, he insisted, except perhaps Cézanne. Braque *le solitaire* was not a joiner. When others joined him, it was time to move on.

10. 'Light like a bird': The Solitaire

In October 1944 Braque did not join the Communist Party. Picasso did, immediately before the Salon d'Automne – the Liberation Salon – a great exhalation, and a celebration of Picasso as hero, the painter-resister, prolific under pressure.[1] The Picasso of legend was being created, but the legend was no more than a convenient fiction, as Christian Zervos pointed out at the time. 'The anecdotes are false, Picasso's participation in the Resistance is false. Picasso quite simply retained his dignity during the Occupation, as millions of people have done here. But he never joined the Resistance . . . His work itself is the greatest resistance.'[2] Plighting his troth to the Party may have worried him more than he allowed. Marcelle was convinced that he did not want to take the plunge on his own. He spent a week with the Braques in Varengeville, trying to persuade his old partner to come in with him, and make a joint declaration.[3] This would have been even more of a sensation, but Braque remained unmoved, even when appealed to by Simone Signoret.[4] He had as much feeling for the workers of the world as Picasso. Some of his best friends were communists. But his realism was too protean for a socialist straitjacket.[5] In any case, done like this, it smacked of a publicity stunt. Gesture politics fell into the same category as current affairs. Demonstration was foreign to him. The loathsome occupiers were on the run at last. This was the time for painting, not pantomime. Picasso's announcement was disappointing, perhaps, but not unexpected. 'It's hardly surprising that he should have joined the Communist Party: it gives him a platform.' The soap box was as unsuitable as the social whirl. 'Picasso used to be a great painter,' he observed. 'Now he is merely a genius.'[6]

As for Braque, according to Picasso, 'What Braque is doing now isn't much like what I'm doing any more. For him the fight is over!' Picasso was inclined to say that Braque's later work had 'charm'. When it came to trading words, he was not about to yield gracefully. 'He too wanted to do apples [*pommes*], like Cézanne,' quipped Picasso, 'and could only ever do potatoes [*pommes de terre*].'[7] The post-war relationship of these two intimate adversaries, Picasso and Anti-Picasso, in René Char's coinage, is popularly recounted as an endless game of one-upmanship, a tournament in which the jousting had become the sole *raison d'être*.[8] 'It's well hung,' said Picasso, of an exhibition of Braque's paintings. 'It's well cooked,' said Braque, of an exhibition of Picasso's ceramics.[9] On a visit to La Californie, Picasso's grandiose villa in Cannes, Braque excused himself from seeing the work in the studio in favour of a ride in the photographer David Douglas Duncan's new gullwing Mercedes. Picasso was furious. When Braque did see the work, on other occasions, he said nothing, provoking the same reaction. Once he was so enthusiastic about some scrap in the courtyard that Picasso told him that he could have it. To everyone's surprise, he did.[10] Exceptionally, they still made each other a present of a painting. Picasso gave Braque a *Sleeping Woman* (1944). Braque gave Picasso a *Teapot and Apples* (1942). There is some suggestion that Picasso would have preferred a black fish. He sent Braque one of his own still-life ceramic plates, with inlaid fish bones and a slice of lemon, hoping possibly to prompt an exchange, only to find that Braque had treated it as a joke.[11] Nevertheless he was fond of his teapot, whatever he might have said about apples. The painting functioned as a kind of barometer. During calm periods it was prominently displayed on a wall of the studio. When a storm blew up – if Picasso was particularly incensed at some act of omission or commission on Braque's part – it vanished. When the air cleared it was restored to its rightful place.

Picasso still followed Braque's every move. Exhibition venues and museum purchases were closely monitored. In 1961 Braque was accorded the signal honour of an exhibition at the Louvre, a remarkably personal one, *L'Atelier de Braque*. 'He is at home in the Louvre,' wrote Jean Cassou by way of introduction, '. . . because this craftsman, this man of the studio, who in his studio patiently develops the implications of his first idea, finds in the Louvre (which is also a continuing construction) the craftsmanship of history, and, for our collective memory, the very image of continuity . . .'[12] The living Braque's apotheosis in the Louvre, the palace of bliss for the souls of the dead, caused Picasso acute discomfort. Nor had time healed the running sore of relative prices. Picasso saw no reason why his prices should be lower than Braque's. Braque saw no reason why his prices should be lower than Picasso's. More often than not the issue resolved itself in Picasso's favour, but not as often as Picasso would have liked.

There were other irritants. Thirty years after Braque's thoughts and reflections first saw the light of day came another war diary, the *Cahier de Georges Braque* (1947), compiled, in the author's words, 'to see how things have evolved'. The *Cahier* appeared in a limited edition of striking format, handwritten and handtooled (or doodled) by Braque, reproduced in black and white photolithography by Mourlot.[13] A second printing quickly followed, equally expensive and equally popular. A mass-market pocket edition, minus doodles, was issued by Gallimard in 1952. 'To the reader, these bitters from a road already long.' (b/w pl. 13)[14]

Increasingly with age, and especially after the publication of the *Cahier*, Braque was prone to produce a maxim without warning in the middle of a conversation, and deliver it, like the punch line to an unspoken story. 'If I want to put my shoe on and I don't have a shoehorn I can use a teaspoon.' This was often used on Picasso in the 1950s. Another variant was reported by Jean Paulhan. 'If we put our shoes on ten times a day and ate only once, spoons would be called shoehorns.'[15] The habit may have functioned in part as a protective screen. Picasso found it tiresome. The mystical turn in his old friend's post-war discourse made him squirm. 'You see, I have made a great discovery,' Braque would say: 'I no longer believe in anything. Objects don't exist for me except in so far as a harmonious *rapport* exists between them, and also between them and me. When one attains this harmony, one reaches a state of intellectual *néant* [nothingness, emptiness, oblivion]. In this way everything becomes possible, everything becomes right, and life is a perpetual revelation. That's true poetry!' Or again, in a late interview, 'I tend towards *le néant*, that is to say to the annihilation of the concept of a thing in order to reach the thing itself. Then words lose their meaning: we're no longer able to say anything in front of a painting. No matter what the end, what counts is the path towards it . . . without ever attaining it. Fortunately.'[16] Picasso had no patience with that sort of talk. 'Next thing, he'll invoke the fourth dimension!'[17]

There was a streak of jealousy in Picasso's show of dismissiveness. 'He doesn't know life,' Picasso had protested to Malraux. Yet he envied Braque his self-sufficiency.[18] He was jealous of the marches Braque had stolen – *Fruit Dish and Glass* (1912), the first *papier collé*, complete with *faux bois* wallpaper purchased in a shop in Avignon while Picasso was away in Paris – and of their claim on posterity. (col. pl. 9)[19] He was jealous of the tricks Braque continued to turn. Whenever he visited Douglas Cooper at the Château de Castille, near Avignon, he would go and study *Studio VIII* (1954–5), hanging in pride of place above Cooper's bed. Asked what he thought, he would only mutter to himself, 'Don't understand, don't understand.' Braque's mysterious *Studios* (1949–56), the refuge of all things and all notions, as Lao Tzu says, challenged Picasso to raise his game. He responded, indirectly, in the first of his own variations on the most celebrated of all studios, Velázquez's *Las Meninas*, in 1957. But he could not match the elemental strangeness, the fathomlessness, the total envelopment achieved by Braque in that dark durance – 'besieged by colours, life, beset by signs', in Celan's phrase.[20]

Ultimately, Picasso was jealous of the *homme intégral*. That Braque could do what he could not was a puzzle and a provocation. That Braque could *be* what he could not was a regular torment. The torment issued in accusation. 'Picasso would even accuse Braque of having imitated him during the Cubist period,' recorded Geneviève Laporte, who loved him.[21] It was not the accused who was diminished by such pettiness. Morally and metaphysically, Braque had a stature that was beyond rivalry, unapproachable. Between Picasso and Anti-Picasso, Picasso was found wanting. He was sufficiently aware to know. To some degree, perhaps, his antics were a mask for that sorrow. John Richardson watched him confront *Fruit Dish and Glass*, forty years on, at the Château de Castille. Picasso glared at it as if staring out an old foe. 'The bastard,' he said, with a theatrical shrug. 'He waited until my back was turned. On my way home, I'll stop at that wallpaper shop and see what they have left.'[22]

In Paris, gamesmanship revolved chiefly around pliancy; that is to say, how far Braque could be made to do Picasso's bidding. The prize was lunch. Not long after Françoise Gilot began living with Picasso, in 1946, they called unannounced on Braque. It was just before twelve, and the aroma of roasting lamb wafted them upstairs to the studio, where Braque showed them his latest work. 'Well,' said Picasso, 'I see you're returning to French painting. But you know, I never would have thought you would turn out to be the Vuillard of Cubism.' Braque, impassive, deployed some more canvases. As the clock neared one, Picasso began to sniff the air appreciatively. 'Oh, that smells good,' he sighed, 'that roast lamb.' Braque continued his tour of the studio. 'I'd like to show you my sculpture, too,' he said. 'Please do,' said Picasso. 'Françoise will enjoy that.' Braque produced some bas-reliefs in the *Theogony* tradition: horses' heads, chariots. 'That lamb smells to me as though it were done,' remarked Picasso. 'Overdone, in fact.' 'I think Françoise might like to see my new lithographs,' suggested Braque, pulling out some samples. From time to time Marcelle would look in, smile, and withdraw. After her third exit, Picasso volunteered, 'You know, you've never shown your paintings of the Fauve period to Françoise.' The Fauve paintings were in the dining room. They trooped downstairs. Diligently Braque showed Françoise every painting in the living room and the dining room. It was observed that one extra place had been laid at the table; Picasso and Françoise were introduced to Braque's nephew, also visiting that day. 'That lamb smells burnt to me now,' said Picasso. 'It's a shame.' Braque resumed his discussion with Françoise. Picasso changed course. 'There's one of your recent paintings up in the atelier that I didn't really get a good look at,' he said to Braque. 'I'd like to go upstairs and see it again.' Back they went upstairs. For over an hour Picasso re-examined the paintings they had already seen. Braque brought out more. Finally they said their goodbyes. It was four-thirty. Picasso was seething. *Teapot and Apples* disappeared from the wall. And yet, as he calmed down, the complexion of the encounter began to alter. It became apparent that Picasso was impressed, in spite of himself, by the way in which Braque had played out his hand. *Teapot and Apples* reappeared, until the next time. 'You know, I like Braque,' insisted Picasso.[23]

Braque kept his distance. Picasso made overtures, without success. 'Why doesn't Braque come and join me?' he asked Leymarie plaintively at Mougins, site of another villa, in 1961. 'In each house I always keep a floor for him.' This sounds far-fetched, but it was essentially true. In the mid-1950s Picasso offered Braque a studio at La Californie, so that they could cook up something together again, as in Céret forty years earlier.[24] Braque preferred to stay with his new dealer, Aimé Maeght, at Saint-Paul-de-Vence. As Braque knew full well, Picasso despised Maeght as an acquisitive upstart, a man with the sensibility of a shark, and pushy with it. Maeght was all of that – he once told Heinz Berggruen that he, Maeght, was to be the next Minister of Culture – but he was also a promoter of brilliance, unafraid of splashing out on people and things, and entirely capable of surrounding himself with the best of both.[25] Immediately after the war, he tried hard to acquire Picasso, but Picasso was not for sale, certainly not on an exclusive basis, and Kahnweiler had prior claims on whatever became available. Undaunted, Maeght took up Braque. The circumstances were propitious; Braque was willing. Rosenberg was ensconced in New York, with no immediate prospect of return. Braque would not abandon Paris, as he put it, despite the encouragement he received. Periodic meetings during Rosenberg's flying visits were friendly but unsatisfactory. Dealing could not be done at one remove.[26] Kahnweiler for his part was back in Paris after a second exile, indomitable, but with reservations about Braque: his prices were too high, his paintings too 'well made'.[27] Kahnweiler was unshakable in his prejudices, as in everything. For him, Picasso came first. For Braque, there was no going back a second time.

Enter Aimé Maeght. Maeght cultivated Braque, with great

respect, and became his friend as well as his patron. He was absorbed into the dealer's *ménage*. The painter took a keen interest in the idea of a foundation for modern art at Saint-Paul; Maeght himself said that it was Braque who urged on him the project that would help him overcome his grief after the death of one of his children. Braque would quiz André Verdet, a local resident, on progress. 'How's it doing? Are things moving down there? Maeght is an obstinate, stubborn devil. We misjudge him, he's thought to be distant, at bottom he's terribly shy. We owe him this museum; it matters.'[28] Braque 'appreciated homage', says James Lord cattily, and he may well have enjoyed the cosseting and the recognition that came with it, but he also enjoyed the contact with Maeght's extended family – Braque loved children – and he remained clear-eyed about his dealer.[29] Maeght was accustomed to taking his pick of the work of his artists for his own collection. In 1955 Douglas Cooper had his heart set on *Studio VIII* (col. pl. 16). Fearing that Maeght would keep it for himself, Cooper struck an underhand but decisive blow by informing Braque that the dealer identified it from the others in the series as 'the one with two large red armchairs'.[30]

Picasso himself cast a green eye on his bounty (a Rolls for Braque), and on his stable – Chagall, Giacometti, Miró, a dozen other blue-chip modernists – and wondered whether it might not be gratifying to assume the leading role in such an enterprise: a fancy pre-empted by Braque, who made it clear that it was Picasso or him.[31] After long experience of running in tandem, first with Kahnweiler and then with Rosenberg, Braque evidently wanted a commercial separation. Picasso was an incorrigible hooligan. Hooliganism was not conducive to asceticism. In the late 1940s there was a period of estrangement. Picasso and Anti-Picasso saw nothing of each other for several years.[32]

'We had quarrelled,' wrote Sartre of himself and Camus. 'A quarrel is nothing . . . just another way of living *together*, without losing sight of one another in the narrow little world where it is our lot to live. It didn't stop me thinking about him, feeling his eyes fixed on the page of the book, or on the newspaper that I was reading, and wondering: "What has he to say about that? What is he saying about it *now*?"'³³ So it was with Braque and Picasso. In spite of all the vexations and frustrations, many severe, the relationship could not be reduced to mere rivalry. At bottom was an ineradicable *tendresse*. In August 1945 Braque underwent a two-hour operation for stomach ulcers. His doctors had been afraid of something even more serious, but this was bad enough to incapacitate him for several weeks. During the worst of it a distraught Picasso came to visit him every day.³⁴ In health, too, there were reasons for Picasso to call. The deliberate focus on Françoise on the day of the lost lunch was part of a larger pattern. Picasso made a point of presenting each of his women to Braque, as if for his approval.³⁵ Naturally Braque did not pass judgment, except for the back-handed compliment on classical beauty and traditional taste that Picasso was so fond of repeating: 'In matters of love, you have kept in line with the masters.'³⁶ Little had changed. Picasso still sought corroboration. Braque was still the gauge. The revelry of the relationship had abated, but the weathering of the past they shared only served to enrich its significance, much as Braque conceived of a painting gaining poetry, like the patina of a bronze, by itself, over time.³⁷

In June 1947 Yvonne Zervos mounted an exhibition of contemporary art in the cathedral-like chambers of the Palais des Papes at Avignon. For two of the artists involved, it was the realization of a dream. The poet René Char (a native of the region), who had a hand in bringing it about, went to see it early one morning. The place was completely deserted, except for 'a curious silhouette' in meditative pose on the steps –

Braque! I was moved when I saw him like that. He didn't get up; he said to me 'Sit down.' He told me how, many years ago, he used to come there with Picasso when the day's work was done. They would buy a sandwich, then prowl around that semi-abandoned palace where the straw spilled out from the gates. The superb walls of the great audience room, that stone, the same as that of the Pont du Gard [nearby] . . . Braque would have liked to ask the Romans how they did it . . . The two painters would imagine their pictures there, making plans for an

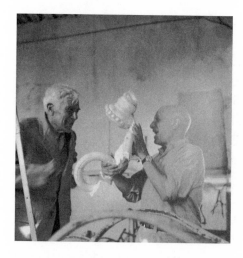

32. Sharing a joke with Picasso at Vallauris in the South of France in 1954, by Lee Miller

exhibition that they punctured with a burst of laughter. But the unhoped-for always happens.[38]

The dialogue was not dependent on physical encounter, but from 1951, after a tense reconciliation, they met again regularly every year. Braque would stay for a month or more at Saint-Paul-de-Vence, not painting but recouping, and visit Picasso at one or other of his abodes on the Riviera. Once in a while, particularly if there was a need for greater circumspection, Picasso would visit Braque at Varengeville. Bonhomie prevailed, though these meetings were not guaranteed free of the occasional barb. 'A lot of Cubists started out as caricaturists,' remarked Braque one day. 'They tried to make us forget it by the narrowness and severity of an Aristotelian discipline.' This was a dig at Gris (long dead), whose intellectual leanings he had always depreciated. It cut closer to home, however, for the one who typified the artist-caricaturist, in Braque's estimation, was Picasso. 'What interested Picasso was the play of forms,' Braque explained to an interviewer a few years later.

He used to play . . . what's more, he's still playing. His great talent is to be a caricaturist in a good and true sense; as always, as he played at that moment [in the Cubist period], as with Velázquez later, as with the famous story of the comb . . . I'd done my apprenticeship in woods and marbles, and I still had an implement, called a comb, that is used to do the grain in the wood. Picasso saw that implement and used it to do the moustaches in his paintings. He has revived the fortunes and novel possibilities of everything to the point of caricature, in the pictorial sense of the word, of course.[39]

Françoise Gilot continued to call on Braque from time to time after she left Picasso in 1953, drawn to his practice and his self-possession. She was struck by his expressivity, and the integrity of his attention: 'All of Braque was always there.'[40] Braque treated her as a fellow-painter. (Gilot herself had been under contract to Kahnweiler, a contract promptly terminated after the break-up.) He spoke to her of Cézanne, and of Cézanne's importance to him, and showed her another painting, one of his treasured possessions, *Bouquet of Peonies in a Green Jar*, by Paul Cézanne. This work hung in his bedroom, together with the landscape by his father and one of his own skull paintings. It was possessed of tutelary properties. First of all, it was unvarnished. Varnish was anathema to Braque. Healthy paintings did not need it. His Cézanne came straight from the studio, he would point out, straight from the hands of the master. More intriguing still, the painting was unfinished, or so people thought. Braque dissented, and delighted in so doing. He must have delighted also in the metamorphic confusions of its identity. The peonies are roses, according to Vollard's stockbook; and in the original *catalogue raisonné* of Cézanne's work, published by Rosenberg in 1936, the green jar is a blue vase.[41] Floral sensations rather than botanical specimens, they explode out of the jar like a rocket out of a bottle. Braque never tired of studying them. The fascination lay in what was painted and what was left unpainted – the fireworks and the blanks in between – not the thing, but the effect it produces. His own late flowerpieces absorbed that lesson. 'The error of so many painters,' he ruminated, 'is that they begin with the flower. For, after the flower, it's over. What is there after the flower? Death, when the flower wilts. While from the root to the flower there is . . . all of life.'[42] What Braque glimpsed in the *Bouquet of Peonies* was the life with which he so passionately identified. 'Cézanne! He swept away the idea of mastery in painting. He was not a rebel, Cézanne, but one of the greatest revolutionaries; this will never be sufficiently emphasized. He gave us a taste for risk. His personality is always in play, with his weaknesses and his strengths. With him, we're poles apart from decorum. He melds his life in the work, the work in his life.' Such was his admiration for Cézanne when he was a young man, Braque told Richardson, that he wanted nothing more than to paint like him. 'Fortunately my wish was never granted – if it had been, I might never perhaps have painted like Braque.'[43]

On one of her last visits, Françoise brought her son with her. Claude Picasso was then a teenager. Braque cried when he saw him. He said he looked like his father when they first met, more than fifty years ago.[44]

The rope frayed but never broke. It was forever – 'I repeat, forever' – as Braque impressed upon André Verdet. The true measure of their connectedness has remained elusive. 'An artistic cooperation,' hazarded Verdet. 'Better than that,' rejoined Braque: 'a union in independence.'[45]

When they met in the South of France, they ate out. One of Picasso's favourite pastimes around the table was baiting Braque about the ceiling decoration he did for the Louvre in 1953: enormous black birds, with a wingspan of 3 metres, in a star-bright cerulean sky. Picasso enjoyed the stories circulating at the time of someone surprising the painter at work on the birds, commenting inanely, 'So *you* do doves, as well', and being unceremoniously shown the door. The joke here was on Braque, as 'copyist' of Picasso, but the joke on Picasso was no less serious. He hated not to be asked.[46] The commission was initiated by the Director of Museums, Georges Salles, a man of unusual enlightenment who went so far as to collect modern art himself (including even the Cubist work of Georges Braque).[47] Salles felt that the Louvre was at risk of losing touch with the present; he was supported by André Malraux, a member of the council. There was reason for concern. The museum was not only walled but ceilinged in the past. For the Louvre, Braque had a hint of danger, as well as a good pedigree.

'Among the great names of today,' ran the briefing notes for the Director, 'his represents a very French art; also an art little discussed. This true revolutionary has something almost reassuring for the man in the street.' Happily, the Director himself managed to improve on this. In answer to the question, 'Why Braque?', he replied with aplomb, 'Because this great artist is also a man of perfect taste. Such a task requires both qualities.'[48]

For Braque, the commission was by no means a foregone conclusion. He took his time about going to inspect the gallery in question, the Salle Henri II, whose existing ceiling was a riot of sixteenth-century wood-carving, not calculated to appeal, and whose exhibits were the Etruscan objects with which he seemed to have some affinity, as the Director did not fail to remind him. Salles left him sitting on a banquette, craning upward, interrogating the possibilities. When he returned, Braque appeared encouraged by his reconnaissance but still guarded about his intentions. His response was characteristic: 'It looks different and better than I'd imagined. I see why you thought of asking me. But I cannot give you my answer now. The answer must come of its own accord.' In fact, when he got home, he told Marcelle, 'They want me to do a ceiling, but I'm not going to.' 'Of course, you're far too old to start doing ceilings,' replied Marcelle in her practical way, before leaving for Varengeville. Three days later Braque telephoned – a rare occurrence – to tell her 'I'm doing it.' Shortly afterwards he remarked: 'Even if one didn't wish it thus, I'll do it for myself.' And so, at seventy, Georges Braque tackled his first ceiling. By a curious circularity, he renewed his apprenticeship. The frieze in the Ceylon Tea House ('very 1900') was followed by the decoration in the Louvre, after an interval of half a century. He did it for himself, for posterity, for the Etruscans, maybe a little for the admirable Georges Salles, and for an asking price of 10 million old francs. 'If they'd wanted a ceiling for a room containing Veroneses and Titians, I wouldn't have accepted,' he told a friend. 'For pottery, it was a different matter.'[49]

The asking price was readily accepted. The design was not. The initiator himself had qualms at the outset. Salles was taken by surprise. He had expected Braque to offer a Braque, enlarged, and rehung. Instead, he found the artist thinking ceilings, as he put it, not easel paintings. As with other commissions, in other media, Braque entered directly into the spirit of the thing. Made-to-measure Braques were still not for him. What he produced was his own thinking-in-keeping. He thought in colour and matter and space. 'Colour needs room to breathe.'[50] For the Salle Henri II, he thought *animation*. He wanted the wide blue yonder to pulsate. He wanted the great black birds to take wing. He wanted people to sense the ceiling as they sense the sky, without looking up. The vision came slowly. Once it crystallized, Braque was not to be deflected from it. 'If you ask me to make changes,' he told Salles amicably, 'I will say to you what I said to [Louis] Jouvet [the impresario] who asked me to introduce a green into a certain décor: "Add green if you want, but for my part I can't, because I don't see it." It's the same for this ceiling. I see it so, and I'm incapable of seeing it otherwise.'[51] He made several models to enable him to establish the tonal values, sending his assistant, Pierre Pallut, up a tall ladder with pieces of sky so that he could consider the effect from below. The vast canvases that would become the decorative panels themselves were painted in another room, on the floor, and fixed in position only at the very end. Braque worried constantly about the blueness of the blue (a difficult tone to mix, especially over a large surface area). 'Ah! That blue, that's what tormented me most! It makes the ceiling. Cold, icy, next to the warm gold of the carved wood; I was afraid it would be too hard. One day I added some black, but I soon came back to the purest shade.' (col. pl. 14)[52]

Two months passed. The blue began to throb. More and more matter was caked on the birds. Close to, it was as if they had real body. They seemed so heavy they might fall. Near the end, Salles was amazed to find them looking more like a relief than a painting, solid and substantial, yet full of life, and strangely mobile. For all their corporeality, they had a lightness that bore them up. 'One should be light like a bird, and not like a feather,' as Valéry aptly said. So with the black birds. On the ceiling, they would fly. 'The amazing virtue of his images derives from the fact that they are not at all threatening,' argued Francis Ponge: 'they share the heaviness, thickness, ungainliness, weakness and precariousness of creatures . . . Braque's birds are much heavier than air, as birds really are, but they fly better than all other painted birds because, like real birds, they start from the ground, come down to feed, and fly back up.'[53]

Braque applied the finishing touches, put away his brushes, and permitted himself a moment of exultation. 'Ah! This has never been done before! A ceiling like this has never been conceived before. For me, it's an event. What would they say, the painters of yesterday, if they could see it? Never mind, we must be of our own time.' Georges Salles confessed that he found something moving about the birds turning in the sky. 'Their truth is the unknown of all creation. Their faithfulness, under many guises, was to incarnate the constancy of the bird.' The artist was delighted. 'What you say is truly rewarding. To do something like that, one must feel that one is being supported. It's an undertaking!'[54]

The undertaking was greeted with a mixture of indifference and hostility. Behind the scenes, the Director had already been forced to stake his personal authority on the continuance of the project. After the unveiling, dissension became open. The Friends of the Louvre were not ready for Braque or for his crudely painted, semi-abstract apologies for birds. If the ceiling was indeed of its own time – very 1950s – they were not ready for that either. There were resignations. With two conspicuous exceptions (Cassou and Leymarie), the museum world was lukewarm, at best, in its re-action.[55] Among the critics, Georges Limbour was almost alone in appraising it sympathetically.[56] The state withdrew its hand as if bitten. Apart from the design of a 50-centime postage stamp in 1961 – perhaps inevitably, a white bird – there would be no more official commissions.[57] The public, or at least that faction disposed to complain, did so with feeling. 'These canvases, hardly worthy of the brush of a six-year-old, dishonour one of the rooms of the Louvre,' wrote a disgusted student.[58] Other artists made snide remarks.[59] Even some of the friends of Braque were ambivalent. 'His ceiling isn't so bad,' thought de Staël, who went to see it in

33. Etruscan antiquity in the Louvre

progress, 'but at the last moment he got scared and risked nothing; I've no idea at all whether it's the glory or his eyes.'[60]

If the perpetrator was aware of the recriminations, he was undismayed. Not to be outdone, Maeght commissioned a mural decoration for his villa in Saint-Paul, and later a stained-glass window for the foundation. Alfred Hitchcock, too, was fascinated by Braque's birds, and ordered from Maeght a huge mosaic on that theme for his garden in Santa Cruz, California, hoping in vain that the artist himself would come and lay it.[61] Duncan Phillips, bowled over by the *Studio* paintings exhibited at the Galerie Maeght in 1956, dearly wanted to buy one, but could not afford $95,000. By way of consolation, he sought and received Braque's permission – for a consideration of one million old francs – to have a bas-relief made after one of his birds in flight. Executed in brown granite by Pierre Bourdelle, it was placed over the door of a new annexe in 1960, and keeps a benevolent eye on the Phillips Collection to this day.[62] In 1966, shortly before his death, Phillips acquired the elegantly simplified *Bird* (1956), observed in suspension in a multifoliate world, a painting with roots worthy of Cézanne. 'At the end of its invisible thread, Braque's bird no more escapes terrestrial fatality than a particle of rock in Cézanne's geology.'[63]

The bird announces Braque's majestic late work. Yet the import of these air-heavers has never been satisfactorily resolved.[64] Their origins are suitably mysterious. A passing resemblance to the decorations on the antiquities in the room beneath the Louvre ceiling

34. The first meeting between Braque and Saint-John Perse, with Paulhan, in 1958, in front of *The Bird and Its Nest* (1955)

appears incontestable, but in truth they are more Braquian than Etruscan. For Saint-John Perse in his hymn to the avian, and the Braquian, *The Order of Birds* (1962) – another telling encounter between painter and poet, with twelve colour etchings by Georges Braque – the birds 'were no longer cranes from the Camargue nor seagulls from the Normandy coasts or Cornwall, herons from Africa or the Ile-de-France, nor kites from Corsica or the Vaucluse, nor wood-pigeons from the Pyrenean passes; but all birds of the same fauna and the same vocation, upholding a new caste and of ancient lineage'.[65]

Braque and Perse met only twice, in 1958 and 1961, yet they had an almost intuitive understanding of each other. Perse broke his rule never to write to order by accepting a publisher's invitation to supply the text for a volume intended for Braque's eightieth birthday. He knew the artist's work – and demonstrated an astonishing command of 'the secret force of its "ecology"'. He also found the man profoundly sympathetic, as he said, a highly developed soul, continually questing: 'For my part, I saw nothing but nobility;

and this distant flash of a dream that seemed to want to describe, uninterrupted, a progression of inalienable things.'[66] Braque in turn was entranced by a fragment from one of Perse's earlier works, which became an epigraph for *The Order of Birds*: 'The bird more vast on its course sees man free of his shadow at the boundary of his estate.'[67]

The two men exchanged compliments and proofs by letter. 'Mon cher grand Braque,' wrote Perse in salutation. Braque followed suit, paying tribute to the poet (who was awarded the Nobel prize for literature in 1960) in his best Zen manner. 'I read *Birds* which moved me greatly. You push literature into the background.'[68] Their collaboration was also a conjunction. Perse had already composed what he called a poetic meditation on birds in general; he interleaved a further meditation on *Bracchus avis avis* in particular. Braque had several etchings ready to hand, before he read the text; he then made three or four more. The result is remarkably seamless: a true concordance, as its printer Aldo Crommelynck has said.[69] Braque's etchings are thrilling. Perse thought them better than beautiful. He was especially taken with the last one, boldly dispersed elements of bird, black on white, analysis and conclusion (col. pl. 16).

Thanks to Crommelynck, Braque had discovered a new freedom in his printmaking. The printer had noticed that 'in Braque's paintings the space separating the objects depicted was as important as the objects themselves, and that this had never been so with his prints . . . Why not, I thought, do this with etchings? It is perfectly possible.' He inducted the painter into the secrets of aquatint.[70] Braque was as patient in this technique as in all the others. His metal plates were dipped in acid as many as five or six times to achieve the required tone and surface texture. Days would pass with each variation; more days would pass while he pondered further emendation. Braque was not interested in quick results. Painting or printmaking, there was no formula but 'to be present', at once exacting and receptive. 'Braque has a terrific eye and he is always right,' marvelled Janine Crémieux, publisher and expeditor of *The Order of Birds*, 'it is marvellous to work with him.'[71] A sour Vlaminck called him the lead and zinc worker. 'One can see him pushing straight ahead like a farmer ploughing his furrow,' wrote Jean Grenier, utilizing one of Braque's favourite images, 'his gaze fixed between the horse's ears.'[72] Time and chance would take care of the rest. 'What gave them substance,' he would say of his etchings, 'was accident.'[73]

Henri Deschamps, Braque's lithographer in Mourlot's workshop, was struck by the sensuality of his art. Inspecting the first version of a lithograph Deschamps had brought him, he said: 'It's good, but it doesn't drip enough!'[74] To achieve the hallucinatory blackness of *Apples on a Black Background* (1954), two different plates were used for the ground, and garlic juice added to the inks to give it a natural lustre (a nineteenth-century technique). This was something more than simply warmed-over drawing, as Francis Ponge remarked. He was thinking prints. 'Braque is the model of that species of genius, more revolutionary than the terrorists and more poetic than the poets – we can see that in the long run – who, under an apparently descriptive guise, sometimes a simple still life, never offer us anything anecdotal, but always something like an example, a law, a watchword, an emblem.'[75]

Bending the process of mechanical reproduction to his needs, he was keen to preserve the maker's mark, the human touch. In his first post-war lithograph, *Phaethon* (*Chariot* I), he had the brown border area printed twice, moving the paper one millimetre to the left for the second printing, to obtain a softened, 'handworked' edge. In the delicately balanced *Amaryllis* (1958), traces of the line drawing are left visible in the print. Even varnish had its place. A light varnishing to enliven the surface of the print is an old trick. Braque applied thick boat varnish to a number of his black and white prints. The amber glow of the varnish lent them colour, and also a certain translucence, a little like stained-glass windows, while the smooth, ceramic quality of *Varnished Bird* (1954) gives the illusion that it has peeled off some ancient pot. Filiations, secret and otherwise, were important to him. Contemplating his own late work, he met an old acquaintance, he said, 'the Braque of yesteryear'.[76] *The Bird in the Foliage* (1961), against a background of newspapers, recalls the *papiers collés*; and the inclusion of a cutting

35. Meditating on *The Bird and Its Nest*, 1955 (col. pl. 15)

headlined MAX ERNST, QUEL OISEAU ÊTES-VOUS? (what bird are you?) resumes their jousting wit. 'People imagine that every bird must be a dove,' observed Braque, innocently.[77]

On a still, grey day in May 1955 he had visited La Tour du Valat, the ornithological station run by his friend Lukas Hoffmann, son and heir to long-standing Braque patrons and to the Hoffmann–La Roche fortune.[78] The experience continued to haunt him, a haunting that fed into the late work he loved best, *The Bird and Its Nest* (1955), a work he would never sell, and from which he was reluctant to be parted even for a short time.[79] When he went to Varengeville, *The Bird and Its Nest* went with him, on the roof of the car, secured with the bare minimum of rope and pitons. (Braque took a craftsman's pride in the economy of his packing.) At Varengeville it lodged next to the fireplace. Braque and Marcelle and Mariette would sit in front of the fire and watch it like television. Mariette saw *le maître* express no greater joy than in communing with that painting, begun in unaccustomed rapture on Easter morning. Here too he may have felt an airborne link with the past. One of the Great War poems he collected from Apollinaire, a poem appropriately entitled 'Silence bombardé', contains a stanza on the same theme.

> Farewell night
> All the birds of the world
> Have made their nests
> And sing in a ring[80]

In the Camargue he saw flamingoes – the firebird of the ancient Greeks – taking off, pinkly, a long-stemmed bouquet in full bloom over the lagoon; and a sudden apparition, a heron, flapping low across the marshes, duty bound.[81] He could not forget how the sky seemed to reflect the water, rather than the other way around, and how the birds seemed to swim through the air.

From that vision I derived aerial forms. The birds inspired me; I am trying to extract the greatest benefit for my painting. Even if they interest me as species of living creatures, however, their natural function as birds must be buried in my memory. After the shock of inspiration that they produced in my mind, even the concept must fade, must be abolished, so that I can get closer to my essential concern: the construction of pictorial fact. Painting alone must impose its presence . . .[82]

Birds were as mutable as everything else in the Braque world. The unclassifiable one with the nest was originally a stork, drawn a little more naturalistically; a rare specimen clearly labelled *The Duck* looks nothing like a duck but something like a snow goose, an after-thought addition or contradiction, in Braque parlance, affixed to the slit-eyed space-age bird jetting towards a black hole in the transcendental *In Full Flight* (1956–61), a canvas brought neatly back to earth by the pull of the pigment itself.[83] After weeks of application, the painting became so heavy with matter that Braque could no longer lift it on and off the easel. Jean Bazaine remembered its intoxicating effect, and its bodyweight, and Mariette, on their way down from the studio: 'It's too much. Isn't it? It's almost unbearable.'[84]

'We must choose,' said Braque. 'A thing cannot be real and realistic at the same time.'[85] Braque's birds were real but not realistic. They were not storks or ducks or any other species – unless poetic compounds like moonswallows and starswifts are admissible – but 'the bird *in itself*', in Jules Michelet's phrase, 'the sublime and divine summit of living concentration, which constitutes the great personal force of the bird, but which implies its extreme individuality, its isolation, its social weakness'. Braque may have known this remarkable nineteenth-century paean to the bird – Perse surely did – with its Braquian imagery and its cosmic address. '*The wing, flight*, a unique power, which is the dream of man. Every other creature is slow. Compared with the falcon or swallow, the Arab horse is a snail. Flight itself does not appertain solely to the wing, but to an incomparable power of *respiration and vision*. The bird is peculiarly the son of air and light. An essentially electrical being, *the bird sees, knows, and foresees earth and sky, the weather, the seasons*. It swoops; it penetrates; it attains what man shall never attain.'[86]

It was not a symbol. Braque avoided symbols, he said, at all costs.[87] Symbols and symbolists came out of the same swamp as theories and theorists; they were fit only for categoric rejection. Guitars were not madonnas, apples were not breasts, skulls were not *memento mori*, birds were not carriers of souls, harbingers of peace, bringers of life, or messengers of gods. They were birds. 'They are simply birds, species unknown,' he told Richardson, 'though maybe an ornithologist would be able to identify them for you.'[88] Nonetheless, they had undeniable poetic potential. Braque was fond of adducing Reverdy's line, 'a swallow stabs the sky', to show how to turn a swallow into a dagger.[89]

Braque had long been fascinated by animals. During the Occupation he had read *Moby Dick* and been much taken with Melville's delight in the unexpected reversibility of things. One of the characters, not knowing any better, carries a wheelbarrow which someone has lent him to transport his belongings. A tomahawk-pipe kills and soothes with equal facility. A coffin becomes a lifebuoy. The narrator's encounter with an albatross anticipates Braque's encounter with the birds of the Camargue.[90]

Through its inexpressible, strange eyes, methought I peeped to secrets which took hold of God. As Abraham before the angels, I bowed myself; the white thing was so white, its wings so wide, and in those for ever exiled waters, I had lost the miserable warping memories of traditions and of towns. Long I gazed at that prodigy of plumage. I cannot tell, can only hint, the things that darted through me then.[91]

Melville spoke powerfully to artists. *Moby Dick*, which has extraordinary chapters on everything from whiteness to whales in paint, is a kind of *Studio* of a book, magnificently irreducible. Like the *Studios*, it can be inventoried but not explained. Maurice Blanchot wrote in the 1940s of 'the simplicity of its mystery'.[92] Something very similar tempted Georges Braque.

Braque would also have been familiar with the Taoist conception of 'Bird-Immortals'.[93] The Immortal bird *par excellence* is the crane. It was believed to live for more than 1,000 years and to be capable of breathing with its neck bent, a technique for making the breath supple that is imitated by Taoists themselves. The immaculate whiteness of its plumage is evidence of its purity, but its cinnabar-coloured head shows that it knows how to preserve its life potency; inwardly it is all yang (light and life). The crane is the Immortals' mount when they frolic in the skies. In 1954 Braque was working on the commission for Maeght's house in Saint-Paul, the Mas Bernard, named for the dealer's youngest son, who had just died from leukaemia, after a long illness, at the age of eleven. The artist was acutely aware of the family's ordeal. He made them a Bird-Immortal, neck bent, contemplating with equanimity an aerodynamic brother.

Birds of some description appear in six of the eight *Studios*, as if to testify to the masterpieces of that genre. They also invade the most audacious of the preceding series of *Billiard Tables* (1944–52), with a flock of oncoming birds and mock birds, and the ghostly presence of a great billiard-table bird spanning the composition (its wing-tip overhanging the table on the right of the painting), to say nothing of the free-floating dado rail, the easel hatstand, the granular fruit-balls, the creased coffin table, and the strange aquarium-like

36. In front of *The Billiard Table* (1947–9), with oncoming birds

presentation, explained to one interviewer as an attempt to suggest motion continuing beyond the canvas.[94] The *Billiard Tables* presaged the stygian ecosystem of the *Studios*. Like their Cubist forebears, these paintings cannot be absorbed in an instant. They are worlds; they invite exploration. But they can also inflame. The collector Jacques Gelman removed one from the wall of Aimé Maeght's dining room and took it home after lunch. 'In the future it will be said of that canvas that it is a Cubist reverie from the century of the great terror,' wrote André Lhote of another.[95]

Asked where the birds came from, Braque himself was playful. 'In one of these *Studios*, the bird arrived naturally to perch on the top, a complete surprise.'[96] In a certain sense they were born on the canvas, as he claimed. A nascent bird form can be seen slicing through the confines of its canvas, as if breaking out of its shell, in a precursor *Studio* of 1939 – a studio with bars on the window – a painting much studied by other artists, including Jasper Johns and Ellsworth Kelly, for its patterns and its shapes.[97] Ten years later, when he embarked on the Studio series proper, the bird had flown, first into another painting of its own (subsequently destroyed), and then into an etching for a text of René Char's, the prototype for the denizens of the Louvre.[98] For Braque at the easel, birds materialized and dematerialized almost at will. Ultimately, it was not the bird in isolation that captured his imagination. When Jean

1. *Marie Laurencin and Georges Lepape at the Moulin de la Galette*, 1904

2. Marie Laurencin, *Georges Braque at the Easel*, 1904

3. Georges Lepape, *Georges Braque*, c. 1905

4. *Large Nude*, 1908

5. *Woman*, 1908

6. *Houses at L'Estaque (Houses and Tree)*, 1908

7. Marie Wassilief, *The Braque Banquet*, 1917. At the table, left to right: Wassilief with carving knife and bowl, Matisse with turkey, the one-armed Blaise Cendrars, Picasso, Marcelle with laurels, Halvorsen, Léger with cap, Jacob, Béatrice Hastings, Pina with revolver, Braque with laurels, Gris, Dufy (?), Modigliani at the door

8. Greeting card: 'No Braquing any time'

9. *Violin: 'Mozart/Kubelick'*, 1912

10. *Homage to J. S. Bach*, 1911–2

11. Picasso, *The Reading of the Letter*, 1921

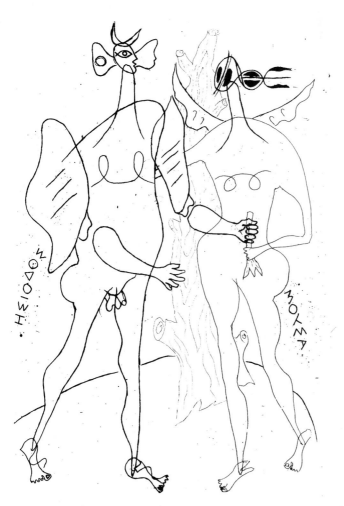

12. *Hesiod and the Muse*, 1932, an
    etching for the *Theogony*

13. A page from Braque's *Cahier*

14. *Death's Head*, 1943

15. *The Stove*, 1942

16. An etching for *The Order of Birds*, 1962

17. Giacometti, *Georges Braque on His Deathbed*, 1963

Leymarie questioned him on the subject in 1958, he replied: 'Birds and space have preoccupied me for a long time. It was in 1929 that the motif came to me for an illustration of Hesiod. In 1950 I painted some birds, but they were incorporated in still lifes, while in my latest things space and movement have been preying on my mind. Other than that, the painting – which is my language – will be able to tell you in more detail.'[99]

Braque was less concerned with birds, as such, than with the miracle of winged flight; that is, with movement in space, progress through a resistant medium.[100] 'The bird is a summing up of all my art,' Braque told Alexander Liberman as they contemplated *The Bird and Its Nest*. 'It is more than painting.' 'It has a hypnotic power,' said Liberman. 'That's it,' Braque responded immediately. 'It's as if one heard the fluttering of wings.'[101]

One December day in 1962, ten years after he commissioned the Louvre ceiling, Georges Salles called on Braque in his Paris studio. There, in that place 'quivering with wings', as they sat on the sofa together, at the painter's request he read aloud from *The Order of Birds*.

Braque's birds, and no one else's . . . Unallusive and untainted by memories, they follow their own destiny, more shadowy than any flight of black swans on the horizon of southern seas. Innocence is their age. They take their chances with man. And rise to dream in the same night as man . . . Braque, you seed Western space with holy species. And the district of man is as though made fertile by them . . . Let the Century's price be paid for us in coin and seed of painted birds![102]

11. 'The prong of the rake': Late Braque

In 1962 Braque turned eighty. His health was failing. He had been under doctors' orders for many years, ever since the stomach ulcers of 1945. In 1947 a severe attack of pneumonia almost killed him. In 1953 he had an operation for appendicitis, followed by a disturbing bout of high fever. He was racked with emphysema. Going upstairs to his studio was a visible effort. He wheezed and coughed and hawked, using a white enamel cup with a lid as a portable spittoon. He had more than a decade of august late work already behind him. 'There are cases in which old age bestows not an eternal youth, but on the contrary a sovereign freedom,' says Deleuze, 'a pure necessity where one enjoys a moment of grace between life and death, and where all the parts of the machine

37. Braque by Lee Miller (1956)

combine to dispatch into the future a trait that traverses the ages.'[1] Braque's moment was long.

The final flowering of his collaborative impulse was *Lettera amorosa* (1963), with René Char. A first version of that poem had appeared ten years earlier: Char pruned and trimmed as Braque did. Painter and poet were by then substantial allies, in Char's words. He was twenty-five years younger than Braque, but despite the difference in age they were profoundly *sympathique*. Temperamentally, they met on common ground. 'Painting,' said Braque, 'is not an art where anything goes.' 'Poetry,' said Char, 'is not chewing-gum.'[2] Both were workmen. Both strove to master the craft while forswearing special effects. Both abhorred tricksiness. 'Nothing fancy, please,' Char instructed the copy-editor on a set of proofs – an instruction which might equally have come from Braque.

Both were steeped in Heraclitus and Pindar. One of the first of Char's manuscripts illustrated by Braque was the poem 'Lyre', an echo of those ancestral voices.

> An eagle feather falls from the sky . . .
> (Rarely found.)[3]

For all their sky-watching, both drew their strength from a certain rootedness. 'Work that is grounded like no other, and yet how it shivers with alchemy!' wrote the poet appreciatively in the catalogue of the painter's first show at the Galerie Maeght in 1947, eliciting a pair of crossed fish from Braque in comradely response.[4] The turning of the earth must have seemed especially appropriate to the painter in this context, for both men loved the Vaucluse, the area where Char grew up and where Braque summered for so many years before and after the Great War. The surprise encounter on the steps of the Palais des Papes while Braque was exhibiting there had a kind of spiritual significance for each of them. 'If it holds up, a painting hung there proves itself,' Char remembered him saying on that occasion.[5] The naming of parts, and poets, only increased his enjoyment. 'Char' (a chariot and more recently a tank) was sufficiently close to 'charrue' (a plough) to make almost a play on words, or pictures. It is surely no coincidence that Braque, who was very attached to ploughs, paired one of his favourite Char poems with a lithograph of *La Charrue*, a classic image of this period, part still life, part landscape, part meditation, the clotted impasto laid on with a trowel, or at least a palette knife, *à la* Nicolas de Staël; the thing perished but imperishable, a discoloured negative, its mute humanity underlined by a Heraclitean observation in his notebook: 'The idle plough rusts and loses its usual meaning.' The observation might have been made, maxim-like, to Char (who had a plough in his garden), and in fact Braque gave the poet a gouache of the same work, in memory of the poem in question, 'The Untold Future'.[6]

Char was a fighter in the Resistance. As a poet, he chose to remain silent during those years, but he too kept a note of his thoughts, later published. 'You look at things directly and stand firm,' Braque congratulated him characteristically. 'All heroism lies there.'[7] The admiration was mutual. Visiting Braque in Varengeville in 1948, Char copied out passages from the painter's notebook, some phrases that sang in his poetic ear – 'the prong of the rake', 'night, dust, sleep' – some maxims and reflections that had not yet seen the light of day: 'A thing can't be in two places at once. One can't have it in one's head and under one's eye.' 'When I watch a painter at work, sometimes I have more admiration for his easel than for him.'[8]

Braque himself singled out *Lettera amorosa* as the poem that he particularly wanted to rework with its author. *Lettera amorosa* (the title borrowed from Monteverdi) is indeed a love letter, of a rather unusual kind. Rewritten by Char for the purpose, it is fragmentary, disconnected, engrossed in the natural world, yet direct in its avowals.

I can only be, want only to live in the space and freedom of my love. Together we are neither the result of surrender nor the grounds for a still more disheartening servitude. So let us wage war, wicked and blameless, against each other.[9]

Both painter and poet were determined that this should not be just another illustrated book, but a genuine dialogue – 'a sovereign conversation' in Char's phrase – in the sense that each would attend very closely to what the other was saying, and fashion his response accordingly.[10] Several years elapsed, however, before the project got under way. Eventually in 1958 the Geneva-based publisher Edwin Engelberts succeeded in corralling them into a contract. Once Char had made some revisions, Engelberts produced a dummy of the book, with the poem set out in widely spaced fragments on the page, the layout and type approved by both contributors. This became a kind of episodic storyboard for Braque to work from. It inspired no fewer than twenty-nine lithographs: sympathetic vibrations or imaginative responses to the hard-won words – a cumulative cross-pollination. The outcome was a triumph. *Lettera amorosa* is one of the great artistic conversations of the twentieth century.

Braque's inspiration was not something that could be hurried. Edwin Engelberts has left a revealing account of how the collaboration proceeded. The principals assembled in Braque's Paris studio: Char, the printer Mourlot, the lithographer Deschamps, Mariette, and Engelberts himself. Deschamps remembered Char taking in the contents of the vast studio and whispering, 'We're in the presence of greatness.'[11] When everyone was ready the poet began to read from the text, commenting on it from time to time. Engelberts sat next to Braque with the dummy book open on his knees, like an amanuensis, writing on a blank page whatever the words evoked for the painter. Char came to the moving declaration at the heart of the work: 'I laugh marvellously with you. That is my unique good fortune.' ('Je ris merveilleusement avec toi. Voilà la chance unique.') Braque bade Engelberts write 'Sun-Springtime'. The lithograph of that evocation, a double-page spread, took over a year to complete. It evolved through five variations. The first showed a section of high wall throwing a long shadow; the presence of the sun indicated by the shadow. The second replied to the first with the outline of an opening in the wall, through which sunlight poured on to the ground; the presence of the sun indicated by the light. The third, more direct, showed a fraction of a disk and its rays. But Braque was still not satisfied.

The following summer, in Varengeville, Engelberts saw a fourth version. This time a sunflower, one of Braque's favourites, stood out in the composition. Some leaves blew, treeless, from one page to the other. The presence of the sun was indicated by a symbol. The publisher rejoiced at this sight; he thought it would make a wonderful lithograph. The artist continued to experiment. Months later Engelberts returned to the Paris studio. '*Voilà*,' said Braque, as if picking up where they had just left off, 'I have finished this lithograph.' In the fifth and final scheme the sun had been simplified to a rough circle. The leaves still blew from page to page. One of them, half within the sun-circle, had turned a lighter shade of green. 'Every allusion, every description, everything picturesque had disappeared.' (col. pl. 17)[12] Braque had been true to one of his earliest precepts. This seven-colour lithograph was not an anecdote but a pictorial fact. It was a response grounded in empathy with his interlocutor, and immersion in his œuvre. In an earlier work Char had written of 'a tree full of laughter and leaves'.[13] The lithograph exemplified the bold reductions of Braque's late style. 'To write is not to describe. To paint is not to depict.'[14]

He was still working as if he had time, but in reality he had none, as he surely knew. 'Following in a great tradition, this artist went to his death in the dignity of silence,' wrote André Verdet, whose late interviews with Braque resonate with candour. 'He had reflected on the nearness of death; he had planned to approach it calmly, with the conviction of the elect who know that where they faithfully accomplished their task their star will continue to shine for other men of heart and spirit.'[15] His calm was legendary. For Jean Grenier it was 'a calm achieved through self-mastery rather than through apathy'. For Saint-John Perse it was an Oriental calm. 'In his work and his life as an artist, Braque bore fine human witness. He is one of those who rank among the "standing stones" on the path of man.'[16]

In May 1963 he celebrated his eighty-first birthday. He went to watch some go-karting. He enjoyed go-karting – it made him

38. With Mariette in the Paris studio, working on *Lettera Amorosa*

laugh. It was to be his last outing. Over the winter of 1962–3 he had weakened perceptibly. 'Braque's frailness worries me,' Paulhan wrote to a friend. 'He doesn't seem to have any energy.' A diet of fruit pulped in a blender (an invention known to Marcelle as 'the Mixter') brought temporary relief but no lasting improvement.[17] He grew very thin. He still worked every day, but not all day. He tired easily. Mariette's presence at the reading of *Lettera amorosa* was not incidental; her ministrations were vital to bringing the project to a conclusion. Mourlot remembered her prompting: 'There, Monsieur Braque, perhaps you could put something there?'[18] No one but Mariette could have produced the same effect – or dared to suggest to Georges Braque where to make his mark.

He became even more reclusive, as if withdrawing, literally, inside himself. The imposing frame remained intact, a little bowed, but he looked increasingly gaunt, and, towards the end, rather yellow – cancer-yellow.[19] He died on 31 August 1963, at home, in Paris, as he might have wished, 'without suffering, calmly, his gaze fixed until the last moment on the trees in his garden, the highest branches of which were visible from the great windows of his studio' – *looking* until the end. The cause of death was given as cerebral infarct: a clot blocking the supply of blood to the brain.[20]

To all outward appearances Marcelle bore his passing with great fortitude. The late paintings were given to him, she said, as if he had been granted a reprieve, a moment of grace, for the purpose. At eighty-four she faced her grief with the same calm courage with which he met his end. Paulhan called at the house as soon as he heard, and saw her often in the days immediately afterwards. Meeting her again a few weeks later, he was struck by how bright she seemed, 'sad no doubt but talkative, animated and almost pretty: happy to be alive'.[21] When Jean Leymarie dined with her, alone, after a memorial ceremony in Argenteuil, she spent the evening reminiscing, not about Braque, but about Picasso. Yet the man with whom she had shared her life for over fifty years was gone, and in two more so was she. Much of the intervening period she spent settling his estate according to his wishes, and revisiting the places they had been to together.[22]

Mariette was devastated. 'The servant with the big heart', as Pierre Reverdy called her, was suddenly rudderless. Braque was dead. He depended on her no longer. His regular morning greeting: 'Have you been up there [to the studio]?' Yes, she would say. 'So, was it OK yesterday?'[23] It mattered to him what some people thought. Mariette-with-the-big-heart was one of them. For the rest of the time they would work in companionable silence. Now that work was over. The studio was dark. Life had lost its purpose. She wondered if she could go on – if she wanted to go on.[24]

In the final analysis the question answered itself. 'I must speak ... of the *domus* of Braque,' Francis Ponge wrote in tribute a few years later, 'I mean his family circle, the admirable Mariette Lachaud, and her mother, who served Georges and Marcelle Braque throughout; at least from the time we met, living with them throughout, to their death. What am I saying? Even beyond their death.'[25]

Artists everywhere stopped in their tracks. '31 August 1963. Death of Georges Braque,' recorded Jean Bazaine numbly in his journal. It was several weeks before he could bring himself to make a résumé of their association, beginning as so often with a visit to the studio accompanied by Paulhan, in the bitter winter of 1942, and ending twenty years later with another visit, accompanied by his son:

Last visit to Braque, very tired, but all joyful and bucked up by the presence of a child, my son. In the studio, there are some of those little landscapes of Varengeville, narrow grey beaches and black skies, so poignant, so deeply moving in their strength and their humility, that are undoubtedly among his greatest achievements. And also *The Plough*. I had already seen it while he was working on it furiously, before it was exhibited, badly lit, in the Louvre [in the special exhibition of 1961]. Braque was already ill and tired when he painted it. That plenitude, power and freedom of the last works of the great masters in a trade that is so physically exhausting is always a mystery. The plough like a kind of great black bird in an immense space, the earth and the sky, seamlessly tilled. Braque had discovered this 'unbroken space' in painting fifty years earlier through Cubism. All his work is a quest, an enrichment of space. But it seems to me that he had never charged it with such life and truth.[26]

'In front of Braque,' reflected Alain Bosquet, 'it is not enough to say that he is a great painter; we are called upon to ask ourselves what it means to be a great painter.'[27]

Chagall:

The death of Braque, it is something strange, empty and disquieting, the death of Braque. It is not only a great world of art that is gone, but an exemplary man, an artist of whom we haven't seen enough, perhaps, in our bustling lives. It is precisely now that we need this exemplary man and artist. And one branch of the tree of today's art stayed as if suspended in mid-air, waiting. His whites and his greys, his blacks and his greens, his browns file past in our memories. His colours which could be placed, just as they are, in a chapel of religious art. After this death above all, one feels all the more keenly this sorrow and one cannot help calling to mind the nobility and the great humanity of Corot, Chardin, or Daumier.[28]

Giacometti:

Georges Braque has just died. For the time being, this news does not strike any chord in me. At this moment Georges Braque is still as alive as in the past, perhaps more alive than ever, somewhere in his house, in his studio, here in Paris, or by the sea, coming and going, from one painting to another, smoking his cigarette. I can see myself with him, listening, talking, a cup of coffee in front of us on the little table as so often since 1930. But at the same time I think nostalgically of the far-off days of Montmartre that I didn't experience. I think of the young people who were Braque, Picasso and their friends, I see them in their daily lives and their paintings called Cubist are for me the very reflection of those daily lives; for them, these paintings were the concrete expression of the tremendous, inspiring opening into the future and the immediate fresh-ness of everything. And then that future became, for each of them, a complex and solitary path.[29]

Bissière:

It was with immense sadness that I learned of the death of Braque. With him disappears a large part of my youth spent in daily contact with the one who is no longer. Later, the distance in space did not mean that I forgot the friendship I felt for him, nor the affection I believe he felt for me. Although our paths were very divergent, near him I found comfort and also a bond that brought us very close. For he was a painter essentially in the French tradition, as I hope to be. He continued, by renewing it, that unbroken chain which runs from the Middle Ages to Cézanne and Renoir, passing through Corot. In everything he created, there is always that rigour, that measured, balanced approach, and also that sober outlook to be found only between the Atlantic and the Rhine, which remains our best, most precious heritage. But beyond that there was, in everything he touched, a profound humanity; the heart was always committed, and that is why he will remain perhaps the most essential painter of that generation, the one who created an œuvre in which every man worthy of the name recognizes what is best and most valuable about himself. I should like my old friend, entering the dark of the tomb, to find in these lines the brotherly love of one who, at the twilight of life, still recalls the perfume of a very old friendship and the affecting memory of an œuvre that remains dear to him.

Farewell, my dear Braque, you carry with you a large part of my past and you will always live in my memory.[30]

Marie-Laure de Noailles:

Before his death, Braque, dressed as a hunter, was lying in wait for his canvases placed on the ground. Earthenware pots stood nearby, brushes arrayed. He was contemplating his work and he was beautiful in contemplation. I tiptoed out of his studio. I brushed against some preliminary sketches of blue birds. 'Are they waiting for the green to arrive?'

'That is the question,' replied Braque.

I would never see him again. . . .

To be or not to be. Braque is. Hamlet is. That's the main thing. Apply a blue that calls for the green.[31]

But the most affecting envoi came from one who famously shunned the pen – and the dead – Picasso:

Braque, you said to me, once, a long time ago, meeting me out walking with a girl whose beauty one would call classical, that I found very pretty: 'In love you haven't yet detached yourself enough from the masters.' In any case I can still say to you today: I love you, you see that I still cannot detach myself.[32]

Giacometti was prevailed upon to continue an ancient tradition and make a drawing of the artist on his deathbed. In the still of the morning after (as it happened a Sunday), with Jean Leymarie in attendance for moral support, he struggled for several hours to discharge this responsibility to his satisfaction – 'trying to get it right'. Famously despairing of his own work, Giacometti considered the result a failure. It was as if his subject refused to give up the ghost. 'Each time I finished a drawing it was a living Braque. Curious, no?' (b/w pl. 17)[33]

39. The state funeral in the Cour Carrée of the Louvre. From the cover story in *Paris-Match*, 14 September 1963

As Minister for Cultural Affairs, André Malraux scripted a state funeral – a remarkable event for any painter, and wholly out of keeping with the tastes of Georges Braque. The torchlit ceremony was strangely Felliniesque, with newsreel cameras and radio microphones. It was staged in front of the portico in the Cour Carrée of the Louvre, opposite Saint-Germain-l'Auxerrois, where Chardin is buried, which tolled its bells as the coffin was carried into the courtyard by selected guards from the state museums, flanked by soldiers. The rain fell solidly as if made by a machine. A silent crowd of several thousand waited patiently for the spectacle to begin. The *garde républicaine* played Beethoven's 'Funeral March for the Death of a Hero'. The plain wooden coffin was placed on a catafalque draped in a tricolour. In front of it stood Marcelle, heavily veiled, supported by Mariette, and a phalanx of ministers, officials, and members of the diplomatic corps. Malraux delivered the eulogy himself, as he did later for Joan of Arc, Le Corbusier, and the Resistance leader Jean Moulin. One might better say he performed it, with classic histrionics, addressing Marcelle directly, and through her the nation and the world.

Before Georges Braque is laid to rest in the little Norman graveyard of his choice, I bring here the solemn homage of France . . .

Never has a modern nation paid homage of this nature to one of its dead painters. The history of painting, which finds a masterly realization in Braque's work, has been a long history of scorn, poverty, and despair. By his death, Braque seems to ensure revenge for Modigliani's pitiful rites, for van Gogh's sinister burial. And since every Frenchman knows that there is a share of his country's honour which is called Victor Hugo, it is right to tell them that there is a share of the honour of France which is called Braque — for a nation's honour also consists in what it gives to the world . . .

But our admiration is not confined to that placated genius which visits so many masters at nightfall. It also stems from the link between this genius and the most important pictorial revolution of the century, the decisive role Braque took in destroying the imitation of objects and of pageantry. Doubtless the most penetrating aspect of his art is that it unites with a brilliant and outspoken freedom a domination of the means of that freedom unequalled in contemporary painting. Indeed, by revealing with contagious power the freedom of painting, Braque and his companions of 1910 revealed as well that whole art of the past opposed to illusion, from our Romanesque painting to the beginning of time: patiently or furiously creating their derided works, these painters brought back to life the world's entire past.

Finally, these paintings expressed France as much as Corot's — but more mysteriously, for Corot had represented our country a great deal. Braque expressed France with a symbolic force so great that he is as legitimately at home in the Louvre as the angel in Reims Cathedral. Last Saturday, our sadness was a remote but recognizable one, the same sadness we felt when we heard: 'Debussy is dead.'

Tomorrow morning, Madame, let this be said to the sailors and the farmers of Varengeville, who loved Georges Braque: 'Yesterday, when he lay in state, before the palace of our kings and the world's finest museum, a faint voice in the rainy night said "thank you", and a simple hand, a worn, peasant-woman's hand which was the hand of France, stirred gently in the darkness to stroke for the last time his white hair.'[34]

With that flourish, Malraux descended from the podium and embraced Marcelle.

Far away in the South of France, Francis Ponge switched off the radio and sent a sorrowful note to Jean Paulhan. 'Bad winter (despite your election to the Academy), bad summer (despite the birth of [his daughter] Armande's third son), bad year, that has killed Braque. I'm thinking of you. I remember the day when you took me to him (and, naturally, *Braque le patron*). Ah! Thank you! Malraux is a nice guy: his intention was good, but he should have left the speech to you.'[35] Ponge was not alone in having reservations about 'the public demonstrations', as the film director Jean Renoir (son of the painter) put it from his outpost in Beverly Hills. 'These are fine for men like Kennedy, who was a public figure, or Louis XIV, but for Molière or Chardin . . . we feel this is inappropriate.' The Renoirs too had their small Braque, and a long acquaintance with the painter. 'Knowing that we shall not see Braque again when we visit Paris is very painful for both of us.'[36]

Paulhan attended damply at the Louvre, and then followed Braque in spirit to Varengeville, unconsoled: 'It is not only someone, it is something deep, powerful, vast that has gone. We shall not get over it.' There, in the church on the cliff, with its Braque windows and packed congregation of villagers and dignitaries, in his paradoxical way he described the scale of their loss, 'for Braque is not only the great painter that everyone recognizes. He represents precisely enough a state of our thinking, and living'.

The masters of art always taught us that there was only one means of introducing light into the canvas: that is by starting with shadows. Thus there is no clear thinking that does not have its share of obscurity, and mystery.

The believers who talk of being able to love *in God*, to want *in God*, to act *in God*, are alluding to this mystery. Braque did not dispel the mystery, he faced it and made room for obscurity. Hence the ringing clarity of his work, and the simplest thing that one can say of him is that he knows how to paint in God.[37]

40. The funeral at Varengeville. Marcelle, heavy in black, follows the coffin, supported on her left by Mariette.

The Mayor of Varengeville owned a small Braque. Interviewed by *Paris-Match*, he explained: 'It happened in 1945. I had invited him to tea with his lady. He arrived with a painting under his arm.' Asked if he knew how much it was worth, the Mayor replied, 'I don't want to know; it is worth a friend.'[38]

A few months later, at Maeght's invitation, Ponge joined an illustrious company paying homage in a special issue of *Derrière le miroir*. He too was preoccupied with Braque's exemplary quality.

Death of Braque. Closure of the catalogue. Assumption of the work . . .

But the fact is that Braque never stopped being good for me . . . ; that each of his masterpieces, in each of his periods, has been like a stage in my 'ethics' . . . ; that he has been for me a great Master of Life . . .

No philosophers in France, as we know. No one we could pit against the greatest philosopher of the century, against Husserl. But we can hold aloft a small Cézanne, a small Braque. 'To think [*penser*] is not to reason,' Braque used to say. He was right, it is to *weigh* [*peser*]. For him, to paint.

For us, to write. Nothing more serious, then, for the perpetuation of thought than this extinction – since that of Cézanne . . .

'Let us not conclude. The present, the accident is going to liberate us.' Ah! Let us believe in that very strongly, let us cocoon it, this near future! Back to work.[39]

Ten years after the painter's death, the remarkable trio of Braque, Char and the philosopher Martin Heidegger appeared together in the pages of the journal *Argile*.[40] Heidegger had turned poet, ruminating suggestively on the fundamental question raised by his engagement with art in general and with Cézanne and Braque in particular, the relationship between *poème* and *pensée*, art and thought. For Heidegger, 'there was certainly more *thought* in one Braque still life than in five hundred pages of Sartre'.[41]

> In the painter's late work, the difference
> of what enters the presence and the presence itself
> is joined in simplicity; it is 'realized' and
> at the same time handed over to itself,
> transformed into the identity of an enigma.
>
> Does a way open here, that would lead to a common
> presence between the poem and the thought?[42]

These lines, dedicated to Char, echo with the 'common presence' of Georges Braque.

Char himself was hard-hit. His own tribute, composed in the days after Braque's death, headed a commemorative issue of the *Nouvelle Revue Française*:

Braque is the one who has placed his hands over our eyes, to teach us to look better and help us see further, past the line of historical facts and tombs . . . His numerous gifts to poems are cores of dark energy, moist plants revealed to themselves, rebellious or delightful deities (was he not shy to extremes?), birds spared nature's butchery and returned to spirit, spared man's humiliating foolery, like Baudelaire's Albatross. Sometimes he seemed as rough as you could wish; he could appreciate an enigma, and revive its dulled fortunes and shine for us. His shade was that of a day won, a day scaled, a mix of very personal inspiration, reflection, self-enlargement, and toil ... We are difficult people; in becoming simple, we needed both the plant in bloom and the gardener. As soon as one leaves us for ever, the other, who remains beside us (thankfully less ephemeral), reduces us to tears, and transports us back to the lands of our incompetence. Transient beings as we are, not so much travellers as temporary guests![43]

The writer Marcel Jouhandeau recalled his dry humour. 'Braque and I are looking at a drawing by [Jean] Dubuffet. I say: "It's a coffee-grinder." Braque: "No, no. He told me that it's a portrait of his wife." Me: "It portrays a horror and I know his wife, she's charming." 'Braque: "That all depends on the image one has of her, and the image one conveys."' For Jouhandeau, perhaps, the story gained from his own domestic hostilities. He too had a small Braque, sold by his wife in a fit of rage and retaliation for the wrongs of her miscreant husband. A period of separation ensued. Recrimination was not far behind:

Marcel Jouhandeau: ... you took revenge, selling a Braque, a painting
    that belonged to me, and not to you.
Élise Jouhandeau: Oh! Excuse me! To me too.
MJ: What? It was signed in my name, it was dedicated to me!
EJ: To you alone?
MJ: To you also.
EJ: I knew Braque well before you!
MJ: But Braque never had the slightest regard for you, while he had
    given me that painting because he had just illustrated one of my books.
EJ: Ah! Luckily I have letters!
MJ: From Braque?
EJ: Exactly, I have two, in the Bibliothèque Doucet.
MJ: I've never seen them.
EJ: And I have six from his wife.
MJ: Yet Braque's pen was not prolix.

EJ: You twist everything, you see everything in your own diabolical
 light! Luckily, there are others that know me.
MJ: Good luck to them![44]

Jouhandeau also dwelt on his personal supremacy:

What strikes me about Georges Braque is that, neither in the world of
letters, nor in that of music, could one find anyone who holds the same
position as he does among painters. Not only does he occupy one of the
first places, he is apart, one of a kind.

Personally he has something of the patriarch. The Sages of old had the
same prestige, and I am not referring only to the nobility of his features,
which remind one of a Norman peasant but also of a lord, nor to the
grandeur of his bearing. I am thinking of the dignity of his life, the
durability of his work. The unique thing about his character, his special
genius, seems to lie essentially in his refusal to make concessions to
whatever falls outside his own line, whatever fails to measure up to his
rigour, his rectitude, the probity of his personal standards. Braque lived
only to paint, to enrich his palette by noting the rarest of visual impressions. He brought to perfection the resources of his craft.[45]

As Director of the Musée national d'art moderne, Jean Cassou
had the bright idea of mounting a major Braque retrospective. The
artist himself was strangely reluctant. 'To all my entreaties Braque
would make Norman responses, rubbing his chin.' Cassou was
nothing if not persistent. He pursued his quarry to Varengeville,
armed with a plan of the exhibition. They went for a walk round
the garden. Cassou made his pitch. Braque continued to prevaricate.
'Listen, it troubles me to appear to refuse it, but you see . . .'
Eventually Marcelle took Cassou to one side. 'I'm going to explain
to you,' she said. '[Braque] doesn't want this exhibition and it pains
him to admit it. He knows that that will disappoint you. But you
must understand. He is afraid.' Cassou was astonished. Braque
afraid? Marcelle continued: 'He shrinks from the posthumous
character of a big retrospective, after so many years' work.' Cassou
assured her that all great artists had retrospectives, and that life went

on. Moreover, there had been other retrospectives, elsewhere, already . . . But the crux of the problem was the examined life – Braque confronted with Braque, in Paris, 'where all his thought, all his work had taken its chances, had fought its fight. And it was not so much the verdict of others that he dreaded, but rather his own. Others would say what they wish, as they always have, for good or ill. And, of course, that would affect him . . . But the judgement that would affect him most irrefutably would be his.'[46] The retrospective had to wait twenty years.

Braque went on working to the end, 'never satisfied, never discouraged', as Mariette said to Jean Grenier, 'in hope'. Visiting the studio for the last time, Malraux quoted to him Cézanne's remark, 'If I were quite certain that my canvases would be destroyed, and that they would never enter the Louvre, I would stop painting.' Braque considered this carefully and replied: 'As for me, if I were certain that all my paintings would be burned, I believe that I would continue to paint, yes, I would continue to paint.'[47]

'Painting is an answer to everything,' he told Nicolas de Staël, 'even success.'[48] His last painting was found, signed, on the easel: *The Weeding Machine*. Around it were stationed several of the elemental landscapes and seascapes of his late years: small canvases caked with paint (number 6s for which Kahnweiler would have paid 100 francs half a century before), laid down in rough strata like a cross-section – 'vast pictures in miniature', inspiring awe in such scrupulous seers as Bazaine and Giacometti.[49] In the studio, Braque left nothing to chance. He had made all the arrangements himself.

As for the painting on the easel, he had been working on it intermittently for two years, inspired by a photograph from a magazine, cut out by Mariette. The weeding machine, curiously disarticulated, is beached in a turbulent wheatfield. The weeding is over. Birds fly overhead in loose formation, as in van Gogh. *The Weeding Machine* is Braque's *Wheatfield under Threatening Skies with Crows*, less ominous but more mysterious than its predecessor. The atmosphere is heavy, and charged with matter, but an insistent white cloud leavens the cracking sky. The cloud, much pondered by the artist, was the finishing touch.

41. With *The Weeding Machine* (1961–3), in progress, as yet without white cloud (col. pl. 18)

12. 'I am here': Master of the Artless Art

Appreciation of Braque was always more of a cult than a mass movement. In his lifetime he was consistently underestimated, except by the few, and patronized with remarkable persistence as a decorator out of his depth. There were other marks of ignorance. At a show of his recent work at the Tate in London in 1946, *The Little Red Table* (1942) was hung upside down. This indignity went unnoticed throughout the press view and official opening, until it was pointed out by Patrick Heron on the first day, fortunately before Braque himself put in an appearance.

Three years later, in 1949, the *The Little Red Table* was still for sale (at a possible £3,000). Heron made a public appeal for the Tate to buy it, to no avail.[1] That summer the British painter spent an unforgettable evening with Braque in Paris, and saw for the first time the *Studios* in the making.

There were five paintings on five easels, ranged round in an arc . . . Braque said 'Do you mind sitting down and waiting a minute or two while I just finish up these bits of paint, before we talk?' For ten or fifteen minutes he transferred, with a small brush, three tiny mounds of mixed oil paint from two palettes – they were café au lait, milk chocolate and mushroom. He walked about with these little brush-loads from one easel to another until he found a place on one or other of the paintings he was working on where he could fit the colour in . . . *Studio V* [as it became] was practically finished. But another canvas of the same size [probably *Studio II*] was only just begun: it had been scribbled all over with a very loose turpsy mixture of ochre-honey colour with a biggish brush. This had dried, and on top of it an immensely complicated linear grid had been drawn in white chalk, and then superimposed on that another grid of stringy black lines of drawing in charcoal. Two interpenetrating grids, a black and a white on the honey-colour. The subject was a mass of outlines of studio objects and furniture and images from other pictures.[2]

After this initiation Heron proclaimed Braque 'the greatest figure in painting today'.[3] The greatness of the *Studios* was immediately recognized by the critic John Richardson, who saw them in progress, and underwritten by Douglas Cooper, who snapped up *Studio VIII* for his own collection at the Château de Castille.[4] In little England, however, the predominant tone was curmudgeonly. In the years after his death Braque came to public attention, if at all, in a spoof advertising slogan by the Liverpool poet Adrian Henri, GO TO WORK ON A BRAQUE!, and in the lyrics of the album *Space Oddity*, by David Bowie:

> And the Braque on the wall
> Slides down your front
> And eats through your belly
> It's very catching.[5]

To this day the Tate has no late work, indeed no painting by Braque later than 1945, and no means now to acquire one. *Studios* are a scarce commodity. They change hands but rarely, and then for several million dollars.[6]

Georges Braque is the third man of modern art. Picasso has an image, a persona, a legend. Matisse too. Braque seems immune to such treatment, unclassified. His work is his own, 'a new continent bearing no other name than that of its creator'.[7] The Braque world bears the stigmata of strangeness: 'strangeness so entire as even to withstand the stock assimilations to holy patrimony, national and other', despite the efforts of André Malraux and others to pin Frenchness on him.[8]

He is resistant to the stock assimilations. This is partly a matter of the company he kept, partly a matter of the distance he travelled. Braque was the only artist ever to sustain a collaborative relationship with Picasso. They were roped together in one of the key international relationships of the twentieth century, the most momentous artistic collaboration of modern times. For both men the conjugal model of 1908–14 was an unrepeatable experience: for Braque, a memory to burnish, but a chapter closed; for Picasso, an ideal to recapture, a dream forever postponed. Picasso's needs were visceral and overwhelming. He craved the stimulus of encounter. His encounter with Braque was in some ways the most satisfying relationship of his entire life. Perhaps Braque was indeed the one who loved him best.

Afterwards Braque went in search of himself, as Heraclitus prescribed.[9] He had to find ways to avoid being crushed by Picasso's monstrous ego. He cultivated a certain fatalism, an active passivity, a grain of superstition.[10] His number was thirteen (the date of his birthday and his post-trepanation recovery day). It offered protection, or brought him luck.[11] In dialogue with Pierre Reverdy, Carl Einstein and the ancient Chinese, he evolved a bric-à-brac philosophy, which found characteristic expression in apothegms that gained wide currency among Continental intellectuals – a wider currency than they knew – thanks to the often uncredited adopting and adapting practised by the likes of Jean Paulhan, Francis Ponge, even Martin Heidegger.[12] When Paulhan wrote of Camus, in 1963, 'there comes a time when life and art are one', he was imitating the conclusion of Braque's *Cahier*, 'with age art and life are one'. And in the year of the artist's death, he was surely thinking of Braque when he added, 'Art, that which is easier to *be* than to define.'[13] Braque invested heavily in *being*. 'Few people can say: I am here,' he reflected wisely. 'They look for themselves in the past and see themselves in the future.'[14] Georges Braque had an almost mystical aura about him, but he was the least delusional of men.

He became *le patron*, the guru, the enlightener – detached, seclusive, inscrutable – master of the artless art. Tales of the mature Braque have a Zen-like ring to them. His explanation of how to paint a picture: 'When I start, it seems to me that my painting is on the other side, only covered by that white dust, the canvas. I need only dust it. I have a little brush to clear the blue, another the red or the green: my paintbrushes. When I've cleaned it up, the painting is finished.'[15] His interaction with the Spanish sculptor Eduardo

Chillida: Braque attended the young Chillida's first exhibition in Paris, and showed great interest in one of the sculptures, offering to buy it. Chillida insisted on making him a present of it. A few days later Chillida and his wife were invited to Braque's studio. Braque was waiting with three canvases laid out side by side. 'Which of these is yours, Eduardo?' he asked. Without a moment's hesitation, Chillida pointed at one of them. 'Quite right. That's yours,' replied Braque, approvingly. 'Go and have a close look: I've already dedicated it.'[16] This was the Braque who knew something, who had found his way. 'His step betrays whether a man is stepping along *his own* path: so watch me walk! But he who approaches his goal, dances.'[17] Braque stepped firmly along his own path. Sometimes, if things sang in the studio, he danced on the tips of his toes.

Braque was patient. Picasso was not. 'Picasso,' guffawed Beckett's favourite painter Bram Van Velde: 'I don't search, I find . . . Producing, producing . . . the great risk is producing for its own sake. You must never force things. You just have to wait . . . He never felt his way . . . Picasso's curse was never being able to do nothing.' Braque understood that guffaw. Privately, he shared in it. 'Picasso doesn't stint himself. He speaks every language. What talent, what vice!'[18] Clement Greenberg, who was grievously disappointed in the arc of Braque's career, weighed *Violin and Pitcher*, *The Portuguese* and *Man with a Guitar*, forty years after they were painted, and found them 'as great as anything put on canvas'.[19] Yet it took the rest of the twentieth century before he began to be given his due as full partner and frequent instigator in the joint venture of the little cubes. Not coincidentally, this shift occurred only after the chief protagonists had finally quit the scene. Picasso lived until 1973, Kahnweiler until 1979. Both kept an iron grip on posterity. Both left a fabulously rich historical legacy – an archive – still largely unexplored. Picasso's archive is in the Picasso Museum in Paris. It has been open to scholars, subject to certain conditions, since 1985 – not long, given that it is open only on Thursdays and, naturally, closed for lunch. Kahnweiler's archive remains in private hands, in the gallery he created. After a period of selective access, it is now closed to everyone. The history of Cubism is still being hammered out. Manifold uncertainties remain. But the old cliché of the solo virtuoso, the great Picasso, will no longer pass muster. Braque cannot be effaced, Trotsky-like, from the record. The second Cubist century will see it differently from the first.

Their subsequent trajectories, so carefully monitored by the artists themselves, are seldom related. To compare the inventive achievement of their late work is to confront a startling disparity. The incorrigible Douglas Cooper exaggerated, no doubt, in describing the very last paintings as 'incoherent doodles done by a frenetic dotard in the anteroom of death', but it is hard to deny that late Picasso is the chronicle of a fixation, on waning powers and imminent extinction, flickering occasionally with the old fire, for the most part a husk of what used to be; a stupendous over-production by the most productive artist in recorded history.[20] More than half of the twenty-three volumes of Picasso's monumental *catalogue raisonné* are devoted to the work of the last twenty years of his life, a prodigality that exerts its own fascination. Late Braque, by contrast, is a conscious summation; at once a set of radical simplifications and a densely populated ethical universe, painted in 'the style of old age' characterized by Hermann Broch as a kind of *abstractism* in which the expression relies less and less on conventional vocabulary, which finally becomes reduced to a few prime symbols – a bird, a plough, a cloud, a jug, a palette, a lemon.[21] This is work of supreme distinction, to rank with the late work of Bach or Rembrandt or Rilke, but hardly yet assimilated, either to the painter's own career or to the common stock of cultural reference.

Braque has been cast as the great corroborator. In the end he corroborates no one but himself. He stands in no one's shadow.

His metaphors are misleading. Gardening and farming serve to emphasize the craft, the métier; they make of him something more stolid than he was. Braque exemplifies the frequently noted paradox, more apparent than real, 'that those artists who are the most inventive, the most astonishing and the most eccentric in their conceptions are often men whose life is calm and minutely ordered'.[22] He was a premeditative artist of Proustian interiority.

42. The grave at Varengeville, with its lapidary legend

He looked into and saw through. But that was not the end of his private toil. 'We must have the time to dream,' he would say. Braque dreamed open-eyed. He was a dedicated experimentalist. 'There are Braques that resemble artistic meditations on the processes of creation,' wrote Beckett.[23] The simplest thing that one can say of him is that he knew how to paint. Georges Braque was a painter. For other painters, young and old, he was *the* painter. 'After him, who?' asked Ozenfant. He was not merely influential. He had a much rarer distinction. He won for himself the kind of glory beautifully described by Paul Valéry: 'To become for someone else an example of the dedicated life, being secretly invoked, pictured, and placed by a stranger in a sanctum of his thoughts, so as to serve him as a witness, a judge, a father, a hallowed mentor.'[24] Such a man was the talentless painter Braque.

He went to the brink of what could not be done. 'That Braque was the greatest formal artist of the twentieth century is hardly in doubt,' Robert Hughes has concluded; 'nor have many painters since Piero della Francesca displayed such a perfect command over a complex pictorial structure. But in the process he made some of the most mysterious images in modern art.'[25] His boldness was as deceptive as his slowness. In the *annus mirabilis* of 1949, after thirty years of premeditation, he was bold enough to paint five *Studios*, two of them immense canvases off the scale of the old-style numbering. He signed the last of the series in 1953 (but continued reworking it for another three years). This surge may eventually be compared to the seasonal harvest of Cubist masterpieces in the summers before the Great War. *The Bird and Its Nest* (1955) and *In Full Flight* (1956–61) were still to come. So too the compact landscapes and seascapes, not so much painted as excavated, pigment by pigment, as if the old artist had followed his own advice and dug down to the root, to 'the foundation of all art: clay'.[26] It was these excavations that seized Giacometti, 'this almost bashful, imponderable painting, this naked painting, of a totally new daring, a much greater daring than that of long ago; painting that is for me at the forefront of innovation of the art of today with all its conflicts'. At the end of the century the same vision haunted Jean Bazaine in his own grand old age: 'Braque, leaning on the railing on the seashore, at Dieppe, pondering his last little canvases, those seascapes with dark skies, so false, so true.'[27]

Yet the seven inadequate volumes of Braque's *catalogue raisonné* peter out in 1957. The last six years of work remain uncatalogued, a symptom of a general state.[28] The reference books are bare, the entries on Braque almost comically abbreviated. *The Oxford Companion to Art* (1970):

On recovering from a serious wound in 1917 Braque went his own way, first concentrating on still lifes in the French classical tradition with the emphasis strongly on structure and during the 1930s painting beach scenes in which patterned arabesque came into greater prominence. His development combined elegance with formal simplification and culminated in a series of *Oiseaux* [birds] done in the 1950s. He was made a Commander of the Legion of Honour in 1951.

The Catalogue of the Tate Gallery's Collection of Modern Art (1981):

His later paintings included many compositions of still lifes and interiors with contrasting patterns and more complex effects of space, including a series of *Studios* begun in 1948. Designed décor for several ballets, including *Les Fâcheux* 1923–4. Awarded First Prize at the Pittsburgh International and the main painting prize at the 1948 Venice Biennale. Died in Paris.

In Paris there was a retrospective at the Orangerie in the winter of 1973–4, and a centenary exhibition at the Musée national d'art moderne in 1982. There has been nothing since. The late work has never been seen in strength in the French capital. In 1997 a revelatory assemblage of that work, master-minded by John Golding, appeared only at the Royal Academy in London and the Menil Collection in Houston. A selection of Braque's Cubism is permanently on show, but institutionally he is invisible. The Braque Museum in Paris is conspicuous by its absence. Pilgrims to Varengeville are few. Georges Braque may be a 'memory place' in French culture, but it is not much visited.[29] 'Art creates I-distantness,' as Paul Celan observed. 'Art in a certain direction demands a certain distance, a certain path.'[30] And so the paintings bide their time, Braque-bereft. They have almost all their life still before them.[31]

According to Proust, the original artist must proceed as oculists do. The paintings are a course of treatment, not always agreeable. 'When it is over, the practitioner says, "Now look." And then the world (which was created not once but as many times as there have been original artists) strikes us as entirely different from the old world yet perfectly clear.'[32] Ellsworth Kelly was one of many artists on both sides of the Atlantic, including all the major American modernists, who spent long hours among the late works at the Menil Collection or the Royal Academy in 1997. 'Recently I was looking at the late Braques, and afterwards for days I would go round the house and say, my God, everything looks like a Braque.'[33] Patrick Heron had a bad case of this hallucination, as he described it, for many years: 'the hallucination which projected Braque's forms and colours, as it were physically *in between* my eyes and *all* the windows, jugs, tables, and chairs with which I came into contact'.[34]

For some it was the Braque-world itself that colonized the imagination. After the misarrayed Tate exhibition, behind the back of the superior critics, under-nourished artists all over England started painting *Still Life with Kippers*. 'What has Braque done to you?' his friends asked Bryan Wynter, aghast.[35] The same question might have been put to Ivon Hitchens, Ben Nicholson, or John Piper. For others it was a part of the whole, an element, an intriguing detail: for William Congdon the colours, for Ellsworth Kelly the shapes.[36] The shape of a light fitting Kelly appropriated from the corner of a Braque still life became *Sneaker or Brooklyn Bridge* (1955) – metamorphism worthy of the master – and thereafter a whole series of *Brooklyn Bridges*. He was hooked. Fifty years later he bought a small Braque of his own, one of the late landscapes. He loved examining the pigment, as if taking soil samples, and revelled in the communion with the unfettered Braque, just as Braque had revelled in the unvarnished Cézanne.[37] Rilke said of Cézanne that he did not paint 'Look at me', but 'Here it is'. So with Braque.

Meanwhile, in twenty-first-century New York, the octogenarian Françoise Gilot could be seen in her studio, resplendent, surrounded entirely by her own paintings, on the walls, on the easels, on the floor . . . with one exception. In a small corner of the kind that Jean Paulhan once hungered for, out of the direct sunlight, glowed a magnificent late Braque. A few blocks away, the famous Juilliard School offered a course on 'Bach to Braque and Beyond', a neat summary. The bracketing would surely have pleased him. Braque is a natural benchmark. The prescient reach for him almost instinctively. 'I used to ascribe that fierce, vain desire for temporal beauty to *man*,' recorded Sartre in his diary. 'Whereas, I now consider it a characteristic of my own. I see that the Beaver [Simone de Beauvoir] is moved, above all, by the presentation outside her of a wholly inhuman aesthetic necessity – let's say, by a Bach fugue or a picture by Braque: she doesn't want her life to form the material of that necessity.'[38] In Beckett's characteristic pronouncement on

Yeats: 'He is with the great of our time, Kandinsky and Klee, Ballmer and Bram Van Velde, Rouault and Braque, because he brings light, as only the great dare to bring light, to the issueless predicament of existence.'[39]

On the occasion of an exhibition at the Maeght Foundation, when he himself was of an age at which Braque died, Francis Ponge immortalized the Master of Life.

During the Second World War, the presence or rather the idea of Braque (that of the man and the work) permitted us, no matter where in France we found ourselves, not only not to despair, but in hope and patience . . . with all its risks, to fight; permitted us, 'we of the future' in the phrase of the Cubists' best friend, . . . Galloping Guy [Apollinaire], the one who so bravely, gallantly . . . left Nîmes for the front the same summer's day in 14 that Braque and Derain left Avignon . . .

Yes, today, just like then, more indispensably and beneficially than then, Braque's presence reassures us. For he is here, always present, as he said one day to Jean Leymarie of his other friend, Reverdy, who had just died: 'But he is here, always present; what else is there to say and of how many others, still living, can one say the same?' . . .

Yes, against all odds, in the dangerous unsteadiness of the world, Braque is still here, Braque holds. In the present terrible confusion, national and global, morals, violence, terrorism, cowardice, atrocities, spinelessness, ignominy, just as during the Occupation I leant on his idea and that of Picasso, today his idea alone reassures me.

I am well aware that Braque said that art is made to disturb, not to reassure. Well, it is precisely by disturbing me that his art reassures me.[40]

Close to death, Braque slipped in and out of consciousness. On one occasion when he came to, he asked for his palette.

'What use would I be, deprived of painting?'

His last palette:

raw umber
burnt umber
raw sienna

burnt sienna
yellow ochre
lamp black
vine black
bone black
ultramarine
orange–yellow
antimony yellow[41]

Appendix A: Prices by Number

With dealers and fellow-artists, Braque habitually used common abbreviations and a standard numerical scale to indicate canvas size (in centimetres) and to negotiate prices (in francs). He would speak of a 'number 6', for example, or a 'NM 6', meaning a still life (*nature morte*) of 41 × 33 cm (measured on the Figure scale), which his dealer would buy from him at the agreed rate of 75 francs, according to his contract of 1912.

Canvas number/ points	1912 price	?1913 price	1916 price	1920 price	Figure [Figure] (F)	Landscape [Paysage] (P)	Seascape [Marine] (M)
1				130	22×16	22×14	22×12
2				260	24×19	24×16	24×14
3				390	27×22	27×19	27×16
4				520	33×24	33×22	33×19
5	60			650	35×27	35×24	35×22
6	75	100	150	780	41×33	41×27	41×24
8	100	150	200	1,040	46×38	46×33	46×27
10	125	200	350	1,300	55×46	55×38	55×33
12	150	250	400	1,560	61×50	61×46	61×38
15	175	300	500	1,950	65×54	65×50	65×46
20	200	350	600	2,600	73×60	73×54	73×50
25	250	450	700	3,250	81×65	81×60	81×54
30	300	550	800	3,900	92×73	92×65	92×60
40	350	650	900	5,200	100×81	100×73	100×65
50	400	800	1,100	6,500	116×89	116×81	116×73
60	400	800	1,200	7,800	130×97	130×89	130×81
80					146×114	146×97	146×89
100					162×130	162×114	162×97
120					195×130	195×114	195×97

1912 contract with Kahnweiler (30 November 1912)
1913? prices agreed with Kahnweiler (22 December 1913?)

1916 contract with Léonce Rosenberg (24 November 1916)
1920 contract with Kahnweiler (11 May 1920)

Sources: Assouline, *L'Homme*, pp. 183, 287–8; *Papiers collés*, p. 41; *P&B* symposium, p. 345; Fonds Léonce Rosenberg, MNAM.

Appendix B: 'Thoughts and Reflections on Painting' (1917)*

1. In art progress consists not in extension but in the knowledge of its limits.

2. The limits of the means employed determine the style, engender the new form and impel to creation.

3. The charm and the force of children's paintings often stem from the limited means employed. Conversely the art of decadence is a product of extension.

4. New means, new subjects.

5. The subject is not the object; it is the new unity, the lyricism which stems entirely from the means employed.

6. The painter thinks in forms and colours.

7. The aim is not to *reconstitute* an anecdotal fact but to *constitute* a pictorial fact.

8. Painting is a mode of representation.

9. One must not imitate what one wishes to create.

10. One does not imitate the appearance; the appearance is the result.

11. To be pure imitation, painting must make an abstraction of appearances.

12. To work from nature is to improvise. One must beware of an *all-purpose* formula, suitable for interpreting the other arts as well as reality, and which, instead of creating, would produce only a style or rather a stylization.

13. The arts that make their effect by their purity have never been all-purpose arts. Greek sculpture and its decadence, among others, teach us this.

14. The senses deform, the mind forms. Work to perfect the mind. There is no certainty except what the mind conceives.

---

* Braque's 'Pensées et réflexions sur la peinture', *Nord-Sud* 10 (1917), pp. 3–5, in Jonathan Griffin's translation, from Edward F. Fry (ed.), *Cubism* (London: Thames and Hudson, 1966), pp. 147–8.

15. A painter trying to make a circle would only make a ring. Possibly the look of it may satisfy him but he will have doubts. The compass will restore his certainty. The *papiers collés* in my drawings have also given me a kind of certainty.

16. *Trompe-l'œil* is due to an *anecdotal* accident that makes its effect through the simplicity of the facts.

17. The *papiers collés*, the imitation wood – and other elements of the same nature – which I have used in certain drawings, also make their effect through the simplicity of the facts, and it is this that has led people to confuse them with *trompe-l'œil*, of which they are precisely the opposite. They too are simple facts, but *created by the mind* and such that they are one of the justifications of a new figuration in space.

18. Nobility comes from contained emotion.

19. Emotion must not be rendered by an emotional trembling. It is not something that is added, or that is imitated. It is the germ, the work is the flowering.

20. I love the rule which corrects emotion.

Appendix C: Prices at Sales

Average price per number of all but the smallest paintings auctioned at the Kahnweiler and Uhde sales of 1921–3, according to the analysis of Malcolm Gee.★

	Braque	Picasso	Derain	Vlaminck	Léger	Gris
Uhde sale	44	177	–	–	25	15
Kahnweiler						
1st sale	66	61	326	39	24	25
2nd sale	34	59	112	46	7	10
3rd sale	15	36	143	39	5	7
4th sale	19	47	86	43	2	4

★ 'The avant-garde, order and the art market, 1916–23', *Art History*, 2 (1979), p. 102 (figures rounded out), founded on his pioneering doctoral dissertation, published as *Dealers, Critics and Collectors of Modern Painting: Aspects of the Parisian Art Market 1910–1930* (NY: Garland, 1981). See vol. II, appendix F.

Abbreviations

Argenteuil	Archives Municipales, Argenteuil
Ateliers	Jean Leymarie, *Braque: Les Ateliers* (Aix: Édisud, 1995)
Beinecke	Beinecke Rare Book and Manuscript Library, Yale
BNF	Bibliothèque Nationale de France
Cahier	*Cahier de Georges Braque* (Paris: Maeght, 1994)
Daix	Pierre Daix and Joan Rosselet, *Picasso: The Cubist Years 1907–1916: A Catalogue Raisonné of the Paintings and Related Works* (London: Thames and Hudson, 1979)
Doucet	Bibliothèque Littéraire Jacques Doucet, Paris
L'Espace	Françoise Cohen et al., *Georges Braque: L'Espace* (Paris: Biro, 1999)
Europe	*Georges Braque en Europe* (Bordeaux: Galerie des Beaux-Arts, 1982)
G. Braque	Arts Council of Great Britain, *G. Braque* (London: Curwen, 1956)
GEM	Galerie de l'Effort Moderne, Paris
Getty	Getty Research Library, Los Angeles
Gianadda	Jean-Louis Prat, *Braque* (Martigny: Fondation Pierre Gianadda, 1992)
Guggenheim	Jean Leymarie, *Georges Braque* (NY: Guggenheim, 1988)
Havre	Archives Municipales, Le Havre
IMEC	Institut Mémoires de l'Édition Contemporaine, Paris
Jour et Nuit	*Le Jour et la Nuit: Cahiers de George Braque* (Paris: Gallimard, 1952)

Kahnweiler	*Daniel-Henry Kahnweiler* (Paris: Centre Pompidou, 1984)
KY	Kettle's Yard, Cambridge
Late Works	John Golding et al., *Braque: The Late Works* (London: RA, 1997)
Légion	Grande Chancellerie de la Légion d'Honneur, Paris
Leiris	Galerie Louise Leiris, Paris
Leiris	*Donation Louise et Michel Leiris* (Paris: Centre Pompidou, 1984)
Louvre	Musée du Louvre, Paris
LRB	*London Review of Books*
Maeght	*Georges Braque* (Saint-Paul: Fondation Maeght, 1994)
Maeght (1980)	*Georges Braque* (Saint-Paul: Fondation Maeght, 1980)
Marcelle	Marcelle Braque
Mariette	Mariette Lachaud
Mariette tapes	tape-recorded recollections, privately held
Menil	Menil Collection, Houston, Texas
Met	Metropolitan Museum of Art, New York
MF	microfilm
MFA	Museum of Fine Art
MNAM	Musée national d'art moderne, Paris
MoMA	Museum of Modern Art, New York
MP	Archives Picasso, Musée Picasso, Paris
n.d.	not dated
NGA	National Gallery of Art, Washington, DC
NM	*nature morte* [still life]
n.p.	not paginated
NRF	*La Nouvelle Revue Française*
NYPL	New York Public Library
NYRB	*New York Review of Books*
Orangerie	*Georges Braque* (Paris: Musées Nationaux, 1973)
Orsay	Musée d'Orsay, Paris

PAB	Pierre-André Benoit
Papiers collés	Isabelle Monod-Fontaine, *Braque: les papiers collés* (Paris: MNAM, 1982)
Patron	Jean Paulhan, *Braque le patron* (Gallimard, 1952)
PC	private collection
Phillips	Phillips Collection, Washington
Picasso	John Richardson, *A Life of Picasso* (London: Cape, 1991–):
	I 1881–1906 (1991)
	II 1907–1917 (1996)
P&B	William Rubin (ed.), *Picasso and Braque* (NY: MoMA, 1989)
P&B symposium	Lynn Zelevansky (ed.), *Picasso and Braque* (NY: MoMA, 1992)
PML	Pierpont Morgan Library, New York
RA	Royal Academy of Arts, London
Ransom	Harry Ransom Research Center for the Humanities, Austin, Texas
RMN	Réunion des Musées Nationaux
Romilly	Nicole Worms de Romilly (Nicole S. Mangin), *Catalogue raisonné de l'œuvre de Georges Braque* (Paris: Maeght, 1959–82):
	I 1948–1957 (1959)
	II 1942–1947 (1960)
	III 1936–1941 (1961)
	IV 1928–1935 (1962)
	V 1924–1927 (1968)
	VI 1916–1923 (1973)
	VII 1907–1914 (1982)
SJP	Fondation Saint-John Perse, Aix-en-Provence
Still Lifes	*Braque: Still Lifes and Interiors* (London: South Bank Centre, 1990)
Tate	Tate [Gallery], London
Thyssen	Tomàs Llorens et al., *Braque* (Madrid:

	Thyssen-Bornemisza, 2002)
Vallier	Dora Vallier, trans. Robert Bononno and
	Pamela Barr, *Braque: The Complete Graphics*
	[*Catalogue raisonné de l'œuvre gravé* (Paris:
	Flammarion, 1982)] (London: Alpine, 1988)
Vincennes	Service historique de l'Armée de terre,
	Vincennes

Note: in contemporary usage, women were almost always referred to by first name only, and men by surname only – Marcelle was always Marcelle, Braque was always Braque, even to each other. On the whole, this usage has been followed here.

Notes

CHAPTER 1: 'Everyone has his own coffee grounds':
         The Apprentice

1. 'Enfoncement du crâne par éclat d'obus (trépanation)', according to
   the entry in his service record. Dossier Braque, Vincennes.
2. 'Georges Braque. Sa vie racontée par lui-même', *Amis de l'art*, no. 6
   (1949); Henriette Chandet and Hubert de Segonzac, 'Georges Braque
   le père tranquille de cubisme', *Paris-Match*, 5–12 June 1954; *Patron*,
   pp. 36–7. His birth certificate records that he was born at 9.00 in the
   evening. It was he who insisted on the coincidental timing. See, e.g.,
   Paul Guth, 'Visite à Georges Braque', *Le Figaro Littéraire*, 13 May
   1950.
3. A tape recorder was disallowed by the artist. For Vallier's recollections
   of the interviews and their circumstances, 'Pour situer les entretiens',
   L'Intérieur de l'art (Paris: Seuil, 1982), pp. 9–15. Braque himself,
   apparently, came to call it his testament.
4. Friedrich Nietzsche, trans. R. G. Hollingdale, *Human, All Too Human*
   [1886] (Cambridge: Cambridge University Press, 1996), p. 83.
5. *Cahier*, p. 23. He adds: 'We exploit him without knowing that it is
   him.' Perhaps a variant on Delacroix, 'We are not understood, we
   are acknowledged,' a remark Matisse liked to quote; but there is a
   strikingly similar (and very apt) passage in Rilke: 'When one speaks
   of solitaries, one always takes too much for granted. One supposes
   that people know what one is talking about. No, they do not. They
   have never seen a solitary; they have simply hated him without
   knowing him.' Interview with Léon Degand [1945], in Jack Flam
   (ed.), *Matisse on Art* (Berkeley: University of California Press, 1995),
   p. 164; *The Notebooks of Malte Laurids Brigge* [1910], trans. M. D.
   Herter Norton (NY: Norton, 1964), p. 160. *Les Cahiers de Malte*

Laurids Brigge, first published in Paris in 1923, were already in their third edition by 1926.

6. See Montaigne, trans. M. A. Screech, 'On glory', in *The Complete Essays* [1580] (London: Penguin, 1993), p. 704 (emphasis in original), citing Plutarch's *Moralia*, in the widely read French translation of Bishop Jacques Amyot, *Les Œuvres morales et meslées* (1572 and much reprinted), works with which Braque could well have been familiar.

7. Cézanne to Joachim Gasquet, 30 April 1896, in Paul Cézanne, *Letters* [1941] (NY: Da Capo, 1995), p. 245, required reading for the older Braque.

8. Interview with Jean Leymarie, 22 December 2000.

9. Henry R. Hope, *Georges Braque* (NY: MoMA, 1949), pp. 13ff. Hope was briefed by Henri-Pierre Roché, of whom more below.

10. Recollections of Mariette Lachaud; see MNAM, p. 134. I am grateful for the assistance of the Archives Municipales and the Cimetière du Centre, Argenteuil. The location of the grave is carré 4, ligne 2, no. 10.

11. Vallier, 'Braque, la peinture et nous' [1954], *L'Intérieur*, pp. 29–31 (suspension marks Vallier's throughout, interpolations in square brackets mine). Cf. *Patron*, pp. 69–72; Hope, *Braque*, pp. 11–15. It is essentially this version that has been recycled ever since. See, e.g., Janet Flanner, 'Master' [1956], in *Men and Monuments* (NY: Da Capo, 1990), pp. 119ff.; Bernard Zurcher, trans. Simon Nye, *Georges Braque* (NY: Rizzoli, 1988), pp. 9ff.

12. John Richardson, *Georges Braque* (London: Penguin, 1959), p. 4. Two early drawings of the male nude, an athlete and an old man (c. 1900–03), the only two he seems to have preserved, are reproduced in Alvin Martin's unpublished doctoral dissertation, *Georges Braque: Stylistic Formation and Transition 1900–1909* (Harvard University, 1979), p. 327; an ink drawing of *Laundry Barges on the Seine* (1902) is reproduced in Guggenheim, no. 91.

13. Cf. Paulhan's retailing of their respective views. *Patron*, p. 46.

14. Ibid., p. 65.

15. Testimony of Maurice Lesieutre, in Bernard Esdras-Gosse, 'De Raoul Dufy à Jean Dubuffet ou la descendance du "Père" Lhullier', *Études Normandes*, XVII (1955), p. 27.

16. See Kirk Varnedoe, 'Caillebotte's will and bequest', in *Gustave Caille-botte* (New Haven: Yale University Press, 1987), pp. 197–204. The Cézannes were *L'Estaque* (1883–5) and *Cour de ferme à Anvers* (1879–83). *Baigneurs au repos* (1875–7), *Vase de fleurs* (1875–7), and an unidentified *Scène champêtre* were rejected. The selected works are now in the Musée d'Orsay.

17. Y, 'Un dimanche d'été', *La Vie Parisienne*, 3 July 1875, quoted in Paul Hayes Tucker, *Monet at Argenteuil* (New Haven: Yale University Press, 1982), p. 118.

18. Armand Salacrou, *C'était écrit* (Paris: Gallimard, 1974), pp. 13–14. After another period of enforced dilapidation, Salacrou's shack (as he called it) has mutated into a smart restaurant, La Villa, where any original feature is a rarity.

19. See Vivien Hamilton, *Boudin at Trouville* (London: Murray, 1982), pp. 36–9, 44. This version of the tree exchange follows Paul Valéry, trans. Martin Turnell, 'About Corot' [1932], in *Masters and Friends* (London: RKP, 1968), p. 153.

20. Records of the Cercle de l'Art Moderne, Fonds Contemporain, Archives Municipales, Le Havre. See Françoise Cohen, 'A gallery which is personal', in Timothy Wilcox and Margot Heller (eds), *Boudin to Dufy* (Aldershot: Scolar, 1996), p. 11; Guillaume Apollin-aire, 'Les Trois Vertus plastiques' (1908), in *Chroniques d'art* (Paris: Gallimard, 1960), pp. 56–8. Apollinaire's text was later incorporated into his celebrated meditations on *Les Peintres cubistes* (1913). Exhibiting artists included Bonnard, Dufy, Friesz, Marquet, Matisse, Monet, Vlaminck and Vuillard. Braque, Dufy and Friesz constituted the Committee on Painting.

21. *Havre Éclair* [1905], in Jean Legoy, 'Georges Braque et Le Havre', *Havre Libre*, 14 September 1994.

22. Albert Herrenschmidt, 'Le Cercle de l'Art Moderne', *Le Havre*, 27 and 28 May 1906. A gouache is a watercolour painting that is opaque rather than transparent. The colour pigments are bound with glue; an admixture of white is used for lighter tones. Unlike transparent watercolours, the ground of the work (the paper or whatever it is painted on) does not usually show through, meaning that *gouaches* tend to lack the luminosity of their transparent counterparts.

23. Charles Braque's painting is evoked by Hope, *Braque*, p. 11, and Leymarie, *Braque*, p. 13. The similarity of signature was noted at the time by Leymarie: interview, 22 December 2000.

24. *Patron*, pp. 60–61 (inserting a rhyming 'Monsieur Braque').

25. Records of Lycée François I, Argenteuil; Braque interviews with Guth and others. 'Stupidity is not my forte' was a favourite formulation of Paul Valéry's. See *Monsieur Teste* [1896] (Paris: Gallimard, 1946), p. 15.

26. Esdras-Gosse, 'Lhullier', pp. 18, 24, 27; Braque, 'Sa vie', no. 4; Louis Vauxcelles, *Le Fauvisme* [1958, composed 1939] (Paris: Olbia, 1999), p. 93.

27. Hope, *Braque*, p. 12; Gelett Burgess, 'The Wild Men of Paris', *The Architectural Record*, 27 (1910), p. 405; *Cahier*, pp. 15 and 41.

28. Quoted in André Verdet, *Georges Braque* (Geneva: Kister, 1956), pp. 10–11.

29. 'Varengeville' [1968], in *Couleurs*, p. 35.

30. 'Seashores' [1942], trans. Margaret Guiton, in *Selected Poems*, p. 51 (my emphasis).

31. See *Harfleur Landscape* (c. 1900) and *The Côte de Grâce at Honfleur* (1905) in Maeght, nos 1 and 3. Cf. Karen Wilkin, *Braque* (NY: Abbeville, 1991), pp. 17–19.

32. Interview with Marc-Antoine (Louttre) Bissière and Laure Latapie Bissière, 15 March 2001.

33. Cf. André Verdet, *Georges Braque le solitaire* (Paris: XX Siècle, 1959), borrowing from his own interview with Fernand Léger: 'Braque, c'est un silencieux, un solitaire'. *Entretiens, notes et écrits sur la peinture* (Paris: Galilée, 1978), p. 62.

34. Herman Melville, *Moby Dick* [1851] (Oxford: Oxford University Press, 1998), p. 106.

35. Fernande Olivier, *Picasso et ses amis* (Paris: Stock, 1933), p. 126. Elsewhere she acknowledges that Braque was born at Argenteuil, 'by accident' (p. 121). The magnificent new edition of Olivier's writings, *Loving Picasso* (NY: Abrams, 2001), edited by Marilyn McCully and translated by Christine Baker and Michael Raeburn, establishes a more reliable text. In this instance I offer a slightly different translation (and interpretation): cf. p. 196.

36. See *Picasso*, vol. I, pp. 126, 168, 173.

37. *Patron*, p. 70; Arthur Symons, *From Toulouse-Lautrec to Rodin* (1929) and *Gil Blas* (1891), in Richard Thomson, *Toulouse-Lautrec* (London: Oresko, 1977), pp. 59 and 63.

38. Rilke, *Malte Laurids Brigge*, pp. 169–70.

39. Chateaubriand, *Mémoires d'Outre-Tombe* [1848–50] (Paris: Flammarion, 1948), strictly, a four-volume work by the time of this centenary edition.

40. He later illustrated Heraclitus, Milarepa and Hesiod: *Héraclite d'Ephèse*, trans. Yves Battistini (Paris: Cahiers d'Art, 1948); *Milarepa*, trans. Jacques Bacot (Paris: Maeght, 1950); Hesiod, *Théogonie* (Paris: Maeght, 1955), Vallier, nos. 42, 63, 23. Milarepa was an eleventh-century Tibetan magician-poet-hermit (as billed in the French edition). The *Theogony* of Hesiod was a long-delayed outcome of a commission from Vollard in the 1930s – one of the most significant of Braque's career. See ch. 8.

41. Vauvenargues, 'Réflexions et maximes' [1797], *Œuvres complètes* (Paris: Alive, 1999), p. 353 (no. 267); La Rochefoucauld, trans. Leonard Tancock, 'Reflections or aphorisms and moral maxims' [1665], *Maxims* (London: Penguin, 1959), p. 93 (no. 439). Vauvenargues is not well served in English. Cf. *The Reflections and Maxims*, trans. F. G. Stevens (London: Milford, 1940).

42. Jean Cassou, 'Préface', *L'Atelier de Braque* (Paris: RMN, 1961), n.p.

43. See Paulhan to Braque, 2 December 1946, in Jean Paulhan, *Choix des Lettres*, 3 vols (Paris: Gallimard, 1986–96), vol. III, p. 39. This was *Justine ou les Malheurs de la vertu* [1787], a new edition with a preface by Paulhan himself.

44. Evariste-Régis Huc and Joseph Granet, *Souvenirs d'un voyage dans la Tartarie, le Thibet et la Chine pendant les années 1844, 1845 et 1846* [1851], trans. William Hazlitt, *Travels in Tartary, Tibet and China* (London: Routledge, 1928).

45. Braque to Paul Rosenberg, 15 December [1939], Rosenberg Collection, PML. Most probably Richard E. Byrd, trans. L. C. Herbert, *Pôle sud* (Paris: Grasset, 1937).

46. Extract from Braque's unpublished notebook, copied by René Char, 26 December 1948, Fonds Char, 906, AE.IV.7bis, Doucet.

47. *Cahier*, p. 35; Vallier, 'Braque', p. 41. Cf. Ponge on the 'qualities or circumstances' of the shrimp. 'La crevette', trans. C. K. Williams, in *Selected Poems*, p. 81.

48. See Eugen Herrigel, trans. R. F. C. Hull, *Zen in the Art of Archery* (London: Penguin, 1985). Pierre Assouline, *Henri Cartier-Bresson* (Paris: Plon, 1999), pp. 175–7; letter from Henri Cartier-Bresson, 12 December 2000.

49. See Gustie L. Herrigel, trans. R. F. C. Hull, *Zen in the Art of Flower Arrangement* (London: Souvenir, 1999). Mariette Lachaud, tape-recorded recollections, in conversation with Anne de Staël, privately held.

50. Valéry, 'Stendhal', in *Masters and Friends*, pp. 185–7.

51. Arthur Rimbaud, 'Voyelles', in Graham Robb, *Rimbaud* (London: Picador, 2000), pp. 135–6 (Robb's translation). The verdicts are from Edmond Goncourt's journal (1889) and Félicien Champsaur's novel, *Dinah Samuel* (1882), in ibid., p. 417. Braque later contributed an original lithograph, 'The Bird in Front of the Moon', to *Arthur Rimbaud vu par les peintres* (privately published, 1958), Vallier, no. 133.

52. 'Roney' in the existing literature is a misspelling (or mishearing).

53. A list compiled largely from pointers in the Mariette tapes. See also Vallier, 'Braque', p. 49; and the emphasis on *matière* and *métier* in the early work of Roger Bissière, *Georges Braque* (Paris: L'Effort Moderne, 1920), clearly derived from Braque's talk. The painting is *The Saint-Martin Canal* (1906); 'a mere puff of smoke' is suggested by Alexander Theroux, *The Primary Colours* (NY: Holt, 1994), p. 44. Sienna is a fine pigment made from ferruginous, ochrous earth, brownish-yellow when raw, a warm reddish-brown when 'burnt' or roasted. Ceruse is white lead. Antimony (stibium) is a brittle, metallic blue-white element.

54. *Patron*, p. 61. And earlier, to Tériade: 'My painting is revealed on canvas as the future is foretold in coffee grounds.' 'Émancipation de la peinture' [1933], in *Écrits sur l'art* (Paris: Biro, 1996), p. 450.

55. Vallier, 'Braque', p. 48. Cf. Ponge: 'Ideas are not my forte.' Margaret Guiton, preface to *Selected Poems*, p. ix.

56. 'Earth' [1942], in *Selected Poems*, p. 161.

57. Fumet, *Braque*, p. 14. See also ch. 9. Braque probably knew the novel by his near-neighbour in Varengeville, Raymond Queneau, *The Children of Clay* [1938] (Berkeley: Sun and Moon, 1997).

58. Jean-Paul Sartre, 'L'Homme et les choses' [1944], in *Situations*, vol. I (Paris: Gallimard, 1947), p. 253; Braque, introduction to 'Hommage à Francis Ponge', *NRF*, 45 (1956), p. 385, an adaptation of his own maxim, 'Start from the lowest point in order to have a chance to rise', and an echo (perhaps unconscious) of Lucretius, a favourite of both men, subsequently identified by Ponge with Braque: 'You, glory of the Greeks, I follow you/And in your footprints plant my footsteps firm.' *Cahier*, p. 107; Lucretius, trans. Ronald Melville, *On the Nature of the Universe* (Oxford: Oxford University Press, 1997), p. 70, addressing Epicurus. *Le Parti pris des choses* (1942) was the title of the collection that made Ponge's reputation, a collection much admired by Braque. See Paulhan to Ponge, 7 September [1942], in *Jean Paulhan/Francis Ponge* (Paris: Gallimard, 1986), vol. I, p. 280. For a parallel reflection on his own situation, and a comparison to Braque, see Francis Ponge, trans. Lane Dunlop, *Soap* [1967] (Stanford: Stanford University Press, 1998), pp. 45–6.

59. An explanation I owe to Paul Edson. Littré nods on the details of the festival.

60. Collected in *Le Grand Recueil*, vol. III (Paris: Gallimard, 1961), pp. 102–21, quotation p. 105.

61. *Five Sapates* (Paris: Tournon, 1950), Vallier, no. 62; François Chapon, *Le Peintre et le livre* (Paris: Flammarion, 1987), pp. 267–70.

62. Guth, 'Visite'; Brassaï, trans. Richard Miller, *The Artists of My Life* (London: Thames and Hudson, 1982), p. 19.

63. Quoted in 'The Salon of 1765', in *Diderot on Art*, trans. John Goodman (New Haven: Yale University Press, 1995), vol. I, p. 5.

CHAPTER 2: 'Memories in anticipation':
     The Confirmed Painter

1. Dossier Braque, Vincennes; records of La Grande Chancellerie de la Légion d'Honneur, Paris. The precise chronology of Braque's early life is extremely difficult to establish, such is the documentary paucity. In this instance, however, despite subsequent confusions (generated not least by Braque himself, whose dating of his own pre-history is highly unreliable), the records are categorical: the initial year of his military service ran from October 1902 to September 1903.

2. Hope, *Braque*, pp. 14–15; Leymarie, *Braque*, p. 15; Chandet, 'Le père'.

3. Braque to Picasso [April 1911], MP; 'Échos', *Le Supplément*, 21 December 1911, in *P&B*, p. 387. Braque underwent further full-time military training in July–August 1905, September 1909, and March–April 1911.

4. *Cousin Johanet* (1900) in Orangerie, no. 2. Cf. Chandet, 'Le père'.

5. Van Gogh (1853–90) had lived in the rue Lepic sixteen years earlier, in 1887, as Braque may well have known – the first van Gogh retrospective was held at Bernheim-Jeune in 1901, and Braque was already interested.

6. Cf. Cézanne to Émile Bernard, 12 May 1904, in John Rewald (ed.), trans. Marguerite Kay, *Cézanne Letters* [1941] (NY: Da Capo, 1995), pp. 302–3.

7. Vallier, 'Braque', p. 31; *Patron*, p. 46; Flanner, 'Master', p. 126 (the source of the anonymous remark about beefsteak).

8. Vallier, 'Braque', pp. 30–31. Lack of records and Braque's rather free-floating status there make the exact dating of his time at the Académie Humbert a hazardous enterprise. The period usually given, 1902–4, now seems too early, and (insofar as it tends to indicate a full two years) too long. Late 1903 to early 1905 is more likely, with time off for bad behaviour (of which more below), and a tailing off towards the end.

9. Vallier, 'Braque', p. 31; Maria Lluisa Borràs, *Picabia* (Paris: Michel, 1985), p. 15. Braque finds a place in Picabia's self-advertising inter-

war review *391*, reproduced in Michel Sanouillet (ed.), *391* [1917–24] (Paris: Belfond, 1975), but not a very interesting one. The crack about Cézanne was given currency by André Breton. See Pierre Daix, introduction to Brassaï, trans. Jane Marie Todd, *Conversations with Picasso* [1964] (Chicago: University of Chicago Press, 1999), p. xvii. See also ch. 6.

10. Claude Lepape and Thierry Defert, *Georges Lepape ou l'élégance illustrée* (Paris: Herscher, 1983), p. 20.

11. On the symbolic importance of cats, see Julia Fagan-King, 'United on the threshold of the twentieth-century mystical ideal: Marie Laurencin's integral involvement with Guillaume Apollinaire and the inmates of the *Bateau Lavoir*', *Art History*, 11 (1988), pp. 88–114, esp. 95–6.

12. Stein, *Toklas*, p. 68. Probably François Clouet (before 1510–72), a portraitist from a line of portraitists, whose work could be seen in the Louvre and at Chantilly. His *Lady in Her Bath* (1570) is thought to represent Marie Touchet, mistress of Charles IX.

13. In Daniel Marchesseau, *Marie Laurencin* (Tokio: Curieux-Do, 1980), p. 163. Cf. *Picasso*, vol. II, pp. 64–5. Other students, and those with competing interests, Fernande Olivier for one, were not so smitten: *Loving Picasso*, pp. 207–9.

14. Lepape and Defert, *Lepape*, p. 22.

15. Stein, *Toklas*, p. 184; 'Marie Laurencin prend des élèves' [an interview], *L'Intransigeant*, 18 November 1932.

16. Laurencin to Roché, 12 and 28 April, 13 June 1906, Roché Papers, Ransom.

17. Roché diary, 26 March, 16 May, 24 June, 13 July, 23 August 1906, ibid.; Flora Groult, *Marie Laurencin* (Paris: Mercure de France, 1987), pp. 84–5. Cf. *Picasso*, vol. II, pp. 61ff.

18. Burgess, 'Wild Men', p. 405, an interview of April 1908.

19. '*Le Malherbe*' was the coinage of René Dalize, co-founder of *Les Soirées de Paris*: *Picasso*, vol. II, p. 62. Of the poet François de Malherbe (1555–1628) it was said that 'he reduces the Muse to rules of duty' (Boileau) – a premonition, perhaps, of Braque's rule that corrects emotion. *Manuel illustré d'histoire de la littérature française* (Paris: Gigord, 1953), p. 198.

20. Roché diary, 21 January 1906. See also his 'Souvenirs de Georges Braque' [1955], in *Écrits*, pp. 337–8; *Picasso*, vol. II, p. 62.

21. Paul Fort, *Mes mémoires* (Paris: Flammarion, 1944), p. 44 (Paulette is 'Manon'); Denys Sutton, *André Derain* (London: Phaedon, 1959), p. 8. Was Paulette also the model for 'the insatiate' Marthe Galland in André Salmon's *roman à clef*, *La Négresse du Sacré-Cœur* (1920), who recites her husband's poetry at the Stranglers' Cabaret and 'achieves a sort of Baudelairian perfection, by being at the same time spider and fly'?

22. André Salmon, *Modigliani* (Paris: Seghers, 1957), p. 71; Jean Mollet, *Les Mémoires du baron Mollet* (Paris: Gallimard, 1963), pp. 93–4.

23. Roché, 'Souvenirs', in *Écrits*, p. 338 (his emphasis).

24. Ibid., pp. 337–8; diary, 18 May 1906.

25. Braque to Reinhart Dozy, 4 August 1904, in Roberta Hilbrandie-Meijer, 'Drie brieven uit 1904 van Georges Braque aan Reinhart Dozy', *Jong Holland* 6 (1990), p. 15. Dozy was also at the Académie Humbert. On Vaillant see Lepape and Defert, *Lepape*, p. 20; Olivier, *Loving Picasso*, p. 202; Salmon, *Souvenirs*, vol. I, pp. 41–2. On Pons see Apollinaire to Picasso, 29 May 1906, in Pierre Caizergues and Hélène Seckel (eds), *Picasso/Apollinaire Correspondance* (Paris: Gallimard, 1992), pp. 44–6; Salmon, *Souvenirs*, vol. I, p. 194. The other man appears simply as Marinier.

26. Paris was full of Gauguin in 1903, the year of his death: the first Salon d'Automne included a memorial exhibition, and Vollard mounted something akin to a retrospective. Braque told Hope in 1948 that he had never liked Gauguin but was much impressed by van Gogh. *Braque*, p. 18. The name of the latter recurs often in his talk, the former almost never. Cf. *Patron*, p. 72; André Verdet, 'Autour du cubisme' [c. 1960], in *Entretiens*, p. 17.

27. Vallier, 'Braque', p. 49. Lake is originally a reddish pigment derived from lac, a dark-red resin secreted by certain coccid insects. Madder lake is from madder root. The ochre was from Port-Rhu in Brittany.

28. Braque to Dozy, 27 May and 4 August 1904, in Hilbrandie-Meijer, 'Drie brieven', p. 15.

29. Salmon, *Souvenirs*, vol. I, pp. 66–7.

30. *Little Breton Girl* (1904), in Orangerie, no. 5. *Luxe, calme et volupté*

[luxury, calm and voluptuousness], the refrain of 'L'Invitation au voyage' in Baudelaire's black book *Les Fleurs du mal* (1857), became the title of a new work by Matisse (1904–5), much admired by young and old alike (and snapped up by Signac). Spurling, *Matisse*, vol. I, fig. 17 and p. 297.

31. Laurencin to Roché, 12 April and 23 August 1906; Braque to Dozy, 4 August and 28 September 1904. On her own vices, opium and others, Paulette to Roché, 5 and 26 January 1912.

32. Atelier Bonnat inscription, 29 May 1905, AJ52 248, Archives Nationales. Following Hope, who spoke at some length to Braque about his early career, his brief interlude with Bonnat is usually dated autumn 1903 (cf. *Braque*, pp. 15–16): evidently too early.

33. Paul Gauguin, trans. Van Wyck Brooks, *Gauguin's Intimate Journals* [1921] (NY: Dover, 1997), p. 23.

34. The records do not show how long he was with Bonnat – according to Hope, 'a scant two months' – nor do they give any clue as to his progress. The Beaux-Arts has become another blank spot. Apart from his enrolment in Bonnat's studio, Braque's name does not appear on the list of registered students. Nevertheless there is a file on him – which is empty of information. Dossier scolaire, AJ52 301, Archives Nationales. I am grateful to Joëlla de Couëssin for help with these impenetrabilities.

35. Thomson, *Lautrec*, p. 7; André Verdet, 'Entretiens avec Henri Matisse' [1952], in Flam, *Matisse*, p. 213.

36. Cézanne to Bernard, 25 July 1904, in *Letters*, p. 306.

37. Rilke to Lou Andreas-Salome, 10 August 1903, in *New Poems: The Other Part*, p. ix (his emphasis); Vallier, 'Braque', pp. 31–2, spliced with Guth, 'Visite'. The God was Cézanne.

38. Tériade, 'Émancipation', in *Écrits*, p. 450.

39. A 1904 sketch of Hermine and a letter from her are preserved in the papers of Braque's fellow-student Reinhart Dozy. I am grateful to his son, Victor, for access to this material. L. M. appears in Inez Haynes Irwin's diary (27 April 1908, Beinecke) with Derain; it may be that she modelled for him, and for Picasso too. Cf. Hope, *Braque*, p. 17; *P&B*, p. 349; *Picasso*, vol. II, p. 85; Judith Freeman, *The Fauve Landscape* (NY: Abbeville, 1990), p. 109.

40. Verdet, 'Autour', p. 17. He sometimes added Poussin. Hope, *Braque*, p. 17.

41. Verdet, 'Rencontre', p. 32.

42. Georges Limbour, 'Georges Braque: découvertes et tradition', *L'Œil*, 33 (1957), p. 27. Cf. Pierre Schneider, *Les Dialogues du Louvre* (Paris: Biro, 1991), pp. 23ff.

43. Cézanne to Bernard, 25 July 1904, in *Letters*, p. 306; Pierre Mazars, 'D'un plafond du Louvre Georges Braque a fait un ciel', *Le Figaro Littéraire*, 25 April 1953. For his later view of Raphael, see Verdet, 'Rencontre', pp. 33–4. For the story of the ceiling, see ch. 10. The connection has been lost in subsequent reorganization: the Salle Henri II is now a hotchpotch of Roman gold and silverwork, and there are few staff who know the whereabouts of the Braque ceiling.

44. Paul Valéry, trans. Stuart Gilbert, *Analects* (London: RKP, 1970), p. 173.

45. *Patron*, pp. 71–2. Characteristically, and unlike his fellows (Dufy, Friesz and others), Braque does not feature in the registers of copyists in the archives of the Louvre. For Matisse's liberating experience as a copyist there see Spurling, *Matisse*, vol. I, pp. 85–7, 195–6.

46. *Picasso*, vol. II, p. 149, citing conversations with the artist.

47. Maurice Raynal, *Histoire de la peinture moderne*, vol. III (Geneva: Skira, 1950), p. 46.

48. Braque, 'Sa vie', no. 4.

49. Quoted in André Masson, 'Origines du cubisme et du surréalisme' [1941], in Françoise Will-Levaillant (ed.), *La Rebelle du surréalisme* (Paris: Hermann, 1976), pp. 20–21.

50. This bestiary is from Jacques Bonjean, 'L'Époque fauve de Braque', *Beaux-Arts*, 8 February 1938.

51. Verdet, 'Autour', p. 17; Louis Vauxcelles, 'Le Salon d'Automne', *Gil Blas*, 17 October 1905, in *Fauvisme*, p. 132. 'L'orgie des tons purs' was a doubtful compliment, at best, but 'Donatello' was not ironic. The name of the fifteenth-century Florentine sculptor, identified by Vasari as foundational for all the rest, was often used in this period as a kind of shorthand for classical sculpture.

52. Tériade, 'Matisse Speaks' [1952], in Flam, *Matisse*, p. 202. Matisse also spoke, *à la* Braque, of 'a necessity within me, not a voluntary attitude arrived at by deduction or reasoning; . . . something that

only painting can do'. 'Rôle et modalités de la couleur' [1945], ibid., p. 155.

53. Étienne Charles, Marcel Nicolle and Jules Flandrin, respectively, in Spurling, *Matisse*, vol. I, p. 331. Cf. Flanner, 'King of the Wild Beasts', in *Men and Monuments*, p. 90.

54. Georges Duthuit, 'Le Fauvisme' [1929–31], in *Représentation et présence* (Paris: Flammarion, 1974), p. 209; Verdet, 'Autour', pp. 17–18. Novelty and energy became, in another interview, novelty and joy. 'Naissance de fauvisme', *Comœdia*, 25 July 1942.

55. Duthuit, 'Fauvisme', p. 208. Cf. Vauxcelles, *Fauvisme*, pp. 93–4.

56. Apollinaire, 'Le Salon d'Automne' [1907], in *Chroniques*, p. 40; Salmon, *L'Art vivant*, p. 67; Vauxcelles, *Fauvisme*, pp. 19, 77 and 133. 'Fauvette' was perhaps Salmon's coinage, or appropriation, though Vauxcelles applied it as a diminutive to Camoin (p. 115).

57. Interview with André Verdet [c. 1952], in Flam, *Matisse*, p. 293.

58. Plato, *Theaetetus*, 183e, in Anthony Gottlieb, *The Dream of Reason* (London: Penguin, 2000), p. 59.

59. Derain to Vlaminck, n.d. [March 1904], in *Lettres à Vlaminck* [1955] (Paris: Flammarion, 1994), p. 175 (misdated).

60. Matisse to Derain, 25 June 1905, in Spurling, *Matisse*, vol. I, p. 316. Matisse had already been refused by Manguin, Marquet and Camoin. Derain was only too willing.

61. Sutton, *Derain*, p. 14; *Picasso*, vol. II, pp. 71 and 447, n. 51. Curiously, Derain retained only a copy after Biagio d'Antonio's *Christ Carrying the Cross* (1490), a work then attributed to Ghirlandaio.

62. Berthe Weill, *Pan! Dans l'œil* (Paris: Lipschutz, 1933), pp. 118–19; Flam, *Matisse*, p. 302.

63. François Bernardi, *Matisse et Derain à Coullioure, été 1905* (Collioure: Musée de Collioure, 1989), p. 26.

64. Stein, *Toklas*, p. 48.

65. According to the catalogue: *Town Hall, Le Havre, The Coast, Le Havre, The Jetty, Honfleur, Interior, Plate and Oranges, Apples and Grapes,* and *Nude*.

66. Apollinaire, 'Le Salon d'Automne' [1907], in *Chroniques*, p. 41. Pre-Picasso, Dufy and Friesz both chased Fernande Olivier, who opted (briefly) for the former. *Loving Picasso*, pp. 99–102.

67. Braque, 'Sa vie', no. 4; *Patron*, p. 73. Axilette owned Braque's *Seated Nude* (1907), a Fauvist landscape of a different sort (reproduced in Maeght, no. 15).

68. Verdet, 'Autour', p. 18. Cf. Hope, *Braque*, p. 21.

69. Jacques Lassaigne, 'Un entretien avec Georges Braque' [1961], *XX siècle*, XXXV (1973), p. 3; 'Naissance de fauvisme', *Comœdia*, 25 July 1942; *Picasso*, vol. II, p. 68, from a conversation with the artist. For a comparison of the atmosphere in Collioure and L'Estaque see Derain to Matisse, 2 August 1906, in *Lettres*, p. 177.

70. Wilhelm Uhde, trans. A. Ponchont, *Picasso et la tradition française* (Paris: Quatre Chemins, 1928), p. 38. Uhde bought *The Large Trees*, *The Olive Tree*, *The Port of Antwerp*, *Boats*, and *The Scheldt*. *Boats*, retitled *Landing Stage, L'Estaque* (1906), is now in the MNAM. The entry limit for the Indépendants went down from ten to six (and then to two) because of restrictions on space.

71. Pierre Assouline, *L'Homme de l'art* [1988] (Paris: Gallimard, 1999), pp. 65–6. This was *The Vale*. The exact date of purchase is not recorded. Cf. Daniel-Henry Kahnweiler, Francis Crémieux, *Mes galeries et mes peintres* [1961] (Paris: Gallimard, 1998), p. 57; Isabelle Monod-Fontaine, 'Georges Braque', in *Donation Louise et Michel Leiris* (Paris: Centre Pompidou, 1984), p. 24.

72. Chandet, 'Le père'. Cf. Guth, 'Visite'; Vallier, 'Braque', p. 32.

73. The other simply conveyed his respects. All Braque–Picasso correspondence in MP unless otherwise indicated.

CHAPTER 3: 'But that's what a nose is like!':
The White Negro

1. Stein, *Toklas*, p. 65.

2. Derain to Matisse, 8/15 July 1907, in *Le Fauvisme* (Paris: Paris-Musées, 1999), p. 437; to Vlaminck, n.d. [July/August 1907], and more puzzlingly, 'they are more involved with achieving a goal different from their personalities, with neutral perfection', in *Lettres*, pp. 187, 189.

3. 'Le Salon d'Automne', *Je dis tout*, 19 October 1907, in *Chroniques*,

p. 46. The painting that was accepted, listed originally as *Red Rocks*, is difficult to identify – as if to collude in the pre-historical obfuscation, Braque's *catalogue raisonné* omits the Fauvist work altogether and begins with Cubism – but it may be *The Cove, La Ciotat* (1907), according to the expert Alvin Martin, 'The Moment of Change', *Minneapolis Institute of Arts Bulletin* LXV (1981–2), p. 92.

4. Apollinaire, 'The Fountain' (1918), a calligramme, the lines arranged in the shape of a spurting fountain, in *Calligrammes* [1918], trans. Anne Hyde Greet (Berkeley: University of California Press, 1980), p. 123. Those invoked in the third line are André Billy, Maurice Raynal and René Dalize, and in the sixth, Maurice Cremnitz, literary members of the Picasso gang.

5. Apollinaire, 'Windows' [1913], in *Calligrammes*, p. 29.

6. Apollinaire, *Les Mamelles de Tirésias* [1917], in Peter Read, *Picasso et Apollinaire* (Paris: Place, 1995), p. 133; preface to 'Catalogue de l'Exposition Braque' [1908], in *Chroniques*, p. 60, tropes repeated in 'Georges Braque', in *Les Peintres cubistes* [1913] (Paris: Hermann, 1980), pp. 80–83. Saul Steinberg employed a very similar turn of phrase about the angelic Braque, sixty years later, in conversation with Pierre Schneider: *Dialogues*, p. 221.

7. Vallier, 'Braque', pp. 42–3. Cf. Richardson, 'Mystery'; Couturier diary, 31 July–4 August 1952, in Marie-Alain Couturier, *Se garder libre* (Paris: Cerf, 1962), p. 147. Picasso said the same. Malraux, *Tête*, p. 113.

8. Valéry, trans. David Paul, 'The Triumph of Manet' [1932], in *Degas, Manet, Morisot* (London: RKP, 1960), p. 112. Cf. Vallier, 'Braque', pp. 39 and 49.

9. *Cahier*, p. 43 (and 53 and 125). Cf. Mallarmé: 'To name is to destroy, to suggest is to create.' In Arthur Symons, *The Symbolist Movement in Literature* (London: Constable, 1899), p. 128. 'Poets suggest,' said Braque, 'that's much better.' Verdet, 'Autour', p. 20.

10. André Malraux, trans. June Guicharnaud, *Picasso's Mask* [1974] (NY: Da Capo, 1994), p. 235.

11. For an example of the transmission of the notion (and the reiteration of the terms, in this instance 'contrôler' and 'vérifier'), see Tériade, 'Les peintres nouveaux', in *Cahiers d'Art* (1927), in *Écrits*, p. 73.

12. Apollinaire to Soffici, 8 December 1911 and 9 January 1912, in 'Vingt lettres de Guillaume Apollinaire à Ardengo Soffici', *Le Flâneur des deux rives*, 4 (1954), p. 2. It is possible that Braque read them much earlier. They were first published by Soffici, with whom he was well acquainted, in Florence (in French) in 1920.

13. Apollinaire, 'Braque' [1913], p. 83.

14. 'Le Salon des Indépendants', *Gil Blas*, 20 March 1908.

15. Verdet, 'Autour', p. 21; Couturier diary, 31 July–4 August 1952, in Couturier, *Se garder*, p. 147. His direct acknowledgement was rather less fulsome than Apollinaire was apt to suggest ('the preface that you wrote for my exhibition [in 1908] could serve as a clarification of certain points'). Braque to Apollinaire, 31 October 1917, BNF; Apollinaire to Roger Allard [1918], in *NRF* 120 (1962), p. 1148. Cf. Étienne-Alain Hubert, 'Georges Braque selon Guillaume Apollinaire', in P. Brunel et al. (eds), *Mélanges Décaudin* (Paris: Minard, 1986), pp. 265–74.

16. Verdet, 'Autour', p. 18; Jean-Paul Crespelle, in MNAM, p. 26. There was a Seurat retrospective at the 1905 Indépendants and another large exhibition at Bernheim-Jeune in 1908. The painting was *The Racket* (1889–90), much admired in Cubist circles, and bought a little later by Braque's wrestling partner, Richard Goetz, who offered it to the Louvre in 1914 – a bad moment – which turned it down. Seurat dead was worth no more than Cézanne alive, it seems. See Salmon, *L'Art vivant*, p. 145; *Picasso*, vol. II, p. 268; *P&B*, p. 357.

17. Gertrude Stein, 'Braque' [1913], in *Geography and Plays* [1922] (Madison, WI: University of Wisconsin Press, 1993), p. 145.

18. Vallier, 'Braque', p. 34.

19. Stein, loc. cit. Cf. *Toklas*, p. 12. For the full measure of her massive condescension, see the interview with René Tavernier, 'La part du destin', in Gaston Diehl (ed.), *Les Problèmes de la peinture* (Paris: Confluences, 1945), p. 76.

20. *Cahier*, p. 54.

21. 'Braque's Late Greatness' [1997], in *Sacred Monsters, Sacred Masters* (London: Cape, 2001), pp. 241–2.

22. Golding, *Visions*, p. 74.

23. The ditty was imported by Steinberg in the service of his debate with William Rubin about the rival claims to precedence. Leo Steinberg, 'Resisting Cézanne: Picasso's *Three Women*', *Art in America*, 66 (1978), pp. 114–33 (ditty p. 131); and 'The Polemical Part', ibid., 67 (1979), pp. 114–27, a response to Rubin's revisionist thesis, 'Cézannism and the beginnings of Cubism', set out in *Cézanne: The Late Work* (NY: MoMA, 1977), pp. 151–202. Read on for Rubin's rejoinder, 'Pablo and Georges and Leo and Bill', *Art in America* 67 (1979), pp. 128–47; and the aftershocks in his 'Picasso and Braque: an Introduction', in the *P&B*, pp. 15–62. The exclusive temper of the debate (a curious mixture of the high-toned, the self-referential and the in-joke) is perpetuated in their contributions to the *P&B* symposium. For a ground-breaking conspectus see John Golding, *Cubism* [1959] (London: Faber, 1988); for a state-of-the-art reappraisal, Neil Cox, *Cubism* (London: Phaidon, 2000).

24. Vallier, 'Braque', p. 34. Cf. *P&B*, p. 55, n. 5.

25. See Robert Rosenblum, 'The *Demoiselles* Sketchbook no. 42, 1907,' in Arnold and Marc Glimcher (eds), *The Sketchbooks of Picasso* (London: Thames and Hudson, 1986), pp. 59 and 79.

26. Braque to Picasso [10 August/September 1907 (postmark indistinct)], MP; Braque to Kahnweiler, n.d., in Assouline, *L'Homme*, p. 168.

27. Verdet, 'Autour', p. 21.

28. Jacob to René Rimbert, March 1922, in *Lettres à René Rimbert* (Montemart: Rougerie, 1983), pp. 20–21.

29. Olivier, *Picasso* [1933], p. 120; Kahnweiler, *Galeries* [1961], p. 52; Salmon, *L'Art vivant* [1920], p. 123. Kahnweiler's first version (the earliest published version) was slightly different: 'And Braque . . . explained to him frankly that painting like that seems to him like guzzling kerosene.' ['Und Braque . . . erklärte ihm offen, so zu malen, komme ihm vor, als ob man Petroleum saufe.'] Daniel Henry, 'Der Kubismus', *Die Weissen Blätter* 3 (1916), p. 214. In later years he settled on something like the one quoted.

30. Olivier, *Picasso*, pp. 119–20. Exegesis of Fernande's version – the best-known by far – was for a long time hindered by the shortcomings of the standard English translation (e.g. 'rope' for 'tow'): *Picasso and his Friends*, trans. Jane Miller (NY: Appleton-Century, 1965), p. 97.

Cf. *Loving Picasso*, p. 259. The exchange is impossible to situate precisely; if it is correctly placed late in 1907, as seems likely, then 'Cubism' (as yet unnamed and undeveloped) is an anachronism, but this hardly affects the thrust of the argument.

31. Picasso to Braque, 18 May 1912, in *P&B*, p. 390. The patsy was Ubaldo Oppi. Picasso absconded with Eva Gouel (Marcelle Humbert).

32. Marcelle Braque to Picasso, 22 January 1957, MP; Gilbert Krill, avant-propos to Fernande Olivier, *Souvenirs intimes* (Paris: Calmann-Lévy, 1988), pp. 8–9; John Richardson, epilogue to *Loving Picasso*, p. 286. The terms of the settlement perhaps prompted by Marcelle's comment on Fernande's plight – 'a millionaire for ten minutes'.

33. As recorded by Kahnweiler in 'Kubismus' [1916], and many times thereafter, e.g. *Galeries*, p. 52. Other reactions are marshalled in William Rubin et al., *Les Demoiselles d'Avignon* (NY: MoMA, 1994).

34. In the case of Max's grandmother and her origins, the joke gained from the story that the Avignon of the title was not the French town but the Barcelona street (carrer d'Avinyó) – a story now discredited. See *Picasso*, vol. II, p. 19.

35. Cf. Pierre Daix, trans. Olivia Emmet, *Picasso: Life and Art* (NY: Icon, 1993), p. 78; *Picasso*, vol. II, pp. 36–7.

36. Derain to Vlaminck, 7 March [1906], in *Lettres*, pp. 173–4.

37. There is one in the Sainsbury Collection at the University of East Anglia. Steven Hooper (ed.), *The Robert and Lisa Sainsbury Collection*, vol. II (New Haven: Yale University Press, 1997), p. 175.

38. Jean Laude, *La Peinture française et 'l'art nègre'* (Paris: Klincksieck, 1968), pp. 116, 322; Guy Habasque, *Les Soirées de Paris* (Paris: Knoedler, 1958), no. 37. The 1905 date has been questioned. See Jean-Louis Paudrat, 'From Africa', and William Rubin, 'Picasso', in Rubin (ed.), *'Primitivism'*, vol. I (NY: MoMA, 1984), pp. 139, 143 and 338, n. 135. In common with much of the pre-history, it cannot be documented conclusively. Habasque for one may have got it from Braque himself; in the 1940s he questioned the artist closely on the thinking behind Cubism. 'Cubisme et phénoménologie', *Revue d'Esthétique*, 2 (1949), pp. 51–61.

39. Laude, *Peinture française*, p. 116.

40. Braque and Picasso to Kahnweiler, 11 and 16 August 1912, in *P&B*, pp. 401–2; *Leiris*, pp. 26 and 169; *Papiers collés*, p. 180.

41. Braque to Kahnweiler, 10 July 1913, in *P&B*, p. 420; Derain to Vlaminck, [July 1913], in *Lettres*, p. 209.

42. Kahnweiler, 'Werkstätten', *Die Freude* 1 (1920), p. 154; in French in *Leiris*, p. 28; in English (a different translation) in *P&B*, p. 427.

43. Apollinaire, 'Roma Hôtel', *Paris-Journal*, 26 May 1914, in ibid., p. 426. The acolyte was Emil Filla.

44. Malraux, *Tête*, p. 20; *Mask*, p. 13. 'The thing is I've never looked for a fight,' Braque replied to André Warnod when the latter remarked that his paintings tend not to scandalize. *Les Peintres mes amis* [1949] (Paris: Les Heures Claires, 1965), p. 82.

45. These were the work of the Dakar-based photographer Edmond Fortier, apparently acquired by Picasso in 1906. See Anne Baldassari, trans. Deke Dusinberre, *Picasso and Photography* (Paris: Flammarion, 1997), pp. 45ff.

46. Cf. *Picasso*, vol. II, p. 83; Pierre Daix, 'The Chronology of Proto-Cubism: new data on the opening of the Picasso/Braque dialogue', *P&B* symposium, pp. 306–21, and 'Le *Grand Nu* de Braque clé de la "cordée en montagne" avec Picasso', in Maeght, pp. 61–3.

47. Maurice Raynal, 'Panorama de l'œuvre de Picasso', *Le Point*, XLII (1952), p. 13; Daniel-Henry Kahnweiler, *La Montée du cubisme* [1920], in *Confessions esthétiques* (Paris: Gallimard, 1963), p. 24. Raynal gave another variant of the nose exchange, this time with 'a group of disciples', in *Histoire*, p. 56.

48. Vallier, 'Braque', p. 34. Cf. Verdet, 'L'atelier parisien', p. 15. At that point in the testimony Vallier interpolated: 'Here I heard Braque's voice tremble for a moment.'

49. Stein, *Toklas*, p. 261; Roland Penrose, *Picasso* [1958] (London: Granada, 1981), p. 155, apropos the difficulty of distinguishing their Cubist pictures; glossed by Penrose '. . . which a Spaniard would find too rich and unnecessary'.

50. Dore Ashton, 'Introduction' to *Picasso on Art* (NY: Viking, 1972), p. xx, citing Pierre Daix.

51. John Golding, who knew the older Kahnweiler well, has noted his continuing unease about the painting; and the dealer himself had

been 'unconvinced' at the outset. Was there some projection of these emotions on to Braque? *Visions*, p. 102; interview with Professor John Golding, 11 February 2002.

52. Namely *Landscape at L'Estaque* (*Landscape with Houses*) and *Viaduct at L'Estaque* (1907), in *P&B*, pp. 79 and 80. The former came up for auction in 1969, from the collection of Marius de Zayas in New York, and failed to reach its reserve price; it was first illustrated in the literature in 1977. The latter emerged in 1979 from an unidentified private collection in Paris; it was eventually acquired by the Minneapolis Institute of Art in 1982.

53. Antonina Vallentin, *Pablo Picasso* (Paris: Albin Michel, 1957), p. 145.

54. Malraux, *Tête*, pp. 17–19. A reconstruction as long as this inevitably raises doubts about the authenticity of expression (or sentiment), especially as it was written in 1973 from notes made in 1937. Some passages in the book have been rumoured to be more Malraux than Picasso. In Gilot's memoirs Picasso makes rather similar speeches (*Life*, pp. 117–18, 248–9); but the very fact that they are speeches has also called them into question. Gilot's work has been severely censured, for inaccuracy as well as inauthenticity, but often by the *parti pris* (e.g. Kahnweiler): pricked, perhaps, by its acuity. Cf. Rubin, *Primitivism*, p. 335, n. 45; Ashton, *Picasso*, pp. xxvi–vii; Penrose, *Picasso*, pp. 455–6.

55. Cf. Lyotard, *Malraux*, pp. 81–2; O'Brian, *Picasso*, pp. 154–5.

56. Malraux, *Tête*, p. 19.

57. Vallier, 'Braque', p. 33.

58. Salmon, *Souvenirs*, vol. I, p. 145.

59. Penrose, *Picasso*, p. 146; John Richardson, *The Sorcerer's Apprentice* (London: Cape, 1999), p. 290.

60. Roché, 'Braque (suite)', and 'Souvenirs', pp. 340 and 349. According to his diary, 25 April 1909.

61. Claude Meunier, *Ring Noir* (Paris: Plon, 1992), p. 49; *L'Écho des sports*, 10 June 1909, in *Picasso*, vol. II, p. 267.

62. Laporte, *Sunshine*, p. 40.

63. Lepape and Defert, *Lepape*, pp. 20–21.

64. 'La Palette' [Salmon], 'Georges Braque', *Paris-Journal*, 13 October

1911, in *Leiris*, pp. 27–8; Braque to Kahnweiler, 14 October 1911, in *P&B*, p. 383.

CHAPTER 4: 'Mon vieux Wilbourg':
The Encounter with Picasso

1. Apparently Salmon translated for him. Interview with Claude Laurens, 4 January 2001.
2. Cf. *Patron*, p. 74. Picasso's 'reading' was perhaps more absorbing, almost by osmosis, from others; but he does seem to have bought the books. See Maurice Raynal, *Picasso* (Paris: Cres, 1922), pp. 52–3; O'Brian, *Picasso*, p. 176.
3. Picasso, *Violin: 'Jolie Eva'* (1912), in *P&B*, p. 234.
4. Picasso to Braque, 10 July 1912, in *P&B*, p. 399; Braque to Picasso [postmarked 10 July 1912], MP; Picasso to Kahnweiler, 11 July 1912, *P&B*, p. 400. Interestingly, it also worked in reverse. Braque's opinion could be invoked by Kahnweiler in disputes with Picasso, e.g. over the illustrations for Jacob's *Saint Matorel* (1910). See Kahnweiler to Picasso, n.d., in Hélène Seckel, *Max Jacob et Picasso* (Paris: RMN, 1994), p. 79.
5. Valéry, trans. Malcolm Cowley and James R. Lawler, 'The Place of Baudelaire' [1926], in *Leonardo, Poe, Mallarmé* (Princeton: Princeton University Press, 1972), p. 195.
6. Interview with Françoise Gilot, 4 September 2001; Salmon, *Souvenirs*, vol. III, p. 182.
7. Marius de Zayas, 'Picasso Speaks', *The Arts*, III (1923), p. 315; David Sylvester, 'Curriculum Vitae', in *About Modern Art* (London: Pimlico, 1997), p. 30.
8. Braque himself rendered it 'Wilburg' and Paulhan 'Vilbure'. 'Wilbourg' appears to be the most consistent version. See Braque and Picasso to Kahnweiler, 11, 15 and 16 August 1912, in *Leiris*, pp. 26 and 169; *Patron*, p. 47. Sceptical of the connection between aviation and Cubism, Kahnweiler maintained that the nickname derived simply from their mangled pronunciation of 'Wright', which made

it sound like 'Braque' (Penrose, *Picasso*, p. 171) – an unconvincing dismissal, phonetically and psychologically.

9. *L'Illustration*, 5 August 1908, in Robert Wohl, *A Passion for Wings* (New Haven: Yale University Press, 1994), p. 11. Braque and Picasso read *L'Illustration*.

10. Wohl, *Wings*, p. 272 (reporting that Braque was nicknamed Vilbour by the aviators at Issy); Douglas Cooper, *The Cubist Epoch* [1971] (London: Phaidon, 1998), p. 59. Cf. Penrose, *Picasso*, p. 171.

11. It has been suggested that the Braque/Wilbur, Picasso/Orville pairing served to identify Braque as the 'safer' and Picasso as the more intrepid partner. Given that Wilbur was the one whose cool head was witnessed and celebrated in France, and that he met his untimely end at forty-five, whereas Orville survived everything and lived on to the ripe old age of seventy-seven, that does not seem very plausible. Cf. Mark Roskill, 'Braque's *papiers collés* and the feminine side to Cubism', *P&B* symposium, p. 225.

12. Hélène Parmelin, *Picasso dit . . .* (Paris: Gonthier, 1966), pp. 40–41. Parmelin was the wife of the painter Édouard Pignon, a fervent Picassoite of the successor generation. For an evocation of the Grands Magasins Dufayel in all their glory, see Jean Renoir, trans. Norman Denny, *My Life and My Films* (London: Collins, 1974), pp. 17–18.

13. Romilly, vol. VII, p. 41.

14. Sabina Santovetti, *Les Sculptures et les plats gravés du peintre Georges Braque* (unpublished *mémoire de maîtrise*, Paris IV, n.d.), p. 135.

15. Christian Zervos, 'Georges Braque et le développement du cubisme', *Cahiers d'Art* 1–2 (1932), p. 23; *Picasso*, vol. II, pp. 252–4.

16. Daix in discussion, *P&B* symposium, pp. 241–2. Cf. *Picasso*, vol. II, p. 254.

17. Jean Signovert, 'Gravure et émulation', *Nouvelles de l'estampe*, 8 (1964), pp. 224–5; Henri Deschamps, 'Braque lithographe par son lithographe', *Georges Braque* (Argenteuil: Desseaux, 1982), n.p.; interview with Aldo Crommelynck, 22 March 2001.

18. Braque to Kahnweiler, [20/27 September 1911], in *P&B*, pp. 58 and 380; *Picasso*, vol. II, p. 238. Cf. Picasso to Kahnweiler, 9 July 1912, in *Leiris*, p. 169.

19. Paulhan, 'Le premier papier collé', in Berne-Joffroy, *Paulhan*, p. 130.

20. Cooper, *Epoch*, p. 58. Picasso said much the same to Richardson. *Picasso*, vol. II, p. 252.

21. Richardson, 'Mystery'; *Picasso*, vol. II, p. 97; Vallier, 'Braque', pp. 34–5; John Berger, 'Past present', *Guardian*, 12 October 2002.

22. *Patron*, p. 44; Habasque, 'Cubisme', p. 154. In another variant, 'After Marseille it would have had to be the Congo.' Duthuit, 'Fauvisme', p. 209.

23. Duthuit, 'Fauvisme', p. 209; Martin, *Braque*, p. 38, as annotated by Cooper in his copy, now in the Getty. Friesz is quoted by Matisse in 'Testimonial', in Flam, *Matisse*, p. 208.

24. Salmon (reporting Vauxcelles), *L'Art vivant*, p. 67; Burgess, 'Wild Men', p. 403.

25. Douglas Cooper, École du Louvre lecture on 'Braque' (1958), Cooper Papers, 39/5, Getty.

26. *Patron*, p. 47. Chiaroscuro: the interplay of darkness and luminosity, perhaps in stark contrast, *à la* Caravaggio, perhaps more 'smudged' (*sfumato*), *à la* Leonardo. Raynal suggested that chiaroscuro was being replaced by stereoscopy. *Histoire*, p. 52.

27. Burgess, 'Wild Men', p. 405; Haynes Irwin diary, 27 April 1908; *Patron*, p. 46. The authenticity of this talk, too, has been called into question. Plainly Burgess did not grasp the import of much that was said to him. Plainly also there was a good deal of grandstanding by the wild men. Possibly he put words into their mouths. One example is the architectural analogy of plan, elevation and section, apropos Braque's attempt to get every aspect, though that is not expressly attributed to Braque. Still, it seems to me that what is attributed rings true enough; and (allowing for Burgess's ignorance) the circumstantial detail hangs together. Cf. Edward F. Fry, 'Cubism 1907–1908', *Art Bulletin*, XLVIII (1966), pp. 71–2; *Picasso*, vol. II, pp. 85–6; Flam in *P&B* symposium, p. 298.

28. Richardson, *Braque*, p. 5.

29. Vallier, 'Braque', p. 36; *Cahier*, p. 12. In conversation with Kahnweiler, in 1933, Picasso appears to credit Braque with 'the imitation of material form . . . objects represented from the front, in profile and from above'. The passage is difficult to contextualize – more difficult for Kahnweiler's intrusiveness – but interesting nonetheless.

'Conversations avec Picasso' [1959], in *Propos*, p. 90 (trans. Isabelle Kalinowski); cf. *P&B* symposium, p. 170 (trans. Orde Levinson).

30. Braque would certainly have been familiar with Cézanne's *Five Bathers* (1885–7), from a reproduction in Derain's studio, and probably also *Three Bathers* (1879–82), then owned by Matisse. The pose of the figure on the left in Braque's drawing echoes that of the bather on the left in each of these paintings. In addition to the wild beasts, the 1905 Salon d'Automne featured a retrospective of Ingres, including the suggestive *Turkish Bath* (1859–63), from which Matisse borrowed for *Le Bonheur de Vivre* (1905–6), the only work he showed at the 1906 Indépendants. Braque's right-hand figure is a sort of Cézannist or proto-Cubist version of the left-hand figure in the Matisse, whose posture derives from a figure or figures in the Ingres.

31. Haynes Irwin diary, 18 April 1908; *Le Rire*, 11 April 1908, in *P&B*, p. 351.

32. *L'Action*, 21 March 1908, in *P&B*, p. 351; Apollinaire, 'Le Salon des Indépendants', *La Revue des Lettres et des Arts*, 1 May 1908, in *Chroniques*, pp. 51–2.

33. Haynes Irwin diary, 27 April 1908.

34. Lassaigne, 'Entretien', p. xviii; O'Brian, *Picasso*, p. 172. Cf. *Picasso*, vol. II, p. 38; *P&B* symposium, pp. 294ff.

35. Lassaigne, 'Entretien', pp. xvi–xvii. Cf. Kahnweiler, trans. Henry Aronson, *The Rise of Cubism* [1920] (NY: Wittenborn Schultz, 1949), p. 11; *Juan Gris* [1946] (Paris: Gallimard, 1990), pp. 207, 215.

36. Matisse, 'Testimony against Gertrude Stein', *Transition*, 23 (1934–5), supplement, p. 6.

37. Vauxcelles, 'Les Fauves' [1934], in *P&B*, pp. 354–5. The story was later denied by Matisse, but it had currency at the time; it was repeated by Apollinaire in the *Mercure de France*, 16 October 1911, and again in *Les Peintres cubistes*; most importantly, it was believed by Braque. Lassaigne, 'Entretien', p. xviii. Cf. Vallier, 'Braque', p. 43. Of course Matisse may not have been the only one. Jacob was heard remarking to Picasso, 'Have you noticed that for some time now Braque has been introducing cubes into his pictures?' Uhde, *Picasso*, p. 39.

38. Matisse, 'Testimony' [1935], p. 6; 'Matisse Speaks' [1951], in Flam, *Matisse*, p. 204. He added: 'Back in Paris, Braque did a portrait of a woman on a chaise longue in which the drawing and values were decomposed.' In the earlier statement, 'a big, wide canvas that had been started in the same spirit and which represented the seated figure of a young woman'. The *Large Nude*, horizontal, in progress?

39. See Kahnweiler, *Galeries*, p. 103.

40. Apollinaire, 'Georges Braque', in *Chroniques*, p. 60.

41. Charles Morice, 'Braque', *Mercure de France*, 16 December 1908, in Fry, *Cubism*, p. 52. The interview with Burgess pre-dated the exhibition by several months, but was not published until 1910.

42. *Harbour* (1908–9, reworked 1910–11?), in *P&B*, p. 113. There is some confusion in the literature between this work and *Harbour in Normandy* (1909?), in *P&B*, p. 126. It is impossible to be sure which one was exhibited (especially if the idea of reworking is accepted); indeed, there is still another *Harbour* of the same period, nowhere illustrated. Cf. Pepe Karmel, 'Notes on the dating of works', *P&B* symposium, pp. 326–7.

43. 'I felt that there was something more secret in that painting...': Vallier, 'Braque', pp. 32–3.

44. Rilke to his wife, 10 October 1907, trans. Joel Agee, in *Letters on Cézanne* [1952] (London: Vintage, 1991), p. 43.

45. Verdet, 'Autour', p. 18 (my emphasis).

46. T. J. Clark, 'Cubism and Collectivity', in *Farewell to an Idea* (New Haven: Yale University Press, 1999), p. 201.

47. Matisse interviewed by Jacques Guenne (1925), in Flam, *Matisse*, p. 80; Picasso quoted by Kahnweiler, in *Galeries*, p. 76. Characteristically, Picasso also had him as a father and grandfather, but usually in protector mode. Cf. Brassaï, *Conversations*, p. 107. Matisse had bought Cézanne's *Three Bathers*, at considerable sacrifice, in 1899; Picasso owned four at his death, *Black Castle* (1903–4), *The Sea at L'Estaque* (1878–9), *Five Bathers* (1877–8), and a watercolour of Aix Cathedral (1902–4), all of them acquired much later, beginning in the mid-1930s.

48. *Gil Blas*, 25 March 1909, and *Mercure de France*, 16 April 1909, in *P&B*, pp. 359 and 360.

49. Braque to Léonce Rosenberg, 13 August 1917, MNAM. See Braque's 'business letters' to Kahnweiler, beginning in the summer of 1909, e.g. extracts in *P&B*, p. 361.

50. Kahnweiler, 'Conversations' (1957), in Picasso, *Propos*, pp. 95–6.

51. Braque to Kahnweiler, n.d. [19/26 September 1912], in Assouline, *L'Homme*, p. 169. See also *P&B*, pp. 403–4, for this letter and the one that preceded it. This was the Modern Art Circle exhibition at the Stedelijk Museum. They asked for ten canvases; against Kahnweiler's inclination not to participate, Braque sent one (a landscape).

52. Romilly, vol. VII, p. 39; Assouline, *L'Homme*, p. 183; *Picasso*, vol. II, p. 269. A letter from Braque to Kahnweiler, dated 22 December [1913?], confirming the terms of a new three-year contract between them is in the Fonds Léonce Rosenberg, MNAM. The agreed prices had almost doubled.

53. Assouline, *L'Homme*, pp. 184–5; *Picasso*, vol. II, pp. 268–9. In 1920 he signed up Laurens, but by then he had lost some of the others. The war upset all these contractual arrangements.

54. Michael C. Fitzgerald, *Making Modernism* (Berkeley: University of California Press, 1995), pp. 32 and 275, n. 41.

55. Braque to Kahnweiler, n.d. [October 1911], in *P&B* symposium, p. 344.

56. Braque to Kahnweiler, [September/October 1911], in *Leiris*, p. 25. *The Portuguese* (*The Emigrant*) (1911), in *P&B*, p. 211, is notoriously difficult to decipher and still controversial. See *Picasso*, vol. II, p. 192.

57. Gertrude Stein, *Picasso* [1938] (NY: Dover, 1984), p. 12; *Patron*, p. 45. What Braque called *cadre en profondeur* was also called *cadre à gorge*.

58. 'Reverse section' was the usual terminology. Cf. Kahnweiler, who seconds Braque's argument, *Gris*, p. 381, n. 115.

59. Braque, trans. Jonathan Griffin, 'Thoughts on Painting' [1917], in Fry, *Cubism*, p. 147; Stella in Wolfe, *Painted Word*, p. 7, who makes the same point. The maxim appears, slightly amended, in Braque's *Cahier*, p. 30.

60. Simone Tery, 'Picasso n'est pas officier dans l'armée française', *Les Lettres françaises*, 24 March 1945, in Marie-Laure Bernadac and Androula Michael (eds), *Picasso propos sur l'art* (Paris: Gallimard, 1998), p. 45.

61. Matisse, 'Statement to Tériade' (1931), in Flam, *Matisse*, p. 95; *Cahier*, p. 12; William Rubin, *Picasso in the Collection of the Museum of Modern Art* (NY: MoMA, 1972), pp. 72, 206.

62. Raymond Chandler, quoted on the back cover of *Smart-Aleck Kill* (London: Penguin, 1964).

63. That Cubism *à la* Braque–Picasso was 'only . . . the débris of their rooms' was the conceit of Wyndham Lewis in *The Caliph's Design* [1919] (Santa Barbara: Black Sparrow, 1986), p. 119.

64. Harriet Grossman Janis and Sidney Janis, *Picasso* (NY: Doubleday, 1946), p. 7. Braque used a gun for real in 1914–15, but not otherwise. Picasso had one of his own in the early days; he liked to fire it occasionally. Laporte, *Sunshine*, p. 40; information from Marilyn McCully.

65. And also perhaps a foothold on (French) tradition, if it is seen as Braque's *Attributes of Music*, *à la* Chardin (1765). Braque could have studied this painting in the Louvre; and there was a Chardin retrospective at the Galerie Georges Petit in 1907. See also ch. 6.

66. *Picasso*, vol. II, p. 55.

67. Vallier, 'Braque', p. 36; Heraclitus, fragment D.51. Charles H. Kahn, *The Art and Thought of Heraclitus* (Cambridge: Cambridge University Press, 1979), pp. 195–9; Marcel Conche, *Héraclite* (Paris: Presses Universitaires de France, 1986), pp. 425–9. Braque will have seen Heraclitus used to similar effect in Francis Ponge, 'Braque le réconciliateur' [1946], in *L'Atelier contemporain* (Paris: Gallimard, 1977), p. 66; and Jacques Guignard, 'Milarepa Braque', *Derrière le Miroir*, 25–6 (1950), n.p. He quoted it himself in a later interview with Georges Charbonnier, 'Entretien avec Georges Braque', *Le Monologue du peintre* (Paris: Julliard, 1959), p. 15.

68. For Braque's retelling of the story of the decorator's comb, see ch. 10.

69. Rilke, 'The Lute', *New Poems: The Other Part*, p. 143.

70. *L'Intransigeant*, 11 October 1911, in *Chroniques*, p. 200.

71. The revolutionary identifications were Apollinaire's, as reported by Alice Halicka, *Hier* (Paris: Pavois, 1946), p. 56. In this scenario, Braque was Talleyrand, and Picasso either Napoleon (on account of his hairstyle) or 'Voltaire and his hideous grin'.

72. A remark made to Richardson. *Picasso*, vol. II, p. 215. Cf. Vallier, 'Braque', pp. 43–4.

73. *Cahier*, p. 24. In Gleizes' case, politics and *la patrie* also intruded. See ch. 9.

74. Salmon, *Souvenirs*, vol. II, p. 68; Lewis, *Caliph*, p. 121. Cf. *Le Petit Parisien*, 23 April 1911, and *Paris-Journal*, 1 January 1912, in *P&B*, pp. 373 and 388.

75. Braque to Kahnweiler, 8 October 1919, in *Leiris*, p. 29; Dunoyer de Segonzac to Pierre Lévy, 1 January 1967, in Lévy, *Artistes*, p. 106.

76. Richardson, 'Mystery'.

77. Georges Ribemont-Dessaignes, 'Salon d'Automne', *391*, 9 November 1919. André Salmon had used the expression in his original report of the recital. *Paris-Journal*, 23 April 1911.

78. *Cahier*, p. 31.

79. Max Jacob, 'Honneur de la Sardane et de la Tenora', *Le Laboratoire central* [1921] (Paris: Gallimard, 1960), p. 51.

80. The tenora, its sister instrument the tiple, and the tiple's nineteenth-century forerunner the tarota, are all members of the shawm family – and difficult to tell apart in Cubist pictures. Shawms are generally obsolete (replaced by the modern oboe) but the tenora and the tiple are still played in the Catalonian cobla, just as they were in 1911. Some experts believe that the instrument in the works of Braque and Picasso is in fact the tarota. Cf. Lewis Kachur, 'Picasso, popular music and collage Cubism', *Burlington Magazine*, 1081 (1993), pp. 252–9; Stewart Buettner, 'Catalonia and the early musical subjects of Braque and Picasso', *Art History*, 19 (1996), pp. 112–13.

CHAPTER 5: '*I* am Madame Braque': Partnership and Marriage

1. Interview with Louttre and Laure Latapie Bissière, 15 March 2001.

2. According to John Richardson, Picasso himself referred 'very glibly' to an early affair with Marcelle; the story was repeated by Douglas Cooper and 'understood' in Picasso's circle. *P&B* symposium, p. 240; conversations with John Richardson. Picasso is far from being a reliable witness in this matter, however, to say nothing of Cooper.

Evidence is difficult, no doubt, but beyond the Picassoites there is even a dearth of rumour. The story is not repeated in Richardson's *Picasso*.

3. Penrose, *Picasso*, pp. 155–6; *Picasso*, vol. II, p. 84.

4. Simone Signoret, *La Nostalgie n'est plus ce qu'elle était* (Paris: Seuil, 1976), p. 123; William S. Lieberman, 'Introduction', *Twentieth-century Modern Masters* (NY: MoMA, 1989), p. 14. Cf. Olivier, *Loving Picasso*, p. 195.

5. Marcelle to Jacob, 31 August 1908, in Seckel, *Jacob*, p. 69, n. 23.

6. Duncan Grant to Vanessa Bell, 22 November 1927, in Mary Ann Caws and Sarah Bird Wright, *Bloomsbury and France* (NY: Oxford University Press, 2000), p. 201; Gilot interview, 4 September 2001; Julian Trevelyan, *Indigo Days* [1957] (Aldershot: Scolar, 1996), p. 61.

7. Mariette tapes.

8. Interviews with Jacques Dupin (poet and one-time lieutenant of Maeght), 28 March 2001; Jean Ferrand (their chauffeur in the 1950s), 23 March 2002.

9. Stein, *Toklas*, p. 18.

10. Alexander Liberman, 'Braque', *The Artist in His Studio* (NY: Random House, 1988), p. 142. Brassaï's impressions mirror Liberman's exactly. *Artists*, pp. 18, 24. After Satie's death in 1925, Marcelle bought one of his two pianos (made by Rinaldi, complete with candleholders).

11. Richardson, *Apprentice*, p. 194; interview with Françoise de Staël, 30 January 2001. Cf. Couturier, *Se garder*, pp. 135, 156, and *La Vérité*, pp. 307, 309; Fernand Mourlot, *Souvenirs et portraits d'artistes* (Paris: Mourlot, 1973), p. 88.

12. Michel Gall, 'En mourant Braque venge van Gogh', *Paris-Match*, 14 September 1963.

13. Interview with Père Laval, latterly a Dominican at the Couvent Saint-Jacques in Paris, 14 March 2001. Cf. Jacques Laval, *Un homme partagé* (Paris: Julliard, 1978).

14. Couturier diary, 19 February 1952, *Se garder*, p. 135.

15. Ibid., [c.1947], p. 24 (his emphasis).

16. Ibid., 5 April 1950, p. 86.

17. Patrick Heron, 'The changing jug' [1951], in *Painter as Critic* (London: Tate, 1998), p. 55.

18. The usual supposition is that he was put on to Lao Tzu and others by Jean Paulhan in the 1940s. Paulhan was indeed an enthusiast, who pressed *les chinois* and *le zen* on his friends. But Braque was already on to them. His mentor was more likely Carl Einstein, who discovered *les chinois* during the Great War (see ch. 6), and his first handbook Léon Wieger, *Les Pères du système taoïste* (1913). Marcel Granet's influential study, *La Pensée chinoise* (1934), which draws heavily on Wieger's texts, is frequently cited by Kahnweiler in his work on Gris (1946).

19. Lao Tzu, trans. D. C. Lau, *Tao Te Ching* (London: Penguin, 1963), pp. 38, 54. Cf. Chuang Tzu, trans. Burton Watson, *The Complete Works of Chuang Tzu* (NY: Columbia University Press, 1968), pp. 119–20, highlighted by Granet for its encompassing of the central tenets. *La Pensée*, pp. 423ff.

20. *Le Tir à l'arc* (Geneva: Broder, 1960), Vallier, no. 153.

21. Richardson, 'Mystery'. Here the locution sounds like Richardson, but the sentiment seems absolutely authentic.

22. D. H. Kahnweiler, trans. Peter Watson, 'Negro Art and Cubism', *Horizon*, 108 (1948), p. 413.

23. D. T. Suzuki, *An Introduction to Zen Buddhism* [1949] (London: Rider, 1991), p. 99.

24. D. T. Suzuki, 'Zen as Chinese interpretation of the doctrine of enlightenment', in *Essays in Zen Buddhism*, first series (NY: Grove, n.d.), p. 61. Suzuki's *Essays*, the principal vehicle of his expository effort in the West, ran to three volumes or series, first published in English in 1927–33 and in French in 1940–46. Of these, the first was the most read; the last the least interesting (according to Braque). Braque to Paulhan [1960], Archives Jean Paulhan, IMEC.

25. Interview with Antoine Tudal, 26 April 2001; Paulhan to Jouhandeau [2 November 1943], *Choix*, vol. II, p. 339; Ponge, 'Feuillet votif' [1964], in *L'Atelier*, p. 249. Antoine Tudal was the child of Nicolas de Staël (then a struggling artist); he benefited from Braque's largesse in the period immediately after the Liberation and saw a good deal of him during the 1950s.

26. Pierre Cabanne, 'Braque se retourne sur son passé', *Arts*, July 1960; Jean Bazaine, *Couleurs et mots* (Paris: Cherche-Midi, 1997), p. 73 (his

emphases). In an earlier version, *reality* is not that. 'Braque: un enrichissement de l'espace' [1964], in *Le Temps de la peinture* (Paris: Aubier, 1990), p. 71. Sometimes Braque and Zen got mixed up. He was also prone to repeat: 'In Zen it is said, "Reality is not this, it is the fact of being this."' Liberman, *Artist*, p. 144.

27. Suzuki, 'Practical methods of Zen instruction', in *Essays*, first series, pp. 272–3, and on contradiction, pp. 279 ff.; *Cahier*, p. 93. This version of Braque's famous rule (1917, the first sentence only), with the negation after Gris, appears in the plain edition of his thoughts published as *Le Jour et la nuit* (Paris: Gallimard, 1952), p. 12. He alludes to it in interviews with Tériade in 1928 and Gaston Diehl in 1945: 'Georges Braque', in *Écrits*, p. 138; 'L'univers pictural et son destin', in *Les Problèmes de la peinture* (Paris: Confluences, 1945), p. 307. His acceptance of the negation (if acceptance is the right word) has been linked to the greater freedom of colour and line in his work of the inter-war period. The rule remained unaltered, however, in his illustrated *Cahier* (1948, augmented in 1956). Cf. Kahnweiler, *Gris*, p. 231; Raynal, *Histoire*, p. 146.

28. *Cahier*, p. 99.

29. Suzuki, *Essays*, first series, p. 274; Paulhan to Roger Callois, [8 September 1962], *Cahiers Jean Paulhan*, 6 (1991), p. 258.

30. Suzuki, 'Painting, Swordsmanship, Tea Ceremony', in William Barrett (ed.), *Zen Buddhism* (NY: Doubleday, 1956), p. 281.

31. See *Violin and Palette* (1909) and *Violin and Pitcher* (1910), in *P&B*, pp. 143 and 149. *Cubisté* was Braque's derogatory term for what the intellectualizers and systematizers like Gleizes and Metzinger did to their canvases. See Vallier, 'Braque', pp. 43–4.

32. *Picasso*, vol. II, p. 195. Richardson, who is inclined to emphasize her piety, also sees it as a portrait of Marcelle. *P&B* symposium, p. 44.

33. *Patron*, p. 37; Couturier diary, [1952], *Se garder*, p. 140; Braque to Picasso [21 June 1912], MP. Puvis de Chavannes (1824–98), the mural painter of such extravaganzas as *Sainte Geneviève veillant sur la ville endormie* (1898) in the Panthéon, was much admired in his day and much derided afterwards. He gets his due (more than his due) in Serge Lemoine, *From Puvis de Chavannes to Matisse and Picasso* (London: Thames and Hudson, 2002). He had a retrospective at

the 1904 Salon d'Automne. He crops up again in the next chapter.

34. James Lord, *Picasso and Dora* (NY: Fromm, 1994), p. 123.

35. *Bulletin de la vie artistique*, 1 November 1924. 'Other means had to be found for my nature.' Vallier, 'Braque', p. 32.

36. *Le Havre*, 30 January 1911; *Le Petit Havre*, 2 February 1911; *Le Havre Libre*, 14 September 1994.

37. Braque to Picasso [10 May 1913], MP.

38. Gino Severini, trans. Jennifer Franchina, *The Life of a Painter* [1983] (Princeton: Princeton University Press, 1995), p. 62. The other occupants included Dufy, Utter, Utrillo and Valadon.

39. This analysis of 'the Braques' draws on the first-hand experience of Françoise Gilot, Mariette Lachaud, Claude and Denise Laurens, Jean Leymarie, Geneviève Taillade and Antoine Tudal, among others. Almost nothing has appeared in print, except a fragment of memoir by Claude Laurens, 'Tous les jours', *Derrière le Miroir*, 144–6 (1964), p. 67.

40. They were married on 23 March 1926, in Paris.

41. Claude Laurens, 'Le sculpteur Henri Laurens', *Revue du Louvre*, 3 (1967), pp. 125–36. Laurens's beliefs are expressed with great simplicity and humanity (two of his cardinal virtues) in his correspondence with Léonce Rosenberg (MNAM). See also Kahnweiler's fond reminiscence, 'Souvenirs sur Henri Laurens', in Werner Hofmann (ed.), *Henri Laurens* (Teufen: Niggli, 1970), pp. 49–51.

42. 'La France perd un artiste illustre dont elle ignorait le nom: Henri Laurens', *Paris-Match*, 29 May–5 June 1954.

43. Paulhan to Grenier [1943], in *Jean Paulhan/Jean Grenier* (Quimper: Calligrammes, 1984), p. 145; quoted in part in *Patron*, p. 63. Retailed by Penrose as 'la femme qui m'a le plus aimé'. Trans. Jacques Chavy and Paul Peyrelevade, *Picasso* (Paris: Flammarion, 1982), p. 273. Probably a response to 'Braque' in *Comœdia*, 31 October 1942.

44. It was also a delayed reprise of the theme of 'justice' for Braque, first picked out by Picasso thirty years earlier, apropos Salmon's *La Jeune peinture française* (1912). 'He is revoltingly unjust to you.' Picasso to Braque, 31 October 1912, in *P&B*, p. 410.

45. See, e.g., Laporte, *Sunshine*, p. 5; Brassaï, *Artists*, p. 24.

46. For the journal *Kunstblatt* (1920). See correspondence in *Leiris*, p. 29. Braque's 'Pensées et réflexions sur la peinture' appeared originally in

Nord-Sud (1917), under the editorial hand of his friend Pierre Reverdy. See ch. 6.

47. Kahnweiler, 'Kubismus', pp. 211, 215; *Kubismus*, p. 16. Parroted by the influential Czech Vincenc Kramár, trans. Erica Abrams, *Le Cubisme* [1921] (Paris: École des Beaux-Arts, 2002), p. 12.

48. Uhde, *Picasso*, p. 39. Interestingly, a different point of departure yields subtly different results. In Janneau's even-handed treatment, it is not Braque ('reflective, level-headed, rationalistic') but Picasso ('fiery, tormented, unstable') who is the 'female' of the pair. *L'Art cubiste*, p. 14.

49. *Patron*, p. 74.

50. *Picasso*, vol. II, p. 195.

51. Loc. cit. (emphasis in original), based on conversations with Dora Maar. Dated to c.1938 in *Apprentice*, p. 181, but perhaps more likely 1945. See ch. 10.

52. Warnod, *Bateau*, p. 26; *Picasso*, vol. II, p. 245.

53. Salmon, *L'Art vivant*, p. 25. Dated to 'around 1910' by Salmon.

54. See Braque's response to an inquiry into art today, *Cahiers d'Art*, 1–4 (1935), p. 24.

55. *Picasso*, vol. II, p. 192. Compare *Le Portugais* (1911) and *Man with a Violin* (1912), in *P&B*, pp. 211 and 223. The 'little patch of yellow wall' is in Vermeer's *View of Delft*. The Proustian rhapsody is in *Remembrance of Things Past*, in the Scott Moncrieff/Kilmartin translation (London: Penguin, 1983), p. 185.

56. A point emphasized by John Golding.

57. Vallier, 'Braque', p. 36; Penrose, *Picasso*, p. 170.

58. *Cahier*, p. 89. Braque's discourse in this vein captivated Jean Dubuffet, for one. See Dubuffet to Jacques Berne, 16 December 1946, in *Lettres à J.B.* (Paris: Hermann, 1991), pp. 2–3.

59. Descartes, *Œuvres et lettres* (Paris: Gallimard, 1963), p. 181. Ideas taken up by Maurice Merleau-Ponty, among others. See his 'Eye and Mind', trans. Carleton Dallery, in *The Primacy of Perception* (Evanston: Northwestern University Press, 1964), p. 170.

60. Poincaré also spoke, Braque-like, of 'reasoning' about objects in painting as if they were in space. See *La Science et l'hypothèse* [1902] (Paris: Flammarion, 1968), pp. 80–82. The argument for that work

(mediated by Princet) as the source of Braque's talk of tactile space is strongly made – too strongly made – in Arthur I. Miller, *Einstein, Picasso* (NY: Basic, 2001), pp. 130ff. Paulhan for one was familiar with Poincaré's formulations: see *La Peinture cubiste* [essays composed in the 1940s and 1950s] (Paris: Gallimard, 1990), p. 83. Quite apart from Descartes, tactility was already familiar in art discourse. Bernard Berenson had introduced the idea of 'tactile values' in his *Florentine Painters of the Renaissance* (1896). In conversation with John Richardson, Braque disclaimed knowledge of Berenson's theories. *G. Braque* (London: Oldbourne, 1961), p. 16.

61. Penrose, *Picasso*, p. 161; Shattuck, *Banquet*, p. 175. For a slighting reference to Princet's lack of originality, see Picasso, 'Lettre sur l'art' [1926], in *Propos*, p. 22. Kahnweiler was adamant that neither Braque nor Picasso (nor Gris) got anything from Princet, except perhaps some free financial advice. *Gris*, p. 185.

62. *Le Carnet de la Semaine*, 1 September 1918. Cf. *Fauvisme*, p. 24.

63. Marius de Zayas, 'Picasso Speaks' [1923], in *Picasso on Art*, p. 6. Cf. Vallier, 'Braque', pp. 36–7.

64. Cocteau diary, 21 June 1953, in *Le Passé défini* (Paris: Gallimard, 1985), pp. 156–7; Richardson, 'Mystery'. Gris (long dead) did illustrations for *L'Assiette au beurre* (*The Plate of Butter*) and other papers to make ends meet. See also ch. 10.

65. Gilot, *Picasso*, p. 69; Hélène Parmelin, *Voyage en Picasso* (Paris: Laffont, 1980), pp. 82–3.

66. Gilot, *Picasso*, p. 69 (emphasis in original). Cf. Vallier, 'Braque', p. 34.

67. Braque, 'Testimony', pp. 13–14; Vallier, 'Braque', p. 40. On recognition trouble, see ch. 8.

68. Gilot, *Picasso*, p. 68 (emphasis in original). Contrast Brassaï, *Conversations*, p. 93.

69. See ch. 6.

70. Pierre Cabanne, *L'Épopée des cubistes* [1963] (Paris: Amateur, 2000), pp. 288–9. Cf. Kahnweiler, *Gris*, pp. 216–18; *Galeries*, pp. 61–2.

71. John O'Neill (ed.), *Barnett Newman: Selected Writings and Interviews* (Berkeley: University of California Press, 1992), p. 298; Richard Shiff, 'Whiteout', in Ann Temkin (ed.), *Barnett Newman* (Philadelphia: Philadelphia Museum of Art, 2002), p. 86. See, e.g., *Eve* (1950).

72. Jacob, draft memoirs; letter to Louis Dumoulin, 30 September 1943; 'La vie artistique', *391* (1915–16), in Seckel, *Jacob*, pp. 65, 121–2 and 271.

73. Kramár's reservations about Braque are plain in his own account (heavily indebted to Kahnweiler): see *Cubisme*, p. 13, a work illustrated with twenty-three Picassos and one Braque (and a rather feeble excuse for the disparity).

74. Stein, *Toklas*, p. 100. Cf. her *Picasso*, p. 12.

75. Anatole France, *La Révolte des anges* [1913] (Paris: Pocket, 1986), p. 48.

76. The Exhibition of International Art took place at the 69th Regiment Armory. Braque and Picasso were not particularly well represented. Cf. Calvin Tomkins, *Duchamp* (London: Pimlico, 1998), pp. 118–19. Braque's first substantial outing in New York was a joint exhibition with Picasso at Alfred Stieglitz's '291' gallery in 1914–15. On this and subsequent occasions critical attention focussed overwhelmingly on Picasso. Marius de Zayas, *How, When and Why Modern Art Came to New York* (Cambridge: MIT, 1998), pp. 39–40.

77. Kahnweiler, *Galeries*, p. 60. For the colourful ensemble, Salmon, *Souvenirs*, vol. III, p. 180.

78. Braque to Kahnweiler [c.24 August 1912], in *Leiris*, pp. 26–7. *Ajo blanco* is usually a starter, not a dessert. See Delia Smith: 'First you need to blanch the almonds. To do this, place them in a bowl, pour in enough boiling water to cover and leave them aside for 3–4 minutes. Then drain them in a colander and simply squeeze the nuts out of their shells into the bowl. After that, put the almonds in the blender and pour in the olive oil ... Then, add the peeled garlic, vinegar and salt and liquidize until everything is smooth. Now, with the motor still running, slowly add the cold water ... Garnish with the grapes and apple slices.' *Delia's How to Cook*, vol. III (London: BBC, 2001), p. 51.

79. Cf. Robert Rosenblum, 'The Spanishness of Picasso's still life', in Jonathan Brown (ed.), *Picasso and the Spanish Tradition* (New Haven: Yale University Press, 1996), pp. 61–2.

80. Jose Ortega y Gasset, trans. anon., *The Revolt of the Masses* (London: Allen and Unwin, 1932), p. 95; John Berger, *The Success and Failure*

of *Picasso* (Harmondsworth: Penguin, 1965), p. 40. Ortega y Gasset himself had borrowed the expression from Walther Rathenau.

81. D. H. Kahnweiler, 'Huit entretiens avec Picasso', *Le Point*, XLII (1952), p. 26, from 1935.

82. Picasso to Braque, 10 July 1912, *P&B*, p. 399. Though it is now known that he applied (unsuccessfully) for French citizenship in April 1940.

83. *Still Life with Banderillas* (1911), in *P&B*, p. 202. The counterpart to this work is Picasso's *Still Life with a Bottle of Rum* (1911) and perhaps (the following summer) *The Aficionado* (1912).

84. Vallier, 'Braque', p. 34. Cf. Verdet, 'Autour', pp. 21–2.

85. Clement Greenberg, 'Braque spread large' [1949], in John O'Brian (ed.), *The Collected Essays and Criticism*, 4 vols (Chicago: University of Chicago Press, 1988–95), vol. II, p. 307, citing also *Violin and Pitcher* (1910) and *The Portuguese* (1911); Albert Murray, 'The visual equivalent to blues composition', in *The Blue Devils of Nada* (NY: Vintage, 1997), pp. 117–40.

86. André Breton, trans. Richard Howard, *Nadja* [1928] (London: Penguin, 1999), pp. xv and 122, where the painting is called *The Guitar Player*. The nail and string (upper left) are more plausibly a peg or stanchion and a cord or rope – repeated in other works – perhaps an echo of the curtain cord found in several of Picasso's paintings, perhaps a suggestion of a nautical mooring.

87. Samuel Beckett, *Molloy* [1950] (London: Calder, 1959), pp. 13–14; Gall, 'En mourant'.

88. John Berger, 'The moment of Cubism' [1969], in *The White Bird* (London: Hogarth, 1988), p. 179. Cf. Patrick Heron, *Braque* (London: Faber, 1958), p. 24.

89. Jean Paulhan, 'Petite aventure en pleine nuit' [1958], in *Peinture cubiste*, pp. 64–5, a trope borrowed perhaps from Diderot.

90. Berger, 'Moment', p. 179.

91. Bissière, Gilot and Leymarie interviews.

92. Gilot, *Picasso*, p. 182.

93. Braque to Kahnweiler, 15 July 1914, in *P&B*, p. 429.

94. Braque to Kahnweiler, 1 August 1914, ibid., p. 430. Kahnweiler was then in Rome, at the beginning of his own long exile.

95. Kahnweiler, *Galeries*, p. 62. In other versions, 'we never saw each other again': Cabanne, *L'Épopée*, pp. 340–41.

CHAPTER 6: 'If I should Die out there': The Great War

1. See Henri Barbusse, trans. W. Fitzwater Wray, *Under Fire* [1916] (London: Dent, 1926), p. 32.
2. Braque to Picasso, 29 November 1914, MP; Braque to Apollinaire, 19 January 1915, BNF.
3. Dossier Braque, Vincennes. Braque served in the 53rd Infantry Division, first in the 329th Regiment (19th Company) and then in the 224th Regiment (17th Company). True to form, there is apparently no war diary for his unit. There is the summary *Historique du 224e Régiment d'Infanterie* (Paris: Charles-Lavauzelle, 1922).
4. *Cahier*, p. 91. See, e.g., Émile-Jean-Horace Vernet (1789–1863), *The Dog of the Regiment Wounded* (1819).
5. *Cahier*, p. 51, a maxim applied to the war in Frédéric Rossif's documentary *Georges Braque ou le temps différent* (1975), written by Jean Lescure; Melville, *Moby Dick*, p. 190.
6. Marc Bloch, trans. Gerard Hopkins, *Strange Defeat* (NY: Norton, 1968), p. 56; *Cahier*, p. 86. A cubit is the length of the arm from the elbow to the tip of the middle finger.
7. Pierre Hamp's formulation, as quoted in Bloch, *Defeat*, p. 89.
8. *Cahier*, p. 42. For the importance of *constance* see Roger Bissière, 'Notes sur l'art de Braque', *Georges Braque* (Paris: L'Effort Moderne, 1920), notes all but dictated by Braque himself.
9. Apollinaire, 'Si je mourais là-bas', in Apollinaire/Braque, *Si je mourais là-bas* (Paris: Broder, 1962), p. 18; *Poèmes*, p. 108. Braque illustrated the book with an exceptional suite of colour wood-engravings – an exacting art – but he also edited the poems, splitting some, retitling others, even altering punctuation. He seems to have worked from an earlier edition sanctioned by Lou herself, *Ombre de mon amour* (Geneva: Cailler, 1947), the title favoured by Apollinaire. This included facsimiles of some of the poet's original letters and drawings; it was one of Braque's treasured possessions. The standard modern

edition is *Poèmes à Lou* (Paris: Gallimard, 1969), cross-referenced here. Several of these poems mutated into the famous *Calligrammes*. The text of *Ombre de mon amour* has recently been republished (Paris: Bibliothèque des Arts, 2003).

10. Ordre du régiment, 20 July 1916. Cf. Ordre de l'armée, 14 August 1917. Dossier Braque, Vincennes.

11. Alberto Giacometti, 'Gris, brun, noir . . .' [1952], in *Écrits* (Paris: Hermann, 1990), p. 70.

12. Chandet, 'Le Père'.

13. Studies showed a remarkably high recovery rate (c. 95 per cent) from the trepanation procedure itself, as opposed to any operations that were carried out subsequently. Fortunately, Braque seems not to have needed any further work. Paul Delvoie, *Histoire, indications et contre-indications, technique et résultats de la trépanation cranienne* (Brussels: Hayez, 1893).

14. Chandet, 'Le Père'; Gris to Kahnweiler, 1 June 1915, in *Letters of Juan Gris*, trans. Douglas Cooper (London: privately printed, 1956), p. 29; Kahnweiler, *Gris*, p. 37.

15. Seamus Heaney, 'Seeing Things', in *Opened Ground*, p. 341. Both men assured Richardson that they parted on the friendliest of terms. *Picasso*, vol. II, p. 345. For the legends: Hope, *Braque*, p. 74; Patricia Leighten, *Re-ordering the Universe* (Princeton: Princeton University Press, 1989), p. 144, a farrago of speculation about politics and war.

16. For Picasso's Braque period see Robert Delaunay, *Du cubisme à l'art abstrait* [1923–4] (Paris: SEVPEN, 1957), p. 101; Lewis, *Caliph*, p. 115.

17. As for example in their still lifes of the early 1920s. Cf. Brigitte Léal, 'Picasso's stylistic "Don Juanism": still life in the dialectic between Cubism and Classicism', in Jean Sutherland Boggs, *Picasso and Things* (Cleveland: Cleveland Museum of Art, 1992), pp. 30–37.

18. Picasso to Roché, misdated August [?24 May] 1915, Roché Papers, Ransom. On the same day Picasso gave Braque's address to the dealer Léonce Rosenberg: Ambulance 1/18, S.P. 96.

19. Gertrude Stein, *Everybody's Autobiography* (NY: Random House, 1937), p. 119.

20. Gris to Kahnweiler, [31 May 1915], in *Letters*, p. 28. See also the

bulletins of 4 August and 7 September 1915, in Kahnweiler, *Gris*, pp. 37 and 38.

21. Léger to Louis Poughon, 17 August [1914] and 6 January 1916, in *Fernand Léger: une correspondance de guerre, Cahiers du MNAM*, hors-série (1997), pp. 9 and 50. Derain really was a cyclist for a while, and had hopes of becoming a driver. He transferred to the artillery in 1915 and was promoted bombardier in time for demobilization in 1918. Léger, who began the war as a sapper and became a stretcher-bearer, was perhaps the one who saw the most, notwithstanding his persistent efforts to move rearwards.

22. *Picasso*, vol. II, p. 358; Verdet, 'Autour', p. 25; Vallier, 'Braque', p. 44. That was all he said to Vallier about the war: her account is both perfunctory and inaccurate.

23. Braque to Léonce Rosenberg, 18 April 1916, Fonds Léonce Rosenberg, MNAM. Cf. Braque to Picasso, 13 May 1916, MP. Bernay was the depot of the 24th Infantry Regiment.

24. Amédée Ozenfant, *Mémoires* (Paris: Seghers, 1968), p. 93. In Max Jacob's version, she was arrested as a spy but released without being violated. Jacob to Kahnweiler, 22 September 1914, in *Correspondance*, vol. I, p. 99.

25. Rosenberg to Picasso, 6 March 1916, in Fitzgerald, *Modernism*, p. 64; to Gris, 28 November 1918, in *Juan Gris, Cahiers du MNAM*, hors-série (1999), p. 195; and to Braque, 31 December 1919, in Braque–Rosenberg correspondence, MNAM. After Braque had left him, he also made trouble between Braque and Léger. See Rosenberg to Léger, 13 May 1924, in *Fernand Léger: une correspondance d'affaires, Cahiers du MNAM*, hors-série (1996), p. 136.

26. Léonce Rosenberg, *Cubisme et Empirisme* (Paris: L'Effort Moderne, 1921), p. 1.

27. Gris to Rosenberg, 2 June 1916, in *Gris*, p. 29.

28. Braque contract, 24 November 1916, in Braque–Rosenberg correspondence, MNAM; Léger contract, 6 December 1917, in *Léger* (1996), p. 22; Laurens contract, 18 April 1916, in Laurens–Rosenberg correspondence, MNAM; Gris contract, 20 April 1916, in *Gris*, pp. 22–4.

29. Bissière, *Braque*, p. 3.

30. Amédée Ozenfant and Charles-Edouard Jeanneret, trans. John Goodman, *After Cubism* [1918], in Carol S. Eliel, *L'Esprit nouveau* (NY: Abrams, 2001), pp. 135, 139, 165.

31. Francis Picabia, trans. William A. Camfield, 'Dada Manifesto' [1920], in *Picabia* (Princeton: Princeton University Press, 1979), p. 140.

32. Roché, 'L'Être Picasso' [1957], p. 117; Georges Charensol, 'Conclusion, pour un musée français d'art moderne', *L'Art vivant*, 1 October 1925; Christopher Green, *Cubism and its Enemies* (New Haven: Yale University Press, 1987), p. 138.

33. The catalogue raisonné has three works for 1916, two small rough-hewn Cubist still lifes and a conventional landscape, the last done in hospital for charity. For 1916–20, in all, its lists eighty-six paintings (possibly an over-estimate) and two *papiers collés* (definitely an under-estimate).

34. For 'King Shell' (*Obus-Roi*) see Apollinaire to Billy, 26 April 1915, in Shattuck, *Banquet Years*, p. 290; the menu is reproduced in Picasso/ Apollinaire, *Correspondance*, p. 202. Apollinaire was wounded on 17 March and trepanned on 9 May 1916.

35. Apollinaire to Raynal, 27 January 1917, in Pierre-Marcel Adéma, *Guillaume Apollinaire* (Paris: Table Ronde, 1968), p. 315.

36. Marie Wassilieff, *La Bohème du XX siècle* (unpublished, 1929), p. 71. The manuscript is in the possession of Claude Bernès; I am grateful to Hilary Spurling for alerting me to it.

37. Wassilieff, *Bohème*, p. 71; Gris to Raynal, 18 January 1917, in Seckel, *Jacob*, p. 142; Braque to Léonce Rosenberg, 5 February 1917, MNAM; *Picasso*, vol. II, p. 427.

38. Braque to Léonce Rosenberg, 4 March 1917, MNAM; to Picasso, 23 March 1917, MP.

39. Braque to Léonce Rosenberg, 29 June 1917, 13 October 1918, 30 August 1919, MNAM.

40. *Cahier*, p. 28, already embedded in his discourse. See Bissière, *Braque*, p. 4.

41. Jean Leymarie, 'Évocation de Reverdy auprès de Braque et de Picasso', *Mercure de France* 1181 (1962), p. 301. Reverdy lived a few minutes away from Braque in Montmartre, in the rue Cortot. In 1926 he left Paris, retreating to the environs of the abbey of Solesmes,

near La Flèche, on the Loire. There he lived like a hermit; but he could never quite leave the fray altogether. On forays to the metropolis he stayed in Braque's guest quarters.

42. Philippe Soupault, 'L'époque Nord-Sud', ibid., pp. 307, 330; Fumet, *Braque* (1965), p. 138.

43. Pierre Reverdy, 'Une aventure méthodique' [1950], in *Note éternelle du présent* (Paris: Flammarion, 1973), p. 78.

44. *Cahier*, p. 33; *Patron*, p. 60. Cf. Étienne-Alain Hubert, 'Pierre Reverdy et la "poésie plastique" de son temps', *Europe* 638–9 (1982), pp. 109–18.

45. John Richardson, 'Au château des cubistes', *L'Œil*, 15 April 1955.

46. André Breton, trans. Simon Watson Taylor, *Surrealism and Painting* [1926] (London: Macdonald, 1972), pp. 10–11 (his emphases). Breton employs the Braque-word *tenir* ('pour voir si elles tiendraient'); his translator gives 'to survive'. For the sake of consistency I have substituted 'to hold' or 'hold up' here.

47. Reverdy, 'Aventure', p. 64. *Homme intégral* is Saint-John Perse's expression: 'Pierre levée' [1964], in *Œuvres complètes* (Paris: Gallimard, 1972), p. 536.

48. Reverdy, 'Aventure', pp. 78–9.

49. Walter Benjamin, trans. Harry Zohn, 'The Storyteller' [1936], in *Illuminations* (London: Fontana, 1992), p. 84.

50. Louis Latapie, *Patafioles* (unpublished typescript memoirs), pp. 66–7. I am grateful to Laure Latapie Bissière (his daughter) for access to this material, and for her own reminiscences. By contrast, one of the most implausible stories in the literature is that, in response to the American collector John Quinn's inquiry about his war wound, Braque 'invited him to lay his fingers in the runnel above his right temple, and Quinn did so'. B. L. Reid, *The Man from New York* (NY: Oxford University Press, 1968), p. 502.

51. *Cahier*, p. 48; Braque to Paulhan, [1951], Archives Jean Paulhan, IMEC. As Braque would have known, Paulhan too had experience of no-man's-land, subsequently fictionalized. See Paulhan, *La Vie*, pp. 161–2; *Le Guerrier appliqué* [1917] (Paris: Gallimard, 1930).

52. Guth, 'Visite'; John Richardson, 'Braque discusses his art', *Réalités*, 93 (1958), p. 30.

53. Leymarie, 'Évocation', p. 301. As Braque would have known, Reverdy himself had written a poem of the same title, 'Always There' (1916); later he wrote of Laurens in exactly these terms the year after the sculptor's death. 'Toujours là', in *Plupart du temps* (Paris: Gallimard, 1969), vol. I, pp. 141–2; 'La plus longue présence' [1955], in *Note*, p. 138.

54. *Les Lettres Françaises* [1946], in *Transition*, 49 (1949), p. 117; Anatole Jakovski, 'Georges Braque', *Arts de France* 8 (1946), p. 36. The slang for gas mask was *groin de cochon* – 'this pig's snout which represented the war's true face'. Roland Dorgelès, *Souvenirs sur les croix de bois* (Paris: Cité des livres, 1929), p. 18.

55. *Patron*, pp. 25–6, 133–4; Stein, *Toklas*, p. 99.

56. Gustav Vriesen and Max Imdahl, *Robert Delaunay* (NY: Abrams, 1949), p. 49; Delaunay to Weichsel, 12 December 1916, in Kenneth E. Silver, *Esprit de Corps* (London: Thames and Hudson, 1989), p. 144; Tomkins, *Duchamp*, p. 153. Delaunay also shared his chilling views on cleansing with Gleizes.

57. Léger to Louis Poughon, 1 October 1915, in *Léger* (1997), p. 48.

58. Braque to Kahnweiler, 8 October 1919, in *Leiris*, p. 29; Blaise Cendrars, trans. Esther Allen, 'I Have Killed' [1919], in *Modernities* (Lincoln: University of Nebraska, 1992), p. 11.

59. Braque to Kahnweiler, 8 October 1919, in Assouline, *L'Homme*, p. 263. Cf. Kahnweiler's notes on a visit to Braque's studio, 25 February 1920, in *Leiris*, p. 29.

60. *Cahier*, p. 111. Cf. Diderot: 'They will talk of La Tour; but they will see Chardin.' 'Salon de 1767', in Else Marie Bukdahl et al. (eds), *Ruines et paysages* (Paris: Hermann, 1995), p. 173. Braque's later discourse gives talent no quarter. 'One appeals to talent for want of imagination.' *Cahier*, p. 28. His conversations with Georges Charbonnier, Pierre Descargues, Alexander Liberman and John Richardson all touch on the same vexed question.

61. Pierre Cabanne, *Le Siècle de Picasso* (Paris: Denoël, 1975), vol. I, p. 318.

62. This is Brassaï's formulation in *Artists*, p. 164, a book published after Picasso's death, and perhaps the franker for it. Penrose, too, is unusually forthright, stating that Braque 'disapproved of Picasso's

new manner of living and *despised* the way he appeared fashionably dressed at the theatre'. *Picasso*, p. 230 (my emphasis). Cf. Tom Wolfe, *The Painted Word* [1975] (NY: Bantam, 1999), pp. 24–5.

63. Man Ray, *Picasso, Olga Khokhlova and Eugenia Errazuriz at the Beaumont Ball for 'Mercure'* (1924); Stein, *Toklas*, pp. 209–10.

64. Gris to Kahnweiler, 3 September 1919, in Kahnweiler, *Gris*, p. 41; Roché, 'L'Être Picasso', p. 117. 'Notre Toréro' is René Char's disenchanted usage. Char to Pierre-André Benoit (PAB), 20 October 1956, in *PIC & PAB* (Alès: Benoit, 1991), p. 17.

65. Braque to Kahnweiler, 8 October 1919, in *Leiris*, p. 29; Leymarie, 'Évocation', p. 301. Reverdy's manuscript notes of the 'Pensées' include multiple drafts of several of them. In Fonds Reverdy, RDY 388–90, Doucet; an extract is reproduced in *Papiers collés*, p. 182. Those published for the first time in December 1917 reappear, sometimes reworked, in later editions of Braque's *Cahier*, but there is no comparable original in Braque's hand. The thinking of the two men corresponds very closely, which is hardly surprising; they had been discussing these things intensively for years. Reverdy edited *Nord-Sud*; he also edited Braque. Braque subsequently picked up some of his poetic language, as did Reverdy in a certain sense from Braque: see their 1950 dialogue in *Derrière le Miroir* 144–6 (1964), pp. 74–6. There was cross-fertilization, but Braque's thoughts were his own. Reverdy's seminal essay, 'On Cubism' (itself influenced by Braque), had appeared earlier in 1917; the texts may be compared in Fry, *Cubism*, pp. 143–8.

66. 'The call to order' was much in vogue at the time. See below. Braque himself was given to reiterating his thoughts in his correspondence, often by way of admonition or instruction, e.g. Braque to Léonce Rosenberg, 13 November 1918, MNAM.

67. Braque to Kahnweiler, 8 October 1919, and Kahnweiler notes, 25 February 1920, in *Leiris*, p. 29. Cf. Braque to Rosenberg, 12 September 1919, in *Léger* (1996), p. 56. Braque's use of 'analysis' and 'synthesis' in 1919 predates by several years the terminology usually associated with Gris in public statements of the 1920s, from which the widespread and rather indiscriminate later usage is often held to derive. See 'Les possibilités de la peinture' [1924] and

'Réponse à l'enquête' [1925], and Kahnweiler's gloss, in his *Gris*, pp. 342–59 and 203. Several of Braque's later maxims pit art against science, e.g. *Cahier*, pp. 18 and 27.

68. See, e.g., Henri Maldiney, 'L'équivoque de l'image dans la peinture', in *Regard Parole Espace* (Paris: L'Age d'Homme, 1973), pp. 211–53, and *L'Avènement de la peinture* (Paris: Encre marin, 1999), p. 11; Maurice Merleau-Ponty, *Causeries* [1948] (Paris: Seuil, 2002), pp. 55–6; Paul Ricœur, 'L'insoluble', in Jean Bazaine, *Couleurs et mots* (Paris: Cherche-Midi, 1997), p. 67; Meyer Schapiro, 'On some problems in the semiotics of visual art' [1969], in *Theory and Philosophy of Art* (NY: Braziller, 1994), p. 29. Maldiney wrote directly about Braque in *Derrière le Miroir* 25–6 (1950). For the discovery of Braque's *Cahier* (1947) by a young American in Paris, see Roger Shattuck, 'Captions or Illustrations: Braque's Handbook' [1989], in *Candor and Perversion* (NY: Norton, 2000), pp. 211–32. On Carl Einstein see ch. 7; on Heidegger, ch. 11.

69. Braque himself speaks of 'retouching' the maxims for publication in a letter to Stanislas Fumet, 11 July 1943, Fonds Fumet, BNF. I am grateful to Marie-Odile Germain for access to this material.

70. Derain to Alice Derain [January 1918], in *Lettres*, pp. 277–8. On Braque–Rochefoucauld see Claude Leroy, 'Braque écrivain ou la signature du peintre', *Europe*, 638–9 (1982), pp. 59–67, and 'Braque pseudonyme', *Cahiers du MNAM*, 11 (1983), pp. 145–59.

71. Braque to Kahnweiler, 30 October 1919, in *Leiris*, p. 29. Cf. Paulhan, 'Une nouvelle machine à voir', *Peinture cubiste*, pp. 109–34, a formulation originating in discussion with Braque.

72. Compare *Café-Bar* (1919), in Maeght, no. 64, and *Bottle, Glass and Pipe* (1914), in *Papiers collés*, no. 41. Salvador Dalí cut his teeth on pastiches of this style a few years later, e.g., *Gran arlequin y pequeña botella de ron* (1925) or *Bodegón al claro de luna* (1927).

73. Félix Fénéon, quoted in *Le Crapouillot*, 16 November 1922.

74. Appendix B, no. 15; Louis Aragon, 'La peinture au défi' [1930], in *Écrits sur l'art moderne* (Paris: Flammarion, 1981), pp. 32–3.

75. *Patron*, p. 82.

76. Vallier, 'Braque', p. 45; Braque to Kahnweiler, 8 October 1919, in *Leiris*, p. 29. The veracious *ton local* was a watchword from pre-war

days. 'Colour absorbs or is absorbed' was another maxim. *Valori Plastici* 2 (1919), p. 2.

77. Jacob to Picasso, 9 June 1919, in Seckel, *Jacob*, p. 169; André Lhote, 'Exposition Braque', *NRF*, 69 (1919), pp. 153–7. Bissière's laudatory review in *L'Opinion*, 29 March and 26 April 1919, included perhaps the first use of the over-worked *rappel à l'ordre*. The expression was then picked up by Lhote.

78. Cf. Gris to Kahnweiler, 3 September 1919, in Kahnweiler, *Gris*, p. 41. Most of the works in the exhibition sold immediately. According to Rosenberg, the price of Braques then rose steeply; he did not hesitate to claim credit for the artist's post-war relaunch. 'Réponses à des abonnés', *Bulletin de L'Effort Moderne*, 33 (1927); Tériade, 'Entretien avec M. Léonce Rosenberg' [1927], in *Écrits*, p. 94.

79. Cendrars, 'Braque', *La Rose Rouge*, 19 June 1919. Cf. André Salmon, 'Georges Braque', *L'Europe Nouvelle*, 29 March 1919, incorporated in *L'Art vivant*, pp. 121–8. Antoine Arnauld (1612–94) was a brilliant philosophical controversialist who cast doubt on the Cartesian argument for the distinctness of mind and body. In 1662 he wrote a celebrated text called *Logic or the Art of Thinking* – the so-called Port-Royal logic.

80. See Gris to Kahnweiler, 31 January 1919, in Kahnweiler, *Gris*, p. 43. Most GEM artists were hung together in one room, including Gris, Hayden, Herbin, Lipchitz, Metzinger. Braque was hung separately, as was Léger, who had a hand in the hanging. The coolness between Braque and Gris continued for several years, but it was not purely one-sided: Gris fell out with many of his friends. Cf. Gris to Kahnweiler, 21 January 1924, in ibid., p. 79; Georges Auric, *Quand j'étais là* (Paris: Grasset, 1979), p. 186.

CHAPTER 7: 'Tous les conforts, pas de téléphone':
Braque–Chardin

1. *Littérature* 18 (1921), p. 1. Tzara may not have forgotten that when he sought to publish more of Braque's *pensées* he was told that there weren't any, other than those appearing under Reverdy's aegis in

Nord-Sud. Braque to Tzara, 15 January 1917 [?1918], Fonds Tzara, Doucet.

2. The exact figures:

	francs
	francs
Uhde sale (May 1921)	168,000
1st Kahnweiler sale (June 1921)	216,335
2nd Kahnweiler sale (November 1921)	175,215
3rd Kahnweiler sale (June 1922)	84,927
4th Kahnweiler sale (May 1923)	227,662
Grand total from all sales	879,139
Of which Derain	295,000
Of which Braque	61,290

3. Assouline, *L'Homme*, pp. 287–8; Fitzgerald, *Modernism*, p. 110. Matisse's 1920–23 contract with Bernheim-Jeune stipulated 7,000 francs for a no. 50. Léonce Rosenberg's brother Paul paid Picasso 7,500 francs for one that size in 1921.

4. Florent Fels, 'La peinture au Salon d'Automne', *Action*, 5 October 1920; André Salmon, 'Le Salon d'Automne', *La Revue de France*, December 1922; Paul Fiérens, 'Georges Braque', *Sélection*, 4 (1924), p. 361.

5. Roché to Quinn, 6 and 20 October 1920, Quinn Collection, MF Reel 32, NYPL. In 1921 Rosenberg was asking 3,000–6,000 francs for paintings priced at 600 francs in 1918.

6. Braque–Rosenberg correspondence, c. 4 and 7 January 1920, MNAM; Rosenberg to Léger, 18 September 1920, in *Léger* (1996), p. 76. Rosenberg had served first as an observer in aerial reconnaissance, then as an interpreter with the Royal Flying Corps Headquarters Wing in France. It was he who translated Reverdy's 'Sur le cubisme' into English in 1917.

7. Braque to Rosenberg, 6 June 1921, MNAM. For the first Kahnweiler sale – 22 Braques, 24 Derains, 9 Grises, 7 Légers, 26 Picassos, 33 Vlamincks and 6 Van Dongens – Rosenberg's estimate was 197,000 francs. The out-turn was 216,335, of which the Braques made 25,114 and the Picassos 36,403.

8. According to Severini – who is not always reliable – Braque said, 'When you risk your neck in the war, you have a right to respect

and to favours,' a reference to Rosenberg's contention that the sending out of catalogues was not the standard practice, merely 'a favour'. *Life*, p. 268.

9. Auric, *Quand*, pp. 194–5; Ozenfant, *Mémoires*, p. 119; Stein, *Toklas*, p. 120. Not everyone took the same view as Matisse. Léger sympathized with Rosenberg and dissociated himself from Braque. Léger to Rosenberg, 17 July 1921, in *Léger* (1996), p. 88.

10. *Écho de Paris*, 13 June 1921; Stein, *Toklas*, p. 120; Braque to Kahnweiler, 17 October 1921, in *Leiris*, p. 30.

11. *Patron*, p. 83. The story of Rosenberg's boxing, the source of much amusement as it got around, appears to be true: Tériade, 'Entretien avec Léonce Rosenberg' [1927], *Écrits*, p. 93.

12. As late as 1938, the Musée du Luxembourg possessed only two small *natures mortes*. Louis Hautecœur to Georges Huisman, 29 November 1938, in MNAM, p. 98.

13. Cf. the later reflections of Kahnweiler, *Galeries*, pp. 95–6; and André Level, *Souvenir d'un collectionneur* (Paris: Mazo, 1959), p. 70.

14. See Douglas Cooper, 'Braque et le papier collé', in *Papiers collés*, pp. 7–11.

15. Robert Desnos, 'La dernière vente Kahnweiler', *Écrits sur la peinture* (Paris: Flammarion, 1984), pp. 64–7.

16. Paul Éluard, 'Georges Braque' [1925], in Annick Lionel-Marie, *Paul Éluard et ses amis peintres* (Paris: MNAM, 1982), p. 83.

17. 'If he had not sold a Braque he owned, Aragon said he would have tried to commit suicide again; the cash financed his escape from Venice and Nancy Cunard.' Peter Everett, *Matisse's War* (London: Vintage, 1997), p. 143.

18. This was *Clarinet* (1913), in *Papiers collés*, no. 29; Ozenfant, *Mémoires*, p. 119.

19. Paulhan to Marcel Arland [December 1946], in *Choix*, vol. III, p. 44 (his emphasis).

20. *Patron*, pp. 20–22 (his emphasis). Paulhan's use of 'common' here may be an allusion to Braque's play on the distinction between the common and the similar in his maxims: 'Commonality is true. Similarity is false. Trouillebert resembles Corot, but they have nothing in common.' *Cahier*, pp. 38 and 78. Trouillebert was a successful

painter in his day (1829–1900). One of his paintings was mistaken for a Corot; the case was brought to trial.

21. Paulhan to Jouhandeau [March 1932] and [April 1939], in *Choix*, vol. I, p. 237, and vol. II, pp. 96–7.

22. *Patron*, pp. 126–7; Assouline, *L'Homme*, pp. 549–50. Cf. Paul Léautaud diary, 7 March 1944, in *Journal Littéraire*, vol. XV (Paris: Mercure de France, 1963), p. 307. The put-down was not confined to Kahnweiler, or to Paulhan. 'Janet Flanner gave me her article on Braque,' wrote the grand panjandrum Harold Acton to James Lord on 3 December 1956. 'It is extremely readable and very well done, but where are the aesthetic standards of such a person? Mere shibboleths, the slogans still in fashion at the moment. I don't know what to tell her in return. Never has greater nonsense been written about painting and sculpture; and it is a tonic to re-read Vasari and Winckelmann, who knew what they were talking about instead of inventing *de la littérature . . .*'. James Lord, *Some Remarkable Men* (NY: Farrar Straus Giroux, 1996), p. 57. The article was 'Master', first published in the *New Yorker*.

23. Paulhan to Braque [1951], in *NRF* 197 (1969), p. 1028. The trailer article concluded, 'alors c'est Braque que je prends pour patron et pour loi'. *Comœdia*, 31 October 1942.

24. *Entretiens de Francis Ponge avec Philippe Sollers* (Paris: Gallimard, 1970), p. 106; 'L'objet, c'est la poétique' [1962] and 'Braque le réconciliateur' [1946] in *L'Atelier*, pp. 221–4 and 59; 'Bref condensé de notre dette à jamais et re-co-naissance à Braque particulièrement en cet été 80' [1980], in *Nouveau Nouveau Recueil* (Paris: Gallimard, 1992), p. 129.

25. Ponge, 'Réconciliateur', in *L'Atelier*, p. 59 (his emphases).

26. Michel Seuphor, *Un Siècle de libertés* (Paris: Hazan, 1996), pp. 264–5. In fact Seuphor was sensitively attuned towards Braque. See his preface to *Braque graveur* (Paris: Berggruen, 1953).

27. Antoine Tudal, 'Nature morte', in *Souspente* (Paris: Godet, 1945), p. 16. Braque in effect made the publication of this volume possible by contributing a lithograph (in eight colours), and securing a preface by Reverdy. See Vallier, no. 29.

28. Braque, 'Sa vie', no. 4; Salmon, *Paris-Journal*, 12 September 1910 and 16 April 1911.

29. Stein, 'Braque', p. 145 ('Brack' prompted perhaps by Vauxcelles' 'Bracke', *Gil Blas*, 25 March 1909). There is some passing correspondence with *Toklas*, pp. 11–12. Could 'neuresthenia' and what follows date from after Braque's return from the war?

30. Braque, 'Testimony', p. 14. Matisse, among others, wrote in the same vein. Braque's text is in English; the original French has not survived. Stein cast doubt on its authenticity for that reason; on her account, Braque disavowed it. *Everybody's Autobiography*, pp. 35–7. The pithy expression at the end means 'we know where we are'. Interestingly, *fixer* is not so far removed from another meaning of *braquer*: to point or aim a weapon (cf. the first line of Stein's portrait), and metaphorically to fix with a stare.

31. Braque/Prévert, *Varengeville*, p. 12; Jacques Derrida, trans. Richard Rand, *Signéponge/Signsponge* (NY: Columbia University Press, 1984), pp. 61–2; Vladimir Nabokov, *Ada or Ardor* [1969] (London: Penguin, 2000), pp. 20 and 464.

32. Ponge, 'Méditatif', in *L'Atelier*, pp. 292–3.

33. Ponge, 'Réconciliateur' and 'Méditatif', in ibid., pp. 64 and 296. See 'Braque, ou l'art moderne comme événement et plaisir' [1947], in ibid., pp. 70–77; 'Braque or modern art as event and pleasure', in *Transition*, 49 (1949), pp. 43–7.

34. Ponge, 'Feuillet', p. 247; Seamus Heaney, *The Redress of Poetry* (London: Faber, 1995), p. 15.

35. Ponge, 'Dessins' and 'Méditatif', in *L'Atelier*, pp. 106 and 283.

36. 'Les artistes au volant', *Le Crapouillot*, February 1930. Friesz went so far as to compose a confused note on 'The Aesthetic of the Automobile'. Fonds Friesz, 697, Bibliothèque Salacrou, Le Havre.

37. Kahnweiler, *Galeries*, pp. 125–6; Françoise Gilot, *Matisse and Picasso* (London: Bloomsbury, 1990), p. 223; Geoffrey Grigson, *The Private Art* (London: Allison and Busby, 1982), p. 4.

38. Bazaine, *Couleurs*, p. 18.

39. Miriam Cendrars, *Blaise Cendrars* (Paris: Balland, 1984), p. 327; interview with Claude Laurens, 4 January 2001. Braque evidently knew enough about what went on under the bonnet to repair Roché's Citroën 5CV. 'Souvenirs', p. 343.

40. Théâtre Serge Diaghilev, *Les Fâcheux* (Paris: Quatre Chemins, 1924),

text by Cocteau and illustrations by Braque (not in Vallier); Poulenc to Picasso, 19 July 1925, in Francis Poulenc, *Correspondance* (Paris: Fayard, 1994), p. 258. Cf. Raymond Cogniat, 'La décoration théâtrale – Braque et les Ballets Russes', *L'Amour de l'art*, May 1931.

41. Poulenc to Diaghilev, 28 April 1919, in *Correspondance*, p. 89.

42. *Patron*, p. 84; Braque, 'Sa vie', no. 7. Cf. Kochno, *Diaghilev*, p. 226.

43. René Char, *Dans l'atelier du poète* (Paris: Gallimard, 1996), p. 515; Roderick MacArthur, 'Georges Braque and the Tartuffe tradition', *Theatre Arts*, April 1950; Théâtre Louis Jouvet, *Le Tartuffe ou L'Imposteur* (Paris: Athénée, 1950). Braque had also done *Salade* (1924) for Count Étienne de Beaumont, with music by Darius Milhaud.

44. Braque to Paul Rosenberg, 11 September 1927, PML; Chandet, 'Le père'. Cf. Olivier Cinqalbre, 'Braque bâtisseur', in *L'Espace*, pp. 97–111.

45. Stein, *Toklas*, p. 11; Malraux, *Mask*, p. 50.

46. Roché, 'Georges Braque (suite)' [1955], in *Écrits*, p. 349; Jean Grenier diary, 4 November 1967, in *Carnets* (Paris: Seghers, 1991), p. 439; interview with Claude Laurens, 4 January 2001. Cf. A. J. Liebling, *Between Meals* [1959] (NY: North Point, 1986), p. 130.

47. Stein, *Toklas*, p. 102.

48. Jim Ede, *A Way of Life* (Cambridge: Kettle's Yard, 1996), p. 58; interview with Laure and Louttre Bissière.

49. Louis Vauxcelles, 'Braque chez Rosenberg', *Carnet de la semaine*, 14 March 1926; Jacques-Émile Blanche, 'Cahiers d'un artiste' [1917], in Fitzgerald, *Modernism*, p. 78.

50. Vauxcelles, 'Chez Rosenberg'. Wallace Stevens wrote of 'the dilapidations' of Braque and Picasso (as a triumph of the imagination) in 'The Nobel Rider and the Sound of Words' [1942], in *The Necessary Angel* (London: Faber, 1984), p. 15.

51. Gimpel diary, 19 January 1936, in René Gimpel, *Journal d'un collectionneur* (Paris: Calmann-Lévy, 1963), p. 452.

52. Interview with Heinz Berggruen, 8 December 2001.

53. Christian Zervos, 'L'exposition d'œuvres de Corot à la galerie Paul Rosenberg', *Cahiers d'Art*, 4 (1930), p. 199.

54. Tériade, 'Entretien avec Paul Rosenberg' [1927], *Écrits*, p. 107.

55. Rosenberg had a similar (but verbal) arrangement with Picasso from 1918; it too lasted until the irruptions of 1940.

56. In 1929, four still-life compositions, designs for inlaid marble panels to be set into the floor of his dining room. Braque chose the marbles and supervised every stage of the fabrication by the mosaicist.

57. Louis Aragon, 'Un soleil noir s'est couché à Solesmes', *Les Lettres Françaises*, 23 June 1960.

58. Robert Hughes, *The Shock of the New* (London: Thames and Hudson, 1991), p. 146; André Malraux, trans. Stuart Gilbert, *The Voices of Silence* [1951] (NY: Doubleday, 1953), p. 295. Malraux was referring to *The Return from Market* (1739). (He calls it *Housewife*.)

59. Verdet, 'Dernier entretien', p. 44.

60. Diderot, trans. Caroline Beamish, in Rosenberg, *Chardin*, p. 288, from *Salon de 1763* (Paris: Hermann, 1984), pp. 219–20. This was *The Jar of Olives* (1760).

61. Giacometti, 'Gris, brun, noir', p. 70; *Cahier*, p. 21. On Braque's later flowerpieces see ch. 10.

62. At the age of twenty-one Cooper came into a trust fund of £100,000, apocryphally said to derive from Cooper's sheep dip in New South Wales – where his ancestors had indeed made their pile – giving rise to jokes about the characteristic sound of the Australian sheep, 'Bra-a-a-que'. Richardson, *Apprentice*, p. 19.

63. Carl Einstein, 'La Collection Reber', *L'Intransigeant*, 1 April 1930.

64. Malraux, *Voices*, pp. 296, 603, 608, 610. Cf. *Mask*, p. 60.

65. A situation only partially remedied by Liliane Meffre, *Carl Einstein* (Paris: Presses de l'Université de Paris-Sorbonne, 2002).

66. Carl Einstein, *Die Kunst des 20 Jahrhunderts* (Berlin: Propyläen, 1926), e.g. pp. 89 and 91. See also 'La peinture est sauvée, les pompiers sont déçus' [1923], in *Cahiers du MNAM* 1 (1979), pp. 19–22; 'Tableaux récents de Georges Braque' [1929], in *Ethnologie de l'art moderne* (Marseille: Dimanche, 1993), trans. Liliane Meffre; and 'Georges Braque' [1933], in Marion Schmid and Liliane Meffre (eds), *Werke*, vol. III (Berlin: Medusa, 1985), pp. 177–80.

67. Against the wishes of the Director of the Kunsthalle, Wilhelm Barth, who did not care for Braque's art – a common sentiment among the Basle bourgeoisie apparently. Meffre, *Einstein*, p. 267.

68. Einstein to Kahnweiler [1922], in Carl Einstein/Daniel-Henry Kahnweiler, *Correspondance* (Marseille: Dimanche, 1993), p. 35. Almost nothing of Einstein's work has been translated into English. French texts include *Bébuquin* (Paris: Réel, 2000), trans. Sabine Wolf; *La Sculpture nègre* (Paris: L'Harmattan, 1998), trans. Liliane Meffre; *Georges Braque* [1934] (Brussels: La Part de l'Œil, 2003), trans. Jean-Loup Korzilius (the edition used here, restored and retranslated from the German original, more fully and more reliably than the 1934 version). Cf. *Werke*, vol. III, pp. 181–456.

69. Einstein, 'Tableaux récents', p. 42. Part of Einstein's copious output in the meteoric journal *Documents*, in which he was a leading figure, with Georges Bataille and Georges-Henri Rivière.

70. Einstein to Kisling [November/December 1923], in 'Lettres de Carl Einstein à Moïse Kisling', *Cahiers du MNAM*, 62 (1997), p. 118.

71. Einstein to Kisling, 11 December 1920, 22 January 1921 [February 1921], in ibid., pp. 82–4. Cf. Liliane Meffre, *Carl Einstein et le problématique des avant-gardes dans les arts plastiques* (Berne: Lang, 1989).

72. Cf. Einstein's 'Notes sur le cubisme' [1929], in *Ethnologie*, pp. 26–33.

73. Jean Laude, 'Un portrait', *Cahiers du MNAM*, 1 (1979), p. 17; Einstein, *Braque*, pp. 32 and 86, and 'Tableaux récents', p. 44 (his emphases).

74. *Cahier*, pp. 28; Einstein, *Braque*, p. 69.

75. Einstein, *Braque*, p. 35. See also pp. 124–5.

76. Ibid., pp. 133ff., 161–2. 'Hallucination' was in the air in Paris in the 1920s. The first author mentioned in André Breton's *Surrealist Manifesto* (1924) was Hippolyte Taine, with particular reference to his treatment of 'true hallucination' in *On Intelligence* (1870), his *magnum opus* on the philosophy and psychology of perception in that period. In response to an inquiry in *Minotaure* in 1933, Miró spoke of his painting being born 'in a state of hallucination'. *Selected Writings and Interviews* (London: Thames and Hudson, 1987), p. 122.

77. Samuel Beckett, *Proust* [1931] (London: Calder, 1999), pp. 83–4.

78. Einstein, *Braque*, pp. 69 and 101. Cf. Braque to Paulhan, [1953], in *Choix*, vol. III, p. 324; Vallier, 'Braque', p. 35.

79. *Cahier*, p. 45. Braque began to talk like this in the early 1930s. See

Tériade, 'Émancipation' [1933], in *Écrits*, p. 450. The Braque section of that compilation is in effect another instalment of his maxims.

80. For most of the twentieth century, MoMA had no Braques later than 1938, and no interest in acquiring any.

81. Duncan Phillips, 'Personality in Art', *American Magazine of Art*, XXVIII (1935), p. 151 (apropos Cézanne); Marjorie Phillips, *Duncan Phillips and his Collection* (NY: Norton, 1982), p. 192.

82. Duncan Phillips, 'Georges Braque' [1945], in Marjorie Phillips, *Duncan*, p. 196. Cf. Kenneth E. Silver, 'Braque, Picasso and other Cubists', in Erika D. Passantino (ed.), *The Eye of Duncan Phillips* (Washington, DC: Phillips Collection, 1999), pp. 233–66.

83. *Pedestal Table* (1929), in Maeght, p. 165. Cf. *The Sun* (NY), 17 March 1934; *Art News*, 17 March 1934.

84. Phillips to Rosenberg, 9 March 1934, and subsequent correspondence in Phillips Collection Archives. I am grateful to Linda Clous and Karen Schneider for access to this material.

85. Phillips, 'Personality', p. 153, quoting William Schack.

86. Roger Fry to Helen Anrep, 1 May 1925, in Denys Sutton (ed.), *Letters of Roger Fry*, vol. II (London: Chatto and Windus, 1972), p. 568. Lady Cunard (Maud Burke) was an American hostess in London, married to Sir Bache Cunard. Curiously, in his own voluminous and influential writings, Fry had almost nothing to say about Braque. There is a fleeting reference in 'On some modern drawings', in *Transformations* (London: Chatto and Windus, 1927), p. 209.

87. Roché diary, 17 April 1930, Ransom.

88. Roché, 'Souvenirs sur Georges Braque' [1955], in *Écrits*, p. 342.

CHAPTER 8: 'The hand that ponders and the eye that fashions': The Studio

1. Roland Penrose, *Scrapbook* (London: Thames and Hudson, 1981), p. 28; Antony Penrose, *Roland Penrose* (NY: Prestel, 2001), p. 24. Penrose did not escape his attention. Meeting him in later life *chez* Picasso, Braque remarked, 'I haven't seen him for some twenty years

and at first sight I didn't recognize him, he's changed so little.'
Scrapbook, p. 213.

2. See Robert Doisneau, *Braque* (1953), the frontispiece to this book.

3. Tudal interview, 26 April 2001. 'Each brushstroke' is Suzuki.

4. H. S. Ede, 'Georges Braque', *Cahiers d'Art* 1–2 (1933), p. 78; Flanner, 'Master', pp. 151–2. Braque admitted the difficulty very candidly, but he too was sometimes inclined to say that 'true connoisseurs were not deceived', which was essentially Kahnweiler's line. Cf. Brassaï, 'Braque', p. 24; Kahnweiler, *Galeries*, pp. 61–2. On the placing of the signature, see ch. 5.

5. Interview with Heinz Berggruen, 8 December 2001.

6. Nicholas Shakespeare, *Bruce Chatwin* (London: Vintage, 2000), p. 102; conversation with Redmond O'Hanlon, 13 December 2001. Cf. Susannah Clapp, *With Chatwin* (London: Penguin, 1999), pp. 87–8.

7. Paulhan to Jouhandeau, April 1935, in *Choix*, vol. I, p. 336.

8. William Boyd, 'Varengeville', *New Yorker*, 16 November 1998; Jorge Luis Borges, trans. Paul Edson, from epilogue to *Dreamtigers* (Austin: University of Texas, 1964), p. 93.

9. Jacques Dupin, 'L'accomplissement' [1964], in *L'Espace autrement dit* (Paris: Galilée, 1982), p. 79.

10. Roché, 'Souvenirs', p. 344.

11. Kahnweiler, *Galeries*, pp. 112–13.

12. André Breton, *L'Amour fou* [1937] (Paris: Gallimard, 1989), p. 128. Cf. Roland Penrose, 'Picasso's portrait of Kahnweiler', *Burlington Magazine*, 852 (1974), p. 133.

13. Heinz Berggruen, trans. Robin Benson, *Highways and Byways* (Yelverton Manor: Pilkington, 1998), p. 178; interview, 8 December 2001.

14. Cf. Baldassari, *Photography*, p. 85; Leymarie, *Braque*, p. 41; Martin, 'Origines', *Papiers collés*, pp. 48–51; Rubin, 'Narrative', pp. 637–8.

15. Joachim Gasquet, *Cézanne* (Paris: Bernheim-Jeune, 1921), p. 13. Cf. Meyer Schapiro, 'The apples of Cézanne' [1968], in *Modern Art* (NY: Braziller, 1979), pp. 1–38. Braque spoke to Brassaï in the 1940s of Zola's 'betrayal', apropos the novel. 'Braque', p. 16.

16. Salmon, *Souvenirs*, vol. II, p. 67; Picasso to Braque, 25 July 1911, in *P&B*, p. 375; Braque to Picasso, 27 July 1911, MP. Second Empire

was the official style of the government of France in 1852–70 (the reign of Napoleon III).

17. Picasso to Braque, 10 July 1912, in *P&B*, p. 399; Laurens, 'Tous les jours'; Laurens interview, 4 January 2001. The Singapores came from La Belle Jardinière, a department store a little like Liberty's or Sears Roebuck.

18. Cf. *Picasso*, vol. II, p. 120. Richardson offers a less personalized and perhaps less traumatized reading, of a 'rueful farewell' to bygone days – to the comradeship of the old *bande à Picasso*, and to reverence for Cézanne himself.

19. Brassaï, 'Braque', p. 16.

20. Roché, 'Braque (suite)', p. 349.

21. Paul Nelson, 'Mon ami Braque', *Les Lettres françaises*, 6–12 September 1962; *Cahier*, p. 59.

22. Vallier, 'Situer', p. 11. Cf. Flanner, 'Master', p. 118.

23. Nelson, 'Braque'. Balthus, similarly, was prone to call him *un simplificateur*, like Cézanne, high praise. Zeki, *Balthus* (Paris: Belles Lettres, 1995), p. 60.

24. Nelson to unnamed correspondent [1964], in Louvet and de Givry, *Varengeville*, p. 42. Also invited was Latapie, who remembered the Braques' delight in the place. *Patafioles*, p. 68.

25. Proust to Marie Nordlinger [August 1903], in Philip Kolb (ed.), *Correspondance de Marcel Proust*, vol. III (Paris: Plon, 1976), p. 391.

26. See Bill Brandt, 'Braque's Beach', *Observer*, 16 September 1956. Germaine Richier, a sculptor appreciated by Braque, foraged on the Varengeville beach for the death's head *Shepherd of Landes* (1951). A catalogue of Richier's work was found in Braque's empty Varengeville studio thirty years after his death. Frances Morris, *Paris Post-War* (London: Tate, 1993), pp. 161 and 168; Jacques-Louis Binet, 'Returning to Varengeville', *Cimaise* 235 (1995), p. 38.

27. René Char, 'The Shark and the Gull' [1948], in Mary Ann Caws and Tina Jolas (eds), *Selected Poems of René Char* (NY: New Directions, 1992), p. 48.

28. Nelson, 'Braque'. See also Cinqualbre, 'Bâtisseur', pp. 106–11.

29. Nelson, 'Braque'; J. M. Coetzee, *Stranger Shores* (London: Secker & Warburg, 2001), p. 73.

30. Brassaï, 'Braque', p. 18.

31. *Cahier*, pp. 10–11.

32. Liberman, 'Braque', p. 143.

33. Gall, 'En mourant'. Cf. Bazaine, *Couleurs*, p. 18.

34. R. G. Collingwood, *An Autobiography* (Oxford: Oxford University Press, 1939), p. 2.

35. Patrick Heron, 'Getting Braque upside down', *Modern Painters*, 2 (1989), p. 122; Jacques Dupin, preface to Prévert, *Couleurs*, p. 22.

36. Nelson, 'Braque'. Cf. his emphasis on the need to avoid routine. Vallier, 'Braque', p. 50.

37. Braque, 'Sa vie', no. 7. Cf. *Patron*, pp. 63–4.

38. *Cahier*, p. 88.

39. The prize went to Braque on the third vote of the international jury. The principal opposition was Rouault; among other contenders were Kokoschka and Picasso. *Verbale della Seduta per l'Assegnazione dei Premi alla XXIV Biennale 1948* (Venice: Fondo Storico delle Arti Contemporanee, 1948). Braque's exhibits included *The Billiard Table* (1944), the first of an important series. See ch. 10.

40. Couturier, *Se garder*, p. 53; Jean-Paul Sartre, trans. Robin Buss, 'Tintoretto: the Prisoner of Venice' [1957], in *Modern Times* (London: Penguin, 2000), p. 344; *Patron*, pp. 69–70. Cf. J. G. Links, *Venice for Pleasure* (London: Pallas Athene, 1999), pp. 119ff.

41. 'Propos de Georges Braque', *Verve*, 27–8 (1952), p. 80.

42. On the latter visit, a week in June–July 1934, he saw Ede almost every day. I am grateful to Jonathan Blackwood at Kettle's Yard for information from Ede's diary and correspondence.

43. Braque, 'Sa vie', no. 8.

44. Grünewald, *Isenheim Altarpiece* (c. 1515). Rilke and Benjamin were similarly fascinated. In Braque's circle, Picasso made drawings after it, and Zervos published a large portfolio of plates of it at around the same time. See *Minotaure*, 1 (1933), pp. 30–32; *Mathias Grünewald – Le retable d'Issenheim* (Paris: Cahiers d'Art, 1936). Subsequently, Ellsworth Kelly and Jasper Johns (both Braque people) were strongly affected by it. Cf. Andrée Hayum, *God's Medicine and the Painter's Vision* (Princeton: Princeton University Press, 1997).

45. Elias Canetti, trans. Joachim Neugroschel, *The Torch in My Ear* [1980] (London: Granta, 1999), p. 230. Max Ferber, W. G. Sebald's Frank Auerbach figure, has a haunting Canetti-like encounter with it in *The Emigrants* (London: Harvill, 1997), pp. 169–71.

46. Braque to Paulhan, [1948], IMEC, from the Pont du Gard.

47. Kahn, *Heraclitus*, p. 126.

48. Braque, 'Réponse à l'enquête sur l'art aujourd'hui', *Cahiers d'Art* 1–4 (1935), p. 22; Beckett, *Proust*, pp. 65–6. Braque's response is strictly speaking Zervos's redaction of their conversations on the subject; it is 'after Braque', as a tiny footnote suggests (p. 21). It sounds like Braque, but retouched, and in paragraphs.

49. Couturier diary, 15 January 1948, in *Se garder*, p. 35.

50. Introduction to Hesiod, trans. M. L. West, *Theogony and Works and Days* (Oxford: Oxford University Press, 1988), p. xx, the standard modern English edition. There were at least three recent and not-so-recent French editions with which Braque may have been familiar: *Hésiode* [1869], trans. Charles-Marie Leconte de Lisle (Paris: Lemerre, 1909); *Hésiode . . .* [1841], trans. Anne Bignan, with woodcuts by Honoré Broutelle (Paris: Antiqua, 1928); *Théogonie . . .*, trans. Paul Mazon (Paris: Belles Lettres, 1928). He had also studied earlier illustrations and engravings, including as like as not John Flaxman's work on Hesiod, engraved by none other William Blake (1817). See David Bindman (ed.), *John Flaxman* (London: Thames and Hudson, 1979).

51. Georges Limbour, 'La Théogonie d'Hésiode et de Georges Braque', *Derrière le Miroir*, 71–2 (1954–5), n.p.; Christian Zervos, 'Braque et la Grèce primitive', *Cahiers d'Art*, 1–2 (1940), p. 3; C. M. Bowra, *Pindar* (Oxford: Oxford University Press, 1964), pp. 365–6. Cf. Sophie Bowness, 'Braque's etchings for Hesiod's *Theogony* and archaic Greece revived', *Burlington Magazine*, 1165 (2000), pp. 204–14.

52. Pythian 8, in Pindar, trans. G. S. Conway and Richard Stoneman, *The Odes and Selected Fragments* (London: Everyman, 1997), pp. 162–3. 'Dream of a shadow' [*onar skias*] is a proverbial phrase, facetiously altered by Aristophanes to 'shadow of a donkey' [*onou skia*], a sleight of hand Braque might have relished (*Acharnians*, 686).

53. *Athena* [*Athénée*] (1932), a colour lithograph printed by Berdon for Braque, in collaboration with the artist (and at his expense); considered by Braque to be one of the most important lithographs he had ever done (Vallier, no. 19). Athena was also an oil painting of the same date. On horses see Christian Zervos, *Georges Braque. Nouvelles Sculptures et Plaques Gravées* (Paris: Cahiers d'Art, 1960), p. 11.

54. *Theogony*, p. 3.

55. Hesiod named 'Clio [history] and Euterpe [music and lyric poetry] and Thaleia [comedy] and Melpomene [tragedy], Terpsichore [dancing] and Erato [love poetry] and Polyhymnia [sacred lyrics] and Urania [astronomy], and Calliope [epic poetry], who is chief among them all; for she even attends august kings.' *Theogony*, p. 5.

56. *Theogony*, pp. 9–11. Fumet sees Braque's interest in dark Night and bright Day, out of the Chasm, as setting the tone for his own work. *Braque* (1965), p. 120.

57. Limbour, 'Théogonie'.

58. Gimpel diary, 13 March 1934, in Gimpel, *Journal*, p. 444.

59. Einstein, 'Collection Reber', and *Braque*, pp. 102 and 130. Cubism's first phase is here termed 'tectonic-analytic'. The Braque book was mostly written in 1931–2.

60. Ovid, *Métamorphoses* (Geneva: Skira, 1931). See Susan Mayer, 'Greco-Roman iconography and style in Picasso's illustrations for Ovid's *Metamorphoses*', *Art International*, 23 (1979), pp. 28–35. Braque would also have been aware that no French artist had attempted the *Theogony* as a whole, though Delacroix, among others, had tried his hand at *Hesiod and the Muse* (pendentive in the Library of the Palais Bourbon, c. 1845).

61. Vollard to Braque, 17 December 1931, in Fonds Vollard, MS 421(9,3), Louvre; Gimpel diary, 13 March 1934, in Gimpel, *Journal*, p. 444.

62. For contemporary efforts to explain the attraction cf. Marguette Bouvier, 'Georges Braque sculpteur', *Comœdia*, 29 August 1942; Fumet, *Braque* (1965), pp. 117–23; Limbour, 'Théogonie'; Zervos, 'Braque et cubisme', p. 20, and 'Braque et Grèce', pp. 3–4.

63. A selection now published: see *G. Braque et la Mythologie* (Paris: Leiris, 1982); *Verve*, 31–2 (1955), n.p.; *Derrière le Miroir*, 71–2 (1954–5), n.p.;

Bowness, 'Theogony', pp. 205–9. The cookery book metaphor was his: Vallier, 'Braque', p. 47.

64. Vollard had suggested another printer (Fort), with no great enthusiasm, and also mooted the idea of looking elsewhere.

65. Jean Leymarie, preface to Daniel Marchesseau, *Diego Giacometti* (Paris: Hermann, 1986), p. 12; interviews with Jean Leymarie and James Lord, 22 and 13 December 2000.

66. *Sao* (1931). Cf. Vallier, no. 20m and *Théogonie*, p. 65. *Heracles* was another panel in the same format, repeated again in the etchings for Einstein's *Braque*. For his Etruscan studies see ch. 2. The derivations are explored in detail in Sophie Bowness, *The Presence of the Past: Art in France in the 1930s, with special reference to Le Corbusier, Léger and Braque* (unpublished doctoral dissertation, Courtauld Institute of Art, University of London, 1995).

67. Flanner, 'Master', p. 167.

68. *Large Brown Still Life* (1932) and *Reclining Nude/Bather IX* (1932–51). *Cahier*, p. 35 (illustrated by a fishy *nereid*-figure). See, e.g., Fautrier to Paulhan, 21 June 1943, in Curtis L. Carter and Karen K. Butler, *Jean Fautrier* (New Haven: Yale University Press, 2002), p. 201. Cf. Kahn, *Heraclitus*, p. 194.

69. *Cahier*, p. 107.

70. Jean Leymarie, in *Copier créer* (Paris: RMN, 1993), p. 335, and in *Georges Braque en Europe* (Bordeaux: Galerie des Beaux-Arts, 1982), p. 54; Tériade, 'Émancipation', p. 450. Artaud was a tortured soul. In 1946 Braque joined with Paulhan, Picasso and Gide in raising money to pay for his treatment in an asylum. Paulhan, *La Vie*, p. 284.

71. Galanis to Vollard, 2 October 1935, Fonds Vollard, MS 421(9,3), Louvre.

72. Jennifer Mundy, *Georges Braque Printmaker* (London: Tate, 1993), p. 20; Dora Vallier, 'A propos de la "Théogonie" de Braque', *Nouvelles de l'estampe*, 66 (1982), pp. 25–6, and 'Braque et la mythologie', in *Mythologie*, pp. 12–13.

73. According to Aimé Maeght's son, Adrien, who helped with the printing done in the 1950s. Mundy, *Printmaker*, p. 21. According to Vallier, it was 'assumed' that Galanis was responsible.

74. These are Antoine Berman's criteria for evaluating a translation.

See Stephen Romer (ed.), *Twentieth-Century French Poems* (London: Faber, 2002), p. xvi.

75. Vallier, 'Mythologie', p. 13; Liberman, 'Braque', p. 141.
76. Rilke, 'The Eighth Elegy', *Duino Elegies*, pp. 50–51.
77. See Bernice Rose, *The Drawings of Roy Lichtenstein* (NY: MoMA, 1987), p. 135.
78. Pindar, *VIIIe Pythique* (Alès: PAB, 1961). Cf. Brigitte Baer, 'Picasso derrière le masque', in *PIC & PAB*, p. 10.

CHAPTER 9: 'Stricken by and seeking reality':
The Occupation

1. Joan Miró, trans. Paul Auster and Patricia Mathews, 'Working Notes, 1941–2', in Margit Rowell (ed.), *Selected Writings and Interviews* (London: Thames and Hudson, 1987), pp. 181, 195.
2. For the reinforcement of Braque's good opinion see Miró to Pierre Matisse, 4 February 1940, *Selected Writings*, p. 168.
3. Ibid., p. 181; interview with Jacques Dupin, 28 March 2001. Cf. André Breton, 'Constellations de Joan Miró', *L'Œil*, 48 (1958), pp. 50–55, praising them as a triumph of resistance and character at a time of menace.
4. Miró to Pierre Matisse, 12 January 1940, in *Selected Writings*, p. 168; *Je travaille comme un jardinier* (Paris: XX Siècle, 1963), pp. 22–3.
5. André Gide, trans. Justin O'Brien, 10 April 1943, in *Journals 1889–1949* (Harmondsworth: Penguin, 1967), p. 714.
6. Braque, 'Réponse à l'enquête sur l'influence des événements environnants', *Cahiers d'Art*, 1–4 (1939), pp. 65–6; reproduced (in French) in Leymarie, *Ateliers*, pp. 158–60. Unlike the previous one, on the art of today (see ch. 8), this response appears to be all his own words. Some of it is echoed in Vallier, 'Braque', e.g. p. 50.
7. *Cahier*, p. 110.
8. Paul Celan to Hans Bender, 18 November 1954, in John Felstiner, *Paul Celan* (New Haven: Yale University Press, 2001), p. 77; Bazaine, 'Enrichissement', p. 69. On Celan and staunchness, see e.g. 'There

Stood', in *Selected Poems and Prose of Paul Celan*, trans. John Felstiner (NY: Norton, 2001), p. 355; and Felstiner, *Celan*, pp. 268–9.

9. Celan to Margul-Sperber, 8 February 1962, in Felstiner, *Celan*, p. 191.

10. Friedrich Hölderlin, trans. Michael Hamburger, 'Remembrance', in *Selected Poems and Fragments* (London: Penguin, 1998), p. 253.

11. Celan, 'Speech on the occasion of receiving the literature prize of the Free Hanseatic City of Bremen' (1958), and 'The Meridian: speech on the occasion of the award of the Georg Büchner prize' (1960), in *Selected Poems*, pp. 396 and 411. Cf. Braque on his *Studio* series, in Verdet, 'Autour du cubisme', p. 24.

12. Gide, 1921 detached pages, in *Journals*, p. 345.

13. Grenier diary, 30 June 1945, in *Carnets*, p. 19.

14. Couturier diary [1952], in *Se garder*, p. 148; Richardson, 'Late Greatness', pp. 243–4.

15. John Berger, 'Giorgio Morandi' [1997], in *The Shape of a Pocket* (London: Bloomsbury, 2001), p. 142; Vallier, 'Braque', p. 50.

16. *Cahier*, p. 76.

17. Cf. Celan (following Büchner), 'The Meridian', in *Selected Poems*, pp. 409–10.

18. Richardson, 'Braque', p. 26; *Braque*, pp. 23–4. For Richardson they are a tribute to Marcelle's piety.

19. Limbour, 'Varengeville', p. 27, and 'Découvertes', p. 29; Steinberg, 'The Skulls of Picasso', in *Other Criteria*, p. 121.

20. Fumet, *Braque* (1965), p. 68; Rilke to Clara Rilke, 23 April 1923, in *Duino Elegies*, p. xii.

21. Braque to Paul Rosenberg, 22 August 1939, Rosenberg Collection, MA3500, PML. There is no further reference to the subject in the extant correspondence. The next letter in the collection in the archive, dated 6 October 1939, is incomplete; though there are no obvious signs that the correspondence has been weeded, in the nature of things one cannot be sure. No other written evidence has emerged, to my knowledge.

22. Braque to Rosenberg, 6 October 1939, PML.

23. Mariette quoted in Santovetti, *Sculptures*, p. 90. Cf. Braque to Mrs Goodspeed of the Arts Club of Chicago, 22 September 1939, in ibid.,

p. 91. In fact he did some painting in April–May 1940, just before the irruption. Braque to Rosenberg, 13 April and 4 May 1940, PML.

24. *Les Événements survenus en France de 1933 à 1945* (Paris: Assemblée Nationale, n.d.), vol. II, p. 548.

25. André Verdet, 'Picasso et ses environs', in *Entretiens*, p. 152. This conversation is re-imagined in Everett, *Matisse's War*, pp. 50–51.

26. Testimony on his movements and state of mind in this period from the Mariette tapes and Braque's letters to Paul Rosenberg.

27. Mariette tapes.

28. Braque's mother died in 1942, aged eighty-three.

29. Alistair Horne, *To Lose a Battle* (Harmondsworth: Penguin, 1979), p. 606.

30. Braque to Rosenberg, 28 May 1940, PML.

31. Interviews with Blanche Lachaud and Odette Constanty, 30 November 2001; Mariette tapes.

32. Braque began one of his rare fully rounded sculptures, *The Vase* (1940), at Gaujac (illustrated in MNAM, p. 180).

33. Braque to Rosenberg, 28 May 1940, PML; interview with Geneviève Taillade (Derain's niece, and a member of the party), 15 January 2001.

34. From New York, out of touch, Rosenberg wrote to his secretary in Paris in March 1941 wondering whether Braque and Picasso could have their work transferred to the US, and whether they themselves intended to come and join him. Hector Feliciano, *The Lost Museum* (NY: Basic, 1997), p. 74.

35. Brigitte Hedel-Samson, 'Les révoltes de Fautrier', in *Jean Fautrier* (Paris: RMN, 1996), p. 24; Bazaine, *Couleurs*, p. 31.

36. Paulhan, *La Vie*, p. 306, elided with his *'guerrier-appliqué'* ('ginger warrior'), quoted in Claude Roy, *Somme tout*, vol. I (Paris: Gallimard, 1969), p. 301. Cf. Jean Lescure, *Poésie et liberté* (Paris: IMEC, 1998), p. 90.

37. Douglas Johnson, 'Too much Gide', *LRB*, 15 November 2001.

38. Roy, *Somme tout*, p. 302.

39. Ibid., p. 303.

40. Richard Rorty, *Contingency, Irony, and Solidarity* (Cambridge: Cambridge University Press, 1989), p. 80.

41. Ponge, 'Feuillet' and 'Méditatif', in *L'Atelier*, pp. 246–7 and 300.

42. Paulhan to Braque, n.d., in Berne-Joffroy, *Paulhan*, pp. 73–4. The painter was Michelangelo. See Giorgio Vasari, trans. Gaston de Vere, *Lives of the Painters, Sculptors and Architects* [1550], 2 vols (London: Everyman, 1996), vol. II, p. 696. Cf. *Patron*, p. 111.

43. *Patron*, p. 60.

44. In France the period of the German Occupation, 1940–44, is known as *les années noires* – literally, the black years.

45. For Picasso, leeks smelled of death, according to his son. Gertje R. Utley, *Picasso* (New Haven: Yale University Press, 2000), p. 227. Cf. Françoise Gilot, 'From refuse to riddle', *Art and Antiques*, 9 (1992), p. 60.

46. Louis Aragon, 'Les poissons noirs' [1943–6], in *Le Nouveau crève-cœur* (Paris: Gallimard, 1948), p. 57.

47. Reverdy, 'Aventure', pp. 92–4.

48. Heron, 'Zenith', in *Painter as Critic*, p. 123; *Cahier*, p. 122; Mallarmé to Henri Cazalis, [1864], in Stéphane Mallarmé, *Correspondance 1862–1874* (Paris: Gallimard, 1959), p. 137.

49. Pierre Cabanne, 'Braque se retourne sur son passé', *Arts*, July 1960; Guth, 'Visite'; *Cahier*, p. 59. Cf. André Masson: 'Great painting is painting in which the intervals are charged with as much energy as the figures that determine them.' 'Peindre est une gageur' (1941), quoted in Kahnweiler, *Gris*, p. 232.

50. Guth, 'Visite'; Richardson, 'Mystery'; dialogue with Reverdy, 10 February 1950, in *Derrière le Miroir*, 144–6 (1964), p. 75.

51. Jean Cassou, *Une vie pour la liberté* (Paris: Laffont, 1981), p. 291. Cf. Jacques Kober, 'La critique – "Le noir est une couleur"', *Derrière le Miroir*, 3 (1947), n.p.

52. Guth, 'Visite'.

53. Fumet, *Braque*, p. 14. See also ch. 1.

54. Ponge, 'Feuillet' and 'Méditatif', in *L'Atelier*, pp. 246 and 296–7 (his emphasis).

55. These prices compared favourably with those of Picasso, but not with their more acceptable predecessors: works by Degas, Renoir, Monet and Pissarro fetched three to five times as much. Laurence Bertrand Dorléac, *Histoire de l'art* (Paris: Sorbonne, 1986), p. 54.

56. Lynn H. Nicholas, *The Rape of Europa* (London: Papermac, 1995), p. 8.

57. Grenier diary, 23 February 1943, in *Sous l'Occupation* (Paris: Paulhan, 1997), p. 318.

58. Hofer to Goering, 26 September 1941, OSS Art Looting Investigation Unit, Consolidated Interrogation Report No. 2, 15 September 1945, copy in Cooper Papers, 42A/3, Getty.

59. Grenier diary, 23 February 1943, in *Sous l'Occupation*, p. 317.

60. See Laurence Bertrand Dorléac, 'Le voyage en Allemagne', in *André Derain* (Paris: Paris-Musées, 1994), pp. 79–83. Arno Breker tells a different story. *Paris, Hitler et moi* (Paris: Cité, 1970).

61. Mourlot, *Souvenirs*, p. 100.

62. Braque to Paulhan, [1951], Archives Jean Paulhan, IMEC; Albert Camus, trans. Robin Buss, *The Plague* [1947] (London: Penguin, 2001), p. 195.

63. Mariette tapes; interviews with Jean Leymarie and Geneviève Taillade, 22 December 2000 and 15 January 2001.

64. Maurice de Vlaminck, *Portraits avant décès* (Paris: Flammarion, 1943), p. 184. Originally 'Opinions libres sur la peinture', *Comœdia*, 6 June 1942. Braque was barely mentioned by name, except as an accomplice. Picasso did not forget, but he could still turn a phrase: 'Vlaminck is dead! He was a fine bastard! But I prefer a live bastard to a dead one.' Parmelin, *Voyage*, p. 145.

65. Drieu La Rochelle, 'La peinture et les siens', *Comœdia*, 23 August 1941. The piece earned him a commendation from Paulhan. *Choix*, vol. II, p. 224. For another favourable perspective on Braque's art from an unlikely source, see Fritz von Hellwag, 'Austellung Französischer Kunst der Gegenwart', *Kunst*, 75 (1937), p. 334; and in general, Michèle C. Cone, 'French art of the present in Hitler's Berlin', *Art Bulletin*, LXXX (1998), pp. 555–67.

66. The clandestine but widely circulated periodical *L'Art Français* ('the organ of the committees of painters, sculptors and engravers of the Front National in the struggle for the independence of France') applauded the return of 'faithfulness to the spirit of honest research and audacity' for which French art was famous, interpreting that as a manifestation of resistance. 'A propos du salon', *L'Art Français*, 4

(1943), p. 2. Jean Bazaine declared that Braque had come once again 'to give us the true measure of French art'. 'Braque au Salon d'Automne', *Comœdia*, 5 June 1943.

67. Bazaine, 'Braque au Salon'; Jean Paulhan, 'Georges Braque dans ses propos', *Comœdia*, 18 September 1943.

68. Interviews with Laure Latapie and Louttre Bissière, 15 March 2001; Françoise Gilot, 4 September 2001; Françoise de Staël, 30 January 2001; Jean Deyrolle in Jean Grenier, *Entretiens avec dix-sept peintres non-figuratifs* (Paris: Folle Avoine, 1990), p. 65; Mariette tapes. Cf. Germain Viatte, 'Staël au souffle du temps', in Françoise de Staël (ed.), *Nicolas de Staël* (Neuchâtel: Ides et Calendes, 1997), p. 9; Gilot, *Matisse and Picasso*, p. 7.

69. Paulhan, 'Braque', *Comœdia*, 31 October 1942. Cf. *Patron*, p. 127. Leymarie noted that Paulhan and Braque used the terms 'exact' and 'just' (in the sense of 'just so'), in art, to indicate that something had gone right or succeeded. Grenier diary, 22 May 1969, in *Carnets*, p. 493.

70. Mary-Margaret Goggin, *Picasso and His Art during the German Occupation 1940–1944* (unpublished PhD thesis, Stanford, 1966), p. 22.

71. Gerhard Heller, *Un allemand à Paris* (Paris: Seuil, 1981), p. 120. Heller was in charge of the literature section of the Propaganda Staff, 1940–42, and subsequently attached to the staff of the German Ambassador in a similar capacity. He had been a member of the Nazi Party since 1934. The mendacity of his own account of his wartime service is explored in Gérard Loiseaux, *La Littérature de la défaite et de la collaboration* (Paris: Fayard, 1995), pp. 504–19.

72. Jünger diary, 30 September and 4 October 1943, in Ernst Jünger, trans. (from the German) Frédéric de Towarnicki and Henri Plard, *Second Journal Parisien* [1980] (Paris: Bourgois, 1995), pp. 171 and 173–4. Jünger was 'Officer with Special Mission attached to the Military Command'; his job was to censor mail and monitor Parisian intellectual life. With regard to Nazism, on his own account, he was above all that. After the war he refused to appear before a 'de-Nazification' tribunal on the grounds that he had never been Nazified. See Bruce Chatwin, 'Ernst Jünger: an aesthete at war' [1981], in *What Am I Doing Here?* (London: Picador, 1990), pp. 297–315.

73. Cocteau diary, 25 June 1942, in *Journal 1942–1945* (Paris: Gallimard, 1989), p. 167.

74. Lucien Rebatet, 'Révolutionnaires d'arrière-garde', *Je suis partout*, 29 October 1943. Gallimard was the publisher of the *NRF*.

75. Letter from Laure Latapie Bissière, 19 May 2001.

76. Youki Desnos, *Confidences de Youki* (Paris: Fayard, 1957), pp. 217–18. The author herself was the petitioner, on behalf of Jacob and her husband Robert.

77. Gleizes' politics, deeply confused and deeply unattractive, are sympathetically analysed in Peter Brooke, *Albert Gleizes* (New Haven: Yale University Press, 2001), pp. 210–12.

78. Breker to Cone, 25 June 1984, in Michèle C. Cone, *Artists under Vichy* (Princeton: Princeton University Press, 1992), p. 168; Georges Papazoff, *Derain* (Paris: SNEV, 1960), pp. 50–51.

79. Hélion diary, 25 May 1948, in *Journal d'un peintre*, 2 vols (Paris: Maeght, 1992), vol. I, p. 132. Hélion was obsessed with differentiating himself from Braque, and not always to be relied upon. He also thought that in 1938 Braque admired Mussolini, which is hardly likely.

80. Mady Menier-Fourniau, *L'œuvre sculpté d'Henri Laurens* (unpublished PhD thesis, University of Paris I Panthéon-Sorbonne, 1966) vol. I, p. 32; interview with Claude Laurens, 4 January 2001.

81. Kahnweiler, *Galeries*, p. 133.

82. Mady Menier-Fourniau, 'Un sculpteur devant la critique', in Université de Saint-Étienne, *Art et idéologies* (Saint-Étienne: CIEREC, 1978), p. 97; Lobo, 'Quisiera decir algo . . .' ['There's something I'd like to say . . .'], *Le Point*, XXXIII (1946), pp. 47–8.

83. Jean Grenier, *La Dernière page* (Paris: Ramsay, 1988); *Cahier*, p. 117. One of Camus' characters remarks on 'the dreadful word "fatalism"': 'Well, he would not shrink from this term, but only if he was allowed to add the adjective "active".' *The Plague*, p. 175.

84. *Tao Te Ching*, p. 65. The quietist aspect of Taosim was much emphasized in the 1930s by Granet. *Pensée chinoise*, pp. 423ff. Cf. Grenier, *Sous l'Occupation*, pp. 8–9, 15–18.

85. *Tao Te Ching*, p. 38; Camus, *The Plague*, p. 195.

86. Louvet and de Givry, *Varengeville*, p. 26; Latapie, *Patafioles*, p. 68;

Mariette tapes. Cf. Bouvier, 'Braque sculpteur'; Grenier diary, 23 February 1943, in *Sous l'Occupation*, p. 318.

87. Braque to Paulhan [1951], IMEC. Additionally, just before the war broke out, he lent his name to a committee formed to support artists persecuted by the Nazis. Laurence Bertrand Dorléac, *L'Art de la défaite* (Paris: Seuil, 1993), pp. 21, 329.

88. *Cahier*, p. 124.

89. See Richardson, *Apprentice*, p. 182. Coming from such an authority, the suggestion has naturally been given credence in the art-historical literature, e.g., Theodore Reff, 'The reaction against Fauvism', in *P&B* symposium, pp. 33 and 42, n. 70. For a sample of the debate about the nature of the movement: Kevin Passmore, 'The Croix de Feu: Bonapartism, national populism or fascism?', *French History*, 9 (1995), pp. 67–92. I am grateful to Sean Kennedy and Kevin Passmore for guidance on the sources and the literature.

90. Manifesto of the Croix de Feu (1929), reproduced in Jacques Nobécourt, *Le Colonel de La Rocque* (Paris: Fayard, 1996), pp. 1127–9.

91. Richardson's account relies simply on Douglas Cooper's table talk. Conversations with John Richardson.

92. Braque was promoted Officier in 1946, Commandeur in 1951, and Grand Officier in 1960 (on the personal initiative of André Malraux, Minister of Cultural Affairs). By the time of his final elevation, the paperwork required the Prime Minister or his representative to attest to 'the comportment' of the candidate during the war of 1939–45, as consistent with appointment to the Legion of Honour.

CHAPTER 10: 'Light like a bird': The Solitaire

1. There were seventy-four paintings and five sculptures by Picasso, not a retrospective but a selection from his wartime œuvre. Abstemiously, Braque submitted only two paintings.

2. Zervos to Barr, 28 March 1945, Barr Papers, 12/VIIIB3, MoMA. For the myth-making see, e.g., Louis Parrot, 'Hommage à Picasso', *Les Lettres françaises*, 9 September 1944; 'Picasso and the Gestapo', *Newsweek*, 25 September 1944.

3. Couturier diary, 19 February 1952, in *Se garder*, p. 135; Mariette tapes.

4. Mariette remembered Signoret calling on Braque (in Paris) and trying to talk him into joining the CP. Signoret herself does not confirm it – it is perhaps not the kind of thing that would be confirmed, or denied – and insists that she herself was not a member but a sympathizer. Mariette tapes; *La Nostalgie*, pp. 103, 108. Picasso's allegiance is the subject of Utley, *Picasso*, which makes no mention of any of this.

5. Braque's notebook contains the unusually direct observation, 'The purer the socialism, the more total the war.' *Cahier*, p. 76.

6. Grenier diary, 1958, in *Carnets*, p. 257; Richardson, *Apprentice*, pp. 182–3. As reported by James Lord, 'Picasso used to be a great artist, but now he's only a genius.' *Giacometti* [1985] (London: Phoenix, 1996), p. 322, from a conversation of 1960.

7. Malraux, *Tête*, p. 105; interview with Kahnweiler (1946), in Picasso, *Propos*, p. 86; Grenier diary, 1958, in *Carnets*, p. 257.

8. Malraux, *Tête*, p. 274; Mechthild Cranston, *Orion Resurgent* (Madrid: Turanzas, 1979), p. 301. André-Louis Dubois among others speaks of Braque as 'the antithesis' of Picasso, especially as to mode of living. *Sous le signe de l'amitié* (Paris: Plon, 1972), p. 149.

9. Claude Laurens interview, 4 January 2001.

10. Richardson, *Apprentice*, p. 182; Cocteau diary, 24 June 1953, in *Le Passé*, p. 167; Gall, 'En mourant'.

11. Richardson, *Apprentice*, p. 182; Gilot interview, 4 September 2001.

12. Cassou, preface to *L'Atelier*, n.p. Cf. Leymarie, *Ateliers*, p. 7.

13. The first printing was only ninety-five exclusive copies, in folio on vellum; the second, 845, to the same standards, in smaller format. See Vallier, nos 36 and 37. Braque's conception of it: Leymarie, *Ateliers*, p. 179.

14. Prefatory note in the Gallimard edition (not in the others). In 1956 the *Cahier* was augmented with a further selection from the intervening years, in the same deluxe production, and then republished in a standard edition, complete with the original decoration, by Maeght. This last is the edition used here; it is still in print. It was translated by Stanley Appelbaum as *Illustrated Notebooks* (NY: Dover, 1971).

15. Gilot interview, 4 September 2001; Paulhan, 'Propos'. Cf. Jean Grenier, 'Braque', in *Essais sur la peinture contemporaine* (Paris: Gallimard, 1959), pp. 24–5.

16. John Richardson, 'The Ateliers of Braque', *Burlington Magazine*, 627 (1955), p. 170; Cabanne, 'Braque'. Cf. Fumet, *Braque*, p. 17. Richardson's rendition of Braque's statement in English, in 'Mystery' and elsewhere, differs somewhat from the version given here. Braque began to talk in terms of *le néant* and of moving towards a position of *le néant intellectuel* during the war. Paulhan, 'Propos'; Grenier diary, 30 June 1945, in *Carnets*, p. 19. Sartre's celebrated inquiry into *L'Être et le néant* (known in English as *Being and Nothingness*) first appeared in 1943; there is no direct indication that Braque ever opened that book – and he was a slow reader, as he said – but *le néant* figures in Pascal and in Chateaubriand, to name but two writers with whom he was familiar.

17. *Picasso*, vol. II, p. 429; Honoré de Balzac, trans. Richard Howard, *The Unknown Masterpiece* (NY: *NYRB*, 2001), p. 27.

18. Malraux, *Tête*, p. 19. Cf. Gilot, *Life*, pp. 117–18. See also ch. 3.

19. Picasso, like Braque, always set a lot of store by the seismic consequences of the *papiers collés*. See, e.g., interview with Kahnweiler (1935), in Picasso, *Propos*, p. 76; Gilot, *Life*, p. 70. Typically, Kahnweiler maintained that the question of who made the first one was of no interest whatsoever.

20. Paul Celan, trans. Ian Fairley, 'Who Rules?', in *Fathomsuns and Benighted* (Riverdale-on-Hudson: Sheep Meadow, 2001), p. 37, substituting 'beset by signs' (*zahlenbedrängt*) for the translator's 'bestead by ciphers'.

21. Laporte, *Sunshine*, p. 5.

22. *Picasso*, vol. II, p. 249. Braque told a similar story. 'Maybe they still have some in stock.' Richardson, *Apprentice*, p. 187.

23. Gilot, *Life*, pp. 135–7. For another version of the Vuillard jibe, *Matisse and Picasso*, p. 211.

24. One of the other Braques in Picasso's collection was the *papier collé Guitar and Programme* (1913), a souvenir of Céret. He also owned the Cubist *Bottle, Glass and Apple* (1910) – an example of anonymity, unsigned on the back or the front. Both of these works passed

through Kahnweiler's hands. It is not known exactly how or when Picasso acquired them; Richardson suggests that he had the second at least by 1912. Seckel-Klein, *Picasso collectionneur*, pp. 62–8; *Picasso*, vol. II, p. 250.

25. Berggruen interview, 8 December 2001. Louis Clayeux, for one, Maeght's artistic eyes and ears, was the epitome of taste and discretion.

26. Braque to Rosenberg, 24 April 1945, 27 February 1946, PML.

27. Kahnweiler interview with Picasso (1955), in Picasso, *Propos*, p. 73; Assouline, *L'Homme*, pp. 343, 572, 583. These reservations dated back twenty years or more. See Kahnweiler to Leiris, 22 March 1932, in *Kahnweiler*, p. 147; Masson to Kahnweiler, 17 December 1938, in André Masson, *Les Années Surréalistes* (Paris: Manufacture, 1990), p. 403.

28. *The Marguerite and Aimé Maeght Foundation* (Paris: Maeght, 1994), p. 29; Verdet, 'Aux clartés d'un adieu' [1964], in *Entretiens*, pp. 49–50. In another of his free-wheeling conversations with Verdet, Braque used exactly the same words of himself: 'Rencontre', p. 12.

29. Lord, *Giacometti*, p. 340, and interview, 13 December 2000; Mariette tapes; interviews with Berggruen, 8 December 2001; Dupin, 28 March 2001; and Leymarie, 22 December 2000. Signoret indicates that Marcelle disapproved of the way in which Picasso all but abandoned his children; Braque may well have felt similarly. *La Nostalgie*, p. 122.

30. Richardson, 'Late greatness', p. 240; *Apprentice*, p. 187. At Braque's request, Cooper also gave an undertaking that the painting would remain in France. In consequence, he bought it at a very advantageous price (around 7 million francs). The undertaking was given in good faith, but on his death in 1984 the painting went to his adopted son Billy (William McCarty-Cooper), who promptly shipped it to Los Angeles. After Billy's death in 1992, it was auctioned at Christie's in New York for $7 million. It now resides in the Collection Masaveu, Oviedo, Spain.

31. Leymarie, 'Évocation de Reverdy', p. 301; Richardson, *Apprentice*, p. 182; Gilot, *Matisse and Picasso*, p. 210, and interview, 4 September 2001.

32. It is difficult to be certain of the exact period: according to Marcelle,

from c. 1947 to 1951. Couturier, *Se garder*, p. 135, and *Vérité*, p. 307. 'Picasso hooligan' was a *mot* of Maïa Plissetskaïa's. Leiris diary, 8 January 1967, in *Journal de Michel Leiris* (Paris: Gallimard, 1992), p. 620.

33. Sartre, 'Albert Camus' [1960], in *Modern Times*, p. 301.
34. Marcelle to the Paulhans, 20 and 28 August 1945, IMEC.
35. Mariette tapes; Gilot interview, and *Life*, p. 134. Gilot also speculates that, like Matisse, Braque subconsciously hoped that she might be instrumental in rebalancing his relationship with Picasso. This may have been true of Matisse – and conceivably also of Picasso himself – but it does not seem very plausible in Braque's case, either as a general *modus operandi*, or as a hope vested in Gilot herself; not because he did not like her, but simply because he hardly knew her. One might add, what he did know was that Picasso had mixed feelings about Gilot herself, even then, and that the prognosis for that relationship was uncertain. Cf. *Matisse and Picasso*, pp. 113–14.
36. Laporte, *Sunshine*, p. 4. As reported by Gilot, 'In love, you still go along with the tradition.' *Life*, p. 257.
37. Malraux, *Tête*, p. 251.
38. Interview with France Huser (1980), in René Char, *Dans l'atelier du poète* (Paris: Gallimard, 1996), p. 527. See also his 'George Braque intra-muros' [1947], in René Char, *Œuvres complètes* (Paris: Gallimard, 1983), pp. 678–9.
39. Cocteau diary, 21 June 1953, in *Le Passé*, p. 159; Parinaud, 'Braque'. For the decorator's comb and other techniques, see also ch. 4. In art, 'caricature' has a more precise and specialized application, to a 'charged' or 'loaded' portrait, than in common usage of burlesque or grotesque. According to Baldinucci, 'the word signifies a method of making portraits aiming at the greatest possible resemblance of the whole of the person portrayed while yet, for the purpose of fun, and sometimes of mockery, disproportionately increasing and emphasizing the defects of the features, so that the portrait as a whole appears to be the sitter himself while its elements are all transformed'. For another snippet of art criticism, contrasting his own practice of 'folding in' to the centre of intensity in a painting with Picasso's of 'opening out' from it, see Verdet, 'Rencontre', p. 15.

40. Gilot interview.

41. 'Painting in oil representing very sketchy roses in a green jar', Vollard stockbook, in Rewald, vol. I, p. 517; *Flowers in a Blue Vase*, in Lionello Venturi, *Cézanne* (Paris: Rosenberg, 1936), vol. I, no. 748, a catalogue with which Braque must have been very familiar. On varnish (and Cézanne) cf. Brassaï, 'Braque', p. 16.

42. Fumet, *Braque*, p. 14. Cf. Leymarie, *Braque*, p. 11. Shown a Rembrandt and a skilful contemporary copy, in the Louvre, Braque said (thinking perhaps of his own beginnings): 'Yes, in copying we catch the flower but not the root. To re-create a work of art one must start at the root.' Georges Salles, 'Histoire d'un plafond', *Preuves*, 148 (1963), p. 24.

43. Verdet, 'Rencontre', p. 14; Richardson, 'Braque', p. 28.

44. Gilot interview. Signoret emphasizes how much Marcelle disliked the racket that accompanied the Picasso of legend. *La Nostalgie*, p. 122.

45. Verdet, 'Autour', p. 21. Cf. Maeght to Picasso, 17 January 1964, in *Picasso collectionneur*, p. 68. Dora Maar insisted on the abiding nature of the friendship with Braque as fundamental, for all its ambivalence. *Picasso*, vol. II, p. 345; James Lord, *Picasso and Dora* (NY: Fromm, 1994), p. 225.

46. Mazars, 'Plafond'; Cocteau diary, 25 August 1953, in *Le Passé*, p. 260; Gilot interview. Cf. Salles, 'Histoire', p. 25.

47. Salles owned, *inter alia*, *Seated Woman* (1909) and *Sheet of Music and Guitar* (1912–13). His own account of the ceiling commission makes plain his warm relationship with Braque.

48. Paul Chavasse, notes for the Director, 23 April 1953, Dossier P30 Braque, Archives of the Louvre; Mazars, 'Plafond'.

49. Salles, 'Histoire', pp. 22 and 26; Dossier Braque, Louvre; Fumet, *Braque*, p. 74. For Braque's early encounters with the Louvre, and the Etruscans, see ch. 2.

50. Braque in Grenier diary, 30 June 1945, in *Carnets*, p. 19.

51. Salles, 'Histoire', p. 23.

52. Ibid., p. 26; Mariette tapes.

53. Ponge, 'Braque lithographe', p. 245.

54. Salles, 'Histoire', p. 25; Saint-John Perse, *Oiseaux* (Paris: Gallimard, 1963), p. 32.

55. See Gérard Monnier, 'Le temps des directeurs de conscience', in *L'Art en Europe* (Geneva: Skira, 1987), p. 34; *Donation Maurice Jardot* (Paris: RMN, 1999), p. 52. Cassou and Leymarie were two of the very few publicly to applaud both the initiative and the outcome. Cassou, preface to *L'Atelier*; Leymarie, *Braque*, p. 113.

56. Georges Limbour, 'Le plafond de Georges Braque', *Le Point*, XLVI (1953), pp. 42–8.

57. Flanner diary, 13 December 1961, in *Paris Journal* (London: Gollancz, 1966), pp. 497–8.

58. Vincent Corso, 19 September 1953, Dossier Braque, Louvre.

59. See, e.g., Henri-André Martin and Annable Audin, *Souverbie* (Paris: Malaval, 1983).

60. Nicolas de Staël to Theodore Schempp, 5 March 1953, in André Chastel (ed.), *Nicolas de Staël* (Paris: Le Temps, 1968), p. 280.

61. See Nathalie Bondil-Poupard, 'Hitchcock, artiste malgré lui', in Dominique Païni and Guy Cogeval, *Hitchcock et l'art* (Milan: Mazzotta, 2000), pp. 179–88. Hitchcock collected chiefly Dufy, Rouault, Vlaminck, and above all Klee. The Braque mosaic has since been removed.

62. Marjorie Phillips, *Duncan Phillips*, pp. 263–4; Cesar De Hauke to Phillips and Phillips to Braque, 20 and 21 July 1959, Phillips Collection Archives. Marjorie Phillips gives the date of the exhibition at the Galerie Maeght as 1958, but I think it must be 'Œuvres récentes de Georges Braque' (1956).

63. Perse, *Oiseaux*, p. 24. See Robert C. Cafritz, *Georges Braque* (Washington, DC: Phillips, 1982), p. 15 and plate 13. A lithograph of this image, *L'Atelier*, was used as the poster for the Louvre exhibition of 1961. Vallier, no. 185.

64. Waterbirds are referred to as air-heavers in Seamus Heaney, 'Ballynahinch Lake', in *Electric Light* (London: Faber, 2001), p. 26.

65. Perse, *Oiseaux*, p. 31. This 'universalist' interpretation of the Braque bird – but not the power of its expression – was anticipated in Frank Elgar, *Résurrection de l'oiseau* (Paris: Maeght, 1958), also illustrated by Braque (Vallier, no. 137).

66. Perse, *Oiseaux*, p. 14; 'Pierre levée', pp. 536–7.

67. Janine Crémieux (the publisher) to Alexis Leger (SJP was a pen

name), 20 January 1962, *L'Ordre des Oiseaux* correspondence, Fondation SJP, Aix. I am grateful to Marie-Jo Duffès for access to this material. The fragment is from the 'dédicace' to *Amers* (1957).

68. Léger to Braque, 24 December 1961; Braque to Léger, 21 March 1962, SJP. Braque continued: 'As Zen has it, reality is not that. It is the *fact* of being that.' The history of the project is recounted in Andrew Small, 'Estivation d'*Oiseaux*', *Souffle de Perse* 8 (1998), pp. 67–81.

69. Léger to Crémieux, 5 March 1962, SJP; interview with Aldo Crommelynck, 22 March 2001.

70. Mundy, *Printmaker*, p. 31; Crommelynck interview, 22 March 2001. Aquatint is a method of etching used to create tone. Where no tone is required, the metal plate is painted with 'stop-out' varnish. A layer of fine grains of resin is applied, either by hand or in a dust box, and fixed with heat. When the plate is placed in an acid bath, the acid bites tiny rings around each grain; these hold sufficient ink to give the effect of a wash when the plate is printed. Subtle gradations of tone can be achieved by further varnishing and biting of the plate. However skilfully done, there is an element of unpredictability to the process, frustrating or intriguing according to temperament. Braque was intrigued.

71. *Cahier*, p. 59; Crémieux to Léger, 5 May 1962, SJP.

72. Mourlot, *Gravés*, p. 121; Jean Grenier, 'Chez Georges Braque', *Combat*, 3 March 1945. Cf. Verdet, 'Rencontre', p. 12.

73. Mariette tapes.

74. Elizabeth Caillet, 'Braque lithographe par son lithographe', in *Georges Braque* (Argenteuil: Desseaux, 1982), n.p.

75. Ponge, 'Braque lithographe', p. 244.

76. Verdet, 'Rencontre', p. 12; Leymarie, *Ateliers*, p. 179.

77. 'The last time I saw him intimately, at home . . . a loose turtle-dove roamed familiarly from his knees to his wrist, on his shoulder, looking for the top of that great tree.' Perse, 'Pierre levée', p. 537. Cf. Georges Boudaille, 'Braque', *Les Lettres françaises*, 16–22 November 1961. Working practices from Mundy, *Printmaker*, pp. 25–7, 33; Crommelynck interview, 22 March 2001. Phaethon was the son of Helios, the Greek sun-god, who came to grief driving his father's chariot.

The lithograph *Bird in the Foliage* was based on a gouache *Bird on a Newspaper Background*; there was also a *papier collé* on the same model, with a different arrangement of newspaper.

78. Hoffmann was the son of Maja Sacher, sometime owner of *Studio IV* (1949), who had organized the Braque retrospective in Basle in 1933 with Carl Einstein. Braque visited La Tour du Valat on 20 May 1955. Perse followed on 25 November 1962.

79. In spite of the three-month separation, Braque chose this painting to represent his work at the 1958 Universal Exhibition in Brussels. He gave a *papier collé* study to Richardson.

80. Apollinaire, 'Silence bombardé', *Si je mourais*, p. 55; *Poèmes*, p. 196. Another possible literary stimulus was Valéry's celebrated essay on the method of Leonardo da Vinci (1895), which concludes with an observation from Leonardo's notebooks about a great bird taking flight and bringing glory to the nest where it was born. *Leonardo, Poe, Mallarmé*, trans. Malcolm Cowley and James R. Lawler (London: RKP, 1972), p. 63. Cf. Leymarie, *Braque*, p. 114.

81. To the suggestion that his birds were really flowers, Braque replied: 'If you see them as flowers, that's fine.' Boudaille, 'Braque'.

82. Richardson, 'Late Greatness', p. 243; Verdet, *Braque* (1959), pp. 18–19. Hoffmann spoke of firebirds; and Braque produced several of his own. Cf. Karl Loeber and Lukas Hoffmann, trans. Ewald Osers, *Camargue* (Berne: Kümmerley and Frey, 1970).

83. The first state of the painting, without the duck, was completed (and exhibited) in 1956; the duck was added after further contemplation in 1961. Braque explained his thinking to Verdet, 'Rencontre', p. 13. He himself mentioned black holes. Richardson, 'Late Greatness', p. 242. His signature is inscribed on a small cumulus cloud, bottom right. Isabelle Monod-Fontaine proposes that *The Bird and Its Nest* and *In Full Flight* are a pair, and can be read like the facing pages of an open book. 'The master of concrete relationships', in *Late Braque*, p. 18.

84. Bazaine, 'Enrichissement', p. 71.

85. *Cahier*, p. 61. Cf. 'Verisimilitude is only *trompe-l'œil*' (p. 39).

86. Jules Michelet, trans. W. H. Davenport Adams, *The Bird* [1856] (London: Wildwood House, 1981), pp. 198, 311, 313–14 (his empha-

ses). This book was phenomenally popular in France, going through nine or ten editions before being collected in a complete works in 1894, republished in 1930, and given fresh currency in *The Poetics of Space* (1958) by Gaston Bachelard. Cf. Perse's 'sickle-shaped wing of a dream', *Oiseaux*, p. 10. The poetic compounds are Celan's, from 'To the Right', *Fathomsuns*, p. 133.

87. Bachelard, *Space*, p. 238; Charbonnier, 'Braque', p. 12; Leymarie, *Braque*, p. 114.

88. Richardson, 'Braque', p. 26.

89. *Cahier*, p. 78. They are 'timid arrows' in Ponge's 'Les hirondelles', *Selected Poems*, p. 176.

90. The albatross too had literary forebears, in Baudelaire and Coleridge. Braque would certainly have known the former. Cf. Perse, *Oiseaux*, p. 32.

91. Melville, *Moby Dick*, p. 170. Melville was admired by French intellectuals, artists included. It is said that *Pierre* made 'an unforgettable impression' on Picasso in the 1930s. Bonnard was a fan of *Moby Dick*, as was Yanko Varda, whose house Braque rented in Cassis in the 1920s. Penrose, *Picasso*, p. 135, and *Scrapbook*, p. 28. Jean Giono's new translation, published in 1941, raised consciousness even further.

92. Maurice Blanchot, trans. Charlotte Mandell, 'The Secret of Melville' [1943], in *Faux Pas* (Stanford: Stanford University Press, 2001), p. 243.

93. See Max Kaltenmark, trans. Roger Greaves, *Lao Tzu and Taoism* (Stanford: Stanford University Press, 1969), pp. 120–21.

94. *The Billiard Table* (1947–9), one of three major works on the theme. The ghostly billiard-table bird is more clearly visible in the preparatory sketches: *Late Braque*, p. 58. For the congruence between the billiard table and Saint-Dominique see ch. 5. For Braque on motion: Alfred M. Frankfurter, 'G. Braque', *Art News*, XLVII (1949), p. 35.

95. *Twentieth-Century Modern Masters*, pp. 14, 30.

96. Verdet, 'Rencontre', p. 14, referring to *Studio VI* (1950–51) reproduced in *Late Braque*, p. 81.

97. See ch. 12. It is not inconceivable that Braque himself took something, consciously or unconsciously, from another painting. There is a bird-like squiggle in Cézanne's *Still Life: Plate of Peaches* (1879–80), for example.

98. Etching for René Char, *Le Soleil des Eaux* (Paris: Matarasso, 1949). Cf. Char, *L'Atelier*, p. 580; Georges Blin, 'Avant-propos', *Georges Braque, René Char* (Paris: Doucet, 1963), pp. 6–7.

99. Braque to Leymarie, 13 May 1958, in *Ateliers*, p. 222. Cf. Richardson, 'Braque', p. 26. Reverdy also refers to Braque's 'language'. When Braque's letter was originally published in *Quadrum*, the same year, it contained the perplexing misprint of 1910 for 1950, which may have afforded him some amusement. The misprint has been repeated ever since.

100. An argument adumbrated in Jacques Dupin, 'Le nuage en échec' [1956], in *L'Espace autrement dit*, pp. 72–3, and Liberman, 'Braque', p. 146.

101. Liberman, 'Braque', p. 146. Sophie Bowness has suggested plausibly that this tree may be derived from the tree in *Hesiod and the Muse*, the first etching for the *Theogony*, from which came the branch given to Hesiod as a token of his poetic calling. Braque would have revisited the *Theogony* in preparing the Maeght edition for publication in 1955. *Late Braque*, p. 98.

102. Salles, 'Histoire', p. 26; Perse, *Oiseaux*, pp. 30, 32.

CHAPTER 11: 'The prong of the rake': Late Braque

1. Gilles Deleuze, 'Introduction to *What Is Philosophy?*' [1991], in Richard Kearney and Mara Rainwater (eds), *The Continental Philosophy Reader* (London: Routledge, 1996), p. 404.

2. Kahnweiler, *Galeries*, p. 88; Jean Voellmy, *René Char* (Seyssel: Champ Vallon, 1989), p. 143.

3. Char, 'Lyre' [1953 version], in *Arrière-histoire du poème pulvérisé* (Paris: Hugues, 1953), p. 55. Braque and Char also collaborated over editions of Heraclitus (1948) and Pindar (1960). Vallier, nos. 42 and 156.

4. Reproduced in Char, *Atelier*, p. 526. Fish were as appropriate for Char, the country boy, as banderillas for Picasso, the torero.

5. Char, 'Braque, lorsqu'il peignait' [1963], in *Œuvres complètes*, p. 678.

6. Char, 'L'avenir non prédit' [1960], in *Les Matinaux* (Paris: Gallimard, 1998), p. 185.

7. Braque to Char, 5 July 1946, in Marie-Claude Char, *René Char* (Paris: Gallimard, 1992), p. 147. This was *Feuillets d'hypnos*, another text of fragments, subsequently translated into German by Paul Celan.

8. Extracts copied 26 December 1948, Fonds Char, 906, Doucet. Cf. *Cahier*, pp. 120–22.

9. *Lettera amorosa* (Geneva: Engelberts, 1963), p. 32, reproduced in Vallier, p. 274.

10. See T. J. Hines, 'The work admired in every age', in *Collaborative Form* (Kent, Ohio: Kent State University Press, 1991), pp. 14–30. Char had already written a dialogue between 'the painter' and 'the poet', based on their actual conversations. 'Sous la verrière' [1950], in *Œuvres complètes*, pp. 674–6.

11. Caillet, 'Lithographe'.

12. Engelberts in Vallier, p. 267.

13. Georges Blin, 'Avant-propos', in *Georges Braque, René Char* (Paris: Doucet, 1963), p. 10.

14. *Cahier*, p. 39.

15. Verdet, 'Aux clartés', p. 50; Leymarie interview, 22 December 2000.

16. Perse, 'Braque', in *Œuvres complètes*, p. 537; Grenier diary, 6 May 1963, in *Carnets*, p. 366.

17. Paulhan to Ungaretti, October 1962, in *Cahiers Jean Paulhan* 5 (1989), p. 601; Marcelle to Paulhan [1962], IMEC.

18. Mourlot, *Gravés*, p. 123.

19. Paulhan to Perse, 23 September 1963, in *Cahiers Saint-John Perse* 10 (1991), p. 268.

20. Raymond Cogniat, 'Georges Braque est mort', *Le Figaro*, 2 September 1963, quoting a statement issued by the family; *New York Times*, 1 September 1963.

21. Paulhan to Ponge, 23 December 1963, in *Paulhan/Ponge*, p. 322.

22. Leymarie interview, 22 December 2000; Laure Latapie and Louttre Bissière interview, 15 March 2001. Marcelle died on 28 November 1965.

23. Mariette tapes.

24. Paulhan to Ponge, 23 December 1963, in *Paulhan/Ponge*, p. 322; Mariette tapes.

25. Ponge, 'Méditatif', p. 299. Mariette died on 27 August 1997.

26. Schneider, *Habiter*, p. 120; Bazaine, 'Enrichissement', pp. 71–2.

27. 'Le mainteneur', *Combat*, 2 September 1963.

28. Chagall, 'Nous faisons d'étranges réflexions', *Arts*, 4–10 September 1963.

29. Giacometti, 'Georges Braque [1964], in *Écrits*, p. 89.

30. Bissière, 'Mon vieux camarade' [1963], in *T'en fais*, pp. 77–8. See also 'Ma première révélation du cubisme', ibid., p. 48.

31. Marie-Laure [de Noailles], *Journal d'un peintre* (Paris: Julliard, 1966), pp. 29–30.

32. Picasso, 'Hommage à Braque', *Derrière le Miroir*, 144–6 (1964), p. 17.

33. Jean Leymarie, 'La justification de l'étrange aventure . . .', and Georges Boudaille, 'L'interview impossible', *Les Lettres Françaises*, 20–26 January 1966.

34. André Malraux, *Oraisons funèbres* (Paris: Gallimard, 1971), pp. 77–81. Malraux's original manuscript is reproduced in Robert Payne, *A Portrait of André Malraux* (Englewood Cliffs: Prentice-Hall, 1970), pp. 405–9. Lyotard has an interesting line about his speciality being 'the rendering of *deeds* by a Braque or a Reverdy'. *Signed Malraux*, p. 283. For commentary on the state funeral see Paulhan to Jouhandeau, 5 September 1963, in *Choix*, vol. III, p. 239; Gall, 'En mourant'; Flanner diary, 4 September 1963, in *Paris Journal*, pp. 565–6; *New York Times*, 4 September 1963.

35. Ponge to Paulhan, 3 September 1963, *Paulhan/Ponge*, pp. 320–21.

36. Jean Renoir to Pierre Gaut, 11 December 1963, in David Thompson and Lorraine LoBianco (eds), *Jean Renoir Letters* (London: Faber, 1994), pp. 450–51.

37. Paulhan to Jouhandeau, 5 September 1963, in *Choix*, vol. III, p. 239; 'Peindre en Dieu', *NRF*, 130 (1 October 1963), p. 585. Complimented afterwards by Leymarie, Paulhan replied magnificently: 'I tried to be exact.' Joffroy, *Paulhan*, p. vii.

38. Gall, 'En mourant'.

39. Ponge, 'Feuillet', pp. 246–50. Ponge gave a memorable public presentation based on this text. Follain diary, 13 March 1964, in Jean Follain, *Agendas* (Paris: Paulhan, 1999), p. 388. 'Let us not conclude . . .' was another maxim of Braque's. Cf. *Cahier*, pp. 11, 72.

40. Heidegger, 'Parole', Char, 'Aromates chasseurs', Braque, 'Dessins', in *Argile*, 1 (1973), pp. 4–32. *Argile* was edited by Claude Esteban, and published by Maeght.

41. François Fédier, 'G. Braque et M. Heidegger', recollections for the author, 18 October 2002.

42. Heidegger, 'Cézanne', in Dominique Fourcade (ed.), *René Char* (Paris: L'Herne, 1971), p. 175; Fédier, 'Braque et Heidegger'; Kostas Axelos in Janicaud, *Heidegger*, vol. II, p. 21. 'Common presence' was a Char phrase, redolent of another common presence (echo answering echo). Heidegger's poem also echoes his letter on Braque. Cf. Char, *Atelier*, p. 791.

43. Char, 'Songer à ses dettes' [1963], in *Atelier*, pp. 790–91.

44. Jacques Danon, *Entretiens avec Élise and Marcel Jouhandeau* (Paris: Belfond, 1966), pp. 67–8, 174, 190–91. Braque illustrated Jouhandeau's *Descente aux enfers* (1961), one of his last illustrated books, with four remarkable lithographs, two of them rare red birds. See Castor Seibel, 'Jouhandeau, ses peintres, ses illustrateurs', *Bulletin du Bibliophile*, III (1978), pp. 361–73.

45. Marcel Jouhandeau, 'Georges Braque', in *Portraits* (Paris: Antoine, 1988), pp. 74–7. See also his journal for September 1963, in *La Possession* (Paris: Gallimard, 1970), pp. 56–7.

46. Cassou, *Une Vie*, pp. 289–90.

47. Jean Grenier, 'Braque dans son atelier', *Derrière le Miroir*, 166 (1967), p. 19; Malraux, *Tête*, p. 276.

48. Quoted in John Russell, *G. Braque* (London: Phaidon, 1959), p. 33.

49. 'Vast pictures . . .' is what Baudelaire said of some Goya lithographs. See Bachelard, *Space*, p. 172. Bazaine's verdict is recorded above; Giacometti's in 'Braque', p. 89.

CHAPTER 12: 'I am here': Master of the Artless Art

1. Douglas Cooper, 'The art of Georges Braque', *Listener*, 25 April 1946; Heron, 'Upside down', pp. 120–21. Braque's visit to the exhibition was recorded in *Picture Post*, 6 July 1946.

2. Patrick Heron to David Thomson, 14 February 1997, Heron Papers,

privately held. I am grateful to Katharine Heron for access to these papers, and to Janet Axten for typed extracts from them.

3. Heron's championing of Braque – writing of tremendous force and clarity by a fellow practitioner – can be followed in 'Braque' [1946], 'Paris: Summer, 1949' [1949], 'The changing jug' [1951], and 'Braque at the zenith' [1957], in *Painter as Critic*, pp. 13–18, 36–8, 54–9, and 122–7. Braque himself read some of this work when it was originally collected in *The Changing Forms of Art* (1955). He wrote Heron a note of which the latter was justifiably proud: 'I have had translated several passages of your book on painting which I have read with interest. You open our eyes to those things that routine criticism mislays. My sincere compliments.' Braque to Heron, 25 November 1955, Heron Papers.

4. See Richardson, 'Ateliers', 'Late Greatness', and *Apprentice*, pp. 185–7. Cf. Cooper on *Studio II* and *Studio VIII* in G. *Braque*, pp. 49–51. Richardson was living with Cooper at Castille at the time.

5. Adrian Henri, 'Liverpool Poems', *The Mersey Sound* [1967] (London: Penguin, 1983), p. 31; David Bowie, 'Unwashed and Somewhat Slightly Dazed', *Space Oddity* (1969). The original slogan was 'Go to work on an egg!'

6. The Tate was unable to purchase *Studio IX*, at an asking price of $290,000, in 1968; nor, thirty years later, *Studio V*, though it was loaned to the gallery for a lengthy period and reportedly offered at a knock-down price by its Swiss owner, before being sold to MoMA for $6 million in 2000. *Studio VIII* was auctioned at Christie's for $7 million in 1992. By way of comparison, *The Violin* (1914) was auctioned at Sotheby's for $3.3 million in 1987, *Bottle and Clarinet* (1911) at Christie's for £3.5 million in 1996. Finally in 2003 a gift from the Kahnweiler family enabled the Tate to acquire one of the *Billiard Tables*.

7. Gaëtan Picon, 'Mort de Georges Braque', *Mercure de France* (October 1963), p. 490.

8. Samuel Beckett, 'Homage to Jack B. Yeats', in *Disjecta* (London: Calder, 1963), p. 149. Braque's quintessential and all-encompassing Frenchness was insistently urged by both Germain Bazin (Conserv-

ateur-en-Chef at the Louvre) and Jean Cassou (Conservateur-en-Chef at the MNAM), especially on foreign audiences. See, e.g., Bazin's introduction to the catalogue of the 1946 exhibition at the Tate; and Cassou's introduction to the catalogue of the 1949 retrospective at MoMA. The pattern of this thinking (or essentializing) is evident in Bazin, *Le Message de l'absolu* (Paris: Hachette, 1964), pp. 289–90, and Cassou, 'Picasso Espagnol' [1966], in *La Création des mondes* (Paris: Ouvrières, 1971), pp. 68–75.

9. See Kahn, *Heraclitus*, p. 116.

10. For Merleau-Ponty's reflections on passivity and creativity, with reference to Braque, see Stéphanie Ménasé, *Passivité et création* (Paris: Presses Universitaires de France, 2003), pp. 72–3.

11. *Cahier*, p. 117; André Verdet, preface to *Braque: Espaces* (Paris: Vent d'Arles, 1957), a book of thirteen images. Verdet also notes the thirteen letters of Braque's name and address (rue du Douanier). Other artists had numbers; Barnett Newman's was eighteen. Golding, *Paths*, p. 204.

12. Heidegger was much taken with the pocket edition of Braque's notebook, published in 1952 and quickly translated into German. Others have noted a family resemblance between the painter's maxims and the philosopher's aphorisms. See Fédier, 'Braque et Heidegger'; Petzet, *Encounters*, p. 146; Jean Beaufret, *Dialogues avec Heidegger*, vol. I (Paris: Minuit, 1973), p. 192.

13. Paulhan in Madeleine Chapsal, *Quinze écrivains* (1963), picked up in turn by Grenier, in *Carnets*, p. 439; *Cahier*, p. 101 (the last page of the original edition). The maxims remained current among artists of a certain age. See, e.g., Balthus in *Balthus: Les dessins* (Paris: Biro, 1998), p. 9.

14. *Cahier*, p. 90, thinking perhaps of Pascal: 'Everyone should study their thoughts. They will find them all centred on the past or the future. We almost never think of the present, and if we do it is simply to shed some light on the future. The present is never our end. Past and present are our means, only the future is our end. And so we never actually live, though we hope to, and in constantly striving for happiness it is inevitable that we will never achieve it.' *Pensées*, p. 21.

15. *Patron*, pp. 64–5. Paulhan told a slightly different version. As both

men well knew, this story also had echoes of one told by Vasari (and retold by Paulhan), of Michelangelo, who cursed the marble that separated him from his statue. See *Patron*, p. 111.

16. Mario Vargas Llosa, 'Peinar el viento' ['Combing the wind'], *Caretas*, 12 July 2001, a reminiscence of Chillida's widow, Pilar. I owe this reference, and the translation, to Paul Edson.

17. Friedrich Nietzsche, trans. R. J. Hollingdale, 'Of the Higher Man', in *Thus Spoke Zarathustra* (London: Penguin, 1969), p. 304.

18. Charles Juliet, trans. Janey Tucker, *Conversations with Samuel Beckett and Bram Van Velde* (Leiden: Academic, 1995), pp. 41, 82, 93; *Patron*, p. 62.

19. Greenberg, 'Braque spread large', p. 307. Greenberg's puzzled essay on Braque in *Art and Culture* (Boston: Beacon, 1961) is a revised version of this earlier piece, originally a review of the MoMA retrospective of 1949.

20. Cooper in Golding, *Visions*, p. 110. Near the end of his life, contemplating the Cubism of c. 1913, Picasso mused that 'it was perhaps there that we went furthest, Braque and I' – a suggestive admission? – though of course he may well have felt that he himself went further. Pierre Daix, *Tout mon temps* (Paris: Fayard, 2001), p. 453.

21. *G. Braque*, p. 50; Hermann Broch, 'The style of the mythical age', in Rachel Bespaloff, *On the Iliad* (Princeton: Bollingen, 1970), pp. 10 ff.

22. Baudelaire, *Complete Poems*, p. 435. Cf. Pessoa, *Book of Disquiet*, p. 74.

23. *Patron*, p. 37; Samuel Beckett, 'La peinture des Van Velde ou le monde et le pantalon' [1945–6], in *Disjecta*, p. 127.

24. Ozenfant, *Mémoires*, p. 584; Valéry, *Analects*, p. 227.

25. Robert Hughes, 'Objects as poetics', *Time*, 9 October 1972.

26. Braque in Fumet, *Braque*, p. 14.

27. Giacometti, 'Braque', p. 89; Jean Bazaine, 'L'étonnement du grand âge', in *Jean Bazaine* (Paris: Carré, 1998), p. 6.

28. One-quarter of the pre-1957 works in the exemplary catalogue of *Late Braque*, by Sophie Bowness, are not to be found in the *catalogue raisonné*.

29. On 'memory places' see Pierre Nora, trans. Arthur Goldhammer, *Realms of Memory*, 3 vols (NY: Columbia University Press, 1996). Nora defines a *lieu de mémoire* as 'any significant entity, whether

material or non-material in nature, which by dint of human will or the work of time has become a symbolic element in the memorial heritage of any community (in this case, the French community)'. It was visited by the *NRF* in 1974, in a special section with contributions from Antoine Terrasse, Renée Boullier, Dora Vallier and Alain Bosquet. 'Georges Braque', *NRF* 253 (1974), pp. 68–83.

30. Celan, Büchner prize speech, in *Selected Poems*, p. 406.

31. This is Merleau-Ponty's formulation, in 'Eye and Mind', p. 190.

32. See Nora, *Realms of Memory*, vol. II, p. 241.

33. Ellsworth Kelly interviewed by Martin Gayford, 'Where the eye leads', *Modern Painters*, 2 (1997), p. 62.

34. Heron, *Braque*, p. 2.

35. Heddi Hoffmann to Bryan Wynter, n.d. [1948], in Chris Stephens, *Bryan Wynter* (London: Tate, 1999), p. 33; cf. his *Still Life with Kippers* (1948). The show also lodged in the mind's eye of the young Howard Hodgkin. Bruce Chatwin, 'Hodgkin', in *What*, p. 73. Like Johns, Hodgkin does not talk Braque – he talks Vuillard – but the Vuillard of Cubism is there.

36. Congdon diary, 27 October 1982, in Peter Selz et al., *William Congdon* (Milan: Jaca, 1995), p. 320; Kelly interview, 31 August 2001.

37. Kelly interview, 31 August 2001; Couturier, *Se garder*, p. 147.

38. Sartre diary, 29 February 1940, in *War Diaries*, p. 283.

39. 'MacGreevy on Yeats', *Irish Times*, 4 August 1945, in Anthony Cronin, *Samuel Beckett* (London: Flamingo, 1997), p. 141.

40. Ponge, 'Bref', pp. 130–31. The passage contains a Pongean play on the word for gallantly, *crânement* ('oh that word!'), an allusion to *le crâne*, the skull, and therefore to the fate of both Apollinaire and Braque on the battlefield.

41. Grenier, 'Son atelier', pp. 14–15.

Bibliography

Books

Abadie, Daniel, *Bissière* (Neuchâtel: Ides et Calendes, 1986).

Apollinaire, Guillaume, trans. Josephson, Matthew, *The Poet Assassinated* [1916] (Cambridge, MA: Exact Change, 2000)

  trans. Greet, Anne Hyde, *Calligrammes* (Berkeley: University of California, 1980)

  trans. Slater, Maya, *The Mammaries of Tiresias* [1917], in *Three Pre-Surrealist Plays* (Oxford: OUP, 1997)

  Poèmes à Lou (Paris: Gallimard, 1969)

  Ombre de mon amour [1947] (Paris: Bibliothèque des Arts, 2003)

  A propos de Georges Braque (La Rochelle: Rumeur des Ages, 1999)

Aragon, Louis, *Le nouveau crève-coeur* (Paris: Gallimard, 1948)

  trans. Stewart, Jean, *Henri Matisse* (London: Collins, 1972)

Arendt, Hannah/Heidegger, Martin, trans. David, Pascal, *Lettres* (Paris: Gallimard, 2001)

Assouline, Pierre, *L'Homme de l'art* [Kahnweiler] (Paris: Balland, 1988)

  Henri Cartier-Bresson (Paris: Plon, 1999)

Auric, Georges, *Quand j'étais là* (Paris: Grasset, 1979)

Bachelard, Gaston, trans. Jolas, Maria, *The Poetics of Space* [1958] (Boston: Beacon, 1994)

Badré, Frédéric, *Paulhan le juste* (Paris: Grasset, 1996)

Baer, Brigitte, trans. Watson, Iain and Schub, Judith, *Picasso the Engraver* (London: Thames and Hudson, 1997)

Baldassari, Anne, trans. Dusinberre, Deke, *Picasso and Photography* (Paris: Flammarion, 1997)

  trans. Collins, George, *Picasso Working on Paper* (London: Merrell, 2000)

  Picasso papiers journaux (Paris: Seuil, 2003)

Balzac, Honoré de, trans. Howard, Richard, *The Unknown Masterpiece* [1837] (NY: *NYRB*, 2001)

Barbusse, Henri, trans. Wray, W. Fitzwater, *Under Fire* [1916] (London: Dent, 1926)

Barker, Michael, et al., *L'Art traverse la Manche* (Brighton: Herbert, 1992)

Barr, Alfred H., *Cubism and Abstract Art* [1936] (NY: MoMA, 1974)
      Picasso: Fifty Years of His Art (NY: MoMA, 1946)

Barrett, William (ed.), *Zen Buddhism* (NY: Doubleday, 1956)

Bazaine, Jean, *Couleurs et mots* (Paris: Cherche-Midi, 1997)

Bazin, Germain, *La Crépuscule des images* (Paris: Gallimard, 1946)
      Le Message de l'absolu (Paris: Hachette, 1964)

Beckett, Samuel, *Proust* [1931] (London: Calder, 1965)

Bell, Clive, *Old Friends* (London: Chatto and Windus, 1956)

Benoit, P. A., *Braque et le divin manifesté* (Alès: PAB, 1959)
      et al., *13 mai 1962* (Alès: PAB, 1962)

Berger, John, *The Success and Failure of Picasso* (Harmondsworth: Penguin, 1965)
      The White Bird (London: Hogarth, 1988)

Berggruen, Heinz, trans. Benson, Robin, *Highways and Byways* (Yelverton Manor: Pilkington, 1998)

Berne-Joffroy, André, *Jean Paulhan à travers ses peintres* (Paris: RMN, 1974)

Bissière, Isabelle and Duval, Virginie (eds), *Bissière: catalogue raisonné de l'œuvre* (Neuchâtel: Ides et Calendes, 2001)

Bissière, Roger, *Georges Braque* (Paris: L'Effort Moderne, 1920)
      T'en fais pas la Marie (Cognac: Le Temps Qu'il Fait, 1994)

Boggs, Jean Sutherland, *Picasso and Things* (Cleveland: Cleveland Museum of Art, 1992)

Bois, Yves-Alain, *Matisse and Picasso* (Paris: Flammarion, 1998)
      et al., *Ellsworth Kelly: The Years in France 1948–1954* (Munich: Prestel, 1992)

Boissonnas, Édith, *Passionné* (Alès: Benoit, 1958)

Borràs, Maria Lluïsa, *Picabia* (Paris: Michel, 1985)

Bourcier, Noël et al., *Denise Colomb* (Besançon: La Manufacture, 1992)

Boyd, William, *Nat Tate* (Cambridge: 21, 1998)

Braque, Georges, *Cahier de Georges Braque* [1948/1956] (Paris: Maeght, 1994)

   trans. Appelbaum, Stanley, *Georges Braque: Illustrated Notebooks* (NY: Dover, 1971)

      Le Jour et la nuit (Paris: Gallimard, 1952)

      Grands Livres Illustrés (Maeght, 1958)

      and Apollinaire, Guillaume, *Si je mourais là-bas* (Paris: Broder, 1962)

      and Char, René, *Georges Braque–Renè Char* (Paris: Doucet, 1963)

      and Paulhan, Jean, *Braque Paulhan* (Paris: Bordas, 1984)

      and Prévert, Jacques, *Varengeville* (Paris: Maeght, 1995)

Brassaï, trans. Todd, Jane Marie, *Conversations with Picasso* [1964] (Chicago: University of Chicago, 1999)

   trans. Miller, Richard, *The Artists of My Life* (London: Thames and Hudson, 1982)

Breton, André, trans. Polizzotti, Mark, *The Lost Steps* [1924] (Nebraska, NE: University of Nebraska, 1996)

   trans. Taylor, Simon Watson, *Surrealism and Painting* [1926] (London: Macdonald, 1972)

   trans. Howard, Richard, *Nadja* [1928] (London: Penguin, 1999)

Brion, Marcel, trans. Molesworth, A. H. N., *Georges Braque* (London: Oldbourne, 1960)

Brooke, Peter, *Albert Gleizes* (New Haven: Yale, 2001)

Brunet, Christian, *Braque et l'espace* (Paris: Klincksieck, 1971)

Cabanne, Pierre, *André Derain* [1990] (Paris: Gallimard, 1994)

   L'Épopée des cubistes [1963] (Paris: L'Amateur, 2000)

Cafritz, Robert C., *Georges Braque* (Washington, DC: Phillips, 1982)

Calder, Alexander and Davidson, Jean, *Calder* (NY: Pantheon, 1966)

Camus, Albert, trans. Buss, Robin, *The Plague* [1947] (London: Penguin, 2001)

Carco, Francis, *L'Ami des peintres* (Paris: Gallimard, 1953)

Carter, Curtis L. and Butler, Karen K., *Jean Fautrier* (New Haven: Yale, 2002)

Cassou, Jean, *Braque* (Paris: Flammarion, 1956)

   Braque (London: Collins, 1964)

   Une vie pour la liberté (Paris: Laffont, 1981)

Caws, Mary Ann, *Picasso's Weeping Woman* (Boston: Little Brown, 2000)

Caws, Mary Ann and Wright, Sarah Bird, *Bloomsbury and France* (NY: OUP, 2000)

Celan, Paul, trans. Felstiner, John, *Selected Poems and Prose* (NY: Norton, 2001)

Cendrars, Blaise, trans. Allen, Esther, *Modernities and Other Writings* (Lincoln, NE: University of Nebraska, 1992)

Cendrars, Miriam, *Blaise Cendrars* (Paris: Balland, 1984)

Cézanne, Paul, trans. Kay, Marguerite, *Letters* (NY: Da Capo, 1995)

Chapon, François, *Le Peintre et le livre* (Paris: Flammarion, 1987)
    Mystère et splendeur de Jacques Doucet (Paris: Lettès, 1984)

Char, Marie-Claude (ed.), *René Char faire chemin avec* (Paris: Gallimard, 1992)
    (ed.) *René Char dans l'atelier du poète* (Paris: Gallimard, 1996)

Char, René, *Œuvres complètes* (Paris: Gallimard, 1983)
    Selected Poems (NY: New Directions, 1992)

Charbonnier, Georges, *Le Monologue du peintre* (Paris: Julliard, 1959)

Chastel, André (ed.), *Nicolas de Staël* (Paris: Le Temps, 1968)

Christie's, *Important Modern Works of Art from the Collection of William A. McCarty-Cooper and property from the Douglas Cooper Collection* (NY: Christie's, 1992)

Cincinnati Art Museum, *The Sculpture of Georges Braque* (Cincinnati: CAM, 1956)

Clement, Russell T., *Georges Braque: A Bio-Bibliography* (Westport, CT: Greenwood, 1994)

Clouzot, Henri and Level, André, *L'Art nègre et l'art océanien* (Paris: Devambez, 1919)

Cocteau, Jean, *Picasso* (Paris: Stock, 1923)
    Journal 1942–1945 (Paris: Gallimard, 1989)
    Le Passé défini II (Paris: Gallimard, 1985)

Cogniat, Raymond, *Georges Braque* (Paris: Nouvelles Éditions Françaises, 1976)

Cohen, Françoise, et al., *Georges Braque: L'Espace* (Paris: Biro, 1999)

Colomb, Denise, *Portraits d'artistes* (Paris: 1986)
    Instantanés (Marseille: La Chambre, 1999)

Cone, Michèle C., *Artists Under Vichy* (Princeton: Princeton University Press, 1992)

Cooper, Douglas, *The Cubist Epoch* (London: Phaidon, 1971)

    Braque: The Great Years (Chicago: Art Institute, 1972)

    and Tinterow, Gary, *The Essential Cubism* (London: Tate, 1983)

Coron, Antoine, *Le Fruit donné* (Alès: Benoit, 1989)

Cottington, David, *Cubism in the Shadow of War* (New Haven: Yale, 1998)

Couturier, Marie-Alain, *Se garder libre* (Paris: Cerf, 1962)

    La Vérité blessée (Paris: Plon, 1984)

    Art sacré (Houston: Menil Foundation, 1983)

Cowling, Elizabeth and Golding, John, *Picasso: Sculptor/Painter* (London: Tate, 1994)

Cowling, Elizabeth and Mundy, Jennifer, *On Classic Ground* (London: Tate, 1990)

Cox, Neil, *Cubism* (London: Phaidon, 2000)

Cranston, Mechthild, *Orion Resurgent* [Char] (Madrid: Turanzas, 1979)

Dagen, Philippe, *Le Silence des peintres* (Paris: Fayard, 1996)

Daix, Pierre, *Tout mon temps* (Paris: Fayard, 2001)

Damase, Jacques, trans. White, Tony, *Braque* (London: Blandford, 1963)

Danon, Jacques, *Entretiens avec Élise et Marcel Jouhandeau* (Paris: Belfond, 1966)

Derain, André, *Lettres à Vlaminck* [1955] (Paris: Flammarion, 1994)

Derrida, Jacques, trans. Rand, Richard, *SignéPonge/SignsPonge* (NY: Columbia University Press, 1984)

Descargues, Pierre, *L'Art est vivant* (Paris: Écriture, 2001)

Diaghilev, Théâtre Serge, *Les Fâcheux* (Paris: Quatre Chemins, 1924)

Diehl, Gaston, *Les Fauves* (Paris: Du Chêne, 1943)

    Les Problèmes de la peinture (Paris: Confluences, 1945)

Doisneau, Robert, *A l'imparfait de l'objectif* (Paris: Belfond, 1989)

Doran, Michael (ed.), *Conversations with Cézanne* (Berkeley: University of California, 2001)

Dorléac, Laurence Bertrand, *Histoire de l'art, Paris 1940–1944* (Paris: Sorbonne, 1986)

    L'Art de la défaite (Paris: Seuil, 1993)

Doty, Mark, *Still Life with Oysters and Lemon* (Boston: Beacon, 2001)

Dubois, André-Louis, *Sous le signe de l'amité* (Paris: Plon, 1972)

Dubuffet, Jean, *Lettres à J.B.* (Paris: Hermann, 1991)

Dumur, Guy, *Staël* (Paris: Flammarion, 1975)

Dupin, Jacques, *L'Espace autrement dit* (Paris: Galilée, 1982)

Duthuit, Georges, *Les Fauves* (Geneva: Trois Collines, 1949)
   Représentation et présence (Paris: Flammarion, 1974)
   Écrits sur Matisse (Paris: Beaux-Arts, 1992)

Einstein, Carl, trans. Wolf, Sabine, *Bébuquin* [1912] (Paris: Réel, 2000)
   trans. Meffre, Liliane, *La Sculpture nègre* [1915] (Paris: L'Harmattan, 1998)
   'Braque der Dichter', *Cahiers d' Art*, 1–2 (1933)
   trans. Korzilius, Jean-Loup, *Georges Braque* [1934] (Brussels: La Part de l'Œil, 2003)
   trans. Meffre, Liliane, *Ethnologie de l'art moderne* (Marseille: Dimanche, 1993)
   and Kahnweiler, Daniel-Henry, trans. Meffre, Liliane, *Correspondance* (Marseille: Dimanche, 1993)

Elgar, Frank, *Braque 1906–1920* (London: Methuen, 1958)
   Résurrection de l'oiseau (Paris: Maeght, 1959)

Eliel, Carol S., *L'Esprit nouveau* (NY: Abrams, 2001)

Éluard, Paul, *Donner à voir* (Paris: Gallimard, 1939)

Evans-Wentz, W. Y. (ed.), *Milarepa* [1928] (Oxford: OUP, 1969)

Everett, Peter, *Matisse's War* (London: Vintage, 1997)

Fauchereau, Serge, trans. Lyons, Kenneth, *Braque* (NY: Rizzoli, 1987)

Felstiner, John, *Paul Celan* (New Haven: Yale, 2001)

Fitzgerald, Michael C., *Making Modernism* (Berkeley: University of California, 1995)

Flam, Jack (ed.), *Matisse on Art* (Berkeley: University of California Press, 1995)

Flanner, Janet, *Men and Monuments* [1957] (NY: Da Capo, 1990)
   Paris Journal (London: Gollancz, 1966)

Follain, Jean, *Agendas* (Paris: Paulhan, 1999)

Fry, Edward F., *Cubism* (London: Thames and Hudson, 1966)

Fuente, Véronique Richard de la, *Picasso à Céret* (Narbonne: Mare Nostrum, 1996)

Fumet, Stanislas, *Braque* (Paris: Braun, 1946)

Sculptures de Braque (Paris: Damase, 1951)

Georges Braque (Paris: Maeght, 1965)

Gateau, Jean-Charles, *Éluard, Picasso et la peinture* (Geneva: Droz, 1983)

Gaubert, Sonia and Peyceré, David, *Les Frères Perret: L'œuvre complète* (Paris: Norma, 2000)

Gauguin, Paul, trans. Brooks, Van Wyck, *Gauguin's Intimate Journals* [1921] (NY: Dover, 1997)

Giacometti, Albert, *Écrits* (Paris: Hermann, 1990)

Gide, André, trans. O'Brien, Justin, *Journals* [1947–51] (Harmondsworth: Penguin, 1967)

Gieure, Maurice, *Braque dessins* (Paris: Mondes, 1955)

G. Braque (Paris: Tisné, 1956)

Gilot, Françoise, *Matisse and Picasso* (London: Bloomsbury, 1990)

Monograph 1940–2000 (Paris: Acatos, 2000)

and Carlton Lake, *Life with Picasso* [1964] (London: Virago, 1990)

Gimpel, René, *Journal d'un collectionneur* (Paris: Calmann-Lévy, 1963)

Gleizes, Albert and Metzinger, Jean, *Du Cubisme* [1912] (Sisteron: Présence, 1980)

Glimcher, Arnold and Marc (eds), *Je suis le cahier* (London: Thames and Hudson, 1986)

Golding, John, *Cubism* [1959] (London: Faber, 1988)

Visions of the Modern (London: Thames and Hudson, 1994)

Paths to the Absolute (London: Thames and Hudson, 2002)

et al., *Braque: The Late Works* (London: RA, 1997)

Gottlieb, Anthony, *The Dream of Reason* (London: Penguin, 2000)

Granet, Marcel, *La Pensée chinoise* (Paris: Renaissance du Livre, 1934) [Michel, 1999]

Green, Christopher, *Léger and the Avant-Garde* (New Haven: Yale, 1976)

Cubism and Its Enemies (New Haven: Yale, 1987)

Juan Gris (New Haven: Yale, 1992)

Green, Eleanor, *John Graham* (Washington, DC: Phillips, 1987)

Greenberg, Clement, *The Collected Essays and Criticism*, 4 vols (Chicago: University of Chicago, 1986–93)

Greff, Jean-Pierre, *Jean Bazaine* (Neuchâtel: Ides et Calendes, 2002)

Greilsamer, Laurent, *Le Prince foudroyé* (Paris: Fayard, 1998)

Grenier, Jean, *Essais sur la peinture contemporaine* [1951] (Paris: Gallimard, 1959)
    La Dernière page (Paris: Ramsay, 1988)
    Entretiens avec dix-sept peintres non-figuratifs (Paris: Folle Avoine, 1990)
    Carnets (Paris: Paulhan, 1991)
    Sous L'Occupation (Paris: Paulhan, 1997)

Gris, Juan, trans. Cooper, Douglas, *Letters of Juan Gris* (London: privately printed, 1956)

Groult, Flora, *Marie Laurencin* (Paris: Mercure de France, 1987)

Habasque, Guy, trans. Gilbert, Stuart, *Cubism* (Geneva: Skira, 1959)

Halicka, Alice, *Hier* (Paris: Pavois, 1946)

Hamilton, Peter, *Robert Doisneau* (Paris: Hoëbeke, 1995)

Hayum, Andrée, *God's Medicine and the Painter's Vision* (Princeton: Princeton University Press, 1997)

Hélion, Jean, *Journal d'un peintre*, 2 vols (Paris: Maeght, 1992)
    Lettres d'Amérique (Paris: IMEC, 1996)

Heller, Gerhard, *Un allemand à Paris* (Paris: Seuil, 1981)

Hemingway, Ernest, *A Moveable Feast* [1936] (London: Arrow, 1996)

Heraclitus, *Fragments* (Paris: Presses Universitaires de France, 1986)

Heron, Patrick, *Braque* (London: Faber, 1958)

Herrigel, Eugen, trans. Hull, R. F. C., *Zen in the Art of Archery* [1953] (London: Arkana, 1985)

Herrigel, Gustie L., trans. Hull, R. F. C., *Zen in the Art of Flower Arrangement* [1958] (London: Souvenir, 1999)

Hesiod, trans. West, M. L., *Theogony and Works and Days* (Oxford: OUP, 1988)

Higgins, Ian, *Francis Ponge* (London: Athlone, 1979)

Hines, T. J., *Collaborative Form* (Kent, OH: Kent State, 1991)

Hofmann, Werner, *Georges Braque – Das Graphische Werk* (Stuttgart: Hatje, 1961)

Hope, Henry R., *Georges Braque* (NY: MoMA, 1949)

Hughes, Robert, *The Shock of the New* [1980] (London: Thames and Hudson, 1991)

Hugo, Jean, *Carnets* (Paris: Actes Sud, 1994)

Hulsker, Jan, *The New Complete van Gogh* (Amsterdam: Meulenhoff, 1996)

Isarlov, George, *Georges Braque* (Paris: Corti, 1932)

Isenmann, Paul, *Oiseaux de Camargue* (Brunoy: SEO, 1993)

Janicaud, Dominique, *Heidegger en France* (Paris: Michel, 2001)

Janneau, Guillaume, *L'Art cubiste* (Paris: Moreau, 1929)

Jedlicka, Gotthard, *Pariser Tagebuch* (Frankfurt: Suhrkamp, 1953)

Jordan, Shirley Ann, *The Art Criticism of Francis Ponge* (Leeds: Maney, 1994)

Jouhandeau, Marcel, *Descente aux enfers* (Paris: Nouveau Cercle Parisien du Livre, 1961)

    La Possession (Paris: Gallimard, 1963)

    La Vie comme une fête (Paris: Pauvert, 1977)

Juliet, Charles, trans. Tucker, Janey, *Conversations with Samuel Beckett and Bram van Velde* (Leiden: Academic, 1995)

Jünger, Ernst, trans. de Towarnicki, Frédéric, *Second journal parisien* [1980] (Paris: Bourgois, 1995)

Kahn, Charles H., *The Art and Thought of Heraclitus* (Cambridge: Cambridge University Press, 1979)

Kahnweiler, Daniel-Henry, *Juan Gris* [1946] (Paris: Gallimard, 1990)

    Confessions esthétiques (Paris: Gallimard, 1963)

    and Francis Crémieux, *Mes galeries et mes peintres* [1961] (Paris: Gallimard, 1998)

Kaltenmark, Max, trans. Greaves, Roger, *Lao Tzu and Taoism* [1965] (Stanford: Stanford University Press, 1969)

Kochno, Boris, *Diaghilev et les Ballets Russes* (Paris: Fayard, 1973)

Kosinski, Dorothy, *Douglas Cooper and the Masters of Cubism* (London: Tate, 1987)

    Picasso, Braque, Gris, Léger (Houston: Museum of Fine Arts, 1990)

Kramár, Vincenc, trans. Abrams, Erica, *Le Cubisme* [1921] (Paris: Beaux Arts, 2002)

Krauss, Rosalind E., *The Picasso Papers* (Cambridge, MA: MIT, 1999)

Laburthe-Tolra, Philippe and Falgayrettes-Leveau, Christiane, *Fang* (Paris: Dapper, 1991)

Lafranchis, Jean, *Marcoussis* (Paris: Éditions du Temps, 1961)

Lake, Carlton and Ashton, Linda, *Henri-Pierre Roché: an introduction* (Austin: HRHRC, 1991)

Lancaster, Rosemary, *La Poésie éclatée de René Char* (Amsterdam: Rodopi, 1994)

Lao Tzu, trans. Lau, D. C., *Tao Te Ching* (London: Penguin, 1963)

Laporte, Geneviève, trans. Cooper, Douglas, *Sunshine at Midnight* [1973] (NY: Macmillan, 1975)

Latapie, Louis, *Patafioles* (unpublished)

Laude, Jean, *La Peinture française et 'l'art nègre'* (Paris: Klincksieck, 1968)

Laurencin, Marie, *Le Carnet des nuits* (Geneva: Cailler, 1956)

Laval, Jacques, *Un homme partagé* (Paris: Julliard, 1978)

Léal, Brigitte, *Picasso—Papiers collés* (Paris: RMN, 1998)

Lee, Jane, *Derain* (Oxford: Phaidon, 1990)

Léger, Fernand, *Lettres à Simone* (Geneva: Skira, 1987)

Leighten, Patricia, *Reordering the Universe* (Princeton: Princeton University Press, 1989)

Leiris, Michel, *Brisées* [1966] (Paris: Gallimard, 1992)
    Un Génie sans piédestal (Paris: Fourbis, 1992)
    Journal de Michel Leiris (Paris: Gallimard, 1992)
    and Paulhan, Jean, *Correspondance* (Paris: Paulhan, 2000)

Lejard, André, *Braque* (Paris: Hazan, n.d.)

Lepape, Claude and Defert, Thierry, *Georges Lepape ou l'élégance illustrée* (Paris: Herscher, 1983)

Level, André, *Souvenirs d'un collectionneur* (Paris: Mazo, 1959)

Lévy, Pierre, *Des artistes et un collectionneur* (Paris: Flammarion, 1976)

Lewis, Wyndham, *The Caliph's Design* [1919] (Santa Barbara: Black Sparrow, 1986)
    The Revenge for Love (London: Methuen, 1937)

Lewison, Jeremy, *Ben Nicholson* (London: Tate, 1993)

Leymarie, Jean, *André Derain* (Paris: Skira, 1949)
    Braque (Geneva: Skira, 1961)
    Corot [1966] (Geneva: Skira, 1992)
    Georges Braque (NY: Guggenheim, 1988)
    Braque – Les Ateliers (Milan: Jaca, 1995)

Lhote, André, *De la palette à l'écritoire* (Paris: Corréa, 1946)

Liberman, Alexander, *The Artist in His Studio* [1960] (NY: Random House, 1988)
    Then (NY: Random House, 1995)

Lieberman, William S. (ed.), *Twentieth-Century Modern Masters* (NY: Metropolitan Museum of Art, 1989)

Lionel-Marie, Annick, *Paul Éluard et ses amis peintres* (Paris: MNAM, 1982)

Lipschitz, Jacques, *My Life in Sculpture* (London: Thames and Hudson, 1972)

Lord, James, *Giacometti* [1985] (London: Phoenix, 1996)
    Picasso and Dora (NY: Fromm, 1994)

Louvre, Musée du, *Copier créer* (Paris: RMN, 1993)

Lucretius, trans. Melville, Ronald, *On the Nature of the Universe* (Oxford: OUP, 1999)

Lussy, Florence de, *Jean Cassou* (Paris: BNF, 1995)

Lyotard, Jean-François, trans. Harvey, Robert, *Signed, Malraux* [1996] (Minneapolis: University of Minnesota, 1999)

Madeleine-Perdrillat, Alain, *Staël* (Paris: Hazan, 2003)

Magritte, René, *Écrits complets* (Paris: Flammarion, 2001)

Mailer, Norman, *Picasso* (NY: Atlantic Monthly, 1995)

Maldiney, Henri, *Regard Parole Espace* (Paris: L'Age d'Homme, 1973)
    Art et existence (Paris: Klincksieck, 1986)
    L'Avènement de la peinture dans l'œuvre de Bazaine (Paris: Encre Marin, 1999)
    Ouvrir le rien (Paris: Encre Marin, 2000)

Malraux, André, trans. Gilbert, Stuart, *The Voices of Silence* (NY: Double-day, 1953)
    Oraisons funèbres [1971] (Paris: Gallimard, 1996)
    trans. Guicharnaud, June, *Picasso's Mask* [1974] (NY: Da Capo, 1996)

Man, Felix H., *Eight European Artists* (London: Heinemann, 1954)

Marchesseau, Daniel, *Marie Laurencin* (Tokio: Curieux-Do, 1980)
    Diego Giacometti (Paris: Hermann, 1986)

Marie-Laure, *Journal d'un peintre* (Paris: Julliard, 1966)

Masini, Lara Vinca, *Braque* (London: Hamlyn, 1969)

Massat, René, *Latapie* (Paris: Prisme, 1968)

Masse, Jean-François and Rodange, Thierry, *Salacrou* (Luneray: Bertout, 1999)

Matisse, Henri, *Écrits et propos sur l'art* (Paris: Hermann, 1972)

Mauner, George, *Manet: The Still Life Paintings* (NY: Abrams, 2001)

McCully, Marilyn (ed.), *Picasso: Painter and Sculptor in Clay* (London: RA, 1998)

Meffre, Liliane, *Carl Einstein et le problématique des avant-gardes dans les arts plastiques* (Berne: Lang, 1989)

    Carl Einstein (Paris: l'Université de Paris-Sorbonne, 2002)

Melville, Herman, *Moby Dick* [1851] (Oxford: OUP, 1988)

Merleau-Ponty, Maurice, *L'Œil et l'esprit* (Paris: 1964)

    Causeries (Paris: Seuil, 2002)

Michelet, Jules, trans. Davenport Adams, W. H., *The Bird* [1856] (London: Wildwood, 1981)

Milhaud, Darius, trans. Evans, Donald, *Notes without Music* (London: Dobson, 1952)

Miller, Arthur I., *Einstein, Picasso* (NY: Basic, 2001)

Mirò, Joan, *Je travaille comme un jardinier* (Paris: XX Siècle, 1963)

    trans. Auster, Paul, et al., *Selected Writings and Interviews* (London: Thames and Hudson, 1987)

Monod-Fontaine, Isabelle, et al., *Daniel-Henry Kahnweiler* (Paris: Centre Pompidou, 1984)

    Donation Louise et Michel Leiris (Paris: Centre Pompidou, 1984)

Mourlot, Fernand, *Souvenirs et portraits d'artistes* (Paris: Mourlot, 1973)

    Gravés dans ma mémoire (Paris: Laffont, 1979)

Mullins, Edwin, *Braque* (London: Thames and Hudson, 1968)

Mundy, Jennifer, *Georges Braque Printmaker* (London: Tate, 1993)

Murray, Albert, *The Blue Devils of Nada* (NY: Vintage, 1996)

Nash, Steven A. (ed.), *Picasso and the War Years* (London: Thames and Hudson, 1998)

Nobécourt, Jacques, *Le Colonel de La Rocque* (Paris: Fayard, 1996)

O'Brian, Patrick, *Picasso* [1976] (London: Harvill, 1997)

Olivier, Fernande, *Picasso et ses amis* (Paris: Stock, 1933)

    Souvenirs intimes (Paris: Calmann-Lévy, 1988)

    trans. Baker, Christine and Raeburn, Michael, *Loving Picasso* (NY: Abrams, 2001)

Orledge, Robert, *Satie Remembered* (London: Faber, 1995)

Ozenfant, Amédée, *Mémoires* (Paris: Seghers, 1968)

Païni, Dominique and Cogeval, Guy, *Hitchcock et l'art* (Milan: Mazzotta, 2000)

Papazoff, Georges, *Derain* (Paris: SNEV, 1960)

Parmelin, Hélène, *Picasso dit . . .* (Paris: Gonthier, 1966)

Voyage en Picasso (Paris: Bourgois, 1994)

Pascal, Blaise, *Pensées* [1670] (Oxford: OUP, 1995)

Passantino, Erika D. (ed.), *The Eye of Duncan Phillips* (Washington, DC: Phillips Collection, 1999)

Passmore, Kevin, *From Liberalism to Fascism* (Cambridge: CUP, 1997)

Paulhan, Jean, *Braque le patron* [1946] (Paris: Gallimard, 1952)

    Fautrier l'enragé [1962] (Paris: Gallimard, 1989)

    La Peinture cubiste [1970] (Paris: Gallimard, 1990)

    La Vie est pleine de choses redoutables (Paris: Paulhan, 1989)

    trans. Laennec, Christine Moneera and Syrotinski, Michael, *Progress in Love on the Slow Side* (Lincoln, NE: University of Nebraska, 1994)

Paulhan, Jean/Grenier, Jean, *Correspondance* (Quimper: Calligrammes, 1984)

Paulhan, Jean/Ponge, Francis, *Correspondance* (Paris: Gallimard, 1986)

Penrose, Antony, *The Lives of Lee Miller* (London: Thames and Hudson, 1985)

    Roland Penrose (NY: Prestel, 2001)

Penrose, Roland, *Picasso* [1958] (London: Granada, 1981)

    Scrapbook (London: Thames and Hudson, 1981)

Perse, Saint-John, *Amers, Oiseaux* [1963] (Paris: Gallimard, 1984)

    Œuvres complètes (Paris: Gallimard, 1992)

Petzet, Heinrich Wiegand, trans. Emad, Parvis and May, Kenneth, *Encounters and Dialogues with Martin Heidegger* [1983] (Chicago: University of Chicago, 1993)

Phillips, Duncan, *A Collection in the Making* (Washington, DC: Phillips, 1926)

Phillips, Marjorie, *Duncan Phillips and His Collection* (Washington, DC: Norton, 1982)

Picabia, Francis, *391* [1917–24] (Paris: Belfond, 1975)

Picasso, Pablo, trans. Penrose, Roland, *Desire Caught by the Tail* (London: Calder, 1970)

    Picasso on Art (NY: Da Capo, 1972)

    Propos sur l'art (Paris: Gallimard, 1998)

    Apollinaire, *Correspondance* (Paris: Gallimard/RMN, 1992)

Pierre, José, *Marie Laurencin* (Paris: Somogy, 1988)

Pignon, Édouard, *La Quête de la réalité* (Paris: Denoël, 1966)

Contre courant (Paris: Stock, 1974)

Pindar, trans. Conway, G. S. and Stoneman, Richard, *The Odes* (London: Everyman, 1997)

Ponge, Francis, *Méthodes* (Paris: Gallimard, 1961)

    Entretiens de Francis Ponge avec Philippe Sollers (Paris: Gallimard, 1970)

    La Rage de l'expression [1976] (Paris: Gallimard, 2000)

    L'Atelier contemporain (Paris: Gallimard, 1977)

    trans. Guiton, Margaret, et al., *Selected Poems* (London: Faber, 1994)

    trans. Dunlop, Lane, *Soap* [1967] (Stanford: Stanford University Press, 1998)

    et al., trans. Howard, Richard, *G. Braque* (NY: Abrams, 1971)

Ponge, Francis/Tortel, Jean, *Correspondance* (Paris: Stock, 1998)

Pouillon, Nadine, *Braque* (Paris: MNAM, 1982)

Poulenc, Francis, *Journal de mes mélodies* (Paris: Cicero, 1993)

    Correspondance (Paris: Fayard, 1994)

Prévert, Jacques, trans. Ferlinghetti, Lawrence, *Paroles* [1949] (San Francisco: City Lights, 1990)

    Couleurs (Paris: Maeght, 1981)

Ray, Man, *Autoportrait* (Paris: Seghers, 1963)

Raynal, Maurice, *Picasso* (Paris: Cres, 1922)

    Georges Braque (Rome: Valori Plastici, 1924)

    Histoire de la peinture moderne, vol III (Geneva: Skira, 1950)

    Picasso (Geneva: Skira, 1953)

Read, Peter, *Picasso et Apollinaire* (Paris: Place, 1995)

    Apollinaire et les Mamelles de Tirésias (Rennes: Rennes, 2000)

Reliquet, Scarlette and Philippe, *Henri-Pierre Roché* (Paris: Ramsay, 1999)

Reverdy, Pierre, *Le Livre de mon bord* (Paris: Mercure, 1948)

    Note éternelle du présent (Paris: Flammarion, 1973)

    Nord-Sud, Self-Defence et autres écrits sur l'art et la poésie (Paris: Flammarion, 1975)

    trans. Ashbery, John, et al., *Selected Poems* (London: Bloodaxe, 1991)

Richardson, John, *Braque* (Harmondsworth: Penguin, 1959)

    A Life of Picasso (London: Cape, 1991–)

    The Sorcerer's Apprentice (London: Cape, 1999)

    Sacred Monsters, Sacred Masters (London: Cape, 2001)

Ricoeur, Paul, *La Mémoire, l'histoire et l'oubli* (Paris: Seuil, 2000)

Rilke, Rainer Maria, trans. Herter Norton, M. D., *The Notebooks of Malte Laurids Brigge* (NY: Norton, 1949)

> trans. Snow, Edward, *The Book of Images* (NY: North Point, 1994)
>> *Uncollected Poems* (NY: North Point, 1997)
>> *New Poems* (NY: North Point, 1984)
>> *New Poems: The Other Part* (NY: North Point, 1987)
>> *Duino Elegies* (NY: North Point, 2000)
> trans. Agee, Joel, *Letters on Cézanne* [1952] (NY: Vintage, 1991)

Roché, Henri-Pierre, *Carnets* (Marseille: Dimanche, 1990)

> *Écrits sur l'art* (Marseille: Dimanche, 1998)

Rochefoucauld, de La, trans. Tancock, Leonard, *Maxims* (London: Penguin, 1959)

Rosenberg, Léonce, *Cubisme et tradition* (Paris: L'Effort Moderne, 1920)

> *Cubisme et empirisme* (Paris: L'Effort Moderne, 1921)

Rosenblum, Robert, *Cubism and Twentieth-Century Art* (NY: Abrams, 1976)

Roussard, André, *Dictionnaire des Peintres à Montmartre* (Paris: Roussard, 1999)

Roy, Claude, *Somme tout*, vol. I (Paris: Gallimard, 1969)

Rubin, William, *Picasso and Braque* (NY: MoMA, 1989)

> et al., *Les Demoiselles d'Avignon* (NY: MoMA, 1994)
> (ed.), *Picasso and Portraiture* (London: Thames and Hudson, 1996)

Russell, John, *G. Braque* (London: Phaidon, 1959)

> *Matisse, Father & Son* (NY: Abrams, 1999)

Saarinen, Aline B., *The Proud Possessors* (London: Weidenfeld and Nicolson, 1959)

Sabartés, Jaime, *Picasso* (Paris: Carré et Vox, 1946)

Salacrou, Armand, *C'était écrit* (Paris: Gallimard, 1974)

Salmon, André, *La Jeune peinture française* (Paris: Trente, 1912)

> *L'Art vivant* (Paris: Cres, 1920)
> trans. Brown, Slater, *The Black Venus* [1920] (NY: Macaulay, 1929)
> *L'Air de la Butte* (Paris: Nouvelle France, 1945)
> *Souvenirs sans fin*, 3 vols (Paris: Gallimard, 1955–61)

Sartre, Jean-Paul, *Modern Times*, trans. Buss, R. (London: Penguin, 2000)

Satie, Erik, *Écrits* (Paris: Champ Libre, 1977)

> *Correspondance presque complète* (Paris: Fayard/IMEC, 2000)

Schapiro, Meyer, *Modern Art* (NY: Braziller, 1972)
    Theory and Philosophy of Art (NY: Braziller, 1994)
Schneider, Jean-Claude, *Habiter la lumière* (Paris: Deyrolle, 1994)
Schneider, Pierre, *Les Dialogues du Louvre* [1972] (Paris: Biro, 1991)
Seckel, Hélène, *Max Jacob et Picasso* (Paris: RMN, 1994)
Seckel-Klein, Hélène, *Picasso collectionneur* (Paris: RMN, 1998)
Selz, Peter et al., *William Congdon* (Milan: Jaca, 1995)
Seuphor, Michel, *Braque graveur* (Paris: Berggruen, 1953)
    Un siècle de libertés (Paris: Hazan, 1996)
Severini, Gino, trans. Franchina, Jennifer, *The Life of a Painter* [1983]
    (Princeton: Princeton University Press, 1995)
Shattuck, Roger, *The Banquet Years* [1959] (NY: Vintage, 1968)
    Candor and Perversion (NY: Norton, 1999)
Signoret, Simone, *La Nostalgie n'est plus ce qu'elle était* (Paris: Seuil, 1976)
Silver, Kenneth E., *Esprit de Corps* (London: Thames and Hudson, 1989)
Sollers, Philippe, *Entretiens avec Francis Ponge* (Paris: Gallimard, 1970)
Spies, Werner, *Picasso: The Sculptures* (Ostfildern: Cantz, 2000)
    (ed.), *Pour Kahnweiler* (Teufen: Niggli, 1965)
Spivey, Nigel, *Etruscan Art* (London: Thames and Hudson, 1997)
Spurling, Hilary, *The Unknown Matisse* (London: Hamish Hamilton, 1998)
Staël, Françoise de, *Nicolas de Staël* (Neuchâtel: Ides et Calendes, 1997)
Stein, Gertrude, *Picasso* [1938] (NY: Dover, 1984)
    The Autobiography of Alice B. Toklas [1933] (London: Penguin, 1966)
    Geography and Plays [1922] (Madison, WI: University of Wisconsin,
    1993)
    Everybody's Autobiography (NY: Random House, 1937)
Stein, Leo, *Appreciation* [1947] (Lincoln, NE: University of Nebraska,
    1996)
Stephens, Chris, *Bryan Wynter* (London: Tate, 1999)
Stokes, Adrian, *Greek Culture and the Ego* [1958], in Gowing, Lawrence
    (ed.), *The Critical Writings of Adrian Stokes*, vol. III (London: Thames
    and Hudson, 1978), pp. 77–142
Sutton, Denys, *André Derain* (London: Phaidon, 1959)
    Nicolas de Staël (NY: Grove, 1960)
Suzuki, D. T., *Essays in Zen Buddhism*, 1st series [1949] (NY: Grove,
    n.d.)

Sylvester, David, *About Modern Art* (London: Pimlico, 1997)

Tardieu, Jean, *Le Miroir ébloui* (Paris: Gallimard, 1993)

Tériade, *Écrits sur l'art* (Paris: Biro, 1996)

Theroux, Alexander, *The Primary Colours* (NY: Holt, 1994)

Thorpe, Adam, *Nineteen Twenty-One* (London: Vintage, 2002)

Tilman, Pierre, *J'aime la période des papiers collés de Braque et Picasso* (Verderonne: Dumerchez, 2003)

Toesca, Maurice, *Cinq ans de patience* (Paris: Émile-Paul, 1975)

Tomkins, Calvin, *Ahead of the Game* [1962] (Harmondsworth: Penguin, 1968)

Trevelyan, Julian, *Indigo Days* [1957] (Aldershot: Scolar, 1996)

Tucker, Paul Hayes, *Monet at Argenteuil* (New Haven: Yale, 1982)

Tudal, Antoine, *Souspente* (Paris: Godet, 1945)

  Nicolas de Staël (Paris: Poche, 1958)

Uhde, Wilhelm, trans. Ponchont, A., *Picasso et la tradition française* (Paris: Quatre-Chemins, 1928)

Updike, John, *Just Looking* (Boston: MFA, 2001)

Utley, Gertje R., *Picasso: The Communist Years* (New Haven: Yale, 2000)

Valéry, Paul, trans. Paul, David, *Degas, Manet, Morisot* (London, RKP, 1960)

  trans. Turnell, Martin, *Masters and Friends* (London: RKP, 1968)

  trans. Gilbert, Stuart, *Analects* (London: RKP, 1970)

Vallentin, Antonina, *Pablo Picasso* (Paris: Michel, 1957)

Vallier, Dora, *L'Intérieur de l'art* (Paris: Seuil, 1982)

  trans. Bononno, Robert and Barr, Pamela, *Braque: The Complete Graphics* [1982] (London: Alpine, 1988)

Varnedoe, Kirk (ed.), *Jasper Johns* (NY: MoMA, 1996)

Vauvenargues, *Œuvres complètes* (Paris: Alive, 1999)

Vauxcelles, Louis, *Le Fauvisme* [1958] (Paris: Olbia, 1999)

Verdet, André, *Braque: Espaces* (Paris: Vent d'Arles, 1957)

  trans. Richardson, Frances, *Georges Braque* (Geneva: Kister, 1956)

  Georges Braque le solitaire (Paris: XX Siècle, 1959)

  Entretiens, notes et écrits sur la peinture (Paris: Galilée, 1978)

Vlaminck, Maurice de, *Poliment* (Paris: Stock, 1931)

  Portraits avant décès (Paris: Flammarion, 1943)

Voellmy, Jean, *René Char* (Seyssel: Champ Vallon, 1989)

Volta, Ornella, *Satie et la danse* (Paris: Plume, 1992)

    trans. Pleasance, Simon, *Erik Satie* (Paris: Hazan, 1997)

    trans. Bullock, Michael, *Satie Seen through His Letters* (London: Boyars, 1994)

Vouilloux, Bernard, *Un art de la figure* (Paris: Septentrion, 1998)

Waldberg, Patrick, *Henri Laurens* (Paris: Sphinx, 1980)

Waldman, Diane, *Ellsworth Kelly* (NY: Guggenheim Museum, 1996)

Warnod, André, *Les Berceaux de la jeune peinture* (Paris: Michel, 1923)

    Ceux de la Butte (Paris: Julliard, 1947)

Warnod, Jeanine, *Le Bateau-Lavoir* (Paris: Connaissance, 1975)

Watkins, Paul, *The Forger* (London: Faber, 2000)

Weber, Karl and Hoffmann, Lukas, *Camargue* (Berne: Kümmerly & Frey, 1970)

Weill, Berthe, *Pan! dans l'œil* (Paris: Lipschutz, 1933)

West, Anthony, *John Piper* (London: Secker and Warburg, 1979)

Westgeest, Helen, *Zen in the Fifties* (Zwolte: Waanders Uitgeverij, 1997)

Wheelwright, Philip, *Heraclitus* (Oxford: OUP, 1959)

Whiting, Steven Moore, *Satie the Bohemian* (Oxford: OUP, 1999)

Wilkin, Karen, *Braque* (NY: Abbeville, 1991)

Wolfe, Tom, *The Painted Word* [1975] (NY: Bantam, 1999)

Young, Julian, *Heidegger's Philosophy of Art* (Cambridge: CUP, 2001)

Zayas, Marius de, *How, When and Why Modern Art Came to New York* (Cambridge, MA: MIT, 1996)

Zeki, Semir, *Balthus* (Paris: Belles Lettres, 1995)

Zelevansky, Lynn (ed.), *Picasso and Braque* (NY: MoMA, 1992)

Zervos, Christian, *L'Art en Grèce* (Paris: Cahiers d'Art, 1934)

Zilczer, Judith, *'The Noble Buyer': John Quinn, Patron of the Avant-Garde* (Washington, DC: Hirshhorn, 1978)

Zola, Émile, *L'Œuvre* [1886] (Paris: Flammarion, 1974)

Zurcher, Bernard, trans. Nye, Simon, *Georges Braque* (NY: Rizzoli, 1988)

Articles

Adrian, Dennis, 'Georges Braque's monumental still lifes', *Artnews*, 71 (1972), pp. 30–33

Ameline, Jean-Paul, 'Funambulisme entre figuration et abstraction', in *Nicolas de Staël* (Paris: Centre Pompidou, 2003), pp. 14–23

Apollinaire, Guillaume, 'Préface', Exposition des peintures de Georges Braque [1908], in *A propos de Georges Braque* (La Rochelle: Rumeur des Ages, 1999), pp. 15–20; extract in English in Fry, *Cubism*, p. 49

'Georges Braque', *Les Peintres cubistes* [1913], in *A propos de Georges Braque*, pp. 39–42

Aragon, Louis, 'La peinture au défi' [1930], in *Écrits sur l'art moderne* (Paris: Flammarion, 1981), pp. 27–47

Arland, Marcel, 'Braque', *L'Âge nouveau* 42 (1949), pp. 27–31

Ashbery, John, 'Georges Braque' [1960], in *Reported Sightings* (Cambridge, MA: MIT, 1991), pp. 149–50

Bailey, Colin B., 'Anglo-Saxon attitudes: recent writings on Chardin', in *Chardin* (London: RA, 2000), pp. 77–97

Barrière, Gérard, 'Un citron est un citron est un citron', *Connaissance des Arts*, 261 (1973), pp. 90–99

Baxandall, Michael, 'Fixation and distraction: the nail in Braque's *Violin and Pitcher* (1910)', in Onians, John (ed.), *Sight and Insight* (London: Phaidon, 1994), pp. 399–415

Bazaine, Jean, 'Braque au Salon d'automne', *Comœdia*, 5 June 1943

'Braque: un enrichissement de l'espace' [1964], in *Le Temps de la peinture* (Paris: Aubier, 1990), pp. 69–72

'Le cubisme et nous' [1950], in *Notes sur la peinture* (Paris: Seuil, 1953), pp. 87–91

'Extraits des carnets, 1945–1965', in Schneider, *Habiter la lumière*, pp. 101–24

'Bonnard, Braque et les autres', in *Couleurs et mots*, pp. 17–21

'L'étonnement du grand âge', in *Bazaine* (Paris: Carré, 1998), pp. 5–6

Bazin, Germain, 'Braque', *Braque–Rouault* (London: Tate, 1946), pp. 5–11

Bazin, Pierre, 'Georges Braque', *Présence Normandie*, 5 (1967), pp. 5–15

Beaufret, Jean, 'L'entretien sous le marronnier' [1963], in Char, *Œuvres complètes*, pp. 1137–43

'En France', in *Erinnerungen an Martin Heidegger* (Pfullingen: Neske, 1977), pp. 9–13

Beckett, Samuel, 'La peinture des Van Velde ou le Monde et le Pantalon' [1945–6], in *Disjecta* (London: Calder, 1983), pp. 118–32

Bellet, Harry, 'Braque, à tire-d'aile', in *Braque* (Martigny: Gianadda, 1992), pp. 23–7

'La Francitude de Georges Braque', in *L'Espace*, pp. 113–28

Benjamin, Roger, 'Ingres chez les fauves', *Art History*, 23 (2000), pp. 743–71

Bernard, Emile, trans. Cochran, Julie Lawrence, 'Paul Cézanne' [1904], in Doran (ed.), *Conversations with Cézanne*, pp. 17–30

'Memories of Paul Cézanne' [1907], ibid., pp. 51–79

Bernstein, Roberta, 'Seeing a thing can sometimes trigger another thing', in Varnedoe, *Jasper Johns*, pp. 39–91

Binet, Jacques-Louis, 'Returning to Varengeville: Georges Braque's studio', *Cimaise*, 235 (1995), pp. 37–42

Bissière, Roger, 'Le gros cahier gris (1910–1947)', in *T'en fais pas*, pp. 85–95

'Mon vieux camarade [Braque]' [1963], ibid., pp. 77–8

'Ma première révélation du cubisme' [1966], ibid., p. 48

Blanchot, Maurice, trans. Mandell, Charlotte, 'The secret of Melville', in *Faux Pas* [1943] (Stanford: Stanford University Press, 2001), pp. 239–43

trans. Rottenberg, Elizabeth, 'The instant of my death', in *The Instant of My Death* [1994] (Stanford: Stanford University Press, 2000), pp. 2–11

Blin, Georges, 'Les attenants', in *Georges Braque–René Char* (Paris: Doucet, 1963); reprinted in Char, *Œuvres complètes*, pp. 1148–53

Blondin, Sylvain, 'Chez Georges Braque, Pierre Reverdy . . .', *Mercure de France*, 1181 (1962), pp. 365–6

Blunt, Anthony, 'Picasso's classical period', *Burlington Magazine*, 781 (1968), pp. 187–91

Bois, Yves-Alain, trans. Streip, Katharine, 'Kahnweiler's Lesson', *Representations*, 18 (1987), pp. 33–68

'The semiology of Cubism', in *P&B* symposium, pp. 169–221

trans. Krauss, Rosalind, 'Cézanne: words and deeds', *October*, 84 (1998), pp. 31–43

Bondil-Poupard, Nathalie, 'Hitchcock, artiste malgré lui', in Païni and Cogeval, *Hitchcock*, pp. 179–88

Bonjean, Jacques, 'L'époque fauve de Braque', *Beaux-Arts*, 8 February 1938

Bosquet, Alain, 'La musique de Braque', *NRF*, 253 (1974), pp. 81–3

Boudaille, Georges, 'Braque', *Les Lettres françaises*, 16–22 November 1961

Boullier, Renée, 'Braque et l'espace', *NRF*, 253 (1974), pp. 72–4

Bouvier, Marguette, 'Georges Braque sculpteur', *Comœdia*, 29 August 1942

Bowness, Sophie, 'Braque and music', in *Braque – Still Lifes and Interiors* (London: South Bank, 1990), pp. 57–67

   'Ben Nicholson et Georges Braque', in Barker, *L'Art traverse la Manche*, pp. 25–32

   ' "Braque le patron": Braque and the poets', in *Late Work*, pp. 21–31

   'Georges Braque', *Tate*, 11 (1997), pp. 18–19

   'Braque's etchings for Hesiod's "Theogony" and archaic Greece revived', *Burlington Magazine*, 1165 (2000), pp. 204–14

Boyd, William, 'Varengeville', *New Yorker*, 16 November 1998

Brandt, Bill, 'Braque's beach', *Observer*, 16 September 1956

Braque, Georges, 'Pensées et réflexions sur la peinture', *Nord-Sud* 10 (1917), pp. 3–5, trans. Griffin, Jonathan, 'Thoughts on painting', in Fry, *Cubism*, pp. 147–8

   'Testimony against Gertrude Stein', *Transition*, 23 (1934–5), supplement, pp. 13–14; and in McCully, Marilyn (ed.), *A Picasso Anthology* (Princeton: Princeton University Press, 1981), p. 64

   'Réponse à l'enquête sur l'art aujourd'hui', *Cahiers d'Art*, 1–4 (1935), pp. 21–4

   'Réponse à l'enquête sur l'influence des événements environnants', ibid., 1–4 (1939), pp. 65–6; in English in *Transition*, 5 (1949), pp. 112–13

   'Réflexions', *Verve*, I (1938), p. 7

   'Réflexions', *Verve*, II (1940), pp. 56–7

   'Naissance de fauvisme', *Comœdia*, 25 July 1942

   'Pensées sur l'art', *Confluences*, 4 (1945), pp. 339–41

'Sa vie racontée par lui-même', *Amis de l'Art*, 4–8 (1949)

'Entretien: Pierre Reverdy et Georges Braque, le 10 février 1950', *Derrière le Miroir*, 144–6 (1964), pp. 74–6

Brassai, trans. Miller, Richard, 'Georges Braque', in *The Artists of My Life*, pp. 16–25

Breton, André, trans. Polizzotti, Mark, 'Ideas of a painter' [1921], in *The Lost Steps*, pp. 62–5

'Constellations de Mirò', *L'Œil*, 48 (1958), pp. 50–55

Broch, Hermann, 'The style of the mythical age', in Bespaloff, Rachel, *On the Iliad* (Princeton: Bollingen, 1970), pp. 9–33

Buettner, Stewart, 'Catalonia and the early musical subjects of Braque and Picasso', *Art History*, 19 (1996), pp. 102–27

Burgess, Gelett, 'The wild men of Paris', *Architectural Record*, 27 (1910), pp. 400–414

Butor, Michel, 'La suite des images', in *Répertoires*, III (Paris: Minuit, 1968), pp. 263–8

Cabanne, Pierre, 'Braque se retourne sur son passé', *Arts*, July 1960

Caillet, Elizabeth, 'Braque lithographe par son lithographe', in *Georges Braque* (Argenteuil: Desseaux, 1982), n.p.

Calas, Nicolas, 'L'apparence', in *Braque* (Martigny: Gianadda, 1992), pp. 54–70

Carmean, E. A., 'Braque, le collage et le cubisme tardif', in *Papiers collés*, pp. 57–63

Carré, Henri, 'L'Offensive d'Artois', in *La Grande Guerre*, I (Paris: Quillet, 1922), pp. 205–14

Cassou, Jean, 'Georges Braque', *Cahiers d'Art*, 1 (1928), pp. 5–11
    trans. Wheeler, Monroe, 'Preface' to Hope, *Braque*, pp. 7–9
    'Préface', *L'Atelier de Braque* (Paris: RMN, 1961), n.p.
    'L'atelier de Braque', *Revue du Louvre*, XI (1961), pp. 279–82
    'Picasso espagnol', in *La Création des mondes* (Paris: Ouvrières, 1971), pp. 68–75

Cendrars, Blaise, 'Braque', *La Rose Rouge*, 19 June 1919, reprinted in *Aujourd'hui* (Paris: Denoël, 1987), pp. 67–8, trans. Allen, Esther, in *Modernities and Other Writings*, pp. 98–9

Chandet, Henriette and de Segonzac, Hubert, 'Georges Braque le père tranquille de cubisme', *Paris-Match*, 5–12 June 1954

Char, René, 'Georges Braque' [1947], in *Œuvres complètes*, pp. 673–74

'Georges Braque intra-muros' [1947], ibid., pp. 678–9

'Sous la verrière' [1950], ibid., pp. 674–6

'Lèvres incorrigibles' [1951], ibid., pp. 676–8

'Octantaine de Braque' [1962], ibid., p. 679

'Braque, lorsqu'il peignait' [1963], ibid., p. 678

'Songer à ses dates' [1963], ibid., pp. 679–80

'Avec Braque, peut-être, on s'était dit . . .' [1963], ibid., pp. 680–81

'Cinq poésies en hommage à Georges Braque', in *Georges Braque: œuvre graphique original* (Geneva: Pezzotti, 1958), n.p.

Charbonnier, Georges, 'Contremots', *Derrière le Miroir*, 115 (1959), pp. 1–18

'Entretien avec Georges Braque', in *Le Monologue du peintre*, pp. 7–18

Chassy, Éric de, 'Braque et la nature morte', in *L'Espace*, pp. 31–46

Chastel, André, 'Georges Braque', *Le Monde*, 3 September 1963

'L'art graphique de Braque', *Médecin de France*, 146 (1963), pp. 17–32

'Braque et Picasso 1912: la solitude et l'échange' [1964], in *Fables, formes, figures*, II (Paris: Flammarion, 1978), pp. 424–33

Chatwin, Bruce, 'Ernst Jünger: an aesthete at war', in *What Am I Doing Here?* (London: Picador, 1990), pp. 297–315

'Howard Hodgkin', in ibid., pp. 70–78

Chave, Anna C., 'New encounters with "Les Demoiselles d'Avignon"', *Art Bulletin*, 76 (1994), pp. 597–611

Chipp, Herschel B., 'Georges Braque: the late paintings', in *Georges Braque: The Late Paintings* (Washington, DC: Phillips, 1982), pp. 13–33

Cinqualbre, Olivier, 'Braque bâtisseur', in *L'Espace*, pp. 97–111

Clark, T. J., 'Cubism and collectivity', in *Farewell to an Idea* (New Haven: Yale, 1999), pp. 168–223

Clouzot, Henri, 'La décoration des tissus au congo belge', *L'Amour de l'art*, June 1923

Cohen, Françoise, 'Un tableau est fini quand l'idée s'efface', in *L'Espace*, pp. 15–30

Cone, Michèle C., 'Circumventing Picasso: Jean Paulhan and his artists', in Nash, *Picasso and the War Years*, pp. 99–112

'French art of the present in Hitler's Berlin', *Art Bulletin*, LXXX (1998), pp. 555–67

Cooper, Douglas, 'The art of Georges Braque', *Listener*, 25 April 1946
    'Braque', in *Braque Paintings 1909–1947* (London: Drummond, 1948),
    pp. 3–7
    'The new Braque ceiling in the Louvre', *Listener*, 3 September 1953
    'Georges Braque: the evolution of a vision', in *G. Braque* (London:
    Arts Council of Great Britain, 1956), pp. 5–15
    'Braque et le papier collé', in *Papiers collés*, pp. 7–11
Costa, René de, 'Juan Gris and poetry', *Art Bulletin*, LXXI (1989),
    pp. 674–92
Cottington, David, 'Cubism, aestheticism, modernism', in *P&B* sym-
    posium, pp. 58–91
Cox, Neil, 'La mort posthume: Maurice Heine and the poetics of decay',
    Art History, 23 (2000), pp. 417–49
Cranshaw, Roger, 'Cubism 1910–1912: the limits of discourse', *Art
    History*, 8 (1985), pp. 467–83
Crowther, Paul, 'Cubism, Kant, and ideology', *Word and Image*, 3 (1987),
    pp. 195–201
Culbert, John, 'Slow progress: Jean Paulhan and Madagascar', *October*, 83
    (1998), pp. 71–95
Dagen, Philippe, ' "Des préoccupations exclusives de technique"? Dufy,
    Cézanne, l'impressionnisme et le fauvisme', in *Raoul Dufy* (Lyon:
    Musée des Beaux-Arts, 1999), pp. 30–37
Dahhan, Bernard, 'Georges Braque ou un judicieux usage de la raison',
    Tendances, 35 (1965), pp. 337–59
Daix, Pierre, 'Braque et Picasso au temps des papiers collés', in *Papiers
    collés*, pp. 12–25
    'Georges Braque et le cubisme', in *Braque* (Martigny: Gianadda,
    1992), pp. 11–18
    'The chronology of proto-Cubism', in *P&B* symposium, pp. 306–21
    'Le *Grand Nu* de Braque clé de la "cordée en montagne avec Picasso',
    in *Georges Braque* (Paris: Maeght, 1994), pp. 61–3
    'Derain et Braque', in *André Derain* (Paris: Paris-Musées, 1994),
    pp. 75–8
Danto, Arthur C., 'Georges Braque' [1988], in *Encounters and Reflections*
    (Berkeley: University of California, 1997), pp. 204–10
Davis, Douglas, 'Bird in flight', *Newsweek*, 23 October 1972

Décaudin, Michel, 'Y a-t-il une littérature cubiste?', *Cahiers du MNAM*, 6 (1981), pp. 128–41

Derouet, Christian, 'Exposition Henri Laurens, décembre 1918', in *Henri Laurens* (Lille: RMN, 1992), pp. 38–53

    'La communauté', in *Jeanne Bucher* (Geneva: Skira, 1994), pp. 29–40

Descargues, Pierre, 'Georges Braque', *Arts*, 3 March 1950

    'Braque à l'Orangerie', *L'Œil* 219 (1973), pp. 32–41

    'Georges Braque', in *L'Art est vivant*, pp. 15–20

Desnos, Robert, 'La dernière vente Kahnweiler', in *Écrits sur la peinture* (Paris: Flammarion, 1984), pp. 64–7

Diehl, Gaston, 'L'univers pictural et son destin', in *Les Problèmes de la peinture* (Paris: Confluences, 1945), pp. 307–9

Doisneau, Robert, 'Braque', in *A l'imparfait de l'objectif* (Paris: Belfond, 1989), pp. 103–4

Dorléac, Laurence Bertrand, 'Le voyage en Allemagne', in *André Derain* (Paris: Paris-Musées, 1994), pp. 79–84

Drieu La Rochelle, Pierre, 'La peinture et les siens', *Comœdia*, 23 August 1941

Dupin, Jacques, 'Le nuage en échec' [1956], in *L'Espace autrement dit*, pp. 71–8

    'L'accomplissement' [1964], ibid., pp. 79–80

    'Les papiers collés de Henri Laurens' [1954], ibid., pp. 63–70

Duthuit, Georges, 'Le Fauvisme' [1929–31], in *Représentation et présence*, pp. 195–231

    'Nicolas de Staël', *Cahiers d'Art*, 25 (1950), pp. 383–6

Dyer, Geoff, 'Henri Cartier-Bresson' [1998], in *Anglo-English Attitudes* (London: Abacus, 1999), pp. 31–8

Ede, H. S., 'Georges Braque', *Cahiers d'Art*, 1–2 (1933), p. 78

Einstein, Carl, 'La peinture est sauvée, les pompiers sont déçus' [1923], *Cahiers du MNAM*, 1 (1979), pp. 19–22

    'Notes sur le cubisme' [1929], in *Ethnologie de l'art moderne*, pp. 26–33

    'Tableaux récents de Georges Braque' [1929], ibid., pp. 41–4

    'Georges Braque' [1933], in Schmid, Marion and Meffre, Liliane (eds), *Werke*, III (Berlin: Medusa, 1985), pp. 177–80

    'Lettres de Carl Einstein à Moïse Kisling', *Cahiers du MNAM*, 62 (1997), pp. 74–123

Elsen, Claude, 'Jean Paulhan et le zen', *NRF*, 197 (1 May 1969), pp. 857–63

Esdras-Gosse, Bernard, 'De Raoul Dufy à Jean Dubuffet ou la descendance du "Père" Lhullier', *Études Normandes*, XVII (1955), pp. 17–40

Esplund, Lance, 'In flight', *Modern Painters*, 2 (2003), pp. 104–7

Esteban, Claude, 'Paulhan, peinture, perception', *NRF*, 197 (1 May 1969), pp. 888–96

'Un espace devenu tactile' [1980], in *Traces, figures, traversées* (Paris: Galilée, 1985), pp. 27–37

Fagan-King, Julia, 'United on the threshold of the twentieth-century mystical ideal: Marie Laurencin's integral involvement with Guillaume Apollinaire and the inmates of the *Bateau Lavoir*', *Art History*, 11 (1988), pp. 88–114

Falgayrettes, Christiane, 'Dans le labyrinthe des fresques portables', in *Au royaume du signe* (Paris: Biro, 1988), pp. 33–47

Fenton, James, 'Becoming Picasso', in *Leonardo's Nephew* (London: Viking, 1998), pp. 185–201

Flam, Jack, 'Another look at Cubism', *Art Journal*, 49 (1990), pp. 194–8

'Georges Braque, "Landscape near Antwerp"', in Drutt, Matthew (ed.), *Thannhauser* (NY: Guggenheim, 2001), pp. 78–81

Flanner, Janet, 'Master' [1956], in *Men and Monuments*, pp. 117–73

Frankfurter, Alfred M., 'G. Braque', *Art News*, XLVII (1949), pp. 24–35

Fry, Edward F., 'Cubism 1907–1908: an early eyewitness account', *Art Bulletin*, XLVIII (1966), pp. 70–73

'Braque, le cubisme et la tradition française', in *Papiers collés*, pp. 26–36

'Convergence of traditions: the Cubism of Picasso and Braque', in *P&B symposium*, pp. 92–128

Fumet, Stanislas, 'Georges Braque peintre contemplatif', *Le Point*, XLVI (1953), pp. 4–23

'Braque octogénaire', *Les Lettres françaises*, 6–12 September 1962

'Ne nous évadons pas, ma peinture', *Derrière le Miroir*, 138 (1963), pp. 1–15

'L'Œil de Braque', ibid., 144–6 (1964), pp. 46–7

Gall, Michel, 'En mourant Braque venge van Gogh', *Paris-Match* 14 September 1963

Gee, Malcolm, 'The avant-garde, order and the art market', *Art History*, 2 (1979), pp. 95–106

Giacometti, Alberto, 'Gris, brun, noir . . .' [1952], in *Écrits* (Paris: Hermann, 1990), pp. 68–70

    'Georges Braque' [1964], ibid., p. 89

Gide, André, 'Promenade au Salon d'automne' [1904], in *Œuvres complètes*, IV (Paris: *NRF*, 1933), pp. 423–31

Gilmour, Pat, 'Prints apart', *RA Magazine*, 53 (1996), pp. 34–5

Gilot, Françoise, 'From refuse to riddle', *Arts and Antiques*, 9 (1992), pp. 57–60

    'Early Work, 1940–1955', in *Françoise Gilot: The Early Years, 1940–1955* (NY: Elkon Gallery, 1998), n.p.

Goldaine, Louis and Astier, Pierre, 'Braque' [1960s], in *Ces peintres vous parlent* (Paris: Temps, 1964), pp. 18–21

Golding, John, 'The Gelman Braques', in Lieberman, *Twentieth-Century Modern Masters*, pp. 37–8

    'Guillaume Apollinaire: the painters' friend' [1962], in *Visions of the Modern*, pp. 11–27

    'Pioneering cubism' [1990], ibid., pp. 66–79

    'Braque and the space of still life', in *Braque Still Lifes and Interiors* (London: South Bank, 1990), pp. 9–26

    'Under Cézanne's Spell', *NYRB*, 11 January 1996

    'The late paintings: an introduction', in *Late Works*, pp. 1–14

Gopnik, Adam, 'A leap in the dark', *New Yorker*, 23 October 1989

    'Escaping Picasso', *New Yorker*, 16 December 1996

Green, Christopher, 'Purity, poetry and the painting of Juan Gris', *Art History*, 5 (1982), pp. 180–204

    'Synthesis and the "synthetic process" in the painting of Juan Gris', ibid., pp. 87–105

Greenberg, Clement, 'Braque' [1949], in *Art and Culture* (Boston: Beacon, 1961), pp. 87–90

    'Braque spread large' [1949], in *Collected Essays*, vol. II, pp. 305–9

Grenier, Jean, 'Chez Georges Braque', *Combat*, 3 March 1945

    'Braque', in *Braque Peintures* (Paris: du Chêne, 1948), pp. 3–8

    'Ainsi de Braque', *Derrière le Miroir*, 48–9 (1952), n.p.

    'Dernière visite à Braque', ibid., 144–6 (1964), pp. 50–54

'Braque dans son atelier', ibid., 166 (1967), n.p.

Griffiths, Richard, 'A certain idea of France: Ernst Jünger's Paris diaries', *Journal of European Studies*, 23 (1993), pp. 101–20

Gris, Juan, 'Correspondances avec Léonce Rosenberg', *Cahiers du MNAM*, hors-série (1999)

Grohmann, Will, trans. Gilbert, Stuart, 'Introduction: the private notebooks of Georges Braque', *Verve*, VIII (1955), n.p.

Guignard, Jacques, 'Milarepa Braque', *Derrière le Miroir*, 25–6 (1950), n.p.

Guth, Paul, 'Visite à Georges Braque', *Le Figaro Littéraire*, 13 May 1950

Habasque, Guy, 'Cubisme et phénoménologie', *Revue d'Esthétique*, 2 (1949), pp. 51–61

'Henri Laurens, le taciturne', *L'Œil*, 13 (1956), pp. 4–13

Halvorsen, Walther, 'Exposition Braque, Laurens, Matisse, Picasso à Oslo, Stockholm, Copenhagen', *Cahiers d'Art*, 6–7 (1937), pp. 218–20

Harrington, John P., 'Samuel Beckett's art criticism and the literary uses of critical circumstances', *Contemporary Literature*, 3 (1980), pp. 331–48

Hellens, Franz, 'Braque et le cubisme', *Le disque vert*, 2 (1953), pp. 64–8

Henning, Edward B. et al., 'Two major paintings by Georges Braque', *Bulletin of the Cleveland Museum of Art*, LXIV (1977), pp. 137–51

Henry [Kahnweiler], Daniel, 'Der Kubismus', *Die Weissen Blätter*, III (1916), pp. 209–22

'Werkstätten', *Die Freude*, 1 (1920), pp. 153–4

Heron, Patrick, 'Braque' [1946], in *Painter as Critic*, pp. 13–18

'Paris: Summer 1949' [1949], ibid., pp. 36–8

'The changing jug' [1951], ibid., pp. 54–9

'Braque at the zenith' [1957], ibid., pp. 122–27

'Getting Braque upside down', *Modern Painters*, 2 (1989), pp. 120–22

Higgins, Ian, 'Shrimp, plane and France: Ponge's resistance poetry', *French Studies*, XXXVII (1983), pp. 310–25

Hilbrandie-Meijer, Roberta, 'Drie brieven uit 1904 van Georges Braque aan Reinhart Dozy', *Jong Holland*, 6 (1990), pp. 12–16

Hines, T. J., 'L'ouvrage de tous les temps admire: *Lettera Amorosa*', *Bulletin du Bibliophile*, 1 (1973), pp. 40–55

Hubert, Étienne-Alain, 'Pierre Reverdy et la "poesie plastique de son temps', *Europe*, 638–9 (1982), pp. 109–18

'Georges Braque selon Guillaume Apollinaire', in Brunel, P. et al., *Mélanges Décaudin* (Paris: Minard, 1986), pp. 265–74

Hughes, Robert, 'Objects as poetics', *Time*, 9 October 1972

Isarlov, Georges, 'Georges Braque', *Orbes*, 3 (1933), pp. 79–97

Jakovski, Anatole, 'Georges Braque', *Arts de France*, 8 (1946), pp. 31–6

Jenkins, O. Winthrop, 'Toward a reinterpretation of cubism', *Art Bulletin*, 50 (1948), pp. 270–78

Johnson, Ron, 'Picasso's musical and Mallarmean constructions', *Arts Magazine*, 51 (1977), pp. 122–7

Jouhandeau, Marcel, 'Georges Braque', in *Portraits* (Paris: Antoine, 1988), pp. 73–7

Kachur, Lewis, 'Picasso, popular culture and collage Cubism', *Burlington Magazine*, 1081 (1993), pp. 252–9

Kahn, Elizabeth Louise, 'Art from the front, death imagined, and the neglected majority', *Art History*, 8 (1985), pp. 192–208

Kahnweiler, Daniel-Henry, trans. Cooper, Douglas, 'The state of painting in Paris', *Horizon*, XII (1945), pp. 333–41

trans. Watson, Peter, 'Negro art and cubism', ibid., 108 (1948), pp. 412–20

'Huit entretiens avec Picasso', *Le Point*, XLII (1952), pp. 22–30

'The creative years', *Art News Annual*, 24 (1955), pp. 107ff.

'Mallarmé and painting', in Raymond, Marcel (ed.), *From Baudelaire to Surrealism* (London: Owen, 1957), pp. 359–63

'Souvenirs sur Henri Laurens', in Hofmann, Werner (ed.), *Henri Laurens* (Teufen: Niggli, 1970), pp. 49–50

Kelly, Ellsworth, 'Where the eye leads', *Modern Painters*, 2 (1997), pp. 60–65

Kennedy, Sean, 'Accompanying the Marshal: La Rocque and the Progrès Social Français under Vichy', *French History*, 15 (2001), pp. 186–213

Kochnitzy, Léon, 'Henri Laurens', *Horizon*, XV (1947), pp. 15–23

Kosinski, Dorothy, 'G. F. Reber: collector of Cubism', *Burlington Magazine*, 1061 (1991), pp. 519–31

Kramer, Hilton, 'Cubism's conservative rebel', *New York Times Magazine*, 20 May 1962

'Elegance in mourning', *New Criterion*, 15 (1997), pp. 17–20

Krauss, Rosalind, 'The motivation of the sign', in *P&B* symposium, pp. 261–305

Labrusse, Remi, 'Beckett et la peinture', *Critique*, 519–20 (1990), pp. 670–80

Lanvin, Chantel, 'Esquisse d'une vie artiste', in *Hommage à Louis Latapie* (Toulouse: Musée des Augustins, 1988), pp. 9–15

Lassaigne, Jacques, 'Entretien avec Braque', in *Les Cubistes* (Bordeaux: Beaux-Arts, 1973), pp. xvi–xviii

    'Georges Braque', in *Georges Braque* (Marcq-en-Baroeul: Fondation Prouvost, 1979), n.p.

Laude, Jean, trans. Pollock, Matthew, 'The strategy of signs', in Romilly, vol. VII, pp. 11–53

    'L'esthétique de Carl Einstein', *Médiations*, 3 (1961), pp. 83–91

    'Picasso et Braque', in *Le Cubisme* (Saint-Étienne: CIEREC, 1971), pp. 7–28

    'Un portrait [Carl Einstein]', *Cahiers du MNAM*, 1 (1979), pp. 10–16

Laurens, Claude, 'Tous les jours', *Derrière le Miroir*, 144–6 (1964), p. 67

    'Le sculpteur Henri Laurens', *Revue du Louvre*, 3 (1967), pp. 125–36

Lawrence, D. H., 'Introduction to his paintings' [1929], in *Selected Essays* (Harmondsworth: Penguin, 1950), pp. 307–46

Léal, Brigitte, 'Picasso's stylistic "Don Juanism"', in Boggs, *Picasso and Things*, pp. 30–37

Léger, Fernand, 'Une correspondance de guerre', *Cahiers du MNAM*, hors-série (1990)

    'Une correspondance d'affaires', ibid. (1996)

Leroy, Claude, 'Sept fragments d'un Léger par Cendrars', *Europe*, 638–9 (1982), pp. 137–43

    'Braque écrivain ou la signature du peintre', ibid., pp. 59–67

    'Braque pseudonyme', *Cahiers du MNAM*, 11 (1983), pp. 145–59

Leymarie, Jean, 'Georges Braque: L'oiseau et son nid', *Quadrum*, 5 (1958), pp. 72–3

    'Évocation de Reverdy auprès de Braque et de Picasso', *Mercure de France*, 1181 (1962), pp. 298–302

    'L'espace et la matière', in *Georges Braque* (Paris: RMN, 1973), pp. v–xv

    'Braque's journey', in *Georges Braque* (NY: Guggenheim, 1988), pp. 9–18

'Diego Giacometti', in Marchesseau, *Diego Giacometti*, pp. 7–22

Lhote, André, 'Exposition Braque', *NRF*, 69 (1 June 1919), pp. 153–7

Liberman, Alexander, 'Braque' [1954], in *The Artist in His Studio*, pp. 140–63

Limbour, Georges, 'Le plafond de Georges Braque' [1953] *Critique*, 351–2 (1976), pp. 885–90

'Georges Braque à Varengeville' [1953], in *Dans le secret des ateliers* (Paris: L'Élocoquent, 1986), pp. 23–7

'L'atelier parisien de Braque' [1956], ibid., pp. 29–33

'La Théogonie d'Hésiode et de Georges Braque', *Derrière le Miroir*, 71–2 (1954–5), n.p.

'Georges Braque, découvertes et tradition', *L'Œil*, 33 (1957), pp. 26–35

Luckett, Helen, 'Georges Braque: illustrations to poems by Guillaume Apollinaire' (London: Arts Council, 1985)

MacArthur, Roderick, 'Georges Braque and the Tartuffe tradition', *Theatre Arts*, April 1950

Magritte, René, 'Georges Braque' [1936], *Écrits complets*, pp. 92–3

Mailer, Norman, 'The white negro' [1957], in *The Time of Our Time* (NY: Random House, 1998), pp. 211–30

Maldiney, Henri, 'G. Braque', *Derrière le Miroir*, 25–6 (1950), n.p.

Maldonado, Guitemie, 'Voir dans l'épaisseur du monde', in *Nicolas de Staël* (Paris: Centre Pompidou, 2003), pp. 211–16

Malherbe, Anne, 'Le peintre et la matière', in ibid., pp. 219–26

Marcenac, Jean, 'La preuve par l'oiseau', *Les Lettres françaises*, 27 December 1962–2 January 1963

Martin, Alvin, 'The moment of change', *Minneapolis Institute of Art Bulletin*, 65 (1981–2), pp. 82–93

'Georges Braque et les origines du langage du cubisme synthétique', in *Papiers collés*, pp. 43–56

'The late Braque at the Phillips and some comments on the Braque centennial', *Art Journal*, 43 (1983), pp. 83–6

Masson, André, 'Jean Paulhan devant la peinture', *NRF*, 197 (1 May 1969), pp. 877–80

'Origines du cubisme et du surréalisme', in *La Rebelle du surréalisme* (Paris: Hermann, 1976), pp. 18–23

Matisse, Henri, 'Testimony against Gertrude Stein', *Transition*, 23 (1934–5), supplement, pp. 5–8

Mayer, Susan, 'Greco-Roman iconography and style in Picasso's illustrations for Ovid's *Metamorphoses*', *Art International*, 23 (1979), pp. 28–35

Meffre, Liliane, 'Lettres de Carl Einstein à Moïse Kisling', *Cahiers du MNAM*, 62 (1997), pp. 74–123

Ménier, Mady, 'Un sculpteur devant la critique: Henri Laurens', in Université de Saint-Étienne, *Art et idéologies* (Saint-Étienne: CIEREC, 1978), pp. 194–208

Merleau-Ponty, Maurice, trans. Dreyfus, Hubert L. and Allen, Patricia, 'Cézanne's doubt' [1948], in *Sense and Non-Sense* (Evanston: North Western, 1964), pp. 9–25

Miller, Simon, 'Instruments of desire', *Musical Quarterly*, 76 (1992), pp. 443–64

Moeller, Magdalena M., 'The conquest of space', in *Georges Braque* (NY: Guggenheim, 1988), pp. 25–30

Monnier, Gérard, 'Le temps des directeurs de conscience', in *L'Art en Europe* (Geneva: Skira, 1987), pp. 25–35

Monod-Fontaine, Isabelle, 'Braque, la lenteur de la peinture', in *Papiers collés*, pp. 37–42

   'Le cubisme de Laurens', in *Henri Laurens* (Paris: Centre Pompidou, 1985), pp. 9–15

   'The master of concrete relationships', in *Late Works*, pp. 15–20

Moon, Mick, 'Echoes and memories', *RA Magazine*, 53 (1996), pp. 32–3

Morice, Charles, 'Braque', *Mercure de France*, 16 December 1908; in English in Fry, *Cubism*, p. 52

Nash, John, 'Braque and cubism', *Listener*, 1 June 1978

Nelson, Paul, 'Mon ami Georges Braque', *Les Lettres françaises*, 6–12 September 1962

Parke-Taylor, Michael, 'Copies de l'album fauve [Derain]', *Cahiers du MNAM*, 5 (1980), pp. 363–77

Passmore, Kevin, 'The Croix de Feu: Bonapartism, national populism or fascism?', *French History*, 9 (1995), pp. 67–92

Paulhan, Jean, 'Georges Braque', *Comœdia*, 7 October 1942

   'Georges Braque dans ses propos', *Comœdia*, 18 September 1943

'Peindre en dieu', *NRF*, 130 (1 October 1963), pp. 583–5

'Correspondance', *NRF*, 197 (1 May 1969), pp. 1027ff.

Perl, Jed, 'Braque the anticlassicist' [1982], in *Paris without End* (San Francisco: North Point, 1988), pp. 66–75

'Latest and greatest' [1987], *Eyewitness* (NY: Basic, 2000), pp. 242–50

Perse, Saint-John, 'Birds', *Origin*, 11 (1963), pp. 1–12

'A la mémoire de Georges Braque', in *Œuvres complètes*, pp. 536–7

Phillips, Duncan, 'Research and stylism in painting', in *The Artist Sees Differently* (Washington, DC: Phillips, 1931), pp. 75–8

'Personality in art', *American Magazine of Art*, 28 (1935), pp. 148–55

'Georges Braque', in *Georges Braque: A Retrospective Exhibition* (Washington, DC: Phillips, 1939), n.p.

Pia, Pascal, 'Livres de peintres', *L'Œil*, 35 (1957), 63–71

Picon, Gaëtan, 'A la place des fleurs', *Derrière le Miroir*, 144–6 (1964), pp. 30–31

Pijaudier, Joëlle, 'Laurens et le cubisme', in *Henri Laurens* (Lille: RMN, 1992), pp. 18–31

Platt, Susan Noyes, 'Modernism, Formalism and Politics', *Art Journal*, 47 (1988), pp. 284–95

Poggi, Christine, 'Mallarmé, Picasso and the newspaper as commodity', *Yale Journal of Criticism*, 1 (1987), pp. 133–51

'Braque's early papiers collés', in *P&B symposium*, pp. 129–68

Ponge, Francis, 'Braque le réconciliateur' [1946], in *L'Atelier contemporain*, pp. 58–69

'Braque ou l'art moderne comme événement et plaisir' [1947] ibid., pp. 70–77; trans. Beckett, Samuel, 'Braque or modern art as event and pleasure', *Transition*, 5 (1949), pp. 43–7

'Braque-dessins' [1950], *L'Atelier contemporain*, pp. 102–8

'Braque-Japon' [1952], ibid., pp. 120–29

'Braque lithographe' [1963], ibid., pp. 237–46

'De la nature morte et de Chardin' [1963], ibid., pp. 228–36

'Feuillet votif' [1964], ibid., pp. 246–50

'Braque ou un méditatif à l'œuvre' [1971], ibid., pp. 283–317; trans. Howard, Richard, 'Braque or the meditation of the work', in *G. Braque* (NY: Abrams, 1971), n.p.

'Bref condensé de notre dette à jamais et re-co-naissance à Braque particulièrement en cet été 80' [1980], in *Nouveau Nouveau Recueil*, III (Paris: Gallimard, 1992), pp. 129–35

'Braque-Argenteuil' [1982], ibid., pp. 151–5

Porteus, Hugh Gordon, 'After Braque', *Listener*, 12 September 1963

Proust, Marcel, trans. Warner, Sylvia Townsend, 'Chardin' [1895], in *Marcel Proust on Art and Literature* (NY: Carroll and Graf, 1997), pp. 323–36

Queneau, Raymond, 'Histoires de Braque et Marcelle Braque', in *Journaux* (Paris: Gallimard, 1996), p. 588

Raynal, Maurice, 'Quelques intentions du cubisme', *Bulletin de L'Effort Moderne*, 1 (1924), pp. 2–4

'Panorama de l'œuvre de Picasso', *Le Point*, XLII (1952), pp. 4–21

'Henri Laurens', ibid., XXXIII (1946), pp. 3–10

Reff, Theodore, 'The reaction against Fauvism: the case of Braque', in *P&B* symposium, pp. 17–57

Reverdy, Pierre, 'Sur le cubisme' [1917], in *Nord-Sud*, pp. 14–21

'Une aventure méthodique' [1950], in *Note éternelle*, pp. 41–104

'La plus longue présence' [1955], ibid., pp. 137–44

Revol, Jean, 'Braque et Villon', *NRF*, 104 and 105 (1 August and 1 September 1961), pp. 321–5 and 524–7

Ribemont-Dessaignes, Georges, 'A propos d'une nature morte', *Le Point*, XLVI (1953), pp. 32–7

'Braque', *Arts*, 3–9 September 1953

'Georges Braque illustrateur', *L'Œil*, 47 (1958), pp. 48–53

Richardson, John, 'The ateliers of Braque', *Burlington Magazine*, 627 (1955), pp. 164–70

'Au château des cubistes', *L'Œil*, 15 April 1955

'Le nouvel "atelier" de Braque', *L'Œil*, 15 June 1955

'The power of mystery by Georges Braque', *Observer*, 1 December 1957

'Braque discusses his art', *Réalités*, 93 (1958), pp. 24–31

'Braque: pre-cube to post-zen', *Art News*, 63 (1964), 29–31

'Braque's Late Greatness' [1997], in *Sacred Monsters*, pp. 237–44

interviewed by Tom Phillips, 'Georges Braque', *RA Magazine*, 53 (1996), pp. 28–32

Richet, Michèle and Pouillon, Nadine, 'Georges Braque', *Revue du Louvre*, XXIII (1973), pp. 319–22

Ries, M., 'Braque's ateliers and the symbolic bird', *Journal of Aesthetic Education*, 29 (1995), pp. 67–78

Rocco, John, 'Drinking Ulysses: Joyce, Bass Ale and the typography of cubism', *James Joyce Quarterly*, 33 (1996), pp. 399–409

Roché, Henri-Pierre, 'Braque' [1950], in *Écrits*, pp. 331–2

    'Braque' [1954–5], ibid., pp. 333–4

    'Souvenirs sur Georges Braque' [1955], ibid., pp. 337–45

    'Georges Braque (suite)' [1955], ibid., pp. 347–9

    'Braque' [1958], ibid., 351–2

    'Adieu, brave petite collection!' [1959], ibid., pp. 417–27

    'Une rencontre Braque–Derain à coups de poing', *Arts*, 23–29 March 1955

Roque, Georges, 'Le fauvisme: première abstraction du XX siècle?', *Critique*, LVI (2000), pp. 202–13

Rosenberg, Harold, 'The cubist epoch' [1971], in *Art on the Edge* (Chicago: University of Chicago Press, 1983), pp. 162–72

Rosenberg, Pierre, 'Chardin: the unknowing subversive?', in *Chardin* (London: RA, 2000), pp. 27–35

Rosenblum, Robert, 'Picasso and the typography of Cubism', in Penrose, Roland and Golding, John (eds), *Picasso in Retrospect* (NY: Praeger, 1973), pp. 49–75

    'The Spanishness of Picasso's still lifes', in Jonathan Brown (ed.), *Picasso and the Spanish Tradition* (New Haven: Yale, 1996), pp. 61–93

Roskill, Mark, 'Braque's papiers collés and the feminine side to Cubism', in *P&B symposium*, pp. 222–60

Rubin, William, 'Cézannisme and the origins of Cubism', in *Cézanne: The Late Work* (NY: MoMA, 1977), pp. 151–202

    'Pablo and Georges and Leo and Bill', *Art in America*, 67 (1979), pp. 128–47

    'From narrative to "iconic" in Picasso', *Art Bulletin*, LXV (1983), pp. 615–49

Russell, John, 'Braque at 80', *Sunday Times*, 13 May 1962

Salles, Georges, 'Histoire d'un plafond', *Preuves*, 148 (1963), pp. 22–6

Salmon, André [La Palette], 'Georges Braque', *Paris Journal*, 13 October
1911
    'Georges Braque – l'artiste et l'artisan', *L'Europe Nouvelle*, 29 March
1919

Salomon, Gabrielle, 'André Derain: notes sur la peinture', *Cahiers du
MNAM*, 5 (1980), pp. 343–62

Sartre, Jean-Paul, 'L'homme et les choses', in *Situations*, I (Paris: Gallimard, 1947), pp. 226–70

Schapiro, Meyer, 'The apples of Cézanne' [1968], in *Modern Art*, pp. 1–38
    'On some problems in the semiotics of visual art' [1969], in *Theory
and Philosophy of Art*, pp. 1–32

Schulz-Hoffmann, Carla, 'Georges Braque: the Cubist phase', in *Georges
Braque* (NY: Guggenheim, 1988), pp. 19–24

Seibel, Castor, 'Jouhandeau, ses peintres, ses illustrateurs', *Bulletin du
Bibliophile*, III (1978), pp. 361–73

Seuphor, Michel, 'Braque graveur', in *Braque graveur*, n.p.
    'L'œuvre graphique de Braque', in *L'Œuvre graphique de Braque*
(Liège: Musée des Beaux-Arts, 1953)

Shattuck, Roger, 'Captions or illustrations? Georges Braque's handbook'
[1989], in *Candor and Perversion*, pp. 211–32

Signovert, Jean, 'Gravure et émulation', *Nouvelles de l'estampe*, 8 (1964),
pp. 224–5

Silver, Kenneth E., 'Braque, Picasso and other Cubists', in Passantino,
Duncan Phillips, pp. 233–66

Solier, René de, 'L'œuvre gravé de Braque', *Cahiers de la Pléiade*, XII
(1951), pp. 39–41
    'L'oiseau de Braque', *Cahiers d'Art* (1956–7), pp. 235–41

Soupault, Philippe, 'L'époque Nord-Sud', *Mercure de France*, 1181 (1962),
pp. 312–34
    'Propos sur Pablo Picasso, Georges Braque et Juan Gris', in *Écrits sur
la peinture* (Paris: Lachenal et Ritter, 1980), pp. 221–3

Spies, Werner, trans. Kaufholz, Eliane, 'Vendre des tableaux – donner
à lire', in *Daniel-Henry Kahnweiler* (Paris: Centre Pompidou, 1984),
pp. 17–44

Staller, Natasha, 'Meliès' "fantastic" cinema and the origins of cubism',
Art History, 12 (1989), pp. 202–32

Stefani, Alessandro de, 'Matisse e il cubismo: per una nova datazione del *Grand Nu* di Braque', *Paragone*, XXXIX (1988), pp. 35–61

Stein, Gertrude, 'Braque' [1913], in *Geography and Plays*, pp. 144–9

Steinberg, Leo, 'Resisting Cézanne: Picasso's "Three Women"', *Art in America*, 66 (1978), pp. 114–33

 'The polemical part', ibid., 67 (1979), pp. 114–27

 'The philosophical brothel', *October*, 44 (1998), pp. 11–74

Suzuki, D. T., 'Painting swordsmanship, tea ceremony', in Barrett, *Zen Buddhism*, pp. 279–94

Sylvester, David, 'Braque in Edinburgh', *Listener*, 30 August 1956

 'Braque's "Still Life with Fish"', *Listener*, 15 February 1962

 'Picasso – I' [1960], in *About Modern Art*, pp. 79–85

 'Still Life: Cézanne, Braque, Bonnard' [1962], ibid., pp. 90–110

 'Picasso – II' [1988], ibid., pp. 399–414

 'Picasso and Braque' [1996], ibid., pp. 445–8

 'Johns – II' [1997], ibid., pp. 463–76

Szirtes, George, 'The late flight of Georges Braque', *Pretext*, 7 (2003), pp. 111–19

Tériade, E., 'Les dessins de Georges Braque' [1927], in *Écrits sur l'art*, pp. 88–90

 'Confidences des artistes' [1928], ibid., pp. 137–8

 'Épanouissement de l'œuvre de Braque' [1928], ibid., pp. 132–5

 'Émancipation de la peinture' [1933], ibid., pp. 448–53

 'Entretien avec Henry Kahnweiler', *Feuilles Volantes*, 2 (1927), pp. 1–2

 'Entretien avec Léonce Rosenberg', ibid., 6 (1927), pp. 1–3

 'Entretien avec Paul Rosenberg', ibid., 9 (1927), pp. 1–2

 'Propos de Georges Braque', *Verve*, VII (1952), pp. 71–80

 'Matisse speaks', *Art News Annual*, 21 (1952), pp. 40–71

Terrasse, Antoine, 'Pierre Bonnard et la lecture', *Bulletin du Bibliophile*, 3–4 (1988), pp. 267–9

 'La règle et l'émotion', *NRF*, 253 (1974), pp. 68–71

Valéry, Paul, trans Turnell, Martin, 'About Corot' [1932], in *Masters and Friends*, pp. 134–54

Vallier, Dora, 'Braque, la peinture et nous' [1954], in *L'Intérieur de l'art*, pp. 29–51

'Braque dans sa force', *NRF*, 253 (1974), pp. 75–80

'A propos de la "Théogonie" de Braque', *Nouvelles de l'estampe*, 66 (1982), pp. 24–6

'Braque et la mythologie', in *Georges Braque et la mythologie* (Paris: Galerie Leiris, 1982), pp. 7–13

'Braque et la sculpture', in *Georges Braque: sculptures* (Paris: Maeght, 1985), pp. 7–10

'Braque au fil de temps', in *Braque* (Martigny: Gianadda, 1992), pp. 19–21

Verdet, André, 'Rencontre dans l'atelier parisien' [1961], in *Entretiens*, pp. 11–16

'Autour de cubisme' [c. 1960], ibid., pp. 17–25

'Rencontre à Saint-Paul' [1950s], ibid., pp. 26–34

'Dernier entretien' [1963], ibid., pp. 39–48

Verhesen, Fernand, 'René Char et ses "alliés substantiels"', *Liberté*, 10 (1968), pp. 147–58

Vlaminck, Maurice de, 'Opinions libres sur la peinture', *Comœdia*, 6 June 1942

Wallard, Daniel, 'Braque en 1943', in Diehl, *Les Problèmes de la peinture*, pp. 93–8

Warnod, André, 'Braque' [1946/1949], in *Les Peintres mes amis* (Paris: Heures Claires, 1965), pp. 81–8

trans. Frechtman, Bernard, 'Georges Braque's notebooks', *Transition*, 2 (1948), pp. 119–21

Warren, Rosanna, 'A metaphysic of painting: the notes of André Derain', *Georgia Review*, XXXII (1978), pp. 94–149

Watt, Alexander, 'With Braque', *Art in America* 3 (1961), pp. 102–3

West, Rebecca, 'The private and impersonal notebooks of Georges Braque', *Verve*, VIII (1955), n.p.

Wilkin, Karen, 'O pioneers!', *New Criterion* (December 1989), pp. 29–35

'Will Georges Braque ever get his due?', *Hudson Review*, L (1997), pp. 444–52

Winkfield, Trevor, 'Braque the enchanter', *Modern Painters*, 1 (1997), pp. 30–37

Wogensky, Robert, 'Celui qui aimait les peintres', *NRF*, 197 (1 May 1969), pp. 881–7

Wollheim, Richard, 'The moment of Cubism revisited', *Modern Painters* 4 (1989–90), pp. 26–31

Zeltner-Neukomm, Gerda, trans Guillain, Alix, 'Un poète de natures mortes', *NRF* 45 (1956), pp. 422–5

Zervos, Christian, 'Georges Braque et la peinture française', *Cahiers d'Art*, 1 (1927), pp. 5–16

'Observations sur les peintures récentes de Braque', ibid., 1 (1930), pp. 5–10

'L'exposition d'œuvres de Corot à la galerie P. Rosenberg', ibid., 4 (1930), pp. 198–203

'Le classicisme de Braque', ibid., 1 (1931), pp. 35–40

'Georges Braque et le développement de cubisme', ibid., 1–2 (1932), pp. 13–27

'Georges Braque', ibid., 1–2 (1933), pp. 1–7

'Georges Braque et la Grèce primitive', ibid., 1–2 (1940), pp. 3–13

'Georges Braque', ibid., II (1950), pp. 388–91

Acknowledgements

Researching is adventuring into the unknown. Blandine Chambost has been my skirmisher, interpreter, and conductor into the strange ways of French archives ('What proof do you have, monsieur, that we hold these papers?') and the Byzantine workings of the Bibliothèque Nationale, 'which in both its entire layout and its near-ludicrous internal regulation seeks to exclude the reader as a potential enemy', as the late W. G. Sebald so aptly remarked. Hilary Spurling solved for me the problem of accommodation for a lengthy sojourn in Paris. Adelheid Scholten and Paul Stoop provided hospitality in Berlin and translations from the German. Polly Howells and Eric Werthman gave me a base of operations in New York and the run of their library. Paul Edson – truly a substantial ally – supervised all translations from the French, and indeed motley-minded perturbations in the English. Needless to say, the final responsibility for both French and English remains mine alone.

In the course of this adventure I have accumulated numerous other debts.

For personal information and documentation on Braque: the late Jean Bazaine, John Berger, Heinz Berggruen, Laure Latapie Bissière, Marc-Antoine (Louttre) Bissière, Henri Cartier-Bresson, the late Denise Colomb, Odette Constanty, Aldo Crommelynck, Victor Dozy, Jacques Dupin, François Fédier, Jean Ferrand, Françoise Gilot, Jasper Johns, Ellsworth Kelly, Blanche Lachaud, Christian Lachaud, the late Claude Laurens, Denise Laurens, Quentin Laurens, Jacques Laval, Albert Loeb, Jean Leymarie, James Lord, Claire Paulhan, Armande Ponge, John Richardson, Anne de Staël, Françoise de Staël, Geneviève Taillade, Antoine Tudal, Jack Youngerman, Marc Yver.

For intelligence and encouragement in the quest: Janet Axten, Ian Barker, Claudine Boulouque, William Boyd, Peter Brooke, James Ashley Cooper, Elizabeth Cowling, Neil Cox, Valentine Cunningham, Julien Dossier, Patrick Duncan, Araceli and Paul Edson, Mary Fedden, Alastair

Finlan, Uwe Fleckner, John Golding, Michael Harrison, Charles Haxthausen, Roberta Hilbrandie-Meijer, Clyde Hopkins, John Horton, Sean Kennedy, James Knowlson, Philippe Lacoue-Labarthe, Florence de Lussy, Marilyn McCully, Bill McGuire, Yoshihiko Mizumoto, Isabelle Monod-Fontaine, Simon Morris, Redmond O'Hanlon, Kevin Passmore, Sandra Persuy, Michael Raeburn, Peter Read, Carol Rigolot, Nicole Worms de Romilly, André Roussard, Jack Shear, Hilary Spurling, Dan Todman.

For access to archival holdings and private collections: Michèle Auric, Claude Bernès, François Chapon, Marie-Claude Char, Victor Dozy, Claude Duthuit, Alain Grenier, Katharine Heron, Claude Laurens, Eric Parry, Jacqueline Paulhan, Jean-Claude Roché.

Among archivists, curators, and librarians: the staff of the Agence Photographique de la Réunion des Musées Nationaux, Paris; the staff of the Centre d'Archives d'Architecture du XXe siècle, Paris; Wanda de Guébriant at the Archives Duthuit, Paris; the staff of the Archives du Louvre, Paris: Mercedes Maya at the Archives Municipales, Argenteuil; Sylvie Barot at the Archives Municipales, Le Havre; Laurence Camous and Anne-Marie Zucchelli at the Archives of the Musée national d'art moderne, Paris; the staff of the Archives Nationales, Paris; Ellen R. Cordes at the Beinecke Rare Book and Manuscript Library, Yale; the staff of the Musée Bibliothèque Pierre-André Benoit, Alès; the staff of the Bibliothèque d'Art et d'Archéologie Jacques Doucet, Paris; the staff of the Bibiothèque Historique de la Ville de Paris; the staff of the Bibliothèque Littéraire Jacques Doucet, Paris; Mauricette Berne, Marie-Odile Germain and Florence de Lussy at the Bibliothèque Nationale de France, Paris; the staff of the Bibliothèque Centre Pompidou, Paris; the staff of the Bibliothèque Sainte-Geneviève, Paris; Dominique Rouet at the Bibliothèque Salacrou, Le Havre; the staff of the Bodleian Library, Oxford; the guardian of the Cimetière du Centre, Argenteuil; the staff of the Courtauld Institute Library, London; Joëlla de Couëssin at the École Nationale Supérieure des Beaux-Arts, Paris; Virginia Funkhouser at the Getty Research Library, Los Angeles; Claire Paulhan at the Institut Mémoires de l'Édition Contemporaine, Paris; the staff of the Keele University Library; Jonathan Blackwood at Kettle's Yard, Cambridge; Jean Beysset at the Grande Chancellerie de la Légion d'Honneur, Paris;

Acknowledgements

the staff of the Fondation Maeght, Saint-Paul de Vence; the staff of the Galerie Maeght, Paris; Susan Davidson and Carol Shanks Price at the Menil Collection, Houston; Sarah Bergh at the Metropolitan Museum of Art, New York; the staff of the Manuscripts and Archives Division of the New York Public Library; McKenna B. Lebens and Sylvie L. Merian at the Pierpont Morgan Library, New York; Anne-Marie Castelain at the Musée Malraux, Le Havre; Anne Distel at the Musée d'Orsay, Paris; Irene Konefal, Patrick Murphy and Kate Silverman at the Museum of Fine Arts, Boston; Michelle Harvey, Angela Lange, Jeremy Melius and Jennifer Tobias at the Museum of Modern Art, New York; the staff of the National Art Library, London; Anne Collins Goodyear, Anne Halpern and Nancy Hubbard Yeide at the National Gallery of Art, Washington, DC; Simon Bailey in the Oxford University Archives; Marie-Jo Duffès at the Fondation Saint-John Perse, Aix-en-Provence; Linda Clous and Karen Schneider at the Phillips Collection, Washington, DC; Sylvie Fresnault, Laurence Madeline and Jeanne Sudour at the Musée Picasso, Paris; Linda Ashton at the Harry Ransom Research Center for the Humanities, Austin, Texas; Ornella Volta at the Fondation Erik Satie, Paris; the staff of the Hyman Kreitman Research Centre at the Tate, London; the staff of the Service Historique de l'Armée de Terre, Vincennes.

At Hamish Hamilton and Penguin in London: Juliette Mitchell and Simon Prosser, for their meticulous and sympathetic editing, and their generous encouragement; Kate Brunt and Eithne Staunton, for their heroic work on picture research; and Helen Campbell, for her attentive copy-editing. At Arcade in New York: Richard Seaver, for the personal interest he has taken in the book.

To Bruce Hunter, without whom this project would not have got off the ground.

Finally, the entire manuscript was read, more than once, by Blandine Chambost, Dee Danchev, and Paul Edson. It has also been scrutinized by John Golding and Marilyn McCully, two of the greatest experts in the field. To all of these readers – my ideal readers – I am deeply grateful.

Index

'B' indicates Braque.
Page numbers in italics indicate integrated photographs.

DATE DUE

DEMCO, INC. 38-2931